The Development of Planning Thought

Planning Thought

A critical perspective

Cliff Hague

Department of Town and Country Planning
Heriot-Watt University/Edinburgh College of Art

Hutchinson

London   Melbourne   Sydney   Auckland   Johannesburg

KU-480-078

Hutchinson & Co. (Publishers) Ltd

An imprint of the Hutchinson Publishing Group

17–21 Conway Street, London W1P 6JD

Hutchinson Publishing Group (Australia) Pty Ltd
PO Box 496, 16–22 Church Street, Hawthorne, Melbourne,
Victoria 3122

Hutchinson Group (NZ) Ltd
32–34 View Road, PO Box 40–086, Glenfield, Auckland 10

Hutchinson Group (SA) (Pty) Ltd
PO Box 337, Bergvlei 2012, South Africa

First Published 1984

© Cliff Hague 1984

Set in Times Roman by Book Ens, Saffron Walden, Essex.

Printed and bound in Great Britain by
Anchor Brendon Ltd, Tiptree, Essex

British Library Cataloguing in Publication Date
Hague, Cliff
    The development of planning thought.
    1. City Planning – Case studies 2. City planning –
    Scotland 3. Edinburgh (Lothian) – City planning –
    History
    I. Title
    711'.4'094134   HT166

ISBN 0 09 158070 6

HERTFORDSHIRE
COUNTY LIBRARY
1938206
711.409

Contents

Acknowledgements

This book took a long time to write. As I began to write it, the section on Edinburgh expanded beyond what was initially intended. What was to be one chapter became five. This was because it seemed arbitrary to select areas and sites in isolation from the overall structure of planning in the city. The study therefore came to focus on the development of planning, and the political difficulties which attended implementation.

From the outset I had hoped to connect the physical and spatial aspects of planning with political analysis and an awareness of planning ideology and urban imagery. This ambitious scope made it difficult to achieve sustained depth and rigour in the analysis. The book is therefore presented as a basis for criticism – a starting point from which contrasting explanations can be advanced, and comparative studies undertaken.

My faltering attempts to write were sustained by a number of people. Above all I must thank my wife, Irene, who both encouraged me, and bore the brunt of the demands of four young children, while I was trying to make progress with the book. I am also indebted to the team at Hutchinson for all their help and support, and particularly to Rab MacWilliam and Doug Fox for being so patient. Professor Mike Bruton and John Ratcliffe also gave valuable advice and guidance, which I greatly appreciated. My employers, the Edinburgh College of Art, also helped by granting me two terms' leave of absence in 1981 which allowed me to get ahead with work for the book.

I must also thank the colleagues with whom I have worked in Edinburgh for their suggestions and ideas. Above all though thanks are due to the students who went through the Heriot-Watt/Edinburgh College of Art Planning Department in the 1970s. In writing the book I have drawn on dissertation work by several of them: Hugh Bingham, George Chree, Steve Crane, Jim Kaucz, Derek Laidlaw, Nick Lewis, David Ward, Alex Waterworth, David West and Petter Wiberg. As well as thanking these people, I would also like to thank the many others with whom I worked closely, and whose scholarship and commitment helped to build and sustain a critical approach within the Department, at times in hostile circumstances. It is perhaps invidious to name a few out of many, but I would like to record my special thanks to Stuart Borrowman, Dave Ferguson, Vivien Green, Inger Haug, Tony Long, Arthur McCourt, Jamie Mackie, Henry McLeish, Keith Moore, Peter Russell and Phil Swann. Special thanks are also due to Tom McCann and Bill Sturrock who did the maps for the book.

Finally, I would like to thank Brian Melville for sharing his ideas and learning through correspondence and meetings in the late 1970s.

Of course, none of these people are in any way to blame for the weaknesses in this book. On that score criticism must be directed to me.

Cliff Hague
Edinburgh
October 1983

Introduction

The separation of fact and value, description and evaluation, science and criticism are the building blocks of our conventional notion of rationality. Concentrated study of how to do things has allowed the human race to dominate its environment in an unprecedented manner. It has also created an unprecedented potential for the destruction of that environment and for the domination of the people who live within it. Such a situation can scarcely be equated with the apex of rationality. Purposive rationality also claims to be objective. One consequence is that concepts have become synonymous with operations, while ideas that cannot be reduced to means of technical manipulation have been rendered increasingly incomprehensible.

Urban growth and planning is both a consequence and a part of this rationality of control. Planners have become participants and victims in the process. The development of planning theory has been a one-sided struggle to come to terms with the dominant form of rationality. The result has been an orthodoxy which seeks to explain planning as a rational decision-making process. Thus Faludi observes, 'Planning may therefore by defined as deciding on a course of action by satisfying oneself that it is possible to present one's choice in a form which could have resulted from a rational planning process, even if this has not actually been the case.'[1]*

In this way the concept 'planning' is reduced to a function, 'deciding on a course of action': any possible distinction between the idea and the contingent function in everyday work is foreclosed. The language and grammar abridge the scope for reflection on action; all that can be contemplated is the form of the presentation. Yet the quotation implicitly acknowledges the tensions between the way decisions are made and what is called a rational planning process, whilst simultaneously banishing the difference between the concept and the operation.

This view of planning as a set of operations came to the fore in the 1960s. It is one particular form that the scientization of politics took within the planning profession. It marked another stage in the debate about the 'nature' of planning. The ambiguities and conflicting interests embodied in that debate, and the oft-lamented misunderstandings of the general public about what planning entails, testify to the conceptual potential encapsulated in the phrase 'town and country planning'. A planning theory which reduces that meaning to a sequence of procedures, while proclaiming its objectivity, is repressive and partial. The

* Superior figures refer to the *References and notes* at the end of each chapter.

present has been eternalized, by severing planning and theorists from any specific analysis of the society in which they are located.

A critical approach to planning theory has no need for one universally applicable theory, one general set of axioms shrinking concern with place and time. The idea of town planning can be emancipatory, carrying the possibility of people fashioning their own living environment with will and consciousness. The struggle is to free the discourse from the shackles of economic, technological and ideological domination, to rediscover the ethical and moral questions in the creation of environments. Existing theories and practices in the name of planning are neither inherently correct, nor self-evidently proper. They are the temporary manifestations of historical, social processes, constrained by the interests that are dominant in the society at the time.

Attempts to establish an approach to planning relating to a higher rationality commit the theorist to a struggle against established planning practice. However, an understanding of that practice is central to any enlightenment. Similarly a dialectical approach requires that the practice is sifted for those fragments of meaning that hold out possibilities for a different practice. The mere dismissal of aggregates is dehumanizing and authoritarian. Interpretation of a textual tradition is therefore important. Texts, plans and places can be studied to understand their meanings and the intentions of their authors. But all texts have a context. Reflection on the social and political context within which those items were fashioned prompts self-awareness of the distortions within and around the theoretician's own practice.

Interpretation is thus an important part of theorizing which has been underdeveloped within the community of planners. Explanation is another. This entails the generation of hypotheses from which deductions are derived and tested, so that conditional predictions can be made about future events, or so that explanations of past events can be sustained. The principal flowering of explanatory theory within planning came with the development of urban and regional models, and the attempts to apply principles of cybernetics. More recently such work has been carried out under the disciplinary headings of economics and geography. In particular there have been notable attempts to explain the processes of urban and regional change in terms of neo-Marxian economic concepts, and to compare developments in different countries.[2]

Theorizing and an awareness of theoretical traditions is thus of real importance. Without it planners are prone to descend into the mire of unreflective assertions of untested assumptions. The vulnerablility to such narrow professional empiricism has been deeply embedded in both planning education and planning practice.[3] It is one reason why the profession has lurched in the facile pursuit of fashions. However, there are also dangers in hypostatizing theoretical propositions, shunning any attempt to relate them to evidence in fear of a descent into positivism. Authoritarianism lurks in that closed circle. These beliefs have structured this book.

In the first part of the book the emphasis is towards the theoretical. The proposition is that to understand town planning, we need to study in three major, interlinked dimensions. First, the building and growth of cities has an economic dimension. There can be no grounds for suggesting that such pervasive phenomena as cities, which represent such an enormous scale of investment, are in some way independent of the mode of production. Their development in relation to the mode of production must therefore be explained. This is the area explored in Chapter 1. Then there is a political dimension. Town and country planning is part of the administrative system of the modern state. The way the political context shapes the planning system is therefore an important area of theorizing, which needs to take account of the specific historical form of the state in question. These themes are developed in Chapter 2. Then there is a socio-cultural dimension, which concerns the way that the production and planning of places has been perceived, and the interests that have structured that perception. Chapter 3 is therefore concerned with the discourse among the planners about their role.

The second part of the book is concerned with the practice of planning. This is studied in one place, Edinburgh, over an extended time period, in order to provide a counterpoint to the generalizations in the first part. A single case study can be dismissed as a mere sample of one, but it is included to illustrate how the strands of theory can be applied, and to open the way to comparative studies of other cities or topics.

The final chapter of the book attempts to reflect on the theory and practice of town planning, and to advance some propositions for the future.

References and notes

1   A. Faludi, *Planning Theory*, (Pergamon, 1973), p. 38.
2   See, for example, J. Carney, R. Hudson and J. Lewis (eds), *Regions in Crisis*, (Croom Helm, 1980).
3   See, for example, R. Glass, 'The evaluation of planning: some sociological considerations', *International Social Science Journal (1959)* vol. XI, no. 3.

Part One Theories and Planning

Preface – A note on planning theory

The word 'theory' is often uttered disdainfully by planners. It made a late and unconvincing entry into planning education, where it blazed briefly then faded. Until the 1960s 'principles and practice' ruled the day; the studio master schooled his apprentices in the art of design. The appearance of 'planning theory' on the syllabus owed something to professional machismo – hopefully suitable doses would produce a scientific (and hence acceptable) basis for planning.

Within a remarkably short space of time, the field of planning theory was monopolized by a particular formulation: planning was a conceptual general system, a science of making decisions. Thus the ethics of neutrality and functionalism, foundation stones of the professional ideology, were retained. The fact that many of the ideas were derived from American texts both gave them an aura of modernity, and also testified to the generality, and hence truly theoretical character of the proposition. Planners began to hope that their art might also be a science.

The transformation was flawed, and floundered. To many practitioners the ever more elaborate abstractions of the theoreticians were bewildering and vacuous. The fragmentation of the work processes of planners as the profession grew in numbers, roles and techniques (but not in self-understanding), ensured the splintering of the utopian concept of the planner as rational decision-maker. Despite the attempts to enshrine a new rationality, practice became more than ever the flotsam of the tides of political conflict and economic recession. One consequence was that by the early 1980s for 'planning theory', as for so many other products, the label gave scant indication of the contents. [1]*

None of this negates the need for theory. Rather, it begs the question of what kind of theory for what kind of practice? If we see planning as a way of extending the ability of ordinary people to control and improve the way in which they live, then we need an understanding of how and why settlements have developed in the way they have. We also need to grasp the practice of planning as it is presently constituted, and that means locating that practice within the context of the state. Radically-minded planners should look to these directions for their theories.

Theory, however, needs some dialogue with evidence if it is not to become

* Superior figures refer to the *References and notes* at the end of each chapter.

apostatized, an assertion of its own 'truth'. Distrust of empiricism should not degenerate into a circular, logical self-confirmation of the necessary 'correctness' of a particular mode of theorizing. That is the path to the type of authoritarianism which has been discernable in much of planning ideology, and it is a path which all planners must be wary of. These then are the premises from which we approach theories and planning in Part One.

References and notes

1   See, for example, the diversity of concerns, as evidenced by the papers in P. Healey, G. McDougall and M. J. Thomas, *Planning Theory: Prospects for the 1980s* (Pergamon 1982).

1 The production of cities

The blatant deformation of urban development since the industrial revolution, has been the unequivocal product of social conditions: private ownership of land; real estate speculation; systematic subordinization of town planning to the 'growth sectors' of private industry; general underdevelopment of socialized services. These societal conditions, far from being suspended or neutralized by any technical logic, in their turn determine technological underdevelopment – for example, the backwardness of the industrial methods in the construction industry – and aberrant development (high rise blocks, dormitory cities and so on).[1]

The obituary of the large industrial city can now be written. Conventional versions recall its energetic and clumsy youth, the cheery though battered face of maturity, and the gaunt outlines of a deserted old age. The demise can be quantified starkly. The population of Birmingham, that archetypal industrial city, declined by almost 100,000 between 1971 and 1981. The proportionate loss was even greater in Liverpool where a population of 610,000 in 1971 withered to 510,000 a decade later, and in Manchester where the drop was from 544,000 to 449,000. Where houses, shops and factories had crowded together acres now stretch empty of all but weeds and litter. In these husks unemployment and social strife have reached levels unmatched for generations.

Today's spectacular urban growth rates are recorded in the smaller, free-standing settlements, the retreats to high amenity 'rural' living. These shifts have confirmed and intensified a pattern that has emerged since the late 1950s. Tables 1 and 2 chart the trends.

Stripped of their familiarity these patterns look surprising, and beg interpretation. Why should the scale and structure of towns and cities vary through time and space? How are settlements produced? What factors shape regional disparities? What aspects of urban and regional development are problematic and why? At one level everybody is involved in these questions, since the experience of place is an integral part of day-to-day living. However, within the division of labour in our society these matters have become the focus for diagnosis by specialists, notably those labelled geographers, economists or planners. As in other branches of the knowledge industry, ideas have been produced and data have been amassed.

The rubric of the theory generated by this tradition is that 'natural' geographical advantages, mediated by technology and human enterprise, create conditions for urban growth. There was no imperative to connect growth in one location to major change or even decline in another. Thus a symposium on the resurgence of non-

Table 1   *Districts losing population*

	Population change (000's)		
Districts	*1961–71*	*1971–81*	*1961-81*
England and Wales			
London boroughs	−540	−756	−1296
Metropolitan districts			
Principal cities	−353	−386	− 739
Towns over 50,000	+318	−329	− 11
Non-metropolitan districts			
Large cities	− 41	−149	− 190
Small cities	+ 37	− 55	− 18
Industrial towns over 50,000			
in Northern England and Wales	+ 32	− 39	− 7
Scotland			
Central Clyde conurbation		−189	
Principal cities of over 175,000		− 65	
Small Industrial Districts		− 1	

Source: OPCS Towns Report 1982

Table 2   *Districts gaining population*

Districts	Population change (000's)		
	1961–71	*1971–81*	*1961–81*
England and Wales			
Metropolitan districts			
Small towns	+ 94	+169	+ 263
Non-metropolitan districts			
Industrial districts (excluding			
industrial towns over 50,000			
in Northern England and Wales)	+ 427	+239	+ 666
New towns	+ 337	+283	+ 620
Resort and seaside retirement	+ 345	+156	+ 501
Mixed urban and rural and			
accessible rural	+1584	+661	+2245
Remote rural	+ 403	+468	+ 871
Scotland			
Small cities of over 5000		+ 10	
Other service centres		+ 11	
Industrial districts of over 50,000		+ 34	
Accessible rural		+ 49	
Remote rural		+ 39	

Source: OPCS Towns Report 1982

metropolitan areas conducted by the International Regional Science Review late in 1977 gave scant attention to metropolitan decline. The early emergence of counter-metropolitan trends in the USA, as catalogued for example by Berry (1973),[2] is used to bolster an interpretation of America as an 'advanced' version of the path which other countries will follow. Similarly, the dramatic growth of Third World cities, with high levels of rural–urban migration, is coded as the first phase of the urban–industrial life-cycle. Thus the interests producing the settlement structures are blurred behind evolutionary analogies. For example Spence (1982) writes,

It is a fact that the evolution of the metropolitan area is most advanced in the United States. The evolutionary process and the nature of the outcomes seem to be providing the model towards which most of the world's metropolitan areas are converging, admittedly at varying speeds.[3]

Thus cities everywhere are depicted as passing through an inevitable sequence of phases, towards an ever superior mode of being, culminating in a form of life after death, an urban civilization without cities. Settlements, things constructed by the labour of human beings, are ascribed biological characteristics such as maturity.[4]

In the age of Empire climatic determinism was invoked to explain the contrast between the indolence of the indigenous population of tropical colonies and the go-getting entrepreneurs from the chilly north. A more sophisticated variant on this long discredited thesis has recently been assembled. The shift in economic activity and settlement in the USA is attributed to the contrasting climatic attractions of the 'frostbelt' and the 'sunbelt'. A version of the thesis, slightly diluted to match the British weather, has been transferred across the Atlantic; the wealth creators seemingly seek the blue skies of southern England and East Anglia and flee from the drizzle of the north (though there are sunny intervals over Cheshire).

The theory embedded in such formulations is neo-classical eonomics. The assumptions are that markets are apolitical mechanisms which ensure an efficient use of resources. Consumer demands are met through rational choice in the market place, while competition creates efficient production. Much of the mainstream work in locational analysis and regional science is an orchestration of these premises in relation to differential production and distribution costs. The strength of the work derives from the fact that markets are indeed important elements in urban and regional development in many countries. Furthermore the theories are frequently constructed in an elegant manner. Nevertheless they remain inadequate because they abstract market processes from the class relationships which are intrinsic to them. This sense of inseparability of politics, economics and ideas is the intellectual foundation stone of a radical approach to urban and regional planning. From it stems the interest in the political economy of places, and of the theories about them.

By strict definition radicals go to the roots of things. 'What is theory?', the question posed by Max Horkheimer in an essay first published in 1937, does just that. He answered his question by setting out the traditional assumptions and then criticising them:

Theory for most researchers is the sum total of propositions about a subject, the propositions being so linked with each other that a few are basic and the rest derive from these. The smaller the number of primary principles in comparison with the derivations, the more perfect the theory. The real validity of the theory depends on the derived propositions being consonant with the actual facts. If experience and theory contradict each other, one of the two must be re-examined. Either the scientist has failed to observe correctly or something is wrong with the principles of the theory. . . . The general goal of all theory is a universal systematic science, not limited to any particular subject matter but embracing all possible objects. The division of sciences is being broken down by deriving the principles for special areas from the same basic propositions. . . . In so far as this traditional conception of theory shows a tendency, it is towards a purely mathematical system of symbols. As elements of the theory, as components of the propositions and conclusions, there are ever fewer names of experiential objects and ever more numerous mathematical symbols.[5]

The priority attached to empirical testing constitutes the core of the claims to objectivity by traditional theories. Indeed, any question of the purposes that the theory will serve is excluded from the definition. The caricature of the detached academic, so immersed in his research as to seem other worldly, owes its kernel of truth to this perspective. Essentially, then, thought and being are separated; the application of deductive logic to a set of axioms that consitute the rules of the game for a particular theory brings its own fascinations, obliterating the tensions that would be generated by any notion that the rules should be altered. Yet theoretical activity, like any other form of social activity, is shaped by the society of which it is a part; the autonomy of the traditional theorists' self-perception is an illusion woven by the internal logic of his theory building. Similarly the notion of a timeless 'pure' theory is illusory, eternalizing the present, which is but one moment in a historical process of change.

Habermas, a pupil of Horkheimer, took the critique of traditional theory a stage further, spotlighting the link between explanation, prediction and control. He argued that empirical testing predicates limited predictions of objective or objectified processes.[6] Scientific knowledge thus brings with it the possibilities for technical manipulation and control, but only so long as the fundamental social relationships remain unchanged, for those relationships are woven into the objectified requirements of the theory. Though control opens the possibility for change, the scope is limited and the pace incremental. Alternative social goals cannot be empirically verified, and are therefore excluded from the realms of science. Thus as Brian Melville and Jim Lewis observed:

The traditional theorist must take social relationships to be 'natural' or invariant to satisfy the methodological requirement that explanations are also prognoses. When such explanations are used as the basis for social engineering or control they thus reproduce the essential features of the existing society. The political consequences of this kind of social theory result from its methodological structure.[7]

Lewis and Melville applied their critique specifically to the work of Isard.[8] There is no shortage of other examples to illustrate the dominance of traditional theory within urban and regional studies. When planners began to flirt with social science in the 1950s and 1960s the debates were about the very legitimacy of such liaisons: there was scant cognisance of the existence of different traditions within the social sciences. Approaches to urban and regional change rooted in Horkheimer's traditional theory were imported without being subjected to radical critique. Authors such as Britton Harris linked the possibilities for progressive change to improved scientific understanding of cities. In an influential paper he wrote:

It is in fact the magnitude of the problems of societal control in a period of rapid change and development which are providing the impetus for a truly scientific development of the social sciences. Problems such as maintaining peace, feeding billions of people, reducing racial discrimination, and organizing great cities require powerful instruments of control over men and machines. These problems of control can no longer be resolved by an engineering approach which is overwhelmingly oriented towards physical, inanimate machine systems. Engineers working in transportation planning must pay increasing attention to problems of human behaviour, and it is rapidly becoming evident that the relevant behaviours are not only in the field of transportation demand and transportation system utilization, but also in the field of land use development and locational choice. In a sense, therefore, and almost willy-nilly, the planning-engineering professions find themselves working on a frontier of science. This is the area of social behaviour and social control in which the application of the scientific method has been unduely retarded.[9]

The scientization that Harris anticipated produced its rash of urban development models. Lowry's formulation, explaining and predicting urban growth in terms of economic base theory, with a spatial distribution achieved by gravity models for journey to work and journey to shop, was developed to a level of considerable statistical elegance and fathered a number of adaptations to the original formulation.[10]

Though the problem of the treatment of time became a major preoccupation for many modellers – Lowry's original model produced an 'instant metropolis' – the ahistorical nature of the models was taken for granted. Acceptable calibration on past data provided the basis for conditional prediction. The theoretical statement was often extremely crude – the Empiric model was so named because it made no pretensions to theorizing.[11] The declared intent was to facilitate instrumental control, especially where models were consciously produced as commodities by teams of consultants, as was particularly the case with much of the work in America. Reaction set in against the models when they were found deficient in this respect – too often their data requirements outstripped the data available, or their assumptions were too crude to withstand scrutiny.

One model in particular attracted great interest because it tried to treat time as a variable within the model. Its creator was Jay Forrester, who had been head of the Lincoln Laboratory for Air Defense at MIT from 1951 to 1955. In 1956 he became Professor of Management, applying servo-mechanics and computing to industrial problems. In 1967 discussions with a former mayor of Boston persuaded him to model the dynamics of urban decay and revival and to use the model to evaluate existing urban policies.[12] Forrester saw the city as a complex system, with the same characteristics of other such systems, such as counter-intuitive behaviour and resistance to policy change. The city was modelled as comprising three categories of business (new, mature, declining); three of housing (premium, worker and underemployed); and three of people (managerial-professional, labour and underemployed). The relationships within the model were specified by Forrester after discussions with men who had 'practical experience in urban affairs'. Simulation of city growth over a period equivalent to 250 years produced an equilibrium 'stagnant condition'. There was high unemployment of the underemployed, a housing shortage for the managerial-professional and labour groups, a housing surplus for the underemployed and an above average per capita tax rate. Testing of policies showed that only contentious programmes such as demolishing slums and replacing them by premium housing and industry would improve the city, a prescription which he confessed might 'give superficial appearance of favouring upper income groups and industry at the expense of the underemployed'.

Forrester's work rested on the notion that social systems conform to timeless 'pure' rules. It is an extreme example of the way political practice can be transmuted into the technical language of system behaviour. His reliance on deductions from meta-principles was so complete that he even eschewed empirical testing of his parameters. The 'urban dynamics' model has been outlined here because it shows in stark relief tendencies endemic in traditional theory in urban development. It is a reminder of the vital insight for all planners provided by Lewis and Melville in their comment that

What the regional scientist passes on to 'key decision makers' is not just a collection of ideas and measurements but a form of knowledge which is so structured by a particular concept of explanation that it may be used by them. By defining knowledge in this way the regional scientist is already formulating policy by reasserting the conventional boundaries within which a choice of policy must be made.[13]

An alternative approach

The cities and environments we wish to study are the products of human work and organization. They do not flourish because of 'natural' advantages, nor are they determined by technology, for what constitutes an advantage, and what technology is used and how are matters susceptible to conscious human decision. Places have a history as well as a present and a future. These are the starting points for an alternative approach to thinking about the development of settlements. Since cities are socially produced their features must be related to the mode of production within the society. If that society is capitalist the cities will only be fully understood by exploring the logic and historical development of capitalism itself. Many will concede that the 'hidden hand' of the freely competitive stage of capitalism sketched the structure and form of nineteenth-century urbanization. A labour force was concentrated close to key raw materials, simultaneously providing an accessible market; competing railway companies carved routes through town and country in pursuit of profit. However, we must go beyond such descriptions in two respects; first to grasp the processes of capitalist accumulation and their antagonistic character, and second to connect such processes to the contemporary city.

Marx started Volume I of *Capital* with an analysis of the elementary form of capitalist wealth, the commodity, a good produced not for direct consumption by the producing community, but for sale. While commodity production is not unique to this mode of production, the scale of it is. The commodity is 'an external object, a thing which through its qualities satisfies human needs of whatever kind'.[14] Since they are useful, commodities possess a use-value; though this can only be realized in use or in consumption.

A system of extended commodity production is based upon a division of labour into mutually independent groups of producers acting in isolation. In these circumstances goods have no direct use-value to their producers, so if the use-values are to be realized, the goods must be exchanged. Thus use-values are also 'the material bearers of exchange-value'[15] – the value for which the use-values of different commodities are exchanged on the market. The commodity then

is the direct unity of use-value and exchange-value, and at the same time it is a commodity only in relation to other commodities. The *exchange process* of commodities is the *real* relation that exists between them. This is the social process which is carried on by individuals independently of one another, but they take part in it only as commodity owners. . . . The commodity *is* a use-value, but as a commodity it is simultaneously *not* a use-value. It would not be a commodity if it were a use-value for its owner, that is, a direct means for the satisfaction of his own needs. For its owner, it is on the contrary a non-use value, that is merely the physical depository of exchange value or simply a *means of exchange*. Use-value as an active carrier of exchange-value becomes a means of exchange. The commodity is a use-value to its owner only so far as it is an exchange-value. The commodity therefore has still to become a use value . . . a use value of others.[16]

Exchange values therefore transform qualitative differences in use-values into quantitative differences. The fact that in the exchange relation one use-value is worth just as much as another, provided it is present in the appropriate quantity, means that the exchange-value of the commodity is abstracted from its use-value. Similarly, exchange-value also obliterates the specific character of the labour that has produced the commodity, replacing it by the common denominator of human labour in the abstract. Marx therefore argued:

> We have seen that when commodities are in the relation of exchange, their exchange-value manifests itself as something totally independent from their use-value. But if we abstract from their use-value, there remains their value, as it has been defined. The common factor in the exchange relation, or in the exchange-value of the commodity, is therefore its value. . . . What exclusively determines the magnitude of the value of any article is therefore the amount of labour socially necessary, or the labour-time socially necessary for its production.[17]

This latter concept is defined as 'the labour time required to produce any use-value under the conditions of production normal for a given society and with the average degree of skill and intensity of labour prevalent in that society'.[18] The argument then is that value varies directly with the quantity of labour and inversely with its productivity.

The exchange of commodities to realize their value creates a social need for a universal equivalent to represent those values. Money then is the means of exchange and is itself a commodity. Labour power is likewise a commodity. Its exchange-value is the value of the consumer goods necessary to keep the worker and his family in condition to continue to work at a given intensity. This value is not simply an economic coefficient, nor is it simply physiologically determined, but rather embodies historical, moral and political dimensions forged out of practice. The use-value of the labour power which the capitalist purchases is the worker's capacity to produce value, a capacity which is of no use-value to the worker if he has no access to the means of production.

The expenditure of labour power in the production process has a twofold effect: it conserves value embodied in the raw material and the fraction of the machinery exhausted in the production by transferring that value to the finished product, while also directly creating new value. The essence of capitalist production then is that workers produce value over and above the exchange-value at which they sell their labour power, while capitalists buy labour power in the expectation that they will be able to appropriate that surplus value which is thereby produced. It is this social relation, expressed in the form of an exchange relation, which divides capitalist society on a class basis and weaves the logic of a class struggle into the fabric of that society.

The production of a surplus and its appropriation by a minority within the society is not unique to capitalism: for example, there were the tithes of feudalism. To that extent surplus value is nothing more than the 'old' social surplus product in a new form, money. The real difference though is that money can be exchanged to allow the capitalist to realize the use-value to him of more machines, raw materials and labour power. In this way surplus value can be transformed into additional capital, a process termed 'valorization'. The rate of accumulation defines the relation between productive surplus value which is reinvested in this way, and surplus value which in unproductively consumed, for example, in luxury goods.

Though the growth of surplus value *in toto* is clearly in the interests of the capitalist class as a whole, its division within that class, and between its various forms (profits, rents, interest) is unplanned and subject to competition. Competition between the 'various capitals' creates the basic drive to accumulation which is central to this mode of production, and can also lead to a devalorization of capital. This process whereby capital loses part of its value takes two main forms. First, there may be a decline in the price of production of commodities and capital invested in these commodities is thereby devalorized. This is especially likely to happen in the sphere of the means of production. Second, value can be destroyed when firms go bankrupt, or close down.

Capital can be divided into two categories, called 'constant' and 'variable'. Constant capital represents that part which is used to purchase buildings, machinery, raw materials, and energy. It is 'constant' in that it is conserved by the activity of labour power during the process of production and is incorporated into the value of the final commodities produced. It thus constitutes an essential precondition for the production of surplus value, but does not directly produce surplus value itself. Constant capital can be further subdivided into a fixed element (buildings and machinery) and a circulating element (raw materials and energy). Since only the labour power of living labour produces additional surplus value, that part of capital used to buy labour power is called 'variable capital'. This part of capital therefore reproduces the equivalent of its own value, plus a surplus value, which can thus vary the amount of this capital between the start and end of the production process.

Thus constant capital is the value of the means of production and variable capital the value of labour power, the sum total of wages. Their relationship is expressed as the 'organic composition of capital'. This is closely associated with, yet distinct from, its technical composition, that is the relation between the mass of the means of production employed and the mass of the labour necessary for their employment. Now increased productivity of labour will cause more raw material to be worked up in the same amount of time, while the provision of new machinery, improved transport facilities, etc. may be necessary conditions to effect an increase in productivity. Either way the growing productivity of labour brings with it a growth in the extent of the means of production as compared to the labour power incorporated in them; in other words, it alters the technical composition of capital. This change will be reflected in the organic composition by an increase in the constant constituent at the expense of the variable constituent. Hence there is a tendency for the relative magnitude of variable capital to decline, though it can, of course, simultaneously rise in absolute terms. Similarly the degree of change of the organic composition will not be a direct replica of that in the technical composition – after all the assumption of an increased productivity of labour implies that though the mass of the means of production consumed by labour will increase, their value, though rising in absolute terms, is relatively diminished.

These relationships are important for they can be shown to influence the rate of profit. Thus the ratio in which variable capital valorizes its value is known as the 'rate of surplus value' or the 'rate of exploitation', and can be expressed algebraically as

$$e = s/v \qquad (1)$$

where e is the rate of exploitation, s is surplus value, and v is variable capital.

By incorporating constant capital into the analysis, it is possible to derive the rate of profit as

$$p = s/(k+c+v) \qquad (2)$$

where p is the rate of profit, k is fixed constant capital and c is circulating constant capital.

The organic composition of capital we know is

$$o = \frac{k+c}{v} \qquad (3)$$

where o is the organic composition.

We know that the ratio defined in equation (3) will tend to increase in association with the increasing productivity of labour, and by dividing the top and bottom of equation (2) by (v) we can see how this tendency affects the rate of profit:

$$p' = \frac{s/v}{\frac{k+c}{v}+1} \quad \text{or} \quad \frac{e}{o+1} \qquad (4)$$

Therefore, if the rate of exploitation stays constant, any rise in the organic composition will reduce the rate of profit.[19] The absolute rate of profit may still increase of course and what actually happens to the rate of exploitation in practice depends on historical factors and political struggles. These equations then are not mechanical determinants of events, rather they portray the dynamic nature of capitalism, and the contradictions inherent in its structure.

The concepts outlined above provide a starting point in building an understanding of the development of capitalism. Mandel[20] argued that such development hinges around six variables.

1   *The organic composition of capital in general and in the most important branches in particular.* This includes both the volume of capital and its distribution between the three main 'departments': Department I, the means of production; Department II, the means of consumption; and Department III, those branches of production which renew neither constant nor variable capital, e.g. luxury goods and armaments. Capital will seek situations where

the organic composition is lower than average; for example, industries that have not been fully operated along capitalist lines.

2   *The distribution of capital between fixed constant capital, and circulating capital* (i.e. circulating constant capital plus variable capital.) As with all the other variables, this needs to be related both to capital in general, and to the main departments. Thus for example if labour productivity in raw material production outstrips that in the production of consumer goods, circulating constant capital will become relatively cheaper than variable capital. In these circumstances the organic composition will grow more slowly than before, notwithstanding the accelerated technological change and the increased investment in fixed capital.

3   *The rate of surplus value.* Other things being equal, capital will seek out locations or activities where surplus value can be maximized. The rate will also vary through time, reflecting specific historical conditions such as the size of the industrial reserve army – those marginal employees hired in times of booms and laid off during recessions – and the development of the class struggle.

4   *The development of the rate of accumulation.* This again reflects the shifts of capital between the different departments in response to specific conditions.

5   *The development of the turn-over time of capital.* This involves the 'tying up' of capital in the circulation process in activities not productive of any surplus value. It is therefore in the interests of the capitalist class as a whole to accelerate this process.

6   *The relations of exchange between the firms producing the means of production and those producing the consumption goods.* This is mainly a function of the given organic composition of capital in the respective departments.

Mandel suggested that: 'The interplay of these different variables and laws of development can be *summed up in a tendency for the various spheres of production and the various component parts of the value of capital to develop unevenly*'.[21]

This notion of the combined and uneven nature of capitalist development, elucidated through the analysis of concrete historical situations, is of particular relevance to studies of the production of cities and environment. Uneven development very aptly characterizes city and regional growth, intra- and inter-nationally and stands in marked contrast to the attempts to bludgeon the temporal and spatial disjunctures of development into the framework of equilibrium analysis which have characterized much of the more sophisticated traditional theory in this field.[22] Recognition of the combined nature of the development contrasts appealingly with the instrumental necessity to achieve 'system closure' in both spatial and substantive terms for which modellers apologize. Concrete historical analysis has more to offer students of real places than the abstractions of rational economic man, acting on perfect information, on flat, isotropic surfaces.

Cities and industrial capitalism

At the start of the nineteenth century the vast majority of the population of Britain still lived in rural areas. *The* city was London, which from 1500 onwards had dominated the internal balance of trade and capital accumulation within the country. The only European city that could compare with London was Paris, though even that did not account for such a high proportion of the national population. London's ascendency was founded upon the appropriation of a colonial surplus by its merchants and financiers, and the capitalization of domestic agriculture. The nascent capitalist economy restructured the settlement pattern, so that throughout the sixteenth century London was frequently accused of causing 'the loss and decay of many (or most) of the ancient cities, corporate towns and markets within this realm, by drawing them to herself alone, say they both of all trade of traffic by sea, and the retailing of wares and the exercising of manual art also'.[23] The reciprocity in exchange of goods and services on a local basis was gradually being replaced by an arrangement by which the remote regions produced commodities for the London market, a process classically exemplified by the coal production in the north-east of England.

Thus the settlement pattern that was reworked by the growth of industrial capitalism in nineteenth-century Britain was itself a historically specific form, developed from the uneven growth of the initial phases of capitalist organization. The transition from feudalism to industrial capitalism was thus a prolonged historical process. The central logic of feudalism was the maintenance of the balance between population numbers and agricultural land use that gave the maximum surplus product. An 'excess' of population meant that either the surplus would be eaten, or the peasants would starve, for the landowners had no reason to diversify their activities into the production of consumer goods that could be sold to an agricultural labour force that they did not need. Foster identified the preconditions of capitalist industrialization as being

... the diversion of a relatively small amount of resources from immediate consumption (like building churches or country houses) to the sustained improvement of production methods. Consequently the prime requirement in capitalist conditions is a rate of profit high enough to attract capital from other uses. On the *demand* side, this means having an unemployed reserve to prevent labour demanding a bigger share in the new wealth than it had in the old. And equally, to prevent primary producers doing the same, there has to be a readily expandable supply of raw material. On the *market* side, things are slightly more difficult.[24]

The difficulty is that industrialization via a low wage economy does not provide the conditions for sustained investment. While the industrialists can undercut the production costs of craft producers, the super-profit is temporary because of the small scale of the domestic market and its restricted purchasing power. A solution exists where there are a number of co-existing economies, at different stages of development, for then it is possible to sell in extended markets.

Thus Foster argues that Britain's industrialization originated in two successive 'lucky breaks'. First, England's population continued to grow while that of continental competitors began to decline at the start of the seventeenth century, so that for over thirty years textile producers had access to plentiful supplies of labour that were not available on the continent. A massive expansion of the capitalist cheap labour sector was a consequence. There then came the second lucky break, empire. The colonial surplus created a need for a bouyant home market, so that it became in the interests of those who controlled the wealth to break with the restrictions of feudalism, thus stimulating continuing industrial and agrarian innovation. Finally, after over-investment in colonial primary production had brought a collapse in profits, investment was switched to the home industrial sector in the 1770s and 1780s.

A concrete illustration of this genesis, and its relation to the settlement pattern is provided by Foster's detailed description of the industrialization of the Oldham area. In the mid-sixteenth century there were less than 700 households and the land was held by seven feudal families who lived off the production of their peasants. The early seventeenth century saw a temporary boom in European demand for low quality 'new draperies', giving merchants the incentive to seek production in previously untouched rural areas such as Oldham, where there was a supply of cheap labour. This disruption of the peasant economy produced a large number of landless cottagers, and a few comparatively rich peasant-yeomanry. By the middle of the century the industry and Oldham were in decline. The re-expansion of the European economy in the early decades of the eighteenth century saw a revival of the industry: with population growth outstripping food production the cottagers were obliged to sell their labour to survive. There was no apprenticeship system in rural places like Oldham and thus no shortage of labour: the weaving was done on an outwork basis, with as many members of the family as possible involved directly in the production process. The industry, though profitable for the capitalists, remained largely unmechanized. By the 1790s, however, the weaving sector was experiencing reduced profits because of increased continental competition. In contrast, the mechanization of cotton spinning and the introduction of factory production opened the way to above-average profit rates. The machines allowed productivity to be increased, without the capitalists being obliged to meet proportionally increasing wage and raw material costs. The factory builders in Oldham were local men who started out with capital. Factory builders needed capital not just for the new machinery, but for power, raw materials, labour and credit; they needed land and the resources that went with it. Foster shows that it was the same families who employed most of the miners and a near-majority of the textile workers. These four families directed the building of the local turnpike system, backed canal construction and jointly enclosed the town's common lands in 1802.

Despite the advent of factory production, outworking was still the major form of employment until the late 1820s and population growth continued in the rural out-townships until that stage. Mechanization of weaving came in the 1830s and with it the transformation of Oldham from a semi-rural area to an industrial settlement. The whole process was punctuated by crises, as the existence of a completely mechanized industry in what was otherwise a technologically underdeveloped economy made for a long-term decline in the rate of profit. The technological advances reduced the exhange value of the output of the cotton industry, without a corresponding reduction in the labour cost of inputs from other sectors.

The development of industrial capitalism was therefore uneven between sectors, between places and over time. Foster's work is an analysis of the growth and decline of class consciousness in three nineteenth-century towns (Northampton and South Shields are the other two). It connects their changing industrial base and politics. Such studies are valuable to planners in three respects. First, they provide an alternative to the conventional histories of the nineteenth-century city, descriptions rooted in liberal anti-urbanism. Second, they show how the fundamental concepts of a critical political economy can be applied to concrete situations. Finally, they help us to read today's physical environment of such places with new insights, unravelling the class relations, the struggles over the surplus value, that are within the edifices.

Some of the best writing in this vein was produced by the Community Development Projects. Their reports connected graphically and in some detail the way the imperatives of capital accumulation created booms and slumps in industrial settlements, leaving places and people in thrall and disarray.[25] In similar vein, but at a regional scale, Carney and his colleagues have analysed the economic and political development of the north east of England.[26]

The blossoming of the capitalist economy restructured both town and country. Not only were rural areas like eighteenth-century Oldham urbanized, but fundamental changes occurred in those areas that continued in agricultural production. The capitalization of agriculture meant enclosures of the common lands and commodity production rather than subsistence farming. Competition from food imports undermined branches of local production. The economic effect was the emergence of a surplus population, whose migration to the towns swelled the ranks of the industrial reserve army, thereby keeping down the exchange value of the commodity labour power. Migration decisions were by no means always the results of abstract deliberations by rational 'economic man', as traditional theorists might suggest. The clearances of Highland Scotland saw the rationality of the landowners forcibly imposed upon the crofters. This transition to a capitalist agriculture required 'improvements', notably consolidation of small crofts into larger holdings and the replacement of subsistence production by sheep farming for markets in the south. Rents increased threefold and reluctant tenants were evicted from their ancestral homes and bodily exported by the landowners.

The only option for the landless labourers was to sell their labour power and to do that they had to move to the areas where there was some demand for labour. These locations were closely tied to the sources of raw materials and power precisely because of the uneven nature of the development process. Transport and energy transmission remained in a primitive state for some decades after the industrial revolution commenced. Spatial separation from sources of raw materials and energy would thus greatly increase the element of constant capital, thus affecting the organic composition of capital and the rate of profit. At the same time it was, of course, in the interests of capitalists to accelerate the turn-over time of capital by speeding up the circulation process through improvements in transport. It is no surprise therefore that the second phase of industrialization began with the great period of railway building and investment, with 6000 miles of track being laid in the UK between 1830 and 1850. This also provided new opportunities for the valorization of capital previously accumulated, for by the 1840s the annual surplus available for investment was in the order of the then enormous sum of £60 million.[27]

At this macro-level then the settlement structure was forged by the movement of capital between branches and places of production in search of opportunities to realize an above average rate of profit. The effect had been not only a restructuring of relations between town and country, but between regions and the metropolis. In England, Manchester and Birmingham even began to challenge London's dominance in finance and trade, while in Scotland Glasgow outstripped Edinburgh and had its own Stock Exchange. Later in the nineteenth century London's financial dominance was re-established, as might be expected both by the economics and the ideology of imperialism, yet the archetypal institution of industrial capitalism, the factory, remained the exception within the capital. Even at the start of this century less than 20 per cent of the industrial labour force there worked in factories. Instead the small workshop typified London production, and faced with provincial competition, and remote from the main sources of energy – the coalfields – London industrialists had to utilize the one major advantage of their location, their access to a seemingly inexhaustible supply of cheap labour. It was precisely this advantage which constituted a major disincentive to mechanized production, and which was almost guaranteed by London's position as the only major urban centre in the heart of the agricultural counties during the final stages of nineteenth-century agricultural rationalizations.[28] Thus metropolitan industry mainly meant sweatshops and outworking, while the city's economy was dominated by finance, trade and the production of luxury commodities. As a consequence, the world's greatest city was also the world's greatest slum, posing a seemingly insoluble problem to reformers and kindling hopes and fears of revolutionary action.[29]

British urbanization differed from that of other emergent capitalist economies because of differences in the type of market, the nature of the labour supply and the availability of capital. Britain's was a 'modest' urbanization in many respects, with a widely dispersed pattern of growth points. The contrasts are summed up in Table 3.

The internal structure of the city was also fashioned by capitalist relationships. Land was allocated to users through market exchange. Engels lucidly described the pattern of land uses in the Manchester of the 1840s, where all routes focussed on the Exchange at the heart of the commercial and financial district.[30] Mills, warehouses and factories commanded sites adjacent to the canals and waterways, while the market segregated the housing of the classes over space.

Typically the working-class housing was adjacent to the industry; the cost of

Table 3   *Conditions of industrialization related to distribution of industrial population*

	Britain	USA	France/Germany
Market	Overseas	Domestic	Domestic/overseas
Labour supply	Plentiful	Scarce	Skilled labour scarce
Capital supply	Adequate	Uneven	Scarce
Capital source	Private (small)	Private (large)	State and institutional
Distribution of urban population	Decentralized provincial	Concentrated in large cities	Concentrated in large cities

Source: R. Mellor, 'The capitalist city: Britain 1780-1920' *Urban Change and Conflict,* Unit 1, (Open University Press 1982), p. 23.

reproducing labour power was less where people could walk to work. In the early stages of industrialization the entrepreneurs also tended to reside close to their factory, though in grander residences: capital accumulation and environmental degradation triggered their retreat. Thus the great employers in Foster's Oldham lived in mansions around the edge of the town, while their operatives lived in housing described by a contemporary journalist as '. . . filthy and smouldering. Airless little backstreets and close nasty courts are common; pieces of dismal wasteground – all covered with wreaths of mud and piles of blackened brick – separate the mills . . .'[31] The workers of South Shields lived 'in a warren of back-to-back terraces built more or less on top. The better off lived further inland: the bankers and shipowners at Westcoe; the tradesmen round a small market place erected (as a property speculation) by the local landowners, the bishops of Durham, in the later eighteenth century'.[32]

Housing for the labour force was a direct factor of production for some industries, where the employer provided the accommodation, so that, in effect, part of the worker's wage was paid in kind.[33] The mining industry was a prominent example, with Marx recording that miners who could not be housed in this way received a compensatory payment of £4 per annum.[34] The houses and the surrounding environment were developed in accord with the principles of capital accumulation: the mines were often worked on leases, so that the employer needed to discount his capital invested in house building over the length of the lease, a formula pointing directly to the construction of cheap houses of minimal standards.

In most cases, though, housing was a commodity, financed, built and managed not to meet social need, but to accumulate capital. Production of a high-value commodity such as a house for consumption by people living at or below the poverty line is evidently problematic. Problems of realization had to be overcome by investors exchanging the commodity on a rental basis. Even then the returns were unlikely to match those in other areas of production and hence working class housing was not an attractive proposition to large-scale capitalists. Small builders therefore carried the risks of the actual development, while the landlords were typically small-scale operators with petty bourgeois backgrounds.[35] The poor housing and insanitary living conditions that this economic relationship inevitably produced were in themselves a problem. Not only did they physically express the misery of a large section of the population, but they also had an effect on productivity. Ill health and premature death had little economic impact in situations where the industrial reserve army was extensive; however, the loss of skilled workers, whose reproduction might involve lengthy training, was more disquieting. Furthermore, the risk of disease spreading from the quarters of the poor to the domiciles of their 'betters' was real enough to provoke concern.

This is not to argue that all the working class lived in conditions of unrelieved squalor. The quality of housing reflected the expectations about the rent-paying abilities of the tenants. Some degree of spatial segregation was achieved both horizontally and vertically (typically poorest at the bottom of the slope, better off at the top where the air and the views were likely to be superior). Indeed, the nuances of status embodied in housing and neighbourhood played their part in incorporating elements of the working class into the ideology of capitalism, after the creation of one class communities had fostered working-class consciousness and organization. Conditions could also vary through time. As Marx observed, 'As a result of the ebb and flow of capital and labour the state of the dwellings of an industrial town may today be tolerable, tomorrow frightful.'[36]

Land was a fundamental requirement both for industry and housing. This allowed the landowning class to appropriate an appreciable part of the total surplus value produced. Marx noted an increase of 38 per cent in income from rents of land subject to taxation in the period of 1853–64,[37] and argued that landed capital was particularly indicative of the emergence of capitalism itself: 'Modern landed property . . . cannot exist without capital as its presupposition, and it indeed appears historically as a transformation of the preceding historical shape of landed property by capital so as to correspond to capital.'[38]

The production of a settlement structure and a physical environment also involved contradictory class relations in the building industry. Not surprisingly, given the growth rates of towns and cities, building constituted an important employment sector: Clapham[39] suggested that building provided more jobs for boys and men than any other industry except agriculture in 1833 and the numbers in the industry increased at a faster rate than the population as a whole for the century before 1914.[40] Though the industry developed largely along craft lines, the proportion of labourers to craftsmen was always high. There was a major strike of London building workers in 1859–60 for the reduction of the working day from nine to eight hours and the later decades of the century saw attempts by the workers in the industry to strengthen their bargaining position by rationalizing the union structure and by decreasing the inter-union conflicts rooted in the craft basis of organization. Similarly, the employers formed a national association in 1899, and attempted more widespread, unified action against strikes. Concentration of capital meant that by 1899 seventeen firms, less than 3 per cent of the total, were building well over 40 per cent of London's new houses.[41]

Thus the transformation of places that occurred during the growth of industrial capitalism cannot be attributed to technological change in isolation, nor to 'natural', linear or evolutionary changes. The exploitation of the natural environment, and the restructuring of relations between town and country, regions and metropolis, house and workplace, residence and social status were expressions of the combined and uneven nature of capitalist development. The whole process of urban development was problematic precisely because it was rooted in antagonistic class relations. This recognition is the starting point for a critical approach to the contemporary city.

Contemporary problems of urban and regional development

Just as the origins of today's settlement structure are attributable to the relations of production in the early, freely competitive stages of capitalism, the subsequent moulding of that structure has been closely linked to the imperialist and late capitalist stages. The theme of combined and uneven development again provides the context within which the problems of urban and regional development can be approached.

The physical spread of cities in countries such as the UK has been very evident during the twentieth century. In England and Wales the amount of land devoted to urban development doubled over the first half of the century, and even during the 1960s the net transfer of agricultural land to urban use in the UK averaged 19,700 hectares per year (48,700 acres). [42] In part this reflects national population growth from 38 million in 1901 to over 55 million in 1971, but demographic change *per se* does not constitute a sufficient explanation, for one of the most rapid phases of urban development coincided with expectations of a static or declining population, in the 1930s. Migration from the rural areas into the cities, such a potent factor in the nineteenth century spread of urban areas, has also been relatively insignificant. The basis of the urban expansion has therefore been demographic growth and developing transport technologies, mediated by the rising affluence which has enable headship rates to fall and car ownership to increase. This affluence was rooted in the relationships between the developed metropolitan countries and their colonies and semi-colonies.

Under the classical phase of imperialism capital began increasingly to move to colonial locations in search of above average levels of profit. The single nation state with its limited market and raw materials became a restriction on growth. Similarly, once the initial advances in technology had been consolidated, it became difficult to dramatically increase levels of productivity at home. In contrast, the colonies offered the opportunity of replacing pre-capitalist ways of producing raw materials by capitalist methods; for example, in plantation agriculture, or mechanization of mining. The transformation of colonial production was by no means absolute, however, for the ready availability of cheap labour militated against capital-intensive production methods. Rationalization rather than mechanization was therefore the norm and the capital accrued from the enterprises circulated back to the metropolitan countries rather than being reinvested in the industrialization of the colonies. Thus the industrial gap between the two widened, as did the divergence in wage levels. As Mandel observed

As soon . . . as the accumulation of capital ceased to advance principally through the displacement of pre-capitalist classes on the internal market (for labour) and turned instead to the expansion of the external market, it started to create more jobs than it destroyed in the metropolitan countries, because the jobs it destroyed were henceforward located in the underdeveloped countries.[43]

Colonial development thus provided an export market for some sectors of domestic production, notably railways and shipbuilding. One indication of the way such dominance of the world markets impacted on urban development can be seen from the case of Clydebank. Between 1901 and 1911 its population increased by 80 per cent. The boom reflected the pre-eminence of the Clyde in world shipbuilding; during 1912 a greater tonnage of ships was produced on the Clyde alone than in any other nation on earth.

   The rationalized production of raw materials in the colonies reduced their costs to imperialist consumers, thereby also reducing the organic composition of capital. These conditions made advances in working-class living standards possible within the major imperialist nations. Writing in 1920, Lenin expressed the situation as follows:

Obviously out of such super profits it is possible to bribe the labour leaders and the upper strata of the labour aristrocracy. And this is precisely what the capitalists of the 'advanced' countries are doing: they are bribing them in a thousand different ways, direct and indirect, overt and covert . . . .[44]

At the macro-level, then, the settlement pattern was consolidated through relations of combined and uneven development that obtained under imperialism. The onset of suburbanization was likewise tied to rising living standards which were dependent on those same relations. The decorous Edwardian suburb and the cantonment town are thus opposite poles of the same development process.

   Since the end of the Korean war, the major form of colonial exploitation has been through unequal relations of exchange, rather than the extraction of colonial surplus profits. The low productivity of colonial labour and the perceived political instability of the colonies and ex-colonies have increasingly persuaded capital in general to produce raw materials within the metropolitan countries, using industrialized production processes and manufacturing synthetic substitutes. This has resulted in a decline in the relative and absolute price of many Third World-produced raw materials on the world market, as those countries lost their position as semi-monopolistic sellers.

   This transfer of value through the changing terms of trade was the foundation upon which was built the rising affluence enjoyed by the rich countries during the 1950s and 1960s. As the share of the 'pure' means of subsistence in the real wages of the mass of their populations declined, mass consumption of what had previously been considered luxuries increased. One form of that consumption was better housing, more space and improved environments in suburbia, and the possession of a car. The rise in world commodity prices in the early 1970s and the ending of cheap oil by the OPEC cartel in particular, exposed something of the problematic nature of the trend towards a lower density, more dispersed settlement structure: calls for protection of agricultural land, self-sufficiency and more compact urban areas achieved a new topicality.

Suburban expansion was a major part of the British post-war consumer boom. It was integral to the promotion of owner occupation, a trend with strong ideological overtones as well as an economic underpinning. Suburban living imposed extra costs on household budgets; to cope, more women went to work, often in part-time jobs. In Britain the proportion of married women working increased from 10 per cent in 1931, to 22 per cent in 1951, to 42 per cent in 1971, and to just over 50 per cent by the end of the 1970s.[45] The consequent dislocation of the organization of domestic labour helped boost demand for a whole array of consumer durables, thus creating new commodities. Major industries have grown to meet this demand. They spend vast sums on advertising, much of it primarily directed at women who are insinuated to conform to the prescribed role of choosing the products to run an efficient and attractive home.

This is not to romanticize the unpaid domestic drudgery endured by previous generations of working class women, or the experience of those whose labour was hired for domestic service. Rather it is to note the specific commodity form in which the labour-saving aids have been introduced; such products have been designed, made and marketed with the aim of ensuring capital accumulation. From that basic fact comes the suppression of other non-commodity forms of reordering domestic labour; for example, through mutual help and shared facilities. Because they are commodities the goods are allocated through markets and hence better off families have been the first to benefit. The psychological imprisonment of the consumers to the 'choices' of the advertising industry likewise derives from the commodity form.

Private transport exemplifies *par excellence* the intimate association of suburban living, new commodities and patriarchy. In the city of freely competitive capitalism workers walked to their places of employment; their descendants in dormitory 'villages' must purchase a means of transport so as to sell their labour. The time and distance involved in travelling to work are unproductive costs of circulation. As such they constitute not just an opportunity to develop new commodities (the basis of the car indsutry), but also an indirect cost to the production process itself. A recurring problem for those seeking to manage urban development has therefore been how to expedite and reduce the costs of the journey to work, whilst maintaining and promoting suburban extension.

The labour carried out in and around the home by women in bringing up a family is not valued. Hence the transport system ignores the spatial requirements of such women, except where they can avail themselves of a car as a commodity. Transport is organized to reduce the time spent on the journey to work, rather than the time spent shopping with young children, taking them to the dentist, nursery, etc. Thus the pattern of urban development within advanced capitalism immobilizes women in a home environment designed for the individualistic consumption of commodities. Old persons and young children are similarly marooned while their safety is permanently threatened by the widespread penetration of motor traffic.

Post-war urban development has therefore been an integral part of the movement of capital into new sectors and new locations, in the drive to generate new sources of surplus value. An important feature of such development has been the separation of home and work, a separation corresponding to the notional division between women and men for primary responsibility for household production and wage labour. The whole process then, while rooted in the dynamics of class relationships, has also involved the reification of domesticity and the manipulation of women, together with the sundering of shared working class experiences which are an important element in class solidarity.

Though the spread of the city has been such a logical feature of the development of capitalism it has also been problematic. The costs of producing new houses remain high; not only must payments be made to landowners, but also the production process itself has remained labour intensive. The increases in productivity that have characterized other areas of commodity production have not been attained in the construction industry, though they have in the building materials industry, as Tables 4 and 5 show.[46]

Needleman noted the effects of this lower rate of productivity on housing costs and quoted a UN survey finding that a working-class dwelling in most Western European countries cost more in terms of average wages in 1959 than at the beginning of the century.[47] The provision of consumer credit has therefore become integral to the realization of the exchange value of housing as a commodity. Its significance is particularly apparent in the spectacular suburbanization of the UK in the 1930s. The 1 million investors in building societies in 1924 had doubled by 1939, while their capital rose from £137 million to £771 million and

Table 4   *Average rate of productivity increase in the UK, per cent per annum, 1907–55*

	1907–24	1924–35	1935–49	1949–55	1907–55
Total manufacturing	2.0	2.0	2.0	3.1	2.1
Building materials	1.9	2.1	2.3	2.5	2.1
Building and contracting	1.7	1.2	−3.6	3.6	0.2

Source: Lomax (1959), Table 8.

Table 5   *Trends in output per employee, 1955–73*

	1955–60	1960–5	1966–71	1971–3
Manufacture	2.2	2.8	3.6	6.7
Bricks, pottery, etc.	n.a.	4.0	4.8	8.7
Construction	2.2	1.2	7.0	−2.2

Source: National Institute Economic Review, February, 1975.

new mortgage advances trebled.[48] The builders pool, guaranteeing purchasers 95 per cent mortgages, was a major innovation. Here again therefore the urban development process embodies the characteristic features of the mode of production as a whole. In late capitalism over-capitalization or non-invested surplus capitals are a fundamental problem, which is countered by extending commodity production into new domains. Consumer credit and extensive advertising play an important role in this process; whereas credit was previously only associated with private consumption in times of misery and was the cause of humiliation to the borrowers, it now plays a key role in the economy as a whole, while also being the basis of permanent inflation.

Major reconstruction of central areas has been another characteristic feature of capitalist urban development. In part it was a response to changing technologies used in production and distribution resulting in the suburbanization of industry, as described later. Technology and management methods have also altered the space requirements of the office sector; air-conditioned open-plan spaces are now the norm, instead of small rooms with high ceilings off long corridors, as was common before the 1950s.

The service sector has itself expanded. Over-capitalization is a major structural problem of capitalism. Idle capital has therefore sought to convert services into commodities.[49] A related problem is the realization of surplus value. Simply, yet fundamentally, consumption cannot be increased at the same rate as the productivity of labour for that would prevent the valorization and accumulation of capital. Advertising and consumer credit have developed into crucial activities in the attempt to overcome these problems and they have located within the central areas. Similarly, retailing methods have been drastically restyled to foster and expedite further consumption and realization. Though these pressures have been generalized, the increasing concentration of capital has been reflected in the concentration of demand in the centres of a few key cities.[50]

The extended administration of the state has also added to the demands for central area floorspace, while also providing new outlets for capital investment. While the process as such is again generalized, it has particularly impacted on central areas within capital cities such as London and Dublin.

Problems of capital over-accumulation had a direct as well as an indirect impact on central area redevelopment. There was major investment in property in the years immediately preceding the recession. Pre-tax profits on industrial investments averaged 13 per cent in the USA and the UK in the late 1950s, but had fallen to 10 per cent and 7 per cent respectively by 1973.[51] Property shares performed consistently better than industrial shares on the London stock market from 1967 onwards and the Financial Times property index rose from 60 in 1967 to 250 in 1973.[52] The Heath government attempted to overcome the chronic problems of realization by a 'dash for growth', with an expansion of M3 (currency, current bank accounts and deposit accounts) by 270 per cent from mid-1970 to early 1974.[53] The relative returns on capital ensured that the main boom took place in the property sector.

Thus new and planned office accommodation in the south-east of England increased from 16.9 million square feet in 1968 to 38.8 million square feet in 1974, with the bulk of it concentrated in central London. At the peak of the boom foreign bank borrowing by the fringe banks, who were heavily involved in property development, stood at £3850 million a sum almost equal to the amount that the clearing banks were lending the whole of manufacturing industry. The balance sheet of London and County Securities leapt from £5 million in 1970 to £129 million three years later, that of Cedar Holdings from £11 million to £128 million.[54]

A situation in which money was borrowed at relatively high interest rates and invested at a low guaranteed annual rate of return, in the hope that expectations of escalating rents would push up the paper valuations of the properties was inherently unstable. The collapse of the boom, like its origins, was rooted in the combined and uneven development of the economic system as a whole. Commodity prices began to rise sharply in 1973: the Economist World Commodity Index rose from 170 in January of that year to 290 in July. In part this represented short-term speculation and a response to inflation, but it also stemmed from real relative scarcities that had been caused by the slower rate of capital investment in the primary producing sector than in the manufacturing sector for a long period.[55] This new situation, culminating in the trauma of the escalation in oil prices, created uncertainty, which hit the property sector where prices had already reached levels that were deterring potential users. That year also saw a sharp rise in interest rates, increasing development costs and creating liquidity problems. There was also political discontent at the exorbitant gains made by the property companies and special taxes were threatened. To avert widespread bankruptcies, and a major crisis of confidence in the financial system, the Bank of England and the big banks launched their 'lifeboat operation', the costs of which are put at £2000 million.[56]

The property market was therefore depressed for a while, but has recovered since 1976 without regaining the heady levels of the boom. In this last decade pension funds and life assurance funds have grown rapidly and have invested between 10 and 20 per cent of their capital in property. Their net investment in land and property shot up from £194 million in 1971 to £945 million in 1977.[57] Though not all of this was directed at central area redevelopment, it is clear that the big investors have been competing for prime developments in major centres and especially in London.

Landowners are clearly a key factor in the urban redevelopment process. They have a common interest in maintaining and increasing the value of land. Marx saw them as a class – landed capital – who had appropriated for themselves monopoly over the land; through private property landlords are therefore able to extract rent from users of the land. Where the rent is levied on capitalists producing on the site, it is paid for out of surplus value, since the mere act of owning and renting land is not itself productive of value. A conflict therefore exists between landed capital (seeking to maximize rents) and industrial capital (seeking to minimize them). Though the composition of urban landed capital has changed since Marx's time, with land in prime locations being increasingly acquired purely as a financial investment by the financial institutions within late capitalism, the basic validity of Marx's analysis remains.[58]

Another response to the problem of excess capital seeking investments productive of surplus value has been the mechanization of all sectors of the economy. Durable consumer goods have replaced living labour in the home; agriculture has been industrialized both at the point of production and in the packaged food industry.[59] Mechanized production processes have created a requirement for single-storey accommodation, especially where production line techniques are involved. Parking for the labour force and space to manipulate larger delivery vehicles, has added to the land requirements of such plants. Extensive sites have been difficult to assemble in the traditional manufacturing zones of multiple ownerships in the inner city. Furthermore, the rents there have remained higher than for newly converted agricultural land at the edge of the city. The result has been suburbanization of industry.

A further consequence of this extended industrialization has been a general equalization of the productivity of labour in and between the main realms of production. This has made industry more footloose, and has meant that the chief source of surplus profits is now the 'technological rents' that derive from a monopolization of technological innovation.[60] The turn-over time of fixed capital has therefore been steadily reduced. Machines and plants are used continuously for a shorter period, rather than continually over a longer period and obsolesce more rapidly. This in itself reduces the inertia exerted by fixed capital, and encourages the relocation of concerns. Furthermore, the reduced turn-over time of fixed capital has repercussions on the turn-over time of circulating capital. At one level it encourages firms to convert circulating capital into fixed capital, while for capital in general it leads to a further acceleration in the turn-over time of circulating capital as a source for the additional production of surplus value. This shift is made all the more necessary by the increased organic composition of capital consequent on the reduced turn-over time of fixed capital. It is these tendencies that underpin the growth of the road haulage and warehousing industries, which are both stimulators and products of the suburbanization of industry. Faster movement and planned distribution of goods speed up the turn-over of that part of capital which they represent: capital previously tied up in stock can be freed for investment in plant and machinery. The production of vehicles and containers, etc. is a source of surplus value, and extra surplus value can also be realized from the increased exchange value that can be a consequence of the movement of goods.[61]

A substantial devaluation of the capital locked in exchange value has therefore been forced. Productivity has been increased by writing off labour. Products have been discontinued, plants closed and production rationalized. Overall this has resulted in an enormous decline in jobs for skilled, semi-skilled and unskilled male manual workers. Thus to reduce wage costs new production methods have been devised, replacing tasks requiring skills by jobs that can be done by fewer, unskilled operatives. The process had already begun well before the current crisis, as the data in Table 6 show.

In branches of industry which have remained labour-intensive, such as the production of light industrial finished goods (for example, clothing, shoes and watches) multi-national capital has tended to relocate production to countries offering a pool of low wage labour. The free production zones offered in South Korea, Taiwan, Malaysia, Indonesia, Hong Kong, the Philippines and some Latin American and African countries offer not only low wages but few restrictions in terms of sickness, insurance, holiday allowance and other conditions of employment. In addition, there are no restrictions on the repatriation of profits. Female labour is especially cheap and malleable to the priorities of the company. This process presents enormous competition to traditional producers located in the inner areas of the metropolitan countries, which can only be effectively countered by protective tariffs, or by reducing the degree of labour-intensity of the production process by introducing automation and rationalizations, to restore profitability. The result, however, is a further loss of jobs.

Massey and Meegan probed some of the detail behind these attempts to restructure production.[63] They showed how the heavy electrical engineering, supertension cable and aerospace equipment industries were dominated by problems of surplus productive capital. The response was a centralization of capital, leading to a co-ordinated reduction in productive capacity, which involved a loss of jobs and deskilling, though not necessarily to a relocation of plants to new sites. The problems in the electronic capital goods industry were rather different. There was pressure to increase and cheapen output because of the important contribution this sector could make to increasing productivity in the rest of the economy. International competition was also a factor. The results were overall growth in the sector, but centralization of research and development into fewer and larger companies, with reductions in labour and skill levels. Again, job loss through relocation was far less than through changes and closures in existing plants.

Massey and Meegan showed how the major cities had borne the bulk of the

Table 6   *Change in skill structure of local residents, 1966–71*

	Skilled		Semi-skilled		Unskilled	
	1966	1971	1966	1971	1966	1971
	(%)		(%)		(%)	
Batley	39.5	38.9	21.9	19.7	9.8	9.3
Benwell	42.6	42.2	19.6	15.4	14.8	17.1
Canning Town	34.4	32.4	21.7	18.9	25.0	24.0
North Shields	40.0	40.2	21.6	18.9	16.0	18.1
Saltley	44.5	37.4	26.6	28.7	16.0	20.3

Source: 1966, 1971 Censuses.[62]

reductions in the labour force that this rationalization entailed. The uneven impact of employment change has also been recorded by Fothergill and Gudgin, whose findings are set down in Table 7.

It is the inner areas of the cities which have been the locus for the most severe de-industrialization. Nevertheless, inner area locations are still attractive to some industries, notably those requiring relatively large amounts of cheap storage space involving minimal investment in fixed capital. Access to reserves of cheap labour is another attraction. The cotton mills that were the cradle of industrial capitalism in the north-west of England now serve as discount warehouses. Where the textile industry continues, its labour is likely to include a high proportion of New Commonwealth immigrants. This immigration had its origins in the acute labour shortages that British industry encountered in the 1950s and early 1960s, and in the widening gap in living standards enjoyed in the mother country and her colonial offspring. While this reconstruction of an industrial reserve army has been economically beneficial to capital, and at the same time has provided a scapegoat by which to explain the spiral of inner city decline to the indigenous inhabitants, the high unemployment rates faced by the British-born 'immigrants' during the current crisis poses problems for social control, as the riots of 1981 indicated.

The equalization of productivity and the phase of labour shortage during the 1950s and 1960s led to the recruitment of more women into the labour force. Much of the increase was in part-time jobs. Thus of the 439,000 female jobs created in the service sector between 1975 and 1980, 309,000 (70 per cent) were part-time. By 1980, 27 per cent of all female jobs were part time compared with 3 per cent of male jobs.[64] Though part-time employment opens opportunities for some women, especially those with young children, the conditions and entitlements of part-time workers are markedly inferior to those of full-timers. Thus, while 72

Table 7   *Employment change in Great Britain by settlement type, 1959–75*

	Change in employment, 1959–75			
Settlement type	All emp. (%)	Service emp. (%)	Manufacturing emp. nos. ('000s)	(%)
London	−11.4	+ 1.9	−586	−37.8
Conurbations	− 4.7	+ 5.9	−434	−15.9
Free standing cities	+12.5	+16.0	+ 79	+ 4.9
Industrial towns	+22.0	+21.1	+255	+16.3
County towns	+18.0	+15.2	+184	+28.8
Rural Areas	+14.3	+11.4	+ 73	+77.2
Great Britain	+ 5.1	+10.8		− 5.2

Source: S Fothergill and G Gudgin, *Unequal Growth: Urban & Regional Employment Change in the U.K.* (Heinemann, 1982), Tables 2.2, 2.4 and 3.7, pp. 16, 22 and 44.

per cent of establishments offer membership of a pension scheme, in only 15 per cent are part-time staff eligible for membership. Similarly, 70 per cent provide sick pay benefits above government minima, but only 35 per cent of establishments extend these rights to part-time workers.[65]

Low pay is another widespread problem for female workers. Over 2.25 million of the 3 million workers in Wages Councils industries are women and even the low minimum wages set in such industries are not always adhered to. Another avenue of low paid female employment is homeworking, with its echoes of the outworking in Foster's Oldham. Between 200,000 and 400,000 are thought to be employed in this way in Britain, the majority being women aged between twenty-five and forty-four with dependent children.[66] Though such workers have found an escape from the home/work split discussed earlier, they suffer very low earnings – the 1980 average figure being 75p per hour.[67]

The employment circumstances confronting women must be seen against the increase in one-parent families and the collapse of male employment. Thus in Manchester by the early 1980s over 30 per cent of female workers were the principal wage earners in their households.[68] Once again, class struggles are interwoven with gender, and reflected in the disarray of the physical environment of the city.

While the struggle over restructuring has been most evident to date in the manufacturing sector, there are signs that it is now being intensified in services too. Thus the big clearing banks have begun to cut back sharply on recruitment: Barclays, for example are targetting a 7 per cent annual growth, but with only 2 per cent being met with extra staff. The Prudential made over 400 of its white-collar workers redundant in 1982, and the Commercial Union was aiming to reduce its UK staff by 7 per cent.[69]

Once again there is an impact on the production of the urban fabric. There are already signs of excess office floorspace in city centres. Between January 1981 and October 1982, available office space in London increased from 5.8 million square feet to over 11 million square feet. Despite this, more than 2 million square feet were still being erected.[70] Large companies wanting to stay in central London are switching to compact premises with room for only 100 employees. Routine office activities are both shedding jobs *in situ* and also decentralizing. Symbolically, the London and Manchester Assurance Company now has its head office in Exeter, in a new £6.5 million development. To make the move the company spent £1.8 million on redundancies and early retirements, but sold its City premises for £11 million and reckons to save over £1000 annually on each of its 700 employees.[71]

The economic crisis and the struggles over restructuring have also affected inter-regional relations. Massey showed that the development areas, the old 'problem' regions, had fared less badly in the process of restructuring than the non-development areas. She interpreted the phenomena as follows: 'Such tendencies, however, do not mean the end of a spatial division of labour, homogenization of the whole country. They imply, rather, a different form of integration and new forms of differentiation.'[72]

The quintessential manufacturing industries of late capitalism are those requiring colossal capital investment, exhibiting a very rapid turn-over time for fixed capital, and dependent on a high level of technology. The petrochemical industry is perhaps the most evident example. The space requirements and the pollution from such industries rule out an inner city location. They are capital-intensive rather than labour-intensive, though a significant part of their labour force is made up of highly skilled technicians. They are therefore not even tied to a location close to the metropolis, and indeed access to high quality rural environments may be an enticement to their key workers. The tendency has been for such concerns to locate within the imperialist nations rather than in the Third World, whose supplies of cheap labour are irrelevant to these enterprises, and whose perceived 'instability' could lead to the expropriation of expensive plant. The peripheral areas of the metropolitan countries are thus sought out, not least because pollution controls are likely to be less demanding there than in the heartlands of such countries. Thus the most technically advanced industry is located in areas previously considered to be backward.

The development of the oil industry in the Shetland Isles and the north-east of Scotland provides a dramatic but not unique example. In Belgium there has been unprecedented industrialization in the Flanders region since 1960, a process led by the establishment of the petrochemical industry in the Antwerp area, and in the Ghent–Terneuzen Canal zone. By 1967 per capital income in the Flanders area exceeded that of the old industrial area of Wallonia.[73] In the remote west of Ireland, donkeys today trot past branch factories of multi-national computer companies that were introduced by the assiduous efforts of the Industrial Development Authority.[74]

When viewed, for example, at a Western European scale, there seems to be a case for interpreting the whole process in terms of theories of underdevelopment and dependency. Though caution must be exercised in applying a body of theory fashioned in respect of truly colonial situations, mainly in Latin America, to variations within the metropolitan countries, they nevertheless provide a kernel of understanding. Thus Dos Santos defines dependency as:

A situation in which the economy of a certain group of countries is conditioned by
the development and expansion of another economy, to which their own is subjected
. . . an historical condition which shapes a certain structure of the world economy
such that it favours some countries to the detriment of others, and limits the
development possibilities of the (subordinate) economies.[75]

The repatriation of profits from the colonies has already been commented upon. The argument is that the process of capital accumulation augments the uneven-ness between classes, sectors of industry, agriculture and industry, town and country within the dependent country. Thus as Amin observes,

. . . as economic growth proceeds, none of these features by which the structure of
the periphery is distinguished lessens; on the contrary, each increases. Whereas at the
centre growth is development – that is it has an integrating effect – in the periphery,

growth is not development, for its effect is to disarticulate. Strictly speaking, growth in the periphery, based on integration into the world market, is development of underdevelopment.[76]

The process described by Amin has been illustrated in Scotland. The closures of the pulp mill at Fort William, and the aluminium smelter at Invergordon, are reminders of how the development of underdevelopment is carried out on terms laid down at the centre and by capital, rather than at the periphery and by labour.

This shift towards raw material production in the metropolitan countries exacerbates the difficulties of the underdeveloped countries proper. There part of the development of underdevelopment has involved the replacement of subsistence agriculture by the growing of cash crops aimed at the world market. In part this represents the extension of commodity production by capital, but it also reflects the growing indebtedness of those countries in their search for foreign exhange. Thus the output of coffee from Africa increased by 300 per cent from 1959 to 1967.[77] One contradictory consequence of this reorientation of agriculture is that while the semi-colonies exported 14 million tons of grain products annually in the 1930s, by the later 1960s they were importing 10 million tons a year.[78]

Development has thus produced a major dislocation of relations between rural and urban areas, expressed by the high rates of rural–urban migration, and the sharp contrasts within the city between the anonymous international architecture of the city centre office blocks and the ramshackle vernacular of poverty in the shanty towns. The social crises that permeate the production of cities under capitalism are most sharply exposed in these dichotomies.

Urban and regional development is thus a function of the mode of production as a whole. To understand that development we must grasp the key features of the mode of production. Within capitalism the ultimate imperative is the appropriation and accumulation of surplus value, while the various spheres of production and component parts of capital develop unevenly. This is the process which underpins the 'old' differentiation between imperialist nations and their colonies, between regions within those nations, and between town and country. It is still the dynamic of this process which has created the 'new' differentiations between neo-colonies and metropolitan countries, between conurbations and free standing country towns and also suburbia and the inner city. Spatial divisions are accompanied by gender divisions and both are rooted in class relationships, while simultaneously fragmenting those same class relationships.

The physical environment is the repository of dead labour and as such, within capitalism, inhibits contemporary capital accumulation. Periodic devaluations of fixed capital are one way that capitalism responds to the falling rates of profit. Thus the crises of capitalism are written in the settlement structure and the built environment, and that structure and environment become the focus for political struggles pitched with varying degrees of consciousness at resisting the offerings and imperatives of capital. The state is therefore involved in steering urban and regional change through a variety of mechanisms, one of which it calls 'town and country planning'.

References and Notes

1   E. Mandel, *Late Capitalism* (New Left Books 1975), p. 504.
2   B. J. L. Berry, *Growth Centres in the American Urban System*. Vol. 1, 'Community development and regional growth in the sixties and seventies'; vol. 2 'Working materials on the US urban hierarchy and on growth centre characteristics, organized by economic region' (Ballinger 1973).
3   N. Spence, 'The evolving metropolitan area', *Urban Change and Conflict*, (Unit 8, The Open University Press 1982), p. 77.
4   See, for example, C. Leven, 'The emergence of maturity in metropolis', in C. Leven (ed.), *The Mature Metropolis* (D. C. Heath 1978). This symposium was funded by the Mercantile Bank Corporation: crude economist interpretations of the evolutionary analogy as ideology have some appeal!
5   M. Horkheimer, 'Traditional and critical theory', in P. Connerton (ed.), *Critical Sociology* (Penguin 1976), pp. 206–8.
6   This theoretical position is developed in a number of works by Habermas. See, for example, his text, *Knowledge and Human Interests* (Heinemann 1972).
7   J. Lewis and B. Melville, 'The politics of epistemology in regional science', a paper presented to the Ninth Annual Conference of the Regional Science Association (British Section), 2 September, 1976, p. 12. The paper was subsequently published in P. W. J. Batey (ed.), *Theory and Method in Urban and Regional Analysis'* (Pion 1977).
8   Notably to his book entitled *General Theory* (MIT Press 1969).
9   B. Harris, 'The uses of theory in the simulation of urban phenomena', *Journal of the American Institute of Planners*, vol. 32 (1966), p. 260.
10   I. S. Lowry, 'A model of metropolis', RAND Corporation, *Memorandum RM-4035-RC, 1964*. The major initial adaptation was that by R. A. Garin, 'A matrix formulation of the Lowry model for intra-metropolitan activity location', *Journal of the American Institute of Planners*, vol. 32 (1966), pp. 361–4. A summary of the main developments of the model was provided by W. Goldner, 'The Lowry model heritage', *Journal of the American Institute of Planners*, vol. 36 (1971), pp. 100–10.
11   D. M. Hill, 'A growth allocation model for the Boston region', *Journal of the American Institute of Planners*, vol. 31 (1965), pp. 111–20.
12   J. W. Forrester, *Urban Dynamics* (MIT Press 1968).
13   J. Lewis and B. Melville, p. 21.
14   K. Marx, *Capital*, vol. I, (Penguin 1976), p. 125.
15   Ibid., p. 126.
16   K. Marx, *A Contribution to the Critique of Political Economy* (International Publishers Edition 1970), pp. 41–43.
17   K. Marx, *Capital*, vol. I, pp. 128–9.
18   Ibid., p. 129.

19 K. Marx, *Capital*, vol. III (Lawrence and Wishart 1970), pp. 211–337.

20 E. Mandel, p. 39.

21 Ibid., pp. 41–2.

22 A critique of such traditional theory is provided by D. Massey, 'Towards a critique of industrial location theory', *Antipode*, vol. 5, no. 3 (1973), pp. 33–9. In this article Massey quotes Richardson on the dilemmas posed by equilibrium analysis thus, 'The dilemma is that it is difficult to formulate a determinate general theory of location without adopting the pedagogic device of the equilibrium concept, yet if this concept is adopted complications arise from the probability that general equilibrium is inconsistent with the implications of the space economy,' H. W. Richardson, *Regional Economics* (Weidenfeld & Nicolson 1969).

23 A writer quoted by Stow in 1598; the full context is given by E. G. Taylor, 'Leland's England', in H. Darby, *An Historical Geography of England before 1800* (Cambridge University Press 1961), p. 335.

24 J. Foster, *Class Struggle and the Industrial Revolution: Early industrial capitalism in three English towns* (Methuen 1977), p. 14.

25 For example, Community Development Projects Inter-project Editorial Team, *The Costs of Industrial Change* (Home Office Urban Deprivation Unit 1977); N. Moor and P. Waddington, *From Rags to Ruins: Batley, Woollen Textiles and Industrial Change* (CDP Political Economy Collective 1980); Benwell Community Project, *Adamsez – The Story of a Factory Closure* (Benwell Community Project 1980).

26 For example, J. Carney, R. Hudson, G. Ive and J. Lewis, 'Regional underdevelopment in late capitalism: a study of the North-East of England', in *Urban Change and Conflict* (Centre for Environmental Studies, Conference Paper 14, 1975). Also, J. Carney, R. Hudson and J. Lewis, *Regions in Crisis* (Croom Helm 1980).

27 Community Development Project Inter-Project Editorial Team, 1977, p. 10.

28 For example, in 1891 half the population resident in Canning Town had migrated from Essex, ibid., p. 15.

29 J. R. Mellor develops this theme in another paper to the 1975 CES Urban Sociology Conference, entitled 'The British experiment: combined and uneven development'.

30 F. Engels, *The Condition of the English Working Classes in 1844* (Panther 1969), pp. 79–80.

31 J. Foster, p. 84.

32 Ibid., p. 88.

33 There was a political dimension to this economic relationship. For example, in the 1844 miners' strike the coalowners evicted the strikers and their families from their cottages, then prosecuted those who camped out for trespassing.

34   K. Marx, *Capital* vol. I, p. 820.
35   Arnold Bennett's fiction provides a characterization of landlordism: 'He owned a hundred and seventy-five cottages in the town, having bought them gradually in half-dozens, and in rows; he collected the rents himself, and was celebrated as a good landlord, and as being almost the only man in Bursley who had made cottage property pay.' 'News of the Engagement', in *The Grim Smile of the Five Towns*, (Penguin 1975 edition), pp. 108–9.

The actual building process was also affected by the cycles of booms and slumps in the wider economy: for a summary of the extensive work done on this aspect see A. A. Nevitt, 'Issues in housing', in R. Davies and P. Hall (eds), *Issues in Urban Society* (Penguin 1978), pp. 185–8. Marx described the process in Volume II of *Capital*,

To what extent capitalist production has revolutionised the building of houses in London is shown by the testimony of a builder before the Banking Committee of 1857. When he was young, he said, houses were generally built to order and the payments made in instalments to the contractor as certain stages of the building were being completed. Very little is now built to order. Anyone wanting a new house picks one from among those built on speculation or still in the process of construction. The builder no longer works for his customer, but the market. Like every other industrial capitalist he is compelled to have finished articles in the market. While formerly a builder had three or four houses building at a time for speculation, he must now buy a large plot of ground (which in continental language means rent it for ninety-nine years, as a rule), build from 100 to 200 houses on it and thus embark on an enterprise which exceeds his resources twenty to fifty times. The funds are procured through mortgaging, and the money is placed at the disposal of the contractor as the building proceeds. Then, if a crisis comes along and interrupts the payment of the advance instalments, the entire enterprise generally collapses. At best, the houses remain unfinished until better times arrive; at the worst they are sold for auction for half their cost. Without speculative building, and on a large scale at that, no contractor can get along today. The profit from just building is extremely small. His main profit comes from raising the ground rent, from careful selection and skilled utilisation of the building terrain.

Abbreviated from the *Report of the Select Committee on Bank Acts*, Part 1, 1857, Evidence, Question 5, 13–18; 5435–36.

36   K. Marx, *Capital*, vol. I, p. 816.
37   Ibid., p. 803.
38   K. Marx, *Grundrisse: Introduction to the Critique of Political Economy* (Penguin 1973) p. 252.
39   J. Clapham, *An Economic History of Modern Britain*, vol. 1 (Cambridge University Press 1930).
40   R. Issacharoff, 'The Building Boom of the Inter-War Years: Whose profits and at whose cost?', paper presented to the 1977 Urban Conflict and Change Conference organized by the Centre for Environmental Studies,

the proceedings of which were published by CES as Conference Paper 19.

41 Ibid.

42 A. G. Champion, 'Issues over Land', in R. Davies and P. Hall (eds), pp. 24–5.

43 E. Mandel, p. 363.

44 Lenin, Preface to the French edition of 'Imperialism', 1920, in *Lenin, Selected Works* (London 1969), pp. 174–5.

45 L. McDowell, 'Class, status, location and life style', *Urban Change and Conflict*, (Unit 13, Open University Press, 1982), p. 30.

46 These tables are included in a paper by M. Ball, 'British housing policy and the house building industry', given to the 1977 Urban Change and Conflict Conference. They are derived from K. S. Lomax, 'Production and productivity movements in the UK since 1900', *Journal of the Royal Statistical Society*, Series A, vol. 122 (1959); and the *National Institute Economic Review* (Feb. 1975).

47 L. Needleman, *The Economics of Housing* (Staples 1965).

48 These figures are quoted in J. R. Mellor (1975).

49 See E. Mandel, Ch. 12, pp. 377–407 for a fuller elaboration of the idea.

50 S. Hymer, 'The multi-national corporation and the law of uneven development', in J. Bhagwati (ed), *Economics and World Order from the 1970s to the 1990s* (Collier Macmillan 1972). A similar point is made by R. Colenutt, 'The political economy of the property market', *Antipode*, vol. 8, no. 2 (1976), pp. 24–30.

51 R. Colenutt, p. 24.

52 Ibid., p. 25.

53 R. Heller and N. Willatt, 'The Bungle that cost the Banks £2,000,000,000', *Business Observer*, 29 May 1977.

54 Ibid.

55 E. Mandel, p. 371.

56 R. Heller and N. Willatt. The same story is told by K. Fleet, G. Sarjeant, and R. Milner, 'To the brink of ruin and back', *Sunday Times*, 22 January 1978.

57 R. Colenutt and C. Hamnett, 'Urban land use and the property development industry', *Urban Change and Conflict* (Unit 9, Open University Press 1982), p. 29.

58 For Marxist debates on rent in urban development see D. Harvey, *Social Justice and the City* (Edward Arnold 1973), Ch. 5, I. Breugel, 'The Marxist theory of rent and the contemporary city: a critique of Harvey', in *Political Economy and the Housing Question*, published by the Housing Workshop of the Conference of Socialist Economists, 1975, pp. 34–46. M. Edel, 'Marx's Theory of Rent: Urban Applications', in *Housing and Class in Britain*, published by the Political Economy of Housing Workshop of the

48   *The development of planning thought*

Conference of Socialist Economists, 1976, pp. 7–23.

59   Some 70 per cent of all food is now processed in one way or another according to a report in the *Guardian*, (6 September 1978) by its Agricultural Correspondent.

60   See E. Mandel, p. 193 et seq. He argues that this process is itself deeply contradictory, tending towards latent over-production of the means of production and, under complete automation, to the non-creation of surplus value.

61   E. Mandel, p. 404.

62   Community Development Project Inter-Project Editorial Team, 1977, p. 25.

63   D. R. Massey and R. A. Meegan, 'Industrial restructuring versus the cities', *Urban Studies*, vol. 15 (1978), pp. 273–288.

64   Manchester City Planning Department, 'Employment and unemployment in Manchester: a context for local economic and employment initiatives', *Economic Information Paper 1/81*, Manchester City Council (1981), p. 21.

65   Ibid.

66   Ibid.

67   Ibid.

68   Ibid.

69   *Sunday Times Business News*, 24 October 1982.

70   Ibid.

71   Ibid.

72   D. R. Massey, 'Capital and locational change: the UK electrical engineering and electronics industries', *Review of Radical Political Economics*, Fall, 1978. Reprinted in A. Blowers, C. Brook, P. Dunleavy and L. McDowell (eds.), *Urban Change and Conflict: An Interdisciplinary Reader* (Harper Row/Open University Press 1982), p. 57.

73   J. Carney, R. Hudson and J. Lewis, p. 44.

74   See, e.g. D. C. Perrons, 'The role of Ireland in the new international division of labour: a proposed framework for regional analysis,' *Regional Studies*, vol. 15, no. 2 (1981), pp. 81–100.

75   T. Dos Santos, 'The structure of dependence', *American Economic Review*, vol. 60 (1970). Quoted in C. Regan and F. Walsh, 'Dependence and Underdevelopment: the case of mineral resources in the Irish Republic', *Antipode*, vol. 8, no. 3 (1976), pp. 46–59.

76   S. Amin, *Accumulation on a World Scale* (Monthly Review Press 1974). Quoted in C. Regan and F. Walsh.

77   E. Mandel, p. 375.

78   Ibid.

2 The state response – the development of the British planning system

Orthodox interpretations of the origins of British town planning can be divided into two categories, idealist and evolutionist. Idealists see the power of the idea of planning as advanced by brilliant individual planners as being sufficient explanation for the development of planning, *per se*. The story of the development of planning therefore flits from Howard to Geddes, Unwin, Abercrombie, etc. While such figures undoubtedly made major contributions, a focus on their roles becomes idealist when their ideas are disconnected from the the political situation in which they were formulated.

In extreme forms idealist interpretations can descend to hypostatized assertions about planning that are totally ahistorical. Contextless claims that 'planning is design', or 'planning is a general decision-making process' are examples. Such statements are best understood as ideology, ideas fashioned by the interests of a particular group. Thus those most trenchant in their defence of planners as a professional elite with a unique expertise are prone to interpret town planning as a coherent, unambiguous idea, which at some blurred point in time an equally coherent 'society' grasps and puts into effect. For example, Kantorowich wrote:

It is only during this century when the pressures of rapidly expanding, industrialized and urbanized populations on fixed land resources has so intensified, that the urgent need consciously to plan and control the use of all land has become generally recognized and accepted by society. Thus our profession, Town Planning (or however else it is described), has emerged fully in response to a social need as a distinct professional process, interposed as a catalyst between the stages of policy-making and implementation in the process of environmental change.[1]

Such authors ascribe planning a virgin birth. It is a professional offspring whose immaculate conception is quite severed from the intercourse of social classes.

The alternative tradition, favoured by planners of more liberal inclination, has been a variant of the Whig theory of history. This involves an evolutionist and social reformist interpretation, in which Ashworth's remains a classic text.[2] The bad living conditions of the Victorian city, charted by researchers such as Booth and authors such as Dickens, shocked the conscience of society. The first response was public health legislation. Then came philanthropist experiments in town planning and the emergence of a town planning lobby, whose aims were eventually translated into legislation. Cherry's works have made important contributions to this tradition.[3] Such authors have stressed the social origins of town planning. They have implied a model of the state as a set of benevolent and rational individuals who have responded progressively to new information or changed situations. Thus Cherry wrote:

This book aims modestly to sketch the development of statutory planning in this country, the growth of the subject matter of town planning and the expansion of the town planning profession. The links between them are traced as well as their relationship to a contextual background. It has not been possible to go beyond this stage. The gaps now need to be filled in: the personal contributions of politicians and technocrats, the parts played by dedicated individuals (Chamberlain or Nettlefold at Birmingham or the Simons at Manchester, for example), or the contributions of certain groundswells in human affairs which carried society along a particular path (represented for instance by the social reformers, civic designers or futurists).[4]

The above quotation is interesting both for what it says and for what it does not say. The implication is that there has been an orderly growth and expansion of town planning. The gaps needing filled exclude any relation of town planning to class conflict, nor is any understanding of the economics of capitalism placed on the agenda. The natural science analogy of evolution substitutes for a materialist analysis of the interests which have defined the practice of town planning.

One strength of the evolutionist interpretation is that it does provide a historical perspective, in contrast to the professional tendency to repress history in favour of the proclamation of eternal truths about the nature of planning. However, the weakness is that while planning is described through the extension of government intervention, there is not a theory of the state at the centre of the analysis. The interests served by the growth of planning are thus obscured, as planning is itself equated with progress. Implicitly the approach draws on Weberian traditions in sociology. Weber distinguished between the economic and the political aspects of a society. Though he accepted that there were influences between the two, the spheres were essentially seen as autonomous. Power was seen as primarily the preserve of individuals and bureaucracies. It is a tradition that can offer some useful insights about the development of planning, but its limitation is its rejection of a systematic connection between political and economic power. Once politics and economics are connected, the perspectives on the state are substantially changed.

The state

A theory of the state is also a theory of the society and of the distribution of power in that society. Thus the state consists not just of the government, but also of the institutions associated with it. These necessarily include the civil service, local government, the police, the military and the judiciary. The form and nature of the state, its role and the relation of the state to social interests is not static. In feudalism that state was the key medium of social control. It expressed the social structure of the monarchy and aristocracy as the ruling class, while its morality and metaphysics regulated behaviour and obligations between classes. Domination was made legitimate from the top downwards.

The development of the productive forces under capitalism was predicated on principles of purposive-rational action. These contradicted the mysterious forms through which power had traditionally been legitimated. Instead, economic exchange became the dominant steering mechanism, the cement welding the society together. Habermas argued that the atomized exchange of commodities in the market and not least the exchange of labour power for wages, was notionally the exchange of equivalence. Thus a relation of communicative action became the basis of legitimation.[5] The pattern of feudalism was therefore inverted. Instead of the relations of production being made legitimate through the political system, the political system of the bourgeois revolutions was justified in terms of the legitimate relations of production. A politically constituted system of social labour was superseded by an economic regulation, in which the form of the state was more muted.

Typically, in the period of freely competitive capitalism, the state was primarily concerned with security both internally and in defence against foreign powers. Marx and Engels emphasized in their writings that this state was not a neutral arbitrator, rather it remained a means of class domination. The *Communist Manifesto* declared, 'The executive of the modern state is but a committee for managing the common affairs of the whole bourgeoisie'.[6] The state was thus seen as acting in the interests of capital as a whole, and thus at times acting against the interests of particular capitalists, a logical corollary of the antagonistic production relations around which capitalism was structured.

Writers in the Marxist tradition have continued to portray the state as an instrument of class domination. In a capitalist society economic power is in private hands and government changes do not alter that fact. For such societies to operate capital accumulation must be facilitated and the state must conform to this imperative. Today the state has a more extended role than in the phase of freely competitive capitalism. It contributes directly to capitalist production, through subsidies, state investments and state-owned industries. It also helps to reproduce a labour force, notably through education, health and housing provision, where such necessary services could not be profitably provided by capital itself. Furthermore the modern state reproduces the relations of production, by repressing dissent and by projecting an ideology which obscures class antagonisms, substituting instead a spurious national unity.[7]

One objection to this thesis is the fact that the most hostile critics of state intervention are the unashamed champions of market forces.[8] Furthermore it is workers rather than capitalists who appear to be the most direct beneficiaries of many state services, such as council housing, the health service, perhaps even town planning. One possibility then is that though the state in the last instance must serve the overall interest of capitalists, the working class, aided by the advent of universal suffrage, have been able to win some victories, or at least wrest some concessions.

The proposition is that the state is relatively autonomous while also acting to maintain the profitability of private capital. This measure of autonomy is necessary if the state is to be able to look after the interests of capital as a whole. However, such propositions can easily slip into a very functionalist and instrumental view of state action, in which any and every activity of the state must ultimately be desired by capital. Such reductionisms understate the significance of the repoliticized role this gives the state. In so far as the state limits itself to market complementing functions, the market can remain the means of social organization and the definitive basis of the class structure. On the other hand, when the state replaces the market, or intervenes because of struggles over dysfunctional tendencies of the accumulation process, then the social basis of organization is altered, the state assumes a political role that needs to be legitimated and the class structure is itself altered.

This state of affairs underpinned the long period of post-war consensus in British politics. The ideology of free exchange was replaced by a legitimation for the actions of government in compensating for the dysfunctions of free exchange, as manifested by housing shortages or recurring balance of payments deficits. A class compromise wedded the working class to capitalism through minimum levels of welfare, secure employment and a stable income with an increasing array of consumer items on which to spend it. The task for government was to achieve economic growth and minimize the risks involved in the whole process. Thus technical problems and marginal adjustments came to dominate politics and a new depoliticization was achieved.

Therefore the modern interventionalist state has not been a 'welfare state' in a 'mixed economy', it has been a capitalist state in a highly developed capitalist economy. Its interventions have not resolved the contradictions which spawned them, rather the contradictions have been displaced and refashioned. Thus Habermas argued that the reactions to one crisis sowed the seeds for another. Faced with recurring economic crises the state intervened to regulate the economy in various ways. Failure to achieve the declared ends of such interventions generated crises of rationality, since the state's capacity for action has been shackled by the imperative of protecting private capital. A further consequence has been the erosion of legitimacy, as market allocations have been replaced and the fairness of the state itself called into question. This has given rise to a legitimation crisis. Finally, expectations associated with traditional capitalist virtues – individualism, competitiveness, hard work, self reliance, career progression – have been blocked and frustrated by the developing logic of capitalism as a whole and boxed in by the constraints on the state itself. The result has been a crisis of motivation.[9]

These propositions provide a starting point for the analysis of one aspect of state intervention – 'town and country planning' – in one state, Britain. However, the suggestion that it is possible to construct *a* theory of *the* state needs to be treated with caution. The idea of combined and uneven development is a reminder of the historically specific character of each state. There are even deep historical differences between the different countries which make up the British state.

Mandel cited Britain as a nation where the state machinery has historically been 'weak'. His argument was that the relations of capitalism were so thoroughly planted so soon that the ruling class had less need than say in France to exert their domination politically through state power.[10] Nairn further argued that a landowner/bourgeois alliance has historically contained capitalism in Britain within a particular hegemony, never favouring the aggressive development of industrialism. Empire and the financial success of the City then sustained the 'backward' state form, which has been further bolstered by the strategy of the working-class movement in seeking piecemeal improvements in conditions within the existing conservative social framework. Consequently the British state has averted revolution both from above and below, and has preserved a remarkable social stability.[11]

The origins of town planning

During the rapid urbanization of the nineteenth century, state intervention in urban development was extended through a series of public health measures. Epidemics characteristically began in the slum districts, but could spread from there to engulf the bourgeois areas also. This, together with the effects of illness and premature death on the productivity and availability of labour, made some form of public health control entirely consistent with the interests of the bourgeoisie. The measures also had an ideological dimension. The Victorians fretted at what the abnormal living conditions of the overcrowded areas would do to the next generation.[12] Furthermore, the extensive nature of the bad conditions challenged the notion of a 'deserved poverty of idleness'.[13] Thus the state, nationally and through the initiatives of urban local authorities, attempted to restrain those aspects of the market economy which ultimately threatened its continuity.

In general the legislation left as much as possible to private enterprise. Nevertheless by the turn of the century age-specific mortality rates were falling, and the reproductive cycle was perceptibly shifting from short (high birth rates, high death rates) to long (low birth rates, low death rates). Another factor aiding this transition had been the developing division of labour between male breadwinners and female housekeepers/nurses. The patterns of change were uneven between places, between classes and between sectors. Thus working-class housing remained a major problem. Landlordism, the prerogative of the small bourgeoisie, was already in decline, as more attractive avenues opened for small investors. Newly elected working-class representatives on local councils pressed for better housing and in 1900 the National Housing Reform Council was founded with strong working-class representation, as a lobbying group.

During the 1890s there was a building boom from which some of the better off workers benefited. A cyclical upswing in the economy coincided with electrification of tramways, and the advent of concessionary workers' fares. Combined with the availability of land these resulted in a spate of suburbanization in which skilled artisans were able to participate. Some industrialists saw the suburbanization as the solution to the housing problem without resort to municipal housing provision.

At Port Sunlight W. H. Lever attempted to build a new settlement adjacent to his relocated soap works. Lever, a strong supporter of Gladstone and Liberalism, saw the village as embodying a new understanding between capital and labour. It was a combination of artistic planning and sound business principles. The trade unions opposed Lever's plan as an attempt to exonerate capitalism, and to reincorporate labour within the hegemony of the employer in all aspects of life. However, this re-creation of the conditions of pre-industrial capitalism as an extension of one of the most advanced capitalist firms of the time was widely admired by advocates of town planning.

Thus domestically town planning was seen as a way of reproducing a more contented and efficient working class, without threatening the private ownership of the means of production. However, capitalism had already become a world system, and international factors were also impinging, creating problems beyond solution by individual capitalists.

Increasing imperialist competition and colonial war prompted concerns for the effect that bad living conditions had not just on unfortunate individuals, but on the economic and military strength of the British Empire. The Boer War began in October 1899 at a time when the British economy was again depressed. The unemployed and unskilled were recruited from the cities to go and fight, but a high percentage had to be rejected as unfit for service. An inter-departmental committee on Physical Deterioration was set up. Its report, published in 1904, blamed urban conditions for the general decline in the British 'race' and for Britain's decline as an imperial power.[14] A few years earlier Masterman had written of the 'lowering of the vitality of the Imperial Race in the great cities of the Kingdom through overcrowding in room and area'.[15]

Germany was a particularly feared competitor and had legislation which permitted the local authorities to plan suburban extensions. T. C. Horsfall, an active housing and social reformer in Manchester, was an ardent admirer of the German planning powers. He had visited Germany in 1897, and afterwards steeped himself in literature on German town planning. Like Lever, he saw town planning not as an alternative to market-based urban development, but as an adjunct to the market system. He argued

Experience has proved that it is only private enterprise which can cope with the vast work of supplying the greater part of the immense number of new houses which must be built in and near a town, the population of which is increasing rapidly; but experience has also shown that, without control and guidance and assistance of many kinds from Town Councils, private enterprise does not, and cannot, provide enough new houses; does not place what houses it does supply in right relation to other buildings; and does not supply the kind of house which the community needs; and, further, does not keep the houses which it supplies in good order.[16]

Horsfall claimed that unless improvements were made in the health of the British people through town planning, the nation was condemning itself to an impossibly unequal imperial struggle with Germany.[17]

These few quotations may not prove that British town planning had its origins in attempts to bolster the Empire and its associated resources and markets against foreign competition. But they do indicate that such arguments held some currency in influential quarters at the time. There seem to be grounds for suggesting that the origins of British town planning lie in attempts by industrial capital to increase the rate of profit and to incorporate better-off workers through the provision of better living conditions. State regulation of the development activities of landowners and builders was the means to achieve the end. Thus the class struggle between labour and capital at the point of production was diverted into questions about the appropriate legislation and technical skills needed to create orderly, low-density suburbanization.

The Housing, Town Planning etc. Act, 1909

The General Election of January 1906 returned a Liberal government with a social reform programme. The advance of the organized working class was marked by the election of twenty-nine Labour MPs. John Burns, a former trade union leader and the first working man to sit in a British cabinet, became President of the Local Government Board. An important housing Bill was widely anticipated. The National Housing Reform Council therefore met the prime minister, Sir Henry Campbell-Bannerman, and Burns in November 1906. As well as urging well-aired housing reforms, they also pressed the case for planning powers. Their arguments drew heavily on the advocacy of T. C. Horsfall, who was a member of their committee.

The lobbyists put forward four main ideas. They said that local authorities, acting singly or in groups, should be empowered to make plans for town extensions, setting out the lines for roads and identifying sites for open space, public buildings and workers' housing. Second, they urged revision of building by-laws, so as to allow the kind of developments that had been carried through at Hampstead Garden Suburb. They also proposed powers for local authorities to purchase peripheral land. Finally, they argued for a central commission or department of the Local Government Board, to study urban growth in relation to existing local authority areas.

Another influential lobby was the Association of Municipal Corporations. Their Town Planning Committee was chaired by a Birmingham industrialist and Unionist, Councillor Nettlefold. He had read Horsfall's writings and had visited Germany. He was a strong advocate of the planning of town extensions and an opponent of municipal housing. Thus key individuals influencing the formulation of town planning legislation were reformist industrialists, who saw state regulation of suburban development as consistent with the interests of their class. Nor should the social reformism of the Liberal government mislead us as to the interests it served: at a tactical level it was intended to hold the line against the ascendent Labour Party, anchoring popular support for a party which explicitly repudiated socialism of any kind. The *bête noire* for the reforming Liberals were the landowners and landlords whom they saw as the main oppressors of working people.

This was the context into which a Housing, Town Planning etc. Bill was introduced by the government in 1908. The Bill failed to get beyond the committee stage during the parliamentary session, and a modified version was reintroduced in 1909. All the political parties were agreed on the need to provide more housing and on the value of town planning, but they disagreed on how to achieve these ends. Over 360 amendments were tabled at the committee stage, which was eventually pushed through by the guillotine procedure. Though planning was only a minor part of the Bill, it did provoke sharp controversies. Conservatives spoke in defence of the interests of landowners, and opposed the betterment levy which would apply to gains in land value accruing from 'planning schemes'. The centralized power being given to the Local Government Board to approve planning schemes was also assailed by the classical arguments of the Right, defending individual liberties against the encroaching powers of the state. The Conservative majority in the Lords returned a heavily amended Bill to the Commons, and the government indicated that it was prepared to compromise. A Commons Committee of three Liberals and two Conservatives drafted a reply to their Lordships. The final legislation therefore retained the betterment levy, but fixed it at 50 per cent instead of the 100 per cent first proposed. Provision was also made for either House to nullify a planning scheme. The schemes would not become law until they had 'lain on the table' for thirty days, during which time either House could object, in which case the scheme would be void.

During the parliamentary debates supporters of planning drew comparisons with Germany, where every town had been required to produce a plan and where land laws allowed a municipality to restructure land ownership. In reply, the Lord Privy Seal observed that town planning involving municipal powers over private interests,

... would interfere in the rights of owners which would go far beyond anything that so far any British government has ventured to suggest. In Germany no man can lay out any part of the outskirts of a town without not only submitting his plans to the local authority, but absolutely having to take their plans, and lay out the land in the way which they prescribe ... it would certainly involve an interference by a central authority with rights of private owners to which, as I think, we are not in this country entirely used.'[18]

Thus planning was seen to run counter to the interests of landed capital and even to challenge the 'unpolitical' nature of land ownership and the powers associated with it. In the particular context of the British state, though not in Germany, such a programme could not be carried through, though it would be in the interests of industrial capital to have a healthy labour force, and of imperialism itself to have men fit to defend its territories. Britain, as the first industrial country, had been able to provide the necessary conditions for industrialization without the power of the landed classes being broken. In Germany the 'catching up' nature of the industrialism and the more archaic landlord class, fashioned a different developmental character, with a stronger state form.[19] In this difference lies the contrast in the early history of British and German planning.

Thus, clearly, the first planning legislation was perceived as a threat to landowners and was passed in an amended form despite, and because of, their opposition. The form that planning took was derived from restrictive covenants in private law. Indeed, just what a planning scheme was remained rather unclear. The Act provided no definition, merely listing nineteen 'matters to be dealt with by the general provisions prescribed by the Local Government Board'. In Scotland even such guidance was not forthcoming. The object of the Act was, 'to ensure, by means of schemes which may be prepared either by local authorities or by landowners, that, in future, land in the vicinity of towns shall be developed in such a way as to secure proper sanitary conditions, amenity, and convenience, in connection with the laying out of the land itself and of any neighbouring land'. Thus the focus was on orderly suburbanization, an attempt to staunch the conversion of good quality agricultural land into poor quality housing environments. Even then, the process of controlling suburbanization was entrusted to, but not made mandatory upon, local authorities.

The most notable features of the first British planning legislation were therefore its minimal nature, and strong continuity with established practices in land management and public administration. The local authorities were not given extra powers to develop land themselves, the development process would still be firmly rooted in the market. Not surprisingly then the legislation made little impact, even allowing for the outbreak of war. By 1919 only thirteen schemes had been submitted in England and Wales, and none in Scotland.[20] Not surprisingly, the city which put most effort into planning was Birmingham, the locus of Joseph Chamberlain's attempt to link industry and labour within a right-wing ideology, a more radical class alliance than the hegemony of the British state. For all that, the introduction of town planning did not lead to more and better housing for the mass of the working class, because the garden suburb housing that was the object of the Act was beyond their means. The workmen's National Housing Council denounced the 1909 Act as a mere publicity stunt, which served to distract attention from the realities of the housing problem. While there was working-class agitation for housing reform, the cause of planning seems to have attracted scant working class commitment. Indeed, some working-class housing campaigners such as Jowett, the Independent Labour Party MP for Bradford West, saw planning schemes as primarily benefiting landowners through increasing land values.[21]

Planning homes for heroes

The next planning Act, again a minor addendum to housing legislation, came in 1919. State intervention in housing after the First World War has been the subject of extensive analysis by those seeking to elucidate the role of the state in urban and regional development. Debate has focussed on how far the introduction of rent controls and housing subsidies can be seen as a victory for militant working-class struggles, notably the Clydeside rent strike of 1915, or a victory in which the opposition did not lose.[22] Within that debate it is instructive to see how the particular planning legislation was shaped by the emergent class compromise over housing.

The degree to which growing organization among the British working class really threatened the existing social order in the period immediately after the First World War is a matter of some debate. In 1919 and 1920 there was an enormous increase in trade union membership and the number of strikes, and the Labour Party was also developing in strength. Whether this seriously amounted to a threat to the British state in any way comparable to events in Russia in 1917 can be disputed. However, a number of official reports made explicit connections between bad housing conditions and industrial unrest. The Royal Commission on Industrial Unrest, which appeared in 1917, pinpointed bad housing as one among a number of factors. In the same year the Report of the Royal Commission on the Housing of the Industrial Population of Scotland had 'Bad Housing as a Factor in Industrial Unrest' as the final chapter, and concluded that bad housing was indeed a major cause of social unrest. The Directorate of Intelligence was also furnishing the Cabinet with reports on 'revolutionary organizations' and noting the extent to which housing was an active source of discontent. Thus problems which fundamentally arose at the point of production, in the class struggle over surplus value, were translated instead into their symptoms, in this case the inability of workers to sustain a market demand for decent housing at a price that made production profitable. The extension of state activity into housing can thus be seen as a means of avoiding a wider crisis in the economic system.

It is not surprising then that Mr Addison described his Housing and Town Planning Bill as being '. . . of the utmost importance from the point of view not only of the physical well-being of our people, but of our social stability and industrial content'.[23] His remarks on planning, like the planning content of the Bill itself, were brief. While the legislation fundamentally restructured housing finance, it made only minor changes to the earlier planning legislation. The National Housing and Town Planning Council had been lobbying for town planning to be made mandatory on local authorities, but the Bill did not go so far. Instead it sought to streamline the administrative procedures in the hope of stimulating the submission of more planning schemes. During the debate on the second reading only three MPs spoke on the planning provisions, though all three urged a strengthening of planning powers. Captain the Honourable W. G. A. Ormsby-Gore (Coalition Conservative, Stafford) wanted town planning to be made compulsory for towns with a population of more than 10,000, as he believed this was the only way to get development on 'clean and healthy lines'. Mr L. F. Scott (Coalition Conservative, Liverpool Exchange, and later to be the chairman of the Committee on Land Utilization in Rural Areas) made comparisons with French proposals to require every town of over 10,000 inhabitants to produce a planning scheme for laying out, beautifying and extending the town. Such schemes were also required in settlements of over 5000 people where there had been a 10 per cent population increase in the previous decade, in watering places where the population influx exceeded 50 per cent of the resident population and for important industrial developments. Mr Scott argued that if the British adopted similar criteria, 'the hideous, haphazard and monstrous growths of grey-brown dull towns would be rendered impossible'. Finally, Sir J. Tudor Walters (Coalition Liberal, Sheffield Brightside) stressed the connection between housing and planning, in terms of open space, fresh air and sunlight.

The reason why planning was accorded such a limited role, despite the pleas of this trio and of the wider planning movement outside Parliament, was that, within the market economy, stronger planning powers, rather than aiding the housing drive, could actually have hindered it. The point had been made explicitly by Mr Addison, when he said, 'I am sure we ought to be very, very careful before we make town planning compulsory, and see that we do not provide something which has an effect which may be quite indirect and unlooked for, but which may be very injurious to the development of housing.'[24] Thus 'homes for heroes' were the top priority, and extended state regulation of the development pattern might provoke land owners to withdraw their land from the market.

The National Housing and Town Planning Council lobbied strongly during the committee stage of the Bill. The result was a successful amendment to make town planning compulsory on boroughs and urban districts of over 20,000. The Local Government Board was also given the power to force the preparation of a scheme if they felt the scheme was essential, a provision that strengthened the powers of central government over local government. A subsequent Lords amendment made planning compulsory on rural district councils with over 20,000 people. However, the prevailing political attitude towards planning can also be judged by some of the proposed new clauses which were defeated in the committee stage. A Liberal, for example, was unsuccessful in proposing density restrictions of twelve houses per acre gross in urban areas, and eight in rural areas. Powers for replanning existing developed areas, and to compel property owners to carry out improvements were likewise rejected. A Labour proposal to give county councils powers to appoint regional planning committees and to prepare regional plans also made no headway. Thus the form of land use planning sanctioned by the state remained essentially local, physical and negative.

Few would dispute that the 1919 Housing, Town Planning etc. Act was a concession by the state to demands from organized labour and at a time of severe housing shortage. Again there seems no reason to doubt that one of the reasons why housing was accorded such priority was because it was seen as a 'women's issue' in the first election after their enfranchisement. However, as Dickens points out, the housing programme also commanded the support of industrial capital; indeed, housing provision was one of the few areas of agreement between organized labour and industrial capital, since the tenure of their employees was a matter of relative indifference to industrialists.[25] Nor did a state-led housing programme damage the interests of financiers, who could either lend at high interest rates to fund the developments, or refuse to finance the programme if the terms were not acceptable. Despite this alliance, the state remained constrained by the ability of the landowners to withhold their land needed for the housing programme and by the direct political power that this class could still wield.

Though strong planning powers to acquire and use land to create good quality environments would have been a logical part of the programme, in reality it could not be risked. Thus the shape planning took in the legislation of 1919 was fundamentally fashioned by the class compromise within the British state at that time, with the international relationships of the state being less significant than in 1909, or than they were to be in 1931.

Pale pink socialism

From about 1922 onwards economic conditions began to favour house building. Inflation levelled off, leaving the cost of living about 60 per cent above the pre-war figure, and there was a slow drop in interest rates. The 1923 Housing Act was intended to encourage house building by private enterprise. The election of the first Labour government in 1924 saw the 'Red Clydeside' MP John Wheatley become the Minister responsible for housing. He set out to get a large number of decent houses built as quickly as possible, and to this end the government pledged the building industry that there would be a fifteen-year building programme.[26] Wheatley's Act succeeded to the extent that 504,500 houses were built under it, and despite the advent of a Conservative government it remained the basis of housing policy until 1930. Thus housing remained an issue of high political priority through the 1920s (despite the defeats of the working class on the industrial front during the same period); the financial climate also favoured house building. The result was a continued spread of the urban areas and consumption of agricultural land, re-emphasizing the problems which had been articulated by the proponents of land use planning.

Concern with housing inevitably impinged upon the question of the slums and how such areas might be treated. Neville Chamberlain was the chairman of the Unhealthy Areas Committee, which was established by the Ministry of Health in 1920. The Final Report in 1921 recognized that the reconstruction of slum areas could only be achieved satisfactorily if housing was treated simultaneously with the other land uses in those areas. Thus the prospect of the redevelopment of an area of mixed uses and multiple land ownerships predicated the need for a stronger land use planning role by the state.

The loss of agricultural land and the incursion of urban trippers into the countryside, led to the formation of the Council for the Preservation of Rural England in 1926. One result of their lobbying was a Bill presented by the Conservative MP Sir Edward Hilton-Young. The Rural Amenities Bill was designed to extend planning powers to rural land.

These moves to extend the state's role in regulating development were further strengthened by the return of a majority Labour government in 1929. The Greenwood Housing Act of 1930 switched the focus of housing policy towards slum clearance, thereby raising again the question of planning controls for replanning built-up areas. During 1929 a Committee of Inquiry was set up to investigate the idea of national parks, under the chairmanship of Addison. There was also the Chelmsford Committee on Regional Development and the Marley Committee on Garden Cities and Satellite Towns.

The apex of this activity was the introduction of a Town and Country Planning Bill during 1931. It received general support from all the parties. For the Conservatives, Neville Chamberlain commented, '. . . there is much in the Bill which undoubtedly might have been the subject of a Bill brought in by the Conservatives'.[27] For the Liberals, Ernest Simon saw it as a 'measure of enduring value to the country'. The long established process of piecemeal adaptation within a conservative social framework seemed set to grind on. The only real dissent was over the question of betterment, where the Bill proposed that the local authorities should be able to take 100 per cent of the betterment, whereas the previous legislation only allowed 50 per cent. More fundamental opposition was voiced by the Marquis of Hartington who castigated his Conservative leaders for 'playing around with this kind of half-baked, pale-pink Socialism'.[28] Though the betterment was pared back to 75 per cent, the Bill emerged largely unscathed from the committee stage, when the international financial crisis brought down the Labour government.

The incoming National government was firmly wedded to the City's calls for large-scale expenditure cuts and strict *laissez-faire* orthodoxy. The work of the Addison, Chelmsford and Marley Committees was sidelined, and the grant to the Greater London Regional Advisory Committee was stopped. In such circumstances the reintroduction of the Town and Country Planning Bill appears somewhat paradoxical at first. One factor in persuading the government to bring in the Bill was the pressure exerted by professional bodies. The Town Planning Institute joined with the Presidents and Chairmen of other professional and environmental propagandist bodies to write a letter to the new Prime Minister regretting the apparent demise of the 1931 Bill. They argued the apolitical nature of town planning and its benefits to the nation as a whole. Chamberlain, now Chancellor, and Hilton-Young, now Minister of Health and thus the Minister responsible for planning, remained enthusiasts for town planning, with seats in the Cabinet. Senior civil servants also pressed the case for planning, notably I. G. Gibbon, the Assistant Secretary at the Ministry of Health, and George Pepler, the Chief Town Planning Inspector.[29]

The Bill was this time fiercely attacked in the Commons. Government backbenchers, crusading against 'socialism', and occasionally ignorant of even the existing planning legislation, took up the cudgels of the Marquis of Hartington. Despite this opposition, a debilitated Act reached the statute book in July 1932. Betterment, though fixed at 75 per cent, was in reality difficult to collect. 'Static areas' were exempted from planning controls and many of the clauses complicated planning procedures. Though the Act extended the powers of local authorities to prepare schemes, the freedom was still subject to a Ministerial proviso. As in 1909, a scheme could not become operative until it had been laid before the Commons and the Lords, during which time its legal validity could be questioned. The adoption of planning schemes had previously been obligatory on some local authorities, though the provision was not operated; the 1932 Act made planning merely voluntary. While a scheme was being prepared, a developer was under no obligation to seek planning permission. However, if the development did not conform to the eventual scheme, the developer could be required to demolish the buildings without compensation.

The origins of the 1932 Act thus lie in a number of factors. The uneven returns between capital invested in agriculture and in private housing resulted in land conversion. In addition, the state's own activity in plugging a necessary gap by public housing added to the loss of agricultural land. It might be possible to present new planning legislation, then, as an attempt by the state to defend a threatened sector and to reproduce a working class. However, the planning legislation was essentially a secondary matter, an indirect method of treating these problems, by tidying up existing legislative provisions. Two further factors therefore need to be taken into account. First, there was the concern for the quality of the environments being produced by private enterprise. To project that concern merely as the attempt by the state to protect market forces from their own self-destructive side-effects is to obscure the particular class dimension involved, the sense of patrician disdain for the bargain basement environmental quality of the nascent consumer capitalism. This was allied with calls to preserve Britain's rural heritage, a symbol of eternal social harmony and the unity of man with nature. Second, there was the concern of the state to extend the efficacy of its own administration, and not least to rationalize the costs which it bore in providing the infrastructure needed for new development.

These internal considerations were then challenged by the repercussions of the international financial crisis. The most notable feature of the 1932 legislation therefore remains the way that the continuity of a previously established consensual position was maintained in the face of a new set of antagonisms that were transforming the form and range of the state's activities. The comparison with housing is again interesting, for the 1933 Housing Act, again the responsibility of Hilton-Young, was a more substantial and systematic assault on the housing standards and ideals established in the 1920s, than was the 1932 Act on planning. The fact that a small number of people were influential in achieving this continuity should not be interpreted as proof that state actions can be adequately comprehended as expressions of the voluntaristic will of individual actors. Rather it demonstrates that given the constellation of interests surrounding town planning at that time, described above, and given the status of planning as a relatively minor activity, and the particular nature of the British state with its traditions of piecemeal adjustment, then a small number of senior administrators and politicians could indeed steer through a continuity in policy.

The fashioning of the 1947 Planning System
Planners are wont to revere the 1940s as the 'golden age' of British planning. After all, the 1947 planning Act was widely hailed as the most comprehensive piece of planning legislation the western world had known. In what was characterized as 'the age of the common man', land use planning could be seen as an important element of the welfare state, the various components of which were linked by the common denominator of land. Such an interpretation begs questions

about how and why a new class compromise emerged and how the new planning activity was moulded by the underlying structures of the British state.

The 1947 legislation was the culmination of a decade of deliberation about how the state should respond to the spatial symptoms of Britain's economic and political problems. The world recession of the 1930s and the rise of protective tariffs around national economies exacerbated the decline in profits of manufacturing industries. The growth industries were those locating close to their domestic markets. Electrical engineering, car production, mass-produced clothing and furniture, and consumer durables were freed from the pull of the coalfields by electricity and from the inner city by the internal combustion engine. The productive base of the nation thus shifted from the coalfield conurbations to the south-east and the suburbs. Between 1923 and 1934 the insured population rose by 44 per cent in the south-east, but fell by 5½ per cent in the north-east and by 26 per cent in Wales. Unemployment in Greater London in 1934 was 8.6 per cent of the insured workers; in Workington it was 36.3 per cent, in Gateshead 44.2 per cent and in Jarrow 67.8 per cent.[30]

The uneven industrial change was paralleled in residential development. By the end of the 1920s building societies had become very competitive with other forms of investment, especially given the collapse of the stock market. Capital was thus available for investment in new housing. The costs of new housing actually began to decline and interest rates fell. Public transport networks were extended and car ownership increased. The result was an unprecedented surge of suburbanization around the English cities in general and London in particular. The aesthetics of this flurry of mass production and consumption of environment and natural resources, attracted widespread criticism from the intelligentsia. Authors as different in outlook as D. H. Lawrence, Evelyn Waugh and George Orwell each poured forth their own distinctive invective against the new townscape.[31] In a more scientific manner, Dudley Stamp, in his monumental land utilization survey, catalogued the sacrifice of good agricultural land that the new settlement structure entailed. The wartime blockade further confirmed the folly.

The increased living standards that were expressed in this suburbanization were bolstered by cheap food and raw materials from the colonies, which also provided a protected overseas market for manufactured goods. However, the Empire was in turn dependent on social harmony at home, a need which became even more acute with the onset of war. In contrast, the emergent settlement structure was extending the spatial segregation of the social classes as considerable areas at the edge of cities were developed either for owner occupation or for council housing schemes. Prominent planners were among those who bemoaned this social spatial gulf; for example, Thomas Sharp saw it as being inimical to the promotion of 'understanding and mutual adjustment' between the classes.[32]

New forms of state intervention in urban and regional development were also prompted by the direct interests of the state itself. The Barlow Commission noted the strains on state expenditures caused by the changed pattern of industrial location.

The movement has proceeded with little or no regard to the fact that it necessarily involves heavy expenditure by the community for the provision of such necessary facilities as new roads, housing accommodation, water supply, sewers, gas and electric mains, schools, churches, increased transport, and all the multifarious services required to meet the needs of the industry itself and of the rapidly growing population. This expenditure, moreover, has to be undertaken at a time when facilities of a similar character are already available in the older industrial areas and where they must be maintained in spite of the fact that much of the labour in the new areas is drawn from the older ones, whose authorities, because of the loss of woiking population, become progressively less able to support the services for their remaining population.[33]

The state also saw that its ability to defend the nation against foreign aggressors was being undermined by the developing pattern of settlement. The bombing of Guernica in 1937 caused great alarm as to the vulnerability of major concentrations of population and industry to air attack. The rise of fascist regimes posed a further challenge; together with the communists they seemed to demonstrate that totalitarian states could work more efficiently than democracies, particularly when it came to carrying through major physical development works. The adoption of a stronger planning role in urban and regional development was thus important to the British state economically, strategically and ideologically.

As Backwell and Dickens have argued, the onset of the war altered the class relationships within Britain.[34] War emphasized the need for national unity and mass loyalty, yet it also revealed just how divided living conditions were. Evacuation from the cities to rural areas breached the British social *apartheid*, while the news coverage of the bombed slums revealed just how bad working-class living conditions were. The shortage of labour during the war strengthened the hand of labour *vis-à-vis* capital. It was therefore necessary to make concessions to working-class needs and to boost morale, assuring the mass of the people that a future could lie ahead which would make their suffering worthwhile. Town planning was doubly important: not only were concessions in terms of urban development less threatening to capital than concessions at the point of production itself, but also the idea of town planning could convey important symbols of a new social order. Town planning was portrayed as the means to secure jobs and decent houses in socially balanced and self-contained new communities.[35]

When in doubt, or in need of legitimation, the British state has customarily set up some independent deliberative committee, which can usually be relied upon to resecure continuity, while fashioning adaptations with a neutral and expert gloss. Should they depart from that canon, or should the problem dissolve in the meantime, their reports can be sidelined with a degree of stoicism. Hence the famous trinity of wartime planning reports. Sir Montague Barlow chaired the Royal Commission on the Distribution of the Industrial Population, Lord Justice Scott headed the Committee on Land Utilization in Rural Areas and Mr Justice

Uthwatt's expert committee got to work on the problems of compensation and betterment.

The scope and agency of planning

Ideology cannot be propagated and sustained if it has not some basis in reality. The notion of rational and comprehensive planning as the democratic alternative to totalitarianism or *laissez-faire* drew its credibility from the correct identification of the inter-related nature of the development problem and from the recognition that market forces could not spontaneously solve the problem. However, the translation of the ideas into practice involved deep conflicts with the interests of capital and of the state itself. Adaptation of the planning system so that it could be used in the future to avoid the kind of crises that had racked pre-war Britain meant a challenge to the 'natural' inevitability of market processes, to capital accumulation through investment in land and to the structure and role of the state itself. The problems are illustrated by the contortions which Ministers and officials went through in trying to fit the new planning function into the administrative system.

The central difficulty was the adoption of a national approach to urban and regional development. The Barlow Commission had been set up in 1937, with a brief to explore the 'social, economic or strategical disadvantages' of industrial concentration, and to set out remedial measures 'in the national interest'. The Commission, completing its work as the war began, recognized that rearmament had given a temporary boost to the industries of the 'Depressed Areas', but that the long-term trend was strongly towards growth in London and the south-east. They recommended decentralization, including the development of new towns, and population dispersal on a national scale. This was despite evidence given by the Federation of British Industries strongly opposing state-directed industrial relocation. However, the FBI were prepared to accept a policy whereby industries were discouraged from locating in some areas, and encouraged to locate in others. Those who had urged the commission to recommend controls over the location of industry included the Trades Union Congress, the Council for the Preservation of Rural England, the Garden Cities and Town Planning Association and the Town Planning Institute. The commission's report gives particular stress to the case made by the local authorities for some, generally limited, powers of state control. Among those quoted are the London County Council, the city councils of Manchester, Leeds, Liverpool and even Birmingham (though they were less enthusiastic). The counties of Durham and Cumberland favoured control, and a national planning authority for Scotland was advocated by the Association of Counties of Cities and the Convention of Royal Burghs, as well as the Scottish Economic Committee.[36]

Barlow recommended that to achieve the redistribution a central planning authority should be established that would be 'national in scope and character'. However, the commission were split on what form the new agency should take and how strong its powers should be. The majority report opted for a 'National

Industry Board', which would essentially be advisory, though three members who supported the majority report expressed reservations to the effect that further powers would be required and also calling for regional bodies to be set up. Abercrombie and two others signed a minority report, urging a new Ministry , with full executive powers. The Barlow Report therefore challenged the free movement of industrial capital and called for extended state intervention. Even so, it did so within a general framework of compromise and adaptation, rather than radically redistributing political and economic power.

The idea of a central planning agency was taken up by Sir John Reith, the Minister of Building and Works, in a memorandum on reconstruction of Town and Country which went to the War Cabinet in December 1940. This led to Sir John Anderson, Lord President of the Council, presiding over a series of committee meetings. At these meetings the question of industrial location was a key issue. It was logically 'the basic element in any positive planning of town and country', yet evidently involved much wider political and economic questions.[37] In April 1941 the Uthwatt Committee produced an Interim Report, under pressure from Reith. This included the idea that a central planning authority should be set up and should immediately proceed to produce a national plan. There followed demarcation disputes between Reith and another ministerial committee, the Greenwood Committee on Reconstruction Problems. The compromise they reached was that national policies would be co-ordinated by a National Development Executive, which would be chaired by a cabinet minister without departmental responsibilities. A new Ministry of Town and Country Planning would be set up, but with the more limited task of approving the planning schemes produced in England and Wales, a job the Secretary of State would do in Scotland. Reith accepted the formula, but still pressed for the National Development Executive to be given a more directive role, with widened terms of reference. The War Cabinet considered the question on 9 February 1942 and opted for less far-reaching changes. They decided against creating new ministries while they were so fully engaged in the war effort. Instead they transferred town and country planning functions to the Ministry of Works and Buildings, which was renamed the Ministry of Works and Planning. Rather than a National Development Executive, the Ministry of Works and Planning would be assisted by a committee of officials representing relevant departments.

Though the Ministry of Works and Planning came into being in June 1942, the matter of how to graft a planning function on to the existing state administration remained unsettled. Sir William Jowitt, the Paymaster General, rehearsed the dilemmas once more in a paper to the Committee on Reconstruction Problems. A genuine planning department would, 'cut across the whole existing organization of government', yet could not conceivably take in 'the most important element of finance – because the Treasury of all departments must remain undivided'.[38] He therefore proposed a committee of ministers concerned with the use of land, chaired by a non-departmental minister, a 'small, skilled staff' and a statutory Land Utilization Commission. In July 1942 the Maxwell Fyfe Committee on a Central Planning Authority reported. They found no administrative objection to the Land Utilization Commission. Nevertheless the Reconstruction Problems Committee eventually decided that while there was a possible need for such a commission, it was premature to decide its functions. This view was endorsed by the War Cabinet. The Minister of Town and Country Planning Bill followed, providing for the appointment of a minister whose task would be to secure 'consistency and continuity in the framing and the execution of a national policy with respect to the use and development of land throughout England and Wales'. The Bill was passed in February 1943 and provided for a statutory commission to assist the minister's work.

Faced with the need for national, co-ordinated and purposeful planning, the state opted for ad hoc adaptations to existing structures. An integrated planning system, with powers to match the locations of housing and jobs, and to link with the necessary infrastructure, would have encroached on the responsibilities of existing ministries and departments. The Ministry of Agriculture was intent on maintaining its primacy in matters concerning agricultural land. The Transport Ministry fought to retain its powers over highway matters. Statutory undertakers were also more than reluctant to play second fiddle to any new central planning body.[39] Innovation also ran headlong into probably the most powerful and conservative department of all, the Treasury. As Cullingworth, the official historian of the planning at this period, observes, 'The Treasury in particular looked upon this new department with anxiety, if not with apprehension. Not only did the ministry lack experience: it was attempting to establish a system of planning which, if implemented, would seriously reduce the powers of traditional departments, if not of the Treasury itself.'[40]

Cullingworth suggests that the idea of a strong central planning authority would probably not have got as far as it did but for the preoccupation of senior ministers with war affairs, the diffuse nature of the impending reconstruction programme and the single-mindedness of Reith.[41] Clearly these factors were important, but they leave unanswered the question of what interests were involved. National planning of the location of industry was not in the interest of industrial capital, though a system of incentives to steer locational decisions could directly aid capital accumulation. The war meant a revival of profits and a more vital role for industry, thus extensive state direction of industry was more easily resisted, though even before the Barlow Commission advocates of such a policy had been notably cautious. For all that the promise that through planning there would be no return to the miseries of the 1930s, was a concession to the interests of the working class, strengthened by the particular conditions of wartime. However, to go to the logical solution of a full planning capability for the state would have been a structural impossibility, not just because of the reaction it could have evoked from capital, but also because of the substantial democratization it would have entailed within the state itself. Even the limited debate about agencies was problematic. To go further would have provoked a crisis.

The planning capacity of the state therefore remained limited and fragmented. In England and Wales the Minister of Town and Country Planning was the supremo for the land-use planning schemes; in Scotland the responsibility remained with the Department of Health for Scotland. In England and Wales the Ministry of Health was responsible for housing, having, like other ministries survived largely unscathed. The Distribution of Industry Act, 1945, was one of the last pieces of legislation of the Coalition Government. It gave responsibility for the location of industry and the operation of regional policy for England, Wales and Scotland to the existing Board of Trade. It was empowered only to build factories, give grants or loans, make provision for basic public services and reclaim derelict land. The stick of the granting of Industrial Development Certificates for new industrial developments of more than 5000 square feet, was added by the 1947 Town and Country Planning Act.

Compensation and betterment
Reith appointed the Uthwatt Committee in 1941, with the original intention that its report would not be made publicly available. The central problem faced by the committee was how to reconcile public planning of land use with the interests of landowners. The committee themselves observed,

It is clear that under a system of well conceived planning the resolution of competing claims and the allocation of land for the various requirements must proceed on the basis of selecting the most suitable land for the particular purpose, irrespective of the existing values which may attach to the individual parcels of land.

They recognized that the system of individualistic land ownership contained inherent 'contradictions provoking a conflict between private and public interest and hindering the proper operation of the planning machinery'. These might best be overcome by unifying existing rights in land so that shifts in value occurred within the same ownership. The logic of this assessment pointed the experts towards land nationalization, a path from which they beat a hasty retreat. Land nationalization, they argued, would probably involve insuperable financial problems and would usher into being a complicated bureaucracy. The report explained,

If we were to regard the problem provided by our terms of reference as an academic exercise without regard to administrative or other consequences, immediate transfer to public ownership of all land would present the logical solution; but we have no doubt that land nationalization is not practicable as an immediate measure and we reject it on that ground alone .... Land nationalization is not a policy to be embarked upon lightly but it would arouse keen political controversy.[42]

The interests of the market therefore again imposed constraints on the planning capability of the state itself and the contradictions from the economic system were transferred into the administration. As well as backing the idea of a central planning authority, Uthwatt came up with three main proposals. These were that powers for the public acquisition of developed land should be tightened; that there should be a five-yearly tax on all increases in annual site values, to secure part of the betterment; and that the state should acquire the development rights in undeveloped land.

Backwell and Dickens argue that Uthwatt and the action that followed need to be seen in relation to the particular situation of urban landed capital at that time. Small landlords, for example, had long been a depressed and declining force. The impact of the blitz on their inner city holdings must have been a further blow. Compensation and acquisition of their properties by local authorities could have seemed the only escape route they had to realize their investment. The other side of the coin was the activity of large property investors. The blitz cleared low value properties on high value sites. Marriott demonstrates how property interests reacted to the potential of redeveloping bomb damaged sites.[43] When the nation was fighting for its survival this speculation was the unacceptable face of capitalism. As Backwell and Dickens note, *The Economist* welcomed the Uthwatt Committee as a way of preventing 'pirates' from making 'the community' 'pay through the nose' for its new cities.[44]

The Uthwatt proposals were strongly attacked by the Property Owners Protection Society, as amounting to concealed nationalization. The Coalition Government introduced a Town and Country Planning Bill in 1944, giving local authorities powers to buy land in areas of 'extensive war damage' and 'bad layout and obsolete development'. However, the Bill did not take up the more controversial development rights question, on which the Coalition partners had been unable to agree. The Bill was bitterly attacked by Labour MPs. Lewis Silkin, for example, described it as 'a victory by the landowning interests over the public interest', and said that if the Labour Party accepted the Bill it would be betraying the movement and passing a death sentence on comprehensive planning. However, the Labour Ministers in the Coalition Cabinet had already agreed to the Bill. It took four meetings for the Labour MPs to agree to abstain on the Second Reading and to seek to strengthen the Bill at the Committee Stage. The Labour Ministers voted with the government. There were Conservative rebels on the Bill also, who felt that its provisions were too harsh on property owners. Because of their pressure, Churchill intervened to drop contentious clauses. Foot argued that planning, and especially the question of land ownership, was 'the real rock on which the Coalition was broken'.[45]

Labour's 1945 election manifesto indicated that land nationalization was the long-term goal to be worked towards. In the short term, though, they would strengthen local authorities' powers of compulsory purchase and would tackle the question of betterment. The proposition then was, in the face of an acute housing shortage, to accept Uthwatt's advice to go for piecemeal change that could be implemented without provoking a major backlash. Even then the progress from 1945 to the 1947 Planning Act was extremely complicated. The detailed proposals for compensation and betterment were drafted by civil servants in the Whiskard Committee and Cullingworth records how the complexity of the legal and administrative details gave those people with time and expertise to master the subject a considerable tactical advantage.[46]

Eventually the 1947 Act nationalized development rights and their associated values. Since changes in value were deemed to be created by the community and therefore recouped by the state, no compensation would be payable to landowners for loss of development value. Even so, a £300 million fund was set aside to make 'payments' to owners who could show that their land had some development value on the appointed day. Their claims were to be processed by a Central Land Board, who would then divide the £300 million between the claimants at whatever proportion of their 1948 value that total would allow.

When introducing the legislation to the Lords, the Lord Chancellor said:

Let me emphasize that we do not seek by this Bill to crush private enterprise in development; on the contrary, we want to mobilize all available methods and to encourage all of them to play their part in the building and rebuilding of the country. We claim that this Bill will encourage private enterprise in two ways. First, it enables land, which is the builder's raw material, to be made available in accordance with the plan instead of leaving the developer at the mercy of the landowner to build only where the landowner is willing to sell; secondly, it encourages building by enabling land to be made available at a price that is covered by considerations of public policy not of private gain.[47]

The Lord Chancellor's attempt to sell the Bill as being tailor-made to suit the builders was probably hyperbole, since many builders were also landowners, but the drift of his comments was clear enough – the prime problem was the landowner, not the system itself. The attack on landed capital was nevertheless contentious and the more controversial provisions were clawed back by the succeeding Conservative government.

Thus two of the most crucial aspects around which the 1947 planning legislation was built, namely the idea of co-ordinated planning and public rights in land, emerged bearing the classic imprint of the British state of a piecemeal adaptation to existing policies and structures. Cullingworth consistently stressed the important role played by a few key individuals in shaping planning at this period and Miliband made a similar point in more general terms and with a more acute perception of the relation of the state to class interests. Miliband said of the Attlee government that it

gratefully accepted from the wartime coalition, and from previous Conservative governments, a body of officials who, by social provenance, education and professional disposition, were bound to conceive as one of their prime tasks to warn their Ministers against too radical a departure from traditional departmental policies. No doubt the experience of war had taught them to view with far less distaste than in the past the enlargement of state intervention and control, and they were, at the end of the war, quite ready to serve the purposes of a government pledged to positive state action. But they were equally ready to try and convince their political masters of the dangers of innovation.[48]

These conflicts over planning in general, and land in particular, were based in the division of interests between landed capital and the working class. The interests of industrial capital divided between seeking cheap and readily available sites for production, as well as keeping a contented and efficient labour force on the one hand, together with the need to protect private ownership and the rights it conferred on the other. The shift in power that the peculiar conditions wartime brought about made possible an attack on landed capital, but not a break in the continuity of the patrician British state itself. The specific resolution of town and country planning questions in the 1947 legislation and the measures leading up to it, was one manifestation of the refashioned class compromise of the 'welfare state'. The state acquired a limited planning capacity, with strengthened powers to regulate private development initiatives. There was administrative rationalization, streamlining the number of planning authorities from 1441 to 145, but there was neither devolution of power nor central co-ordination. Through Ministerial approval of the new Development Plans, and the system of planning appeals, central government retained the final veto. However, it did not produce a national plan, nor did it really attempt any co-ordinated central planning of housing, employment, transport, etc. [49] Nor were there any regional planning agencies with executive powers and democratic accountability.

The logic of uneven development meant that the relevance of the 1947 planning legislation was uneven too, both spatially and sectorally. Because of the nature of the class compromise that had defined the planning system, that system was more effective at arbitrating between demands generated by market forces than providing an alternative to market-led development. Thus Robert Grieve, as a young civil servant trying to implement the 1947 Act within the Department of Health for Scotland, quickly realized that it 'could not be applied except as a kind of administrative ritual in the Highlands and Islands'. [50] In such areas there was no competition for the use of land, so planning premised on the assumption of such competition was an irrelevancy.

Nor should we overlook the extent to which the workings of the more positive aspects of the system were constrained by the powers of the City and international finance capital. The balance of payments deficit in 1947 was £443 million, and as speculators moved money out of sterling, government expenditure on housing programmes and the new towns was cut back.

In summary, the 1947 planning system was fundamentally about an attempt by the state to contain and manage contradictory class interests by extending state intervention through piecemeal adaptation to existing structures. The system was therefore logically incapable of resolving those contradictions and thus predicated their re-emergence in distorted forms within the planning system in practice.

Modernizing the planning system

Major changes to the 1947 planning system did not come until the mid-1960s. The financial provisions of the 1947 Act were repealed in legislation passed in 1953 and 1954, thus restoring a free market in land and land values. In England the Ministry of Town and Country Planning was dismantled and merged into Housing and Local Government.

Perhaps the most notable features of the revamping of planning in the 1960s are the extent to which the changes were a response to problems within the administrative system itself and how politically uncontroversial the transition was. Modernization of the planning system was necessary for the planning system was itself a means by which the state attempted to manage the modernization of Britain, modernization to fit the changing structure of capital and the dynamic of the class compromise.

The long wave of affluence, based on the electronic technological revolution and the supply of cheap raw materials and energy from underdeveloped countries, had a substantial impact on the settlement structure and the physical environment. Consumption of land and environment was part of a wider consumer boom, which was compounded by demographic growth. The most obvious indicators which the planning system administered were increasing car ownership, suburban spread and increasing use of the countryside. The state was thus faced with increasing costs of infrastructure provision, as one aspect of rising expenditure. Extra land was needed for power stations, water supplies and schools. Above all the rise in car ownership, and more especially the extrapolations of the rise, pointed to the need to improve the road networks. Thus the state was extensively engaged in planning and implementing physical works which were not in themselves attractive market propositions, albeit the actual contractors' tenders were based on commercial criteria. Such works were integral to the logic of the creation of new commodities, as the expanding galaxy of commodities became the basis of capital's struggles to create new sources of surplus value, and was also an essential component of the new class compromise. Urban renewal was a critical part of the programme. Areas of obsolete environment had to be upgraded to reflect the standards of consumption that were the new norms.

A part of the new consumption was a change in retailing methods and shopping patterns. From 1949 until 1966, Ravenseft Properties invested £60 million into over 400 new shopping developments in 150 different towns and cities in England, Wales and Scotland. Capital invested in property derived an appreciation from the devaluation and inflation of the late 1940s and could manipulate the loopholes attributed to errors of drafting in the 1947 Act. The shift in emphasis from making goods to marketing them, and the centralization and internationalization of capital created the demand for office development. The boom, boosted by the amendments to the provisions of development charges of the 1947 Act by the 1953 Town and Country Planning Act, got under way in the late 1950s and early 1960s. The political reaction against speculative fortunes led to a further attempt to confront 'the land question' in the form of the Land Commission and to a further failure.[51]

The changes in the pattern of industrial location noted in the pre-war period were compounded, as Barlow had anticipated. Faced with technological change, the ending of the Empire and growing foreign competition, traditional industries collapsed, while the new 'growth' industries sought locations close to London and where there was an attractive environment for their key staff to enjoy. The boom in South Hampshire, which provoked a major planning study,[52] is a most evident exemplar, for the area provided no significant advantages of location in terms of raw materials or markets.

The planning system had to confront the two faces of modernization. On the one hand there was the need to fuel the motor of growth and change, especially in sectors and locations where 'spontaneous' growth through market forces was lagging behind. On the other hand, the dysfunctional effects of the growth had to be controlled: land and cherished symbols had to be protected from the devouring appetite of the capital accumulation process. The exchange value locked away in physical assets had to be devalued in the drive to restore profitability. Recent production processes had to be introduced in new locations. Furthermore, the modernization problems had a strong spatial element as areas, cities and whole regions 'lagged behind' the production and consumption forms of the changing economy. Thus the state's attempts to manage the restructuring process necessarily forced a reappraisal of the practice of town and country planning. The catalogues of sites and acreages and proposed land uses that constituted the Developmental Plans were manifestly inadequate for the tasks. At the same time the ambiguities integral to the limited but extended form of state involvement through planning, with a physical and statutory base but economic and social associations, made the strengthening of planning an undemanding course of action, something eminently manageable within the political consensus of the early 1960s.

Within Scotland restructuring was necessary on a massive scale: there was obsolete capacity in most industrial sectors, coal mining and associated activities were contracting, and a large part of the housing stock was physically crumbling. These factors made Scotland a particular forcing ground for new experiments with planning. The Labour Party in Scotland and the Scottish Trades Union Congress had long seen state action as the only basis for improving the economy and working-class living conditions. By the early 1960s business interests were also articulating a case for state-led economic modernization and a necessary fusing of physical and economic planning. The Scottish Council for Development and Industry drew up a programme calling for increased state expenditure to restore the profitability of existing industry, attract new investment and raise levels of personal and collective consumption.[53] The Scottish Development Department was set up in 1962, bringing the existing planning and development functions of the Scottish Office into one department. At about the same time the Scottish Development Group was formed within the Scottish Office as a special inter-departmental team. They produced a White Paper for the Conservative Government, setting out policies for the location and allocation of resources and accepting the essentials of the Scottish Council for Development and Industry's proposals.[54] A planned, public expenditure-led growth in 'depressed regions' such as Scotland was seen as integral to boosting economic performance in the UK as a whole.

The Labour Government elected in 1964 carried these policies further. In January 1966 they published a White Paper. 'The Scottish Economy 1965-70: A

Plan for Expansion'.[55] This looked beyond the central belt and set out a strategy for each of the eight statistical and planning regions within Scotland. It was premised on the assumption that a publicly financed renewal of infrastructure and the productive base would create conditions of self-sustaining growth, where enhanced profitability would be possible without continued high levels of public investment.

The White Paper led into a cycle of regional plans. Reports were prepared for the eight Scottish regions and there were also two major transport studies which covered the central belt. Designation and development of new towns at Livingston and Irvine, as well as a continued promotion of the earlier new towns, were important parts of the approach. However, the modernization was not limited to the central belt. The Highlands and Islands Development Board was set up in 1965, as a regional equivalent of a new town development corporation, though with wider and more flexible economic development powers. Thus planning in Scotland gained a distinct style, as the leading edge of what was necessary and permissible in the state's attempts to modernize the spatial economy of the United Kingdom.

Crucially this modernization did not simply involve the state in a planning role, rather it was directly engaged in implementing the plans, building and managing the new environments. The problems contained in the contradictory imperatives on the planning system (growth promotion and avoidance of crises endemic in that growth), were compounded by the rising expectations which were an integral part of the class compromise and of the creation of new commodities. By the 1960s in Britain problems of rationality and legitimation had become an integral feature of the planning system. The limited planning capability and the final imperative of capital accumulation meant that the planning system could not achieve its declared intents. A consequence of this deficiency in rationality was a loss of public confidence in the planning system itself, and thus increasingly militant challenges to the legitimacy of that system. The problems were most succinctly expressed in one of the seminal plans of the period, the Liverpool Interim Planning Policy Statement, which appeared in 1965: 'The essence of the planning problems of Liverpool is the increasing disparity between what people want and what the city offers in its housing, its range of activities and its total environment.'[56]

The problems of rationality and legitimation were interpreted as technical and procedural matters resolvable by expert review. To this end the then Minister of Housing and Local Government, Sir Keith Joseph, set up the Planning Advisory Group in 1964. His successor, Richard Crossman, happily inherited the group, describing them as a 'stunningly able and successful group of town clerks, treasurers and planners'.[57] Joseph has since become one of the gurus of unrestrained, unapologetic capitalism, bent on rolling back the state. That he and Crossman from the Left of the Labour Party could acquiesce in an identical approach to the problems indicates the strength and breadth of the political consensus of the time. The state was beholden by its own ideology – classless technocracy would adjust what had to be marginal problems, since such problems were seen as quite disconnected from any fundamental cleavages.

The Planning Advisory Group's task was to review the workings of the Development Plan system. Their report argued that public confidence in the planning system was being undermined by the delays in processing the development plans through the centralized apparatus of the Ministry.[58] They emphasized the need to strengthen the technical content of plans and to separate out matters of overall policy from local detail, so that only the main issues need go to the Minister, thus facilitating speedier decisions. The detailed land use zoning of the 1947 system was depicted as being too restrictive and inflexible, tending to submerge the policy content of the plans.[59] In all these respects the PAG tried to restructure the administration of planning to overcome deficiencies of rationality, while making the system capable of being more responsive to market forces as major initiators of change. At the same time improved administrative rationality was envisaged as bolstering public confidence and hence re-establishing the legitimacy of the planning system as an efficient and neutral means of steering development in the public interest. To this was added the idea of public participation, which would improve the technical information available on consumer preferences, legitimate the removal of the statutory right to object to the Minister on detailed, local planning matters and also serve to incorporate those mushrooming amenity associations who were protesting about the planning system.[60]

Another central theme of the report was the integration of land use and transport planning, a proposition also advanced by the Buchanan Report on 'Traffic in Towns'. Again, therefore, the aim was to boost the administrative performance of the system by addressing an evident deficit of rationality. Modernization of the highway system was an integral part of the transformation of the city to meet the changes in production and realization strategies of capital. The state itself also had to ensure that its costly investment in the new infrastructure was at least cost-effective. Land use planning could help to achieve this intent and also held the hope of managing the highway planning process so as to minimize social and environmental damage.

Prominent members of the PAG made clear that their own experience in planning practice had convinced them of the need for proposals like those contained in the Group's report. For example, Dr Wilfred Burns commented,

Six years ago I was given the responsibility for working out a plan for the centre of Newcastle so that the tide of would-be developers that had been held back by the far sighted vision of the Council could be diverted into the most socially beneficial channels. I suppose that we could have started off on the long trek of statutory development plan review; if we had done so our lives would have been unbearable and the development forces would have submerged us. We therefore prepared a policy plan for the central area that was a statement of policies for preservation, character development and tall buildings and an illustrative diagram. We survived.[61]

Walter Bor commented in similar vein about the enormous problems he inherited when he became Liverpool's first City Planning Officer. One third of the city was slums, with two thirds of the central area ripe for redevelopment. Yet there was no effective overall plan, as the development plan had been approved years before and was outdated. The adoption of the ideas in PAG allowed for a much speedier drafting of policies than would have been possible under the traditional system of plan-making. Bor particularly stressed the successes of the new approach in winning consent. The plan had been unanimously approved by the city council. There had been widespread public consultation but no major clashes either with the public in general or with individual owners and interested parties. The only dissidents were 'a small but vigorous group of people' who were opposed to any and every change in the city.[62]

Therefore, in this case, the desire of the central state administration to expedite its own bureaucratic procedures coincided with pressures from local authorities who sought to restyle their planning in an attempt to bridge the gap between the pressures they faced and the limited powers of co-ordination and control at their disposal. At the time Thomas Sharp pointed out that the PAG proposals had been fashioned by the state itself for its own convenience. Nineteen of the group's twenty-one members were drawn from central or local government and there was not a single councillor or ordinary member of the public. Sharp argued that the report would make life easier for the Ministry at the expense of the individual: 'Where are we living? In Russia? In China?', he asked.[63]

The Planning Advisory Group's recommendations were substantially transferred into the 1968 Town and Country Planning Act and its 1969 Scottish equivalent. It is interesting to note that the major innovations had already been rehearsed in 1947. The first draft of the Bill leading to the 1947 Act had spoken of 'A plan indicating the general principles upon which development in the area will be promoted and controlled'. This contrasted with the definition in the Act itself, where a development plan was 'A plan indicating the manner in which the local planning authority propose that land in their area should be used'.[64] Similarly, Lewis Silkin had spoken enthusiastically of the need for public involvement during his speech on the second reading of the 1947 legislation.[65] Thus even the innovations safeguarded continuity.

The modifications to the planning legislation in the 1960s provoked nothing like the political controversies with which planning had been associated in the 1930s and 1940s. Richard Crossman acknowledged that the Bill leading to the 1968 Act had been entirely fashioned by his civil servants and was in no sense a Labour Party measure; rather it was the kind of legislation which any government might pass.[66] In part this was because the controversies about land ownership were now being treated in a separate measure with the creation of a Land Commission. However, the issues in restructuring the city were derived from class relationships, involving the power of finance capital, the movement of industrial capital, the creation of new commodities and the struggle over the division of surplus value. The extended involvement of the state in urban development had fragmented these contradictions so that they appeared, depoliticized of their class basis, as problems of rationality and legitimacy within the administrative system itself, challenged by splintered quasi-groups based on area, sentiment for the past which was being expropriated in the physical demolitions, and individual property owners. The state was thus faced with the unintended effects of its own planning activity. The allegedly democratic and comprehensive planning system, which had been the envy of other capitalist countries and which had been exported almost intact to the colonies, both impeded the restructuring of settlements, and had its legitimacy threatened by its failure to suppress the physical, social and financial crises created by that same restructuring.

The economic crisis and the planning system
The crisis-ridden path from PAG to the collapse of British town and country planning in the late 1970s is encapsulated in a quotation from the Final Report of the Birmingham Inner Area Study, which remarked:

In 1965, and in 1968, when the PAG proposals were enacted, we were still, or so it was thought, in a growth situation. Unemployment was seen as a purely regional phenomenon and the problems of the inner city were seen simply as a backlog of unfit housing which could be remedied largely by new construction in 10 years or so, and there was little, if any, awareness of the complex economic and social issues of the inner city. Last, but not least, no constraints on public expenditure were foreseen right up to 1973.[67]

British planning from the early 1970s onwards has in fact been shaped by the chronic weakness of industrial capital and by the mounting fiscal crisis in the state itself. The faith placed in procedural reform along the lines of the Planning Advisory Group proved unfounded. Indeed, a similar attempted reform, the reorganization of local government, undermined the capabilities of the nascent structure planning system, particularly in England and Wales. Planning powers were divided between two tiers of local government and the boundaries around the urban areas were drawn too tightly to allow city-region planning to operate. The division of other local government functions between the tiers further compounded the difficulties of co-ordinated public sector planning.
   It was not structure planning which shaped the development of British cities in the early 1970s, but a property boom, a boom with its origins in the declining profitability of manufacturing industry. By 1975 the real rate of return, after stock appreciation, for industrial and commercial companies had fallen to 3.9 per cent, compared to about 12 per cent in 1960.[68] Not surprisingly then, the 'dash for growth' of the Heath government, boosting the money supply to encourage the 'risk takers' and the 'wealth creators', resulted in a massive speculative property boom. In 1972–3 lending to manufacturing industry increased by 19 per cent, while bank loans to property companies increased by 75 per cent.[69] The political outcry against speculators together with the destabilizing effect of the collapse of the property boom on the whole financial system, led to the Community Land Act. This was the third unsuccessful attempt to regulate the property market without resort to land nationalization.[70]
   Though the Community Land Act had its origins in political campaigns against

property speculators, the Act in its final form and the advice from central government to local authorities on how they should interpret the Act, ensured the continuity of land development guided by market values. Indeed, financial success for the Act, and fiscal success for the Development Land Tax, depended on a buoyant property market. Ironically the boom had collapsed before the Act reached the statute book. Thus though the state sought to constrain the most provocative aspects of property development it remained beholden to the need to bolster private capital accumulation through such developments. Not surprisingly, then, a recurring theme through the 1970s was the need for the planning system to expedite the development process. This theme had also been central to the deliberations of the Planning Advisory Group a decade earlier.

The property boom strained the capacities of the planning system. There was a 47 per cent increase in decisions on planning applications in England and Wales in 1972 compared with 1970. Planning appeals rose even more sharply, from less than 9000 in 1970 to over 14,000 in 1972.[71] Mr. George Dobry, QC, was therefore asked to review the system of development control and planning appeals to see how they might be improved. His appointment was announced on 3 October 1973, just as the property boom was toppling. His proposals for speeding up planning by instituting a two-category system of applications were sidelined, though the Department of the Environment continued to urge planning authorities to achieve faster decisions by more efficient working methods, and to ponder the possibilities of amending the General Development Order as a means to the same end. Similarly the Examination in Public was instituted as an attempt to reduce delays in the structure planning process, the removal of the objectors' statutory rights to public inquiry being explicitly justified in terms of the scope afforded by public participation.[72]

The years following the collapse of the property boom saw a substantial change in the relationships between local authorities and the property industry. Many of the major property firms of the boom years went into liquidation or had to sell their assets to survive. The major purchasers in this big money buyers' market were the pension funds and insurance companies. From 1973 to 1976 they increased their investment in property from £555 million to £963 million and their share of all investment in property went up from 38 per cent to 96 per cent.[73]

The transition then was from buccaneering self-made millionaires to stable and reliable financial organizations of a massive scale and with an assured long term supply of capital. In contrast, the local authorities were experiencing the first round of expenditure cuts and rate support grant reductions that followed the prescriptions of the International Monetary Fund. The power of the permanent financier was strengthened *vis-à-vis* the local authority contemplating gap sites and derelict buildings.

Co-operation between local authorities and property developers was urged by the Pilcher Committee, set up by Anthony Crosland when he was Secretary of State for the Environment. Their report on Commercial Property Development appeared in November 1975. It argued that a healthy property market was vital to the achievement of the Labour Government's social and economic objectives.

Their successors, the Property Advisory Group, have continued to present the property industry's case within the Department of the Environment.

The ending of the property boom did not signal the switch of capital from property to industrial investment, rather it was the onset of recession. The ability of the state to intervene to offset the loss of jobs and manufacturing capacity was limited not just by the internationalization of capital, but also by the mounting fiscal crisis within the state itself. The costs of the extended welfare programme were particularly apparent in the growth of local authority spending which had jumped from £1528 million in 1954 to £12,778 million in 1974.[74] An increasing proportion of this money, as well as an increasing absolute amount, had come from central government. Local rates constituted 41 per cent of local authority revenue in 1954, but only 30 per cent in 1974.[75]

The change in urban planning policy, giving priority to the inner cities, was announced by Peter Shore, Secretary of State for the Environment, in a speech in Manchester in September 1976. It was the logical outcome of almost a decade of experiments to find relatively low cost solutions to the problems of poverty. There had been the Urban Aid programme, the Community Development Projects, the 'total approach' studies, Neighbourhood Schemes, Inner Area Studies, Transmitted Deprivation Studies, Quality of Life Studies and Area Management Trials and Combined Community Programmes.[76] The new emphasis on the inner cities built on them, and on the theme that had emerged in social planning in the 1960s of selectivity in the allocation of resources, implying means testing rather than flat rate provision. The significance of economic decline to the inner city problem was acknowledged, indeed it could scarcely have been ignored. The response was defined within the constraints on state action. Thus the White Paper 'Policy for the Inner Cities' noted:

Some of the changes which have taken place are due to social and economic forces which could be reversed only with great difficulty or at an unacceptable cost. But some of the movement of jobs and people has been facilitated by policies aimed at reducing the overcrowding of the older parts of the cities. In the post-war years this was an essential part of public policy, but in most cities it has largely been achieved. It should be possible now to change the thrust of the policies which have assisted large scale decentralization and in course of time to stem the decline, achieve a more balanced structure of jobs and population within our cities, and create healthier local economies.[77]

The new towns and the effects of redevelopment on existing industries were thus held up as major influences on inner city decline. The planning system was to carry the can for the long-term collapse in profitability of British manufacturing and its impacts on employment. The new towns were a cause of the inner city problem only to the extent that they were a minor, state administered stimulant to the changing spatial imperatives of the capital accumulation process. It was the uneven nature of that process itself which could only be reversed at 'unacceptable' costs. The resources for the new initiative were therefore to come from within existing budgets and to be of a limited scale. The redistribution was to yield £125 million in England and Wales for 1979–80 and £20 million in Scotland by 1980–81 for the Urban Programme. The increase on the previous funding of the Urban Programme came from an adjustment of the rate support grant to the disadvantage of the rural counties. The March 1977 budget also made a further £101 million available for the UK as a whole for inner city construction works. This money was found by redirecting cash already cut from general capital programmes.

In April 1977 Inner City Partnerships were offered to Liverpool, Manchester and Salford, Birmingham, Lambeth and the London Docklands. Hackney, Islington and Gateshead were added subsequently. Fifteen other authorities were then given extra powers to make loans and to declare Industrial Improvement Areas, the loans being for the erection and improvement of industrial buildings. 'Partnership' carried overtones of harmonious working relationships between local authorities and residents, but also meant the linking of local government with private capital.

Though the major job losses in inner areas were attributable to rationalizations and closures of large firms, the revival of the inner city was increasingly depicted as a correlate of the revival of small businesses. Harold Lever, appointed by the Prime Minister to conduct a special study of small firms, said:

If something is to be done for the pool of a million and a half unemployed, then small businesses are one of our best hopes. In the last ten years a million extra people have been taken on by public authorities. I cannot see them taking up a million in the next decade. Nor can we expect much from the nationalized industries, who are suffering from over-manning. And the larger firms in the private sector are also likely to be shedding labour with the introduction of new technology. It is vital that we help small businesses to expand.[78]

He made the connection between small businesses and the inner city: 'only a vigorous and self-confident small business sector can provide this extra push of effort we require in inner city areas'.[79]

For want of better, inner city planning had to be geared to promoting small firms, meeting their needs and subsidizing their development costs in an attempt to keep existing firms in being or to conjure new ones. Central government urged local authorities to give industrial applications priority over all other types of planning application and to be 'flexible' in relation to non-conforming industrial uses. Planners were urged to provide sites for industry and to use the Local Authorities (Land) Act, 1963, to improve the immediate environment and to provide necessary infrastructure. Similar policies giving priority to the needs of industry were also urged in relation to transport and housing.

By the late 1970s the British land use planning system was one means used by the state to try to redress the declining rate of profit of industrial capital. During this time the Scottish planning system was again developed in some distinctive directions. The collapse of the old political consensus and the mounting economic crisis held out new political possibilities within Scotland. The British state had failed to meet both the demands of Scottish capital for increased profitability and the aspirations of the Scottish working class for better living conditions. The way was therefore open for a new alliance of interests around nationalism, an alliance bolstered by the prospects of North Sea oil revenues.

These factors impinged upon the planning system both directly and indirectly. Exploitation of the oil reserves as quickly as possible was essential to the British state's attempts to grapple with fiscal and balance of payment problems. The development programme therefore needed to be carried through expeditiously, yet in a manner which could contain controversies within manageable limits. Control of a major Scottish resource by multi-national companies was itself provocative. Risks of pollution, or oil-related developments destroying landscapes evocative of Scottish nationality itself, and disrupting local social structures – all pointed towards the crisis potential within the great opportunity of oil.

The land use planning system played a major role in mediating these crisis tendencies. The system of public inquiries allowed both the technical feasibility and notional desirability of development proposals to be scrutinized. The development pressures also pushed the Scottish Development Department into adopting a more national form of planning. Dr Derek Lyddon, Chief Planner at the SDD, explained what happened as follows:

The wide range in the type of land-based developments and their location – some 14 different communities stretching from Shetland to the Clyde – led to a demand for some form of national overview or strategy. This need was also highlighted by the national requirement for quick decisions coupled with the local impact often on rural communities and, above all, the uncertainty associated with exploration and discovery. In response a coastal survey was undertaken and the Coastal Planning Guidelines issued by SDD. Thus, the precedent was established for further summaries of nationally significant land resources accompanied by planning guidelines.[80]

In producing guidelines the SDD was both steering a different path from that followed by the Department of the Environment and feeling towards a new set of relations with local government. In Scotland the momentum of 1960s regional planning had been carried through into the local government reorganization, producing regional elected councils of a scale which permitted integrated physical and economic planning. The Scottish Office was therefore faced with potentially a more powerful challenge from these councils than was the case for the DoE south of the border. The power of the central state within Scotland was further destabilized by the rise in electoral support for the Scottish National Party and by the attempts of the Labour Government to contain that support by creating a Scottish Assembly. The SDD thus achieved greater autonomy from Whitehall, while simultaneously practising 'disengagement' in its relations with local authorities.

The most important innovation in Scottish planning created by the political circumstances of the mid-1970s was the Scottish Development Agency. For the first time the Secretary of State for Scotland was directly involved in and responsible for the development of the Scottish economy. Some of the groundwork for such an agency had been done in the West Central Scotland Plan, one of the regional strategies of the late 1960s and early 1970s. Its major proposal was to set up an Economic Development Corporation for Strathclyde.[81] The plan had demonstrated that traditional approaches to industrial promotion, through provision of sites and buildings, were not adequate to restore profitability to the industry of the region.

In Scotland the class alliance that had carried through the modernization planning of the 1960s was sustained longer than in England because it could be focussed around national demands opposing the failures of the British state. So by 1977 the DoE was looking on Scottish planning as no longer an adaptation of English practice, but a significantly different system.[82] The reality was more ambiguous: there were limits on how far that state could or would alter its practices and on the willingness of the Scottish *bourgeoisie* to follow a radical political path. The British state proved incapable of delivering even the limited reform of an Assembly. Within Scotland business interests were prominent in the campaign against an Assembly, opposing even limited powers over the Scottish economy, while support for it was strongest in working-class urban areas. The planning system remained similarly unreformed. As Wannop pointed out, there have been no National Planning Guidelines for resources which were not natural, and financial resources for urban renewal were not covered. The Scottish Office showed scant enthusiasm for another round of Regional Reports and the structure plans failed to serve as integrated economic and physical planning documents.[83] By the start of the 1980s the Scottish planning system, like that of England, was being restructured by ideologues of monetarism.

The monetarist attack

The economic crisis is hinged on the declining rate of profit. Faced with such a crisis a capitalist state must attempt to restore profitability. In Britain in the early 1980s this meant redirecting actions and expenditures so as to boost assistance to capital and to reduce the value of labour power. The primary beneficiaries of the strategy were to be finance capital and international industrial capital. The strategy required the driving down of living standards for substantial sections of the population and massive closures of production capacity so as to increase the overall rate of profit. It meant severing the class compromise at the heart of the British state and reconstructing a new version. The ideological prop to pursue this end was monetarism.

Monetarist ideology attributes the loss of profitability to the interventions of the state itself. The prescription is that the state should hold down the money supply, provide 'defence' against foreign enemies and secure 'law and order' at home. Beyond that its only role is to ensure that market forces can operate in an unconstrained manner. Monetarism can be seen as an attempt to extricate the state from the crises of rationality and legitimation described by Habermas. An ideology of individual achievement has been refashioned to address the crisis of motivation, while the underlying intent is to resolve the economic crisis in the interests of capital.

Aspects of monetarism had already impinged on the planning system in the 1970s. As outlined above there were attempts by the state to expedite the development process and to make land use planning a means of promoting industrial profitability. The central tenets of monetarism are the reduction of state action that is considered illegitimate, and privatizing those public assets which can yield profits. They were expounded with a new conviction and directed at the land use planning system by the Conservative government elected in 1979. The Secretary of State for the Environment, Mr. Heseltine, addressed the Town and Country Planning Summer School in September 1979.[84] He told the planners that his overall aims were the regeneration of the economy and the revitalization of society. He identified the planning system as one of the causes of national decline. It was guilty of delaying development and thus holding back much needed jobs. The costs of running the system were themselves a drain on expenditure, gobbling up funds which under the monetarist model would otherwise have been used productively. Mr Heseltine's view of the role of the planning system encompassed four tasks for it. These were to ensure that there was always an adequate supply of suitable and serviced sites to meet the needs of industry and the housebuilders; to conserve the special areas such as national parks; to safeguard land required for a special purpose, notably agricultural land; and to promote the interests of society at large, not any one section of it, by ensuring a fair balance between conflicting interests. The two faces of planning – promoting and restraining development – were thus reiterated, as was the ideological justification of the system as a neutral arbitrator.

The amendments to the planning system that have followed were largely rehearsed by Mr Heseltine in his York speech. The planning system has not been scrapped, but it has been trimmed. The aim has been to retain those aspects that directly assist the private accumulation of capital. At the same time the government has espoused a concern for conservation of historic areas and valued landscapes and has sought to improve the quality of architectural design through competitions (the importation of a market metaphor into the arena of aesthetics.) The attempt, then, is to retain and create an environment which can command a popular identity.

The aspects of planning which have been abandoned are those which are seen as impeding private accumulation. Thus the Community Land Act was repealed and Industrial Development Certificate controls were abandoned. The scope for planned intervention at a strategic level has also been reduced by the paring back in regional policy and by the removal of the development control powers of the structure plan authorities. Rigid though arbitrary controls have been imposed on local government spending, making any strategic planning of investment impossible for local authorities over anything but the shortest term. The development control system has also been altered by relaxing the General

Development Order and increasing the size limit for permitted development. What remains of the planning system is meant to make money by the imposition of charges for the submission of planning applications.

Potentially profitable public assets have been turned over to the private sector. Thus the New Towns have been forced to sell off land and buildings and the planning authorities have had to compile registers of publicly owned land which could be available for development – there is no provision to include similar privately owned land in such registers.

The aim then has been to align the planning system with the interests of the property industry. Where local authorities appear unenthusiastic the Secretary of State has been prepared to issue a Special Development Order, a device which in effect takes the granting of outline planning permission out of the hands of the local authority. The Secretaries of State in both Scotland and England have also been to the fore in deleting social policy statements from structure plans and in using ministerial decisions on such plans to make extensive land areas available to the volume house builders. Elsewhere decisions on planning appeals have fitted the same pattern.

Two measures in particular indicate the way the monetarists have adjusted rather than abandoned the state's planning role in relation to the use and development of land. These are the introduction of enterprise zones and of urban development corporations. In both cases a heavy rhetoric of the free market has disguised virtually unprecedented state powers and intervention mechanisms. In both cases these powers are aimed to assist the profitability of private developers, notionally so that the 'area' can benefit from new investment, though actual residents appear to gain little recompense for the loss of some democratic rights.

At York Mr Heseltine had spoken of recreating the conditions within which small firms could thrive. Predictably this did not launch him on a crusade to combat the centralization and concentration of capital, but rather to relax planning controls. The most complete translation of the idea into practice has been the creation of 'enterprise zones'. Professor Peter Hall had enthused at the 1977 Royal Town Planning Institute Annual Conference about the possibility 'Hong Kong-type free ports' in selected inner city areas.[85] The Chancellor of the Exchequer in announcing the enterprise zone experiment paid explicit tribute to Professor Hall. He also explicitly blamed the planning process for the devastation of whole areas of major cities. The first suggestions were that the new zones would be freed of all planning restrictions; however, faced with the possible deleterious impact on adjacent land owners and the necessity of retaining safety requirements, a mere 'simplification' of planning procedures was eventually chosen.

Those locating in an enterprise zone also reap financial benefits. Firms here are exempt from rates and from Development Land Tax, and receive 100 per cent capital allowance for corporation and income tax purposes for commercial and industrial buildings. The intention behind the allowances is twofold. It represents a direct attempt to make companies profitable thus complementing the strategy in the inner city partnerships and indeed with the previous traditions of regional policy incentives. However, it also holds out the possibility that if the zones are thereby a 'success', attracting new firms, the case will then be strengthened for extending the principles on which the success is based to other areas. This would mean a further attack on the social investment expenditures of central and local government in an attempt to cut rates and taxes on capital. It would also mean a further dismantling of those aspects of the land use planning system which can provide some environmental protection in working-class areas.

There are early signs that the rate and tax concessions in the zones are having unintended, though perfectly logical side-effects. The tax and rate concessions have pushed up the market value of the land in enterprise zones. Thus rents are increasing and the landowners are substantial beneficiaries of the concessions. In the Lower Swansea Valley zone 40 per cent of the development will be carried through by the local council and the Land Authority for Wales, both of whom are required by law to get the best price or rent for their land. The English Industrial Estates Corporation is likewise quoting higher rents in the Gateshead zone than for comparable properties nearby. There seems no reason to expect private landowners to be any more philanthropic. Indeed, the Department of the Environment view the prospect with equanimity. A spokesman was quoted as saying, 'The DoE will expect the rents to be slightly higher in the zones than outside. And we would expect those fortunate enough to own land to share some of the benefits with those who are deriving benefits from rate-free periods.'[86]

The early signs are that one of the most successful enterprise zones will be one at Clydebank. The town had suffered massive job losses through the closure of shipbuilding and the Singer sewing machine factory. The Scottish Development Agency had therefore moved a task force into the town before the enterprise zone was declared. Since declaration the Scottish Development Agency has played a crucial role in preparing sites and in promoting the zone. Thus an experiment intended to show how well the market could revive depressed urban areas if freed from the yoke of state control in fact depends on massive state subsidies to those locating in the zone and on a major state agency's masterminding of the development process. State planning has thus been retained, but as a development activity for a private client.

Similar points can be made about the two Urban Development Corporations. The idea was not new: in the late 1960s the Shelter Neighbourhood Area Project had suggested there was a need for an 'old town development corporation'. Because of the parallels with the new town model, the idea had drawn continuing support from the Town and Country Planning Association. The belief was that a strong executive body, with a clear cut brief to get ahead with development could get this done. In many ways the UDCs were to be the antithesis of the over-extended partnership committees under the Inner Urban Areas Act. Such committees had frequently comprised more than fifty members, there were a plethora of sub-committees and the hopes of co-ordinated working had not been fully realized.

The Local Government, Planning and Land Act gave the UDCs sweeping powers at the expense of the local authorities. It made them responsible for land, planning, building control, housing, highways and finance in their areas. It might be argued that since the Merseyside UDC area comprised almost entirely derelict docks with no residents, then there was no real erosion of local accountability. However, such an argument cannot be sustained for the London Dockland UDC, which included substantial residential areas.

It has been clear from the outset that the UDCs intend to channel funds from the state to property capital. The man appointed to be chairman of the London Docklands Development Corporation was Nigel Broackes, chairman of Trafalgar House Ltd, a major property group. LDDC's Chief Executive, Reginald Ward, declared that the organization would be geared to the needs of the private sector, seeking to persuade companies that profitable enterprises could be made out of social needs and social regeneration.[87] To achieve these aims the LDDC has an initial budget of £65 million and is responsible for an area of 5500 acres. It intends to encourage housing development on the riverside sites, and to attract industry to the Isle of Dogs enterprise zone. Encouraging housing means private housing on land the local authorities intended for public housing. As the *Guardian* reported, 'the London Dockland Development Corporation's plans to offer developers land previously scheduled for public sector housing represent an amazing opportunity for profitable business'.[88] The priorities of the Merseyside UDC are the same. Its chairman, a prominent local industrialist, Mr Leslie Young, put it bluntly, 'Our job is not to solve the unemployment problem. Our job is to ensure the area is redeveloped.'[89]

Two inter-related features characterized these changes to the British planning system. Planning was restructured to make it more directly responsive to the development priorities of private capital. This meant pruning planning to the essentials of land assembly and site design. Second, the state attempted to depoliticize the planning process, by-passing democratic accountability through local government. Planning was subsumed again within private philanthropy, in a remarkable piece of atavism. Thus Mr King, when Minister of State for Local Government, was host to the directors of thirty leading British and American firms at a private conference at Sunningdale in April 1980. The purpose was to examine the possibilities of expanding private investment in the decaying inner cities. Mr King was reported as telling his guests that they should hand over some of their profits to the inner cities, both because it was in their interests to improve such areas and because government had done the businessmen themselves a good turn by setting up enterprise zones. Mr King said, 'If British Petroleum, which made £1600 million this year, were to hand over £100,000 to the inner cities it would make a big difference. Yet that sum of money is within the margin of error accountants accept in drawing up the balance sheets and would pass unnoticed.'[90]

The problems of rationality and legitimacy which racked attempts to plan the reconstruction of British cities have been inverted so that they are not expressions of the limited capacity of the planning system, but rather of its over-extension. The failures have been severed from any connection with the state as a capitalist state and held instead to be eternal to the nature of planning itself. In a sense the ideological role that planning played in the war time and immediate post-war years has been resurrected, but turned upside down. Then planning as a method of rational executive action was portrayed as the way to solve problems in the interests of all, unbeholden to any class interest. Now planning as a method of bureaucratic action is the source of problems for all, though it is still unbeholden to any class interest, benefiting only the bureaucrats themselves.

The changes to land use planning are part of the much wider structural changes in the British state which began in the 1970s. The *modus vivendi* between capital and labour and its expression in crisis avoidance and a 'welfare state' broke down. The fundamental causes were the crisis of profitability within industry, initially in Britain then increasingly in the world as a whole, and the associated fiscal crisis in the state itself. These were overlain by the other contradictions from the economic system which were displaced into the state itself and which emerged as a crisis of legitimacy. The struggle to re-establish profitability through remodelling the form of state domination has been waged in terms defined by the strongest fractions of capital, financial and international industrial, rather than domestic industrial, capital, like the small firms which planners are now trying to promote. The current crisis in the planning system can only be resolved in relation to this wider struggle.

The British planning system: an overview

A crude impression of the interests that have shaped the development of the British planning system can be gained from the names of the ministries responsible for its administration. Thus there was the early association with the Ministry of Health, suggesting that the prime rationale for town planning was the reproduction of a healthy labour force. Then there was the Ministry of Works, when the post-war reconstruction of the productive base of the country was the priority. The short-lived Ministry of Town and Country Planning in its very title unified one of the divisions in the nation, bringing together town and country into a rational common purpose. Through the 1950s and 1960s planning was subsumed in Housing and Local Government, reproducing workers and consumers through the social investment policies of the refashioned class compromise. Extended state activity and the legitimation problems associated with it, saw planning co-ordinated into the Department of the Environment in the eco-conscious 1970s. By the late 1970s the main role of that department had shifted far from environment, being instead a key adjunct to the Treasury in seeking to establish central control over local government spending; so unless the title is retained for sentimental reasons another change could be due.

Such an analysis is, of course, an over-simplification, and this chapter has tried to suggest that the planning system has been shaped by more than one intention at any one time, and by conflicting and fragmented interests which have developed over the years. Despite the changes in the planning system, some notable continuities remain. Above all the planning system has remained tied to land use, with little positive control over the two key factors in planning the equitable development of towns and regions, namely land ownership and the movement of industry and employment. At times when landed capital has been weak, or has provoked economic and political resistance because of its unstable pattern of growth, stronger planning controls on the rights of land owners have been prepared. However, landed capital has managed to restrict such extended controls. In part this was achieved through the direct presence of land-owning interests in the House of Commons and the House of Lords. In part there was the sympathy of civil servants reluctant to risk political crises. Furthermore the legal system is more geared to protecting private property rights than to democratizing them. But beyond all these overt and semi-overt influences there has always been the direct economic power of capital. Landowners could withdraw their land from the market, or convert their assets into another form of capital. Furthermore the logic of the market system has meant that even where land is controlled by public bodies, it is administered on market principles, and indeed many public agencies are actually bound by law to operate their lettings and disposal of land in such a commercial way.

Similar constraints have applied in relation to industry and employment. Within a capitalist state the planning strategies had to be limited. The 'unacceptable costs' of reversing the 'economic forces' causing inner city decline, that the Inner Cities White Paper of 1977 referred to, were unacceptable to capital and to the state itself. British town planning has thus remained a limited and bureaucratic form of state intervention. Town planning as such has been only an indirect means of promoting private capital accumulation. By vetoing the development of some land it has boosted the value of other land, through the effect of scarcity within the market. Thus landowners have been a beneficiary of the planning system. However, the planning legislation and the structure of local government have meant that planning is not a capital-spending activity, rather that it is an adjunct to those departments of local and central government which do invest directly in the production of the built environment. Town planning therefore only assists the process of capital accumulation indirectly and should be seen rather as a means by which the state itself attempts to organize its intervention in a more cost-effective and publicly acceptable manner.

The practice of town planning has thus been separated from the processes of capital accumulation, while remaining subservient to them. It is in this relation that planning has necessarily taken on an ideological character, bearing always the promise of things that it cannot deliver. The recurrent theme in the development of British planning has therefore been crisis, that is a situation where a change of form is forced by irreconcilable demands. Planning has been shaped by crises in the production system and by the re-emergence of those repressed crisis tendencies in a fragmented and distorted form within the planning system itself.

British planning has also been shaped not just by the historical shift in the balance between the power of the classes and within the classes over time, but also by the historical balance that has occurred in the particular place. Thus while we would hypothesize that a similar pattern of development might be expected to obtain in other advanced capitalist nations, especially given the growing internationalization of capital, the specificity of political forms is a logical consequence of the dynamic of uneven development. Even within Britain it might be argued that the form of the planning system has been fashioned more by English problems and attitudes than those of the rest of the country. The cherishing of an arcadian rural landscape in the face of suburbanization pressures was essentially an English rather than a Scottish experience, while planning in Northern Ireland only really came of age in the 1960s in an attempt to force modernization and economic growth. It is interesting to speculate how a Scottish Assembly might have developed its planning system in the face of the changes initiated since 1979, and in the light of the way the Scottish planning system was developing in the mid 1970s.

Comparative studies of planning systems are therefore needed to elucidate whether there is indeed *a* theory of *the* state which can provide the basis for understanding town planning practice. Comparisons of local authority planning can also supplement the national pictures, if we are to elucidate how far those authorities are 'simply' arms of the state, inextricably beholden to the same priorities. Do the particular productive bases and class structures of an area affect the workings of the planning system, and if so, how? The deluge of articles about the state in recent years have tended to be written by people who are not planners and who are, perhaps for that reason, prone to generalize about planning in such a way as to portray it as highly functional to the state and the interests of monopoly capital. As this chapter has shown, the development of planning has been deeply problematic within the context of the British state. Though a satisfactory theory of planning as an activity of the state has yet to be articulated, it is at least becoming clear to planners that such a theory is needed and that they have to take some account of classical social science concepts like interests, class, power, ideology and historical development if they are to understand themselves. As the next chapter shows, British planners have previously interpreted their practice in a very different manner.

References and notes

1   R. H. Kantorowich, 'Education for planning', *Town Planning Institute Journal*, vol. 53 (1967), p. 176.
2   W. Ashworth, *The Genesis of Modern British Town Planning* (Routledge and Kegan Paul 1954).
3   In particular, G. E. Cherry, *The Evolution of British Town Planning* (Leonard Hill 1974).
4   G. E. Cherry, (1974), p. 5.
5   J. Habermas, *Towards a Rational Society* (Heinemann 1971), p. 96.
6   K. Marx and F. Engels, 'Manifesto of the Communist Party', in L. S. Feuer (ed.), *Marx and Engels: Basic Writings on Politics and Philosophy* (Anchor Books 1959), p. 9.
7   See, for example, C. Cockburn, *The Local State: Management of Cities and People* (Pluto Press 1977).

8   See, for example, M. Friedman, *Capitalism and Freedom* (University of Chicago Press 1962).

9   J. Habermas, *Legitimation Crisis* (Heinemann 1976).

10   E. Mandel, *Late Capitalism* (New Left Books, 1975), pp. 478–9.

11   T. Nairn, *The Break-Up of Britain* (New Left Books, 1977), notably Ch. 1, 'The twilight of the British State'.

12   For example, in the Eighth Public Health Report, 1866, Dr Hunter observed: 'people are not now alive to tell us how children were brought up before this age of dense agglomerations of poor began, and he would be a rash prophet who should tell us what future behaviour is to be expected from the present growth of children, who, under circumstances never before paralleled in this country, are now completing their education for future practice, as 'dangerous classes' by sitting up half the night with persons of every age, half naked, drunken, obscene and quarrelsome.' (p. 56).

13   The 1863 Public Health Report painted the archetypal Dickensian picture of inadequate diets, overcrowding and insanitary living conditions, and observed: ' These are painful reflections, especially when it is remembered that the poverty to which they advert is not the deserved poverty of idleness. In all cases it is the poverty of working populations.' Sixth Report, pp. 14–15.

14   *Report of the Interdepartmental Committee on Physical Deterioration, 1904*, Cmnd. 2175. This is quoted in P. L. Garside, 1979, 'Evolution or Genesis? The British Town Planning Movement, 1900–1940', paper presented to the Planning History Group meeting at Sheffield.

15   C. F. G. Masterman, 'The Heart of Empire', in *British Empire: Discussions of Problems of Modern City Life in England* (T. Fisher Unwin 1901), quoted in P. L. Garside.

16   T. C. Horsfall, *The Improvement of the Dwellings and Surroundings of the People: The Example of Germany* (Manchester University Press 1904), pp. 27–8.

17   See T. C. Horsfall, *The Improvement of the Dwellings and Surroundings of the People: The Example of Germany* (Manchester University Press 1904), pp. 27–8.

18   *Parliamentary Debates*, 1907, vol. 170, col. 204.

19   T. Nairn, (1977), especially pp. 24–52.

20   G. E. Cherry, 'The Housing, Town Planning Etc. Act, 1919' in *The Planner*, vol. 60 (1974), p. 681.

21   G. McDougall, 'State, capital and land: the history of town planning revisited', *International Journal of Urban and Regional Research*, vol. 3, (1979), pp. 361–80.

22   See, for example, the paper by Peter Dickens, 'Social Change, Housing and the State: some aspects of class fragmentation and incorporation, 1915–46', Centre for Environmental Studies, Urban Change and Conflict Conference, York (1977). Also P. Corrigan and N. Ginsburg, 'Tenants' struggle and class struggle', in *Political Economy and the Housing Ques-*

tion, Housing Workshop of the Conference of Socialist Economists (1975), pp. 134–46.

23 *Parliamentary Debates*, 1919, vol. 114.
24 Ibid.
25 P. Dickens, (1977), p. 11.
26 Wheatley agreed that his proposals were not socialist proposals. To get houses built quickly he saw it as necessary for the state to protect private enterprise from itself. See P. Dickens, (1977), p. 16.
27 *Parliamentary Debates*, 15 April 1931.
28 S. Ward, 'The Town and Country Planning Act, 1932', *The Planner*, vol. 60 (1974), p. 686.
29 Ibid.
30 J. B. Cullingworth, *Town and Country Planning in Britain* (George Allen & Unwin, 1974), rev. 5th ed, p. 23.
31 The real tragedy of England, as I see it, is the tragedy of ugliness. The country is so lovely: the little man-made England is so vile . . . make a new England. Away with little homes! Away with scrabbling pettiness and paltriness. Look at the contours of the land, and build up from these with a sufficient nobility. The English may be mentally or spiritually developed. But as citizens of splendid cities they are more ignominous than rabbits. And they nag, nag, nag all the time about politics and wages and all that, like mean, narrow housewives.'
D. H. Lawrence, *Nottingham and the Mining Country,* (1929).

Ginger looked out of the aeroplane: 'I say, Nina,' he shouted, 'When you were young did you ever have to learn a thing out of a poetry book about this scepter'd isle, this earth of majesty, this something of other Eden? D'you know what I mean? — this happy breed of men, this precious stone set in a silver sea . . . .
This blessed plot, this earth, this realm, this England.
This nurse, this teeming womb of royal kings,
Feared by their breed, and famous by their birth.
Well, I mean to say, don't you feel somehow, up in the air like this and looking down and seeing everything underneath, I mean don't you have a sort of feeling like that, if you know what I mean?'
Nina looked down, and saw, inclined at an odd angle, an horizon of straggling red suburb; arterial roads dotted with little cars; factories, some of them working, others empty and decayed; a disused canal; some distant hills sown with bungalows; wireless masts and overhead cables; men and women were indiscernible, except as tiny specks, they were marrying and shopping and making money and having children. The scene lurched and tiled again as the aeroplane struck a current of air.
'I think I'm going to be sick,' said Nina.
Evelyn Waugh, *Vile Bodies* (1930).

Do you know the road I live in — Ellesmere Road, West Bletchley? Even if you don't you know fifty others exactly like it. You know how these streets fester all over the inner-outer suburbs. Always the same. Long, long rows of little semi-detached houses – the numbers in Ellesmere Road run to 212 and ours is 191 – as much alike as council houses and generally uglier. The stucco front, the creosoted gate, the privet hedge, the green front door. The Laurels, The Myrtles, The Hawthornes, Mon Abri, Mon Repos, Belle Vue. At perhaps one house in fifty some anti-social type who'll probably end in the workhouse has painted his front door blue instead of green!

George Orwell, *Coming up for air*, (1939).

32   T. Sharp, *Town Planning* (Pelican 1940), p. 89.
33   *Report of the Royal Commission on the Distribution of the Industrial Population*. Cmnd. 6153 (HMSO 1940), p. 95.
34   J. Backwell and P. Dickens, 'Town planning, mass loyalty and the restructuring of capital: the origins of the 1947 planning legislation revisited', *Urban and Regional Studies Working Paper 11*, Sussex University (1979).
35   See, for example, *The Picture Post*, 4 Jan. 1941. The whole issue was devoted to the theme of 'A plan for Britain'.
36   *Royal Commission on the Distribution of the Industrial Population*, pp. 189–191.
37   J. B. Cullingworth, *Environmental Planning, 1939–69*, vol. 1, 'Reconstruction and land use planning, 1939–47' (HMSO, 1975) p. 58.
38   Cabinet Committee on Reconstruction Problems, 1942. 12 Annex. para. 8.
39   The question of statutory undertakers is dealt with in detail in J. B. Cullingworth (1975), Ch. V, pp. 145–58.
40   J. B. Cullingworth, (1975), p. 252.
41   Ibid., p. 51.
42   *Final Report, 1942, Expert Committee on Compensation and Betterment*, Cmnd. 6386, p. 27.
43   O. Marriott, *The Property Boom* (Pan 1969).
44   See J. Backwell and P. Dickens, pp. 13–14.
45   See M. Foot, *Aneurin Bevan 1897–1945* (Paladin 1975), pp. 470–3.
46   J. B. Cullingworth (1975), 254–5.
47   *Hansard*, House of Lords, 4 June 1947, col. 136.
48   R. Miliband, *Parliamentary Socialism* (Merlin Press 1972), second ed., pp. 293–4.
49   The Labour government did seek to carry out some economic planning, in the face of post-war shortages. However, decisions on the quantity and kind of industrial output required were to be left substantially to market forces. See A. A. Rogow, *The Labour Government and British Industry 1945–51* (1955), p. 25.
50   R. Grieve, 'In retrospect: 40 years of development and achievement' *The Planner, Journal of the Royal Town Planning Institute*, vol. 66, no. 3, (1980), p. 62.
51   See D. Massey and A. Catalano, *Capital and Land: Land ownership by capital in Britain* (Edward Arnold 1978).

52　C. Buchanan & Partners, *South Hampshire Study: Report on the Feasibility of Major Urban Growth* (HMSO 1966).

53　Scottish Council for Development and Industry, *Inquiry into the Scottish Economy* (James Paton 1961).

54　Scottish Office, *Central Scotland: A Programme for Development and Growth*, Cmnd. 2188 (HMSO 1963).

55　Scottish Office, *The Scottish Economy 1965–1970: A Plan for Expansion*, Cmnd. 2864 (HMSO 1966).

56　Liverpool City Council, *Interim Planning Policy Statement* (1965), p. 56.

57　R. H. S. Crossman, *Diaries of a Cabinet Minister*, vol. 1, entry for 21 March 1965. The planners on the Planning Advisory Group were Walter Bor, Wilfred Burns, Ronald Nicoll, Hugh Wilson, Robert Grieve and Jimmy James.

58　See The Planning Advisory Group, *The Future of Development Plans*, (HMSO 1965), para. 1.29.

59　Ibid., para. 1.1.

60　For a fuller discussion, especially of the Skeffington Report which followed, see S. Damer and C. Hague, 'Public participation in planning: a review', *Town Planning Review*, vol. 42 (1971), pp. 217–32.

61　*Journal of the Town Planning Institute*, vol. 52 (1966), p. 213.

62　*Journal of the Town Planning Institute*, vol. 52 (1966), pp. 214–5.

63　T. Sharp, 'Planning planning', *Journal of the Town Planning Institute*, vol. 52 (1966), pp. 209–15. The other two members of the Planning Advisory Group were planning consultants.

64　See the Planning Advisory Group, paras. 1.21-2.

65　Silkin said:

The provisional plan will be exhibited and submitted to public opinion by such means as maps and pamphlets, travelling exhibitions, talks by planning technicians, and films and models of more important parts of the area. The people whose surroundings are being planned must be given every chance to take an active part in the planning process . . . Too often in the past the objections of a noisy minority have been allowed to drown voices of other people vitally affected. The housewife who will use the new shops, and whose children will go to the new school, the trade union branch whose members will work on the new factory estate, the farmer, the motorist, the amenity society – these too must have their say and when they have had it the provisional plan may need a good deal of alteration, but it will be all the better for that since it will reflect actual needs democratically expressed. In the past plans have been too much the plans of officials and not the plans of individuals but I hope we are going to stop that.

Hansard, Commons, 29 Jan., 1947, col. 963.

66　R. H. S. Crossman, p. 621.

67　Llewellyn Davies and Partners, 'Unequal City', the *Final Report of the Birmingham Inner Area Study* (HMSO 1977), pp. 284–5.

68　*Financial Times*, 5 Oct. 1976.

69   The Labour Party, *Banking and Finance* (1976), p. 14.
70   For a critique of the Community Land Act see The Land Campaign Working Party, 'Lie of the Land', *Shelter Community Action Team.*
71   Department of the Environment/The Welsh Office, 'Streamlining the Planning Machine', Circular 142/73 (DoE), 227/73 (Welsh Office), 9 Nov. 1973 (HMSO), pp. 1–2.
.72   The Pilcher Committee on Commercial Property Development argued that public participation caused delays which affected the profitability of development schemes. They recommended that participation should be limited to 'planning matters', and should not extend to the financial aspects of any scheme.
73   Community Development Project Political Economy Collective and Publications Distribution Cooperative, *The State and the Local Economy* (1979) p. 17.
74   Current and capital expenditure at current prices. These figures exclude debt interest to central government. The source is National Income and Expenditure, Annual, (HMSO).
75   Ibid.
76   For a critique of the poverty programme see Community Development Project, Inter-Project Editorial Team (1977), *Gilding the Ghetto*, The Home Office (Urban Deprivation Unit).
77   *Policy for the Inner Cities*, White Paper, 1977, Cmnd. 6845 (HMSO), para. 2.
78   *The Sunday Times*, 27 Nov. 1977.
79   The *Guardian*, 26 Nov. 1977.
80   W. D. C. Lyddon, 'Scottish planning in practice: influences and comparisons', *The Planner, Journal of the Royal Town Planning Institute*, vol. 66, no. 3 (1980), p. 66.
81   West Central Scotland Plan Steering Committee, 'West Central Scotland Plan,' 1974.
82   W. D. C. Lyddon, (1980), p. 67.
83   U. Wannop, 'Scottish planning in practice: four distinctive characteristics', *The Planner, Journal of the Royal Town Planning Institute* vol. 66, no. 3, (1980), p. 65. Regional Reports were produced by the new regional councils in 1976, and were widely hailed as an important move towards better co-ordinated public sector planning. See, for example, S. T. McDonald, 'The Regional Report in Scotland', *Town Planning Review*, vol. 48, no. 3, (1977), pp. 215–32.
84   M. Heseltine, 'Secretary of State's Address', *Report of the Proceedings of the Town & Country Planning Summer School*, University of York, The Royal Town Planning Institute, London (1979), pp. 25–30.
85   Professor Hall's speech is reported in *Planning Newspaper*, p. 221.
86   *The Sunday Times Business News*, 5 July 1981.
87   Talk at the Polytechnic of Central London, 5 February 1981, reported in A.

Thornley, 'Thatcherism and town planning', *Planning Studies No. 12*, School of the Environment Planning Unit, Polytechnic of Central London, 1981.

88   The *Guardian*, 20 Aug. 1981.
89   P.B. Swann, 'Dock Revival?', *Planning Newspaper*, no. 363, 11 April 1980.
90   The *Guardian*, 3 April 1980.

3 The professional discourse

'Planner-bashing' has been one of Britain's few growth industries in recent years. The golden age, in which the planners of the new Jerusalem achieved an exalted status, was short-lived. Accusations of bureaucratic interference were bolstered by waves of popular discontent, as the refashioned city of late capitalism began to emerge from the comprehensive development areas. Given this turbulence, a monumental self-esteem would have been necessary to prevent planners undertaking some reassessment of the nature and content of their practice.

The task then is to interpret how the British planning profession responded to the contradictions in the extension of state intervention in the production of cities. This may appear to be a form of navel-gazing. A more pertinent critique would be that the ideology of the professionals is peripheral to the real determinants of urban development under capitalism. However, such an assertion begs the empirical question of just what legitimating role professionals play within a particular state form, and how they do it. It also represses self-understanding among the professionals, and thereby obscures the potential for locating and exploiting the contradictions between ideology and rational action that are the basis of a radical professional praxis. As Brian Melville observed, 'If a form of life is to be altered, the barriers of the language games must be breached, the structure of compulsion assimilated, and the repressed dialogues reconstructed.'[1] To understand the behaviour of a group such as town planners, we must understand the rules which delimit behaviour within that group. It would be absurd to suggest that such rules are developed in a totally autonomous manner. The participants are already aware of rules which structure rewards and punishments in other areas of life. The profession has to interact with other bodies, an interaction with further rules of expected behaviour. Nor is the situation static. However, the process of establishing the norms relating the actions of the individual to the groups and the society involves more than just socialization.

The work of Jurgen Habermas provides a theoretical framework within which the development of ideologies can be treated.[2] He argues that when human beings engage in discourse rather than adopt force to resolve a question, they are appealing to some concept of rationality, anticipating the possibility of rational agreement. The possibility is premised on the 'ideal speech situation'. This presupposes that the participants to the discourse are equal partners, equally free to question, argue and decide without duress or coercion. In such an idealized situation, truly rational decisions can be reached. Established power relations in social reality violate this ideal. Since such relations cannot be justified through rational discourse, they are sustained by ideologies. Thus the communication process is not free, but is distorted by the social interests embodied in these power relations.

The discussion in Chapter 2 depicted the state as seeking to achieve stable conditions for economic growth, avoiding risks and dysfunctions, and sustaining a depoliticized mass loyalty through the scientization of politics. The interaction within that state between expert officials and elected politicians might therefore be expected to be rich in distorted language games. The politicians, with their subjective value orientations, confront a world of facts, where volition is depicted as the realm of irrationality. They are torn between manifestos and technical memoranda; between political aspirations and the imperatives of managing the system. The scope for reference to public debate as a forum for rational choice is severely constrained by the manipulation of 'public opinion' to secure the system against threats to its stability. On the other hand, the very expertise of the officials is defined only in proportion to which they submit to the dominant value systems. Furthermore, the experts, obliged to short-circuit the political system, risk blowing a fuse. This will happen where the repressed political content of a decision breaks through the layers of techniques and professional judgement.

Planners have not been to the fore in identifying the inhibitions to communication that have developed around the idea of town and country planning in Britain. Back in 1959, Glass accused the profession of a lack of self-awareness, arguing for more consideration of the ideology of planning rather than the advancement of techniques of design and administration.[3] Reflection and interpretation, essentials for such understanding, were made inaccessible to planners by the professionals' own self image as men of action rather than contemplation. Thus the fashions that so easily jerked the professional rudder led to reformulations of space, administrative structures and methodologies. A textual tradition remains underdeveloped, despite the recent interest in planning history.

The ascendancy of the professionals

When the 1909 planning legislation was passed, there were only four men practising in the United Kingdom as professional planners. They were Adams, Parker, Unwin and Mawson. The land and construction professions were quick to claim that town planning was an expert activity that should be undertaken by professionals. Their only difficulty was in deciding just which professionals should do the job. The scrapping brought out definitions by the professionals of what was valid knowledge for the practice of planning towns.

The professional engineers set up a Town Planning Committee in 1909. The City Engineer of Birmingham, Henry Stilgoe, saw town planning as a matter of engineering. In June 1910 he observed,

I think the people who will administer it [the 1909 Act] will be the borough engineers and surveyors of this country. It is their right. They are the officials, appointed under the Public Health Act, and without their co-operation, and, in fact, without their intimate knowledge of their districts, this Act cannot be put into proper and efficient working order. . . . Those people who talk so much about town planning do not know what they want; would not know what to do with it if given the opportunity.[4]

The architects, one rung up the status ladder of Edwardian England from the engineers, organized their lobbying in a manner befitting their self-perception as artists and gentlemen. While the Institute of Municipal and County Engineers organized Town Planning conferences in Cheltenham, Great Yarmouth and even West Bromwich, scarcely venues to attract the unconverted, the Royal Institute of British Architects launched a metropolitan extravaganza in October 1910. Their Town Planning conference had a glittering guest list, of whom none was more splendid than the Maharaja of Baroda. The King was patron, while the backing of the Almighty was secured by making the Archbishop of Canterbury one of sixty-four honorary vice-presidents, alongside Kitchener of Khartoum. This was the social milieux within which the discussion of the nature and scope of town planning was conducted. The sentiment of the gathering, ensconced in an 800-page volume of *Transactions*, was amply expressed by Beresford Pite: 'The town is too precious a possibility, if not already a possession of beauty to be entrusted to the consideration only of its expert surveyors and engineers. The problems are architectural, and will ultimately be judged as such.'[5]

The surveyors were less strident in their claims. In his presidential address in 1909, Alexander Stenning assured his members that while town planning was a step away from private estate development is was not socialism. Thus fortified, the surveyors saw a contributory role for themselves in the new planning system.

The founding of the Town Planning Institute in 1914 represents both the coming together of like-minded men from different disciplines, and the failure of any one of the founding professions to completely resist the claims of the others. What is certain is that a group of people perceiving of themselves as professional men (the first woman was not admitted to professional membership of the TPI until 1928), set up to define the nature and skills of the planning activity. They were principally from the construction professions and the law, and their definitions were orientated to techniques and action.

Cherry argues that 'radical leanings were much in evidence' among these founder members of the planning profession.[6] However, none of their parent professions, not least the lawyers, can seriously be thought of as radical. Equally the social background and the employment status of these first planners appears overwhelmingly middle class. A reading of the early papers presented to the Institute confirms this thesis, and reveals how quickly the basic ideology of the fledgling profession was shaped. 'This Institute is in no sense a propagandist body,' E. R. Abbott declared in his 1917 presidential address; rather it was made up of 'practical people'.[7] The practical men defined the basis of their competence in an examination system, which filtered entry to the profession from July 1920. Thus, as Cherry acknowledges, the propagandists and idealists became a minority as the profession was fashioned.[8]

The ascendancy of the professionals was a corollary of the way that town planning was established in the 1909 Act as an extension of state intervention at the level of local government. In this sense town planning is just one illustration of a very general phenomenon. As state activity increased, and universal suffrage became widespread, problems were shifted into the area of bureaucratic decision. The proclamations by the professionals of the expert nature of the planning activity thoroughly complemented the bourgeois ideal of civil privatism.

Clearly, then, town planning as part of British local government was going to be a professional matter. If planners were to establish a toehold in the career structures they had to demarcate their own professionalism. To resist the predatory claims of the other professions, planners had to define the tasks which they alone could undertake. The intellectual interest in defining the nature of town planning relates to this material context, and sparked debate between the founding fathers. Adshead argued for a carving up of the new jobs between the existing professions. The surveyor would have control during the preliminary work, after which he would hand over to the engineer, until finally the architect would furnish the plan with buildings.[9] Mawson rejected such a compromise; rather, '... there must be some person whose training has been not that of a specialist, but of that general nature which will place him in sympathy with all the specialists employed, to exercise the judicial faculty, to co-ordinate and correlate the work of each, and to see that every interest is adequately met.'[10]

That person would be the Town Planner or Landscape Architect, terms which were synonymous to Mawson. In the discussion after the paper, Professor Adshead suggested that things had changed since his paper. A clientele was developing for town planning. They were coming to a situation where a man was needed at the helm to control all the other professionals whose interests encompassed town planning.[11] Such discussions built up an intellectually respectable argument for the existence of an independent planning profession with a unique expertise in co-ordinating development. The endurance of this viewpoint, despite and because of hostile attacks from other professions, testified to its importance.

Political neutrality in the interests of all

Professional planners, as expert advisors to politicians on potentially controversial issues of land development, faced problems about the ambiguous relation between their expertise and political judgements. They might, in principle, have asserted that a private market in land produced intolerable inequities in wealth and living conditions, and hence argued that planning was a means of demo-cratizing the development process. Conversely they might have argued that no resolution of the contraditions in urban development was possible within the statutory limits of town planning; hence each and every plan would be defined by the political priorities of elected members. The planners would thus interact with the politicians to help them exercise political choice in an open, informed and self-aware manner. In reality the resolution was the claim by most planners that their technical expertise allowed them to design plans that would benefit society as a whole. The ethical and political questions were thus rendered void by asserting a technocratic route to consensus. Over a long period the planning profession has denied any systematic cleavage of interest along class lines in matters pertaining to the development of cities. But to deny such cleavages and to act on that premise is itself a deeply political practice. Such a practice legitimizes simultaneously the role of planners, the particular and restricted form of their practice within the statutory framework and the depoliticization of the substantive issues themselves. It is thus consistent with the dominant ideology of the state itself.

This not to deny that early planners were intent on improving working-class housing conditions. However, their priorities were consistent with those of the imperial state in reproducing a labour force, rather than in challenging and restructuring existing social relations. Thus Thomas Adams, the first president, addressed the Institute in 1915, and argued that planning was essential to secure healthy living conditions. Rather than probing why such conditions had been denied to so many for so long, he asserted the Empire's needs for:

a strong and healthy race of men and women to fight its battles and to maintain its strength. Whenever, on the one hand, good environment and healthy conditions have contributed to the staying power of our soldiers or those engaged in making munitions of war, or, on the other hand, the absence of these things has impaired the efficiency and strength of our men, they have been contributing factors for or against us at the front.[12]

In the same year Pepler presented a paper which set out to consider whether town planning was 'financially sound as regards land development'.[13] He explicitly ruled out discussion of 'the rights and wrongs of the present property laws'.[14] Having refuted the notion that 'landowners as a class think only of their own interests',[15] Pepler argued that town planning schemes could overcome 'particular difficulties of estate development [that] all meant expense to the owner', and in addition would 'provide settled conditions which are a great attraction to purchasers'.[16] In the subsequent discussion, Professor Adshead saw the loss of development value due to planning schemes as something that would wane with public education of the real value of the restrictions. So when the developers realized that, '. . . the mass of the public, the majority of the public, interested in occupying houses and in investing in land and property realised the benefits of restrictions – as they were rapidly coming to do – they clearly saw that the time was not far distant when restricted land would be regarded as the most valuable.'[17]

The notion that the majority of the people were interested in property investment is empirically questionable, given that the majority of the population owned no property at all. However, the tenor of the paper and the discussion is clear enough: planning does not challenge private ownership of land or property, nor did the professionals particularly want it to. Rather the idea of planning is constituted as a technical method of effecting development, which could overcome difficulties posed by unprofitable aspects of private development.

The notion that planning was a neutral and effective means of furthering the interests of everybody was consolidated by the particular political conditions of the 1930s and the war. Rational executive action was a bulwark against the alternatives of *laissez-faire* and totalitarianism. The economic problems of recession and then reconstruction, and the political problems of refashioning the class compromise, strengthened the credibility of an expertise that could manipulate the processes of urban and regional change so as to eliminate dysfunctions. In this situation planners did advance a critique of the disarray of the pre-war capitalist economy. Even so, the terms of that critique were strictly circumscribed by the ideology of professional expertise. The contradictions in the emergent pattern of urban development were ascribed to mistakes and muddle, to failures to fully apply purposive rationality. Since such a path could no longer be followed in the face of the totalitarian threat, planning, and hence purposive rationality, became virtually synonymous with democracy itself.

The case for planning was well put by Thomas Sharp, in his popularizing paperback that appeared in 1940:

For fifteen years and more in places like Rhondda, Jarrow and Bishop Auckland hundreds of thousands of Englishmen have been eating their hearts out in squalid, dole-supported unemployment spent among fouled landscapes and filthy slum-built towns with hardly a hand lifted to help them. And all the while the new industries they require have been piling up in prosperous places like the Midlands and the South; and our governments have done practically nothing.

It is no overstatement to say that the simple choice between planning and non-planning, between order and disorder, is a test-choice for English democracy. In the long run even the worst democratic muddle is preferable to a dictator's dream bought at the price of liberty and decency. But the English muddle is nevertheless a matter of shame. We shall never get rid of its shamefulness unless we plan our activities. And plan we must – not for the sake of our physical environment only, but to save and fulfil democracy itself.[18]

Glass[19] and Foley[20] in their classic articles, commented on the ambivalence of planning ideology in the years after the war. The ambivalence facilitated an appeal to a wide political spectrum, a factor which in itself helped to depoliticize the form and scope of town planning. The planning package included powerful and comprehensible symbols that were projected on to local cinema screens—war-damaged housing being swept away; new, better housing being planned; space to play in; work to go to; the countryside to enjoy; new schools for a new generation. Their strength was that they did connect with the aspirations of the mass of the population. Yet the terms in which the symbols were paraded remained patrician and ultimately repressive. In the movies and in the plans nobody ever rejected what was offered and demanded more, while speculative property developers were unheard of. The planners were portrayed at their drawing boards, or sweeping their hands across the model of the new city, as if their skill and charisma were itself sufficient to conjure a transformation in social relations and living conditions. It never was and it still is not.[21]

The films are now in the archives. The plans of the period with their carefully coloured maps and twee sketches are collectors' pieces. It all seems impossibly naive. Yet the fundamental idea survived fashions in urban form and the graphics of plan-making. The profession has consistently claimed that its members have the technical skills to manipulate urban and regional development so that functional criteria are met, thereby improving the lot of society as a whole rather than reinforcing inequalities. An illustration was the evidence submitted by the Royal Town Planning Institute to the Royal Commission on the Distribution of Income and Wealth (the 'Diamond Commission'). The Institute stressed that planning could produce wealth for all, but firmly rejected the notion that the distribution of the wealth was a matter worth pursuing. By stimulating economic growth the skills of the planner could create wealth, and 'satisfy human needs and aspirations without harm to other groups or individuals – least of all those least able to fend for themselves'.[22]

It would be easy to ridicule a document which is so banal. Sentiments such as 'The richest of people sometimes choose to end their own lives, while the poorest can fill a room with joy'[23] scarcely prompt serious analysis. However, the important point is that the basic premises of the 1976 memorandum are totally consistent with the mainstream thinking within the planning profession over six decades about the effects of planning and its relations to private property. There is thus a clear distinction between matters arising out of the ownership of property, and the sphere of concern of environmental planning. The memorandum rejects the practice of using development control to guide 'capital gains towards the public purse', since this would curtail investment, thereby inhibiting the 'global creation of wealth', which would therefore threaten physical planning objectives.[24]

Functionalism
The self-image of the planner serving all equally has been buttressed by the language of functionalism, a view of the world firmly ensconced in the construction disciplines, and well to the fore in the design philosophy of the modern movement. The analogy of the city as an organism needing to function properly to survive has been a popular one. In practice it has been used to legitimate the transformation of the city to meet the infrastructure requirements of capital.[25]

This particular facet of the professional ideology appeared in a very pure form in planning education, as indeed did other aspects of that ideology. The central feature of that education has always been studio work, focussed on plan-making at ascending spatial scales, from village up to city region. The intention has been to introduce the trainee planner to the range of problems, and to develop skills in solving them. The implication then is that the problems are primarily related to the spatial scale, rather than to any wider political economy. Likewise, the solutions lie in the manipulation of the land uses by the expert planner. Thus the Royal Town Planning Institute's examination syllabus for 'Social Factors' was strongly functionalist in orientation, including studies of the land use and location requirements of schools, clinics and police stations.[26]

The language of functionalism represses the ethical questions in town planning. The promotion of efficiency, economy and beauty is not the starting point for debates on social justice. Keeble, in his best-selling book, saw the promotion of accessibility as probably the most crucial task that the planner faced. He advised his readers that the ability to drive to the heart of a town along uncongested roads was 'a basic requirement of good town planning'.[27] Such sentiments extend technical control well into the field of political choice, pre-empting even pluralist questions about who benefits from such facilities and at whose expense. Rejection of such professional advice is implicitly ascribed the status of irrationality, for nobody can seriously argue in favour of bad town planning. The language games of the professionals have thus impossibly distorted the basis on which others could participate.

Thus there has been a consensus within the planning profession around a coherent and internally consistent set of ideas. These establish the parameters for the validity claims of knowledge about town planning. The essentials persist from the ruminations of the founding fathers to the profession today. In a nutshell the orthodox position has been, and is, that town planning is a unique professional activity, concerned with the design of the physical environment, so as to achieve functional efficiency and amenity, aims which are in the interests of society as a whole and thus outside the political arena. These propositions have been fashioned and sustained by the interests of the planners themselves in demarcating an employment base to which they can claim preferential access, and by their need for identity and self-esteem. The education and membership policies of the professional institute have bolstered the ideology, through socialization and a measure of coercion. The rewards and punishments of the professional career structure further sustain the orthodoxy. The professional discourse has thus been structured in a way that excludes the possibility of a critical analysis of the role of the planner. The unequal structure of land ownership and the power conferred by land ownership, is perceived as something that is both fixed and unproblematic, and hence not a matter for debate. Society is a unity and so the bedrock social science concepts such as class, interest, the state and power are rendered irrelevant to professional discussions. The one aspect of the ideology which retained some potential for critique concerned the design of the physical environment itself. The idea of redesigning settlements implies a dissatisfaction with the existing environment. In part the planning movement in Britain developed out of the Romantic tradition, with its critique of nineteenth-century capitalism. The links go through the Town and Country Planning Association, back through the Garden Cities and to the stream of moral and literary criticism with Morris and Ruskin and back to Blake. However, this critical potential was suppressed: the patterns of land-use consumption of late capitalism were equated with rational town planning; the profession's traditional interest in aesthetics and settlement structure was then increasingly set aside in favour of management and decision-making. The distortions embedded in the professional discourse have thus served the dominant interests in the capitalist state.

Professional ideology and motivation crisis

One consequence of the distorted language games of the profession has been the frustration and disillusionment of many who entered with high, albeit naive, hopes that they were embarking on a career founded on social, even socialist, reform. Further results, less immediately apparent, have been the doubts and disappointments of those subscribing to the dominant ideology. These derive from the distortions themselves, and from the developing contradictions within the administrative system. They are made manifest in the bitter debates that have taken place within the planning profession, and the adjustments that have consequently been made to the professional ideology.

In analysing these tendencies it is again useful to draw on the work of Habermas. One of the crisis tendencies of advanced capitalism which he identifies is a 'motivation crisis'. This occurs when a mismatch develops between the requirements of the state apparatus and the occupational system on the one hand and the interpreted needs and expectations of members of society on the other. Such crises derive from changes in the socio-cultural system itself, where they are stirred by developments in the mode of production and state activity, rather than being voluntaristic.

An important element of bourgeois ideology has been the achievement ethic, the idea that social rewards are distributed on the basis of individual achievement. The market was the classical mechanism to allocate such rewards. However, the concentration and centralization of capital and the widening experience of the social force present in allegedly neutral market functions undermined the credibility of the argument in its purest form. Hence individual achievement became increasingly identified with education and occupational status as well. Even so, in late capitalism the achievement ideology has been further eroded, not least because there are more and more areas where production structures and labour processes make evaluation according to individually accountable achievement increasingly improbable. Furthermore, fragmented and monotonous labour processes even penetrate sectors where identity could previously be formed through the occupational role.[28]

The struggles to establish planning as a profession and to create career paths for those within it can be interpreted as a reaction to and consolidation of the tendency towards a structure of individual achievement tied to education and occupation; and one aspect of planning practice in the post-war period has been a loss of individual control over work processes and a reduced scope for individual identity with the outputs of the planning system. The corresponding disillusionment has had two notable consequences: there has been a withdrawal of legitimation from the practice of planning as expressed through the statutory system; the other has been a loss in the sense of confidence and identity among the professionals.

The impending disillusionment was catalysed in the evidence presented to the Schuster Committee. The intended role of town and country planning in post-war reconstruction created an instant shortage of manpower with the qualifications to do the job. The state needed more planners quickly, the vast majority to work in local government. The Town Planning Institute was intent on protecting the status and esteem of its qualifications, and had a vested interest in maintaining a scarcity in the supply of qualified labour. It had even managed to rebuff the formidable figure of Dudley Stamp, who had lobbied for geography graduates to be given exemption from the Institute's intermediate examinations. Lewis Silkin, the Minister responsible, therefore set up a departmental committee under Sir George Schuster to investigate the training and qualifications that planners would need to operate the new 1947 planning system.

The Town Planning Institute and its past president, Thomas Sharp, forcefully presented its case to the committee. It argued that physical planning was a unique technical exercise, the kernel of which was the skill of designing two-dimensional plans for the development of land: 'Emphasis is placed on design, because that must be the focus of knowledge; but the designer must obviously understand that which is to be focussed, even if only to enable him to appreciate the free scope that must be provided for the specialists in those other arts, sciences and crafts.'[29] In essence, then, the institute was reiterating the position about the nature of planning that had been put forward by Thomas Mawson over thirty years earlier. The acid test for entry to the profession would therefore continue to be the ability of the individual to prepare a plan 'in the sense of something to be set out on a drawing board'.[30]

Sharp argued that the planner had a distinct professional skill, which was the sole guarantor of good planning. In particular he refuted the proposition that good planning could result from equal collaboration within a team of specialists drawn from a variety of disciplinary backgrounds.[31] Instead he asserted that 'Planning is design: design is one man's responsibility (with, of course, the subordinate help of assistants).'[32] Thus Sharp transmuted the activity of the state in regulating the process of urban development into the non-negotiable private property of the chief planner. The proposition is elitist, authoritarian and difficult to fit to practice within the bureaucracy of central or local government. Presumably Sharp envisaged the Director of Planning of a big city sitting at a super drawing board, receiving bits of information from his subordinate assistants, and translating them on to his plan: 'We'll need another fifty acres of housing land, sir.' 'Fifty acres is it, lad? Pass me my brush and the red-brown 2:1 and I'll work it into my design.'

The basis of reality which Sharp's view did touch was the practice before the 1947 Act, where all the major plans had been produced by consultants, such as Sharp himself. These men were not mere local government servants, rather they were charismatic figures who sold their expertise to clients.[33] Schuster interpreted planning as a social and economic activity, that was limited but not determined by the technical possibilities of design. Administrative skills were adjudged to be at least as important as technical know-how. It was a team job, requiring a sound basic university education. Thus the committee's findings linked the shift by government towards a social welfare programme with the traditions of the administrative civil service and the aura of Oxbridge.

The irony of course is that the high watermark of British town planning, the passing of the 1947 legislation, threatened both to undermine an important aspect of planning ideology (the claim to a unique expertise) and to sweep away important aspects of job satisfaction for members of the profession. The idea that 'planning is a team job' can only partly compensate egos dented by the fragmentation of the process of plan-making within the growing bureaucracy. Not surprisingly then the 'one man, one plan' ideology remained bouyant, despite its unreality. Furthermore, the dissonance between the professionals' expectations and self-perception on the one hand, and the experience of practice on the other, does contain some potential for enlightenment through critical reflection. Thus the contradiction between the prescription of the planner and what is acceptable to the state could develop into critique. How, then, has that contradiction been treated?

The reassertion of civil privatism
A recurring strand of opinion has interpreted the dissonance as an affirmation of the correctness of the professional viewpoint. Defects in the output of the planning system have been thereby attributed to elements of democracy (elected members, ignorant of good planning and politically motivated) or bureaucracy (the legal framework, bargaining between departments, the demeaning nature of administrative work). Thus Keeble argued: '. . . we very badly need to give [the planner] a somewhat freer hand, at any rate . . . to the extent of confining lay intervention to the approval of each important item of proposed policy and each stage in plan-making, rather than continuing a system that has as an important feature month by month lay dabbling'.[34]

The first major polemic against the visual environment associated with the 1947 planning system appeared in the *Architectural Review* in 1955. 'Outrage' depicted the British planning system as bureaucratic and as inhibiting good design, while failing to protect standards. The reasons why hopes of a brave new world had been dashed were enunciated:

Any hope of intelligent interpretation was lost when planning was tied down step by step with local government and made into another unrewarding office job. This chained it to the very points where democracy is most likely to give the lowest common denominator, not the highest common multiple: corporate subtopia, with all the planning rules as its armoury, perverted to make every square mile indistinguishable.[35]

The solution to this standardized environment of consumer capitalism was high-density development in the settlements, and strict protection of the rural areas as countryside, a re-establishment of urbanity. The planners also needed to be extracted from the standardized work processes and their expertise reaffirmed. The prescription was for 'someone who stands outside all specialization and does the visual thinking', who would be given real power. He would be responsible for topographical areas, not administrative units, and to national not local government. The notion that a focus on the visual thinking is not itself a specialization is itself a sign of the distorted language game.

An equally significant expression of disillusionment came two years later.

Thomas Sharp, one of the most distinguished members of the profession, was invited to address the TPI ten years after the passing of the 1947 Act. He spoke of the widespread feeling that planning had become less interesting, hopeful and important.[36] He despaired of the 'endless trivialities' that the work now comprised, and of the domination of that work process by 'the great goddess Admin'. Plans had been debased into mere surveys, 'small and dreary' negative things, concerned with control not creation. He spoke disparagingly of County Planning Officers who defined their function as 'adjudicators between claimants for the use of land'. If planners really were no more than adjudicators and administrators, they did not deserve to survive as a distinct professional body. Thus, in Sharp's eye, immersion in bureaucratic practice had fundamentally undermined job satisfaction and the ability to create a distinctive output as the fruits of a planner's labour.

Sharp's perception ranged more widely, however, for he noted also the mounting hostility of the public towards planning. He saw this as being something quite new. He connected it to the control that planners exercised 'over other people's activities with so little obvious and acceptable result'. He bitterly attacked the private plans that planning officers kept in their bottom drawers away from the public, 'which can be used for bargaining and if necessary for bullying, but which cannot be challenged because they do not legally exist'. He concluded that there was little worth while to show in return for 'the mountain of cost' that had gone into the planning system. So Sharp questioned not just the destruction of motivation among planners, but also the legitimacy of the planning system itself. He even noted that the failure of planning was one manifestation of a much wider malaise in British life. But his critique remained firmly rooted in orthodox professionalism. He pinpointed the problem as the abdication by the professional planners of their role as creative designers. He still saw planning as essential to the nation's civilized survival, but the way to attain real planning was for the profession to regain its lost ground.

Thus Sharp's seminal reflections on planning practice during the first decade of the 1947 system raised fundamental questions about the legitimacy of planning and about the motivation and identity of the planners themselves. The essence of his polemic has been reiterated over the years thereafter. The simplicity of its 'back to basics' call appealed particularly to a generation of planners who became increasingly bewildered by the accretion of a social science jargon into the profession in the subsequent years. Variants on the incantation came from architect–planners attempting to establish urban design as an area of practice that reflected Sharp's prescription. The doubts he raised about the legitimacy of the planning system were most likely to be echoed by those planners engaged in private practice, and by their private sector clients, and in recent years they have become a familiar accusation from the architectural press and prominent architects. Alice Coleman's attacks on the results of the planning system and her calls for a return to basic principles and techniques likewise fit that tradition.[37] In a less dramatic way, the analysis is reflected in the low status traditionally ascribed to development control within the planning profession, where it has been seen as a negative and bureaucratic task that must frustrate the truly creative mind.

Sharp's broad stance was vindicated and he himself won a considerable personal victory in the contentions over the membership issue in the TPI in 1964–5. The controversy was sparked by a report from a working party under Mr L. W. Lane, which went to the Council and to the branches of the Institute. By a majority the working party recommended changes to liberalize membership and education requirements for entry to the planning profession. Their case was essentially pragmatic. They argued that the scope of planning had become so broad that it was no longer possible for any one person to gain an expertise of all its varied aspects. In other words, the labour process had become fragmented, and planning was now in practice a 'team job'. The proposition then was that all the team should be able to become members of the TPI. The distinctive nature of the profession would be retained by ensuring that all entrants had a basic knowledge of the essential elements of planning practice, theory and law.

In December 1964, the Council of the TPI circularized its members with a memorandum on membership policy, and a voting card which contained three propositions. These were (1) to extend membership to all persons making a professional contribution to planning, whether of a general or a specialist kind; (2) to revise the examination requirements accordingly; and (3) to admit people over forty and qualified in a related discipline who were contributing substantially to planning, subject to an interview and other tests as required by Council; this scheme would run for two years. Within weeks Sharp and twenty-eight other corporate members had requested an Extraordinary General Meeting, which was convened on 29 January 1965. Sharp and Keeble were among those who spoke vehemently against the Council and in favour of a separate and distinct profession. Sharp proposed that no further action should be taken on the memorandum and that the questionnaire should be disregarded. The meeting supported him by a 75 per cent majority. When the results of the questionnaire were eventually tallied they revealed:

	Agree	Disagree	Indefinite
Resolution 1	784	914	20
Resolution 2	880	812	24
Resolution 3	532	1158	16

A slate of candidates was organized to fight the Council elections on an 'independent profession' ticket, and after an energetic campaign they were elected, sweeping aside some prominent names in the process.[38] Membership and education policies were then recast by the victors in accord with their own philosophies.

Without doubt a major factor affecting the outcome of the controversy was the fear among the grassroots that their status and career prospects would be threatened by allowing other professions ready entry to the Institute. Their defensive response was to reassert the undiluted primacy of the individual planner with his professional expertise in design, a stance which the Schuster Committee had rejected as outmoded in terms of practice some fifteen years earlier.

The scientization of planning

The other response within the profession to the lack of fit between its ideology and experience in practice was that reflected in the Buchanan–Lane proposals which were battered in the 1964–5 debate. In essence this involved attempts to restructure aspects of the orthodoxy so as to retain the claims to professional status, while reinterpreting the nature of planning so as to more closely approximate to the emergent practice. In this lay the moves to generate new motivation and legitimation by providing an intellectually respectable basis of theory from which a superior practice could be built.

The revamping of ideas about planning to fit a bureaucratic practice necessitated some critique of what had gone before. The critique was couched in terms of positivist social science. Planning had been unscientific, over-reliant on intuition, subjectivity and aesthetics, when what was needed was scientific method, objectivity and empirical studies of the behaviour of the consumers. George Chadwick in his clarion call for planners to adopt a systems view put it like this:

planning was an 'art': one 'flew by the seat of one's pants', and planning skills were regarded as personal, intuitive. It may be no coincidence that for several decades town planning libraries have been conspicuous for their shelves of dusty, unread, unacted upon reports, in handsome binding and format, but obviously, in hindsight, quite unrelated to the real needs and possibilities of their time.[39]

Thus failures in practice were ascribed to the dominance of ideology over method, a one-dimensional view which constrained explanation to the socio-cultural level only, thereby negating any problematic at the political or economic levels. The reductionist analysis led to an equally ideological remedy, the adoption of an allegedly value-free methodology. The hard nosed ideologues prescribed a more realistic, empirical social science approach, with better techniques of forecasting, plan evaluation and monitoring and, in particular, goal setting. The appeal of the critiques was fourfold. First, the experience of planning inquiries, where planning officers had to defend their proposals under cross examination from lawyers acting for an increasingly voluminous number of objectors, clearly pointed to the need for better information and tighter reasoning to sustain planning proposals. Second, there was the simple fact that much of the day to day work of planning officers was indeed administrative, and involved making decisions of a piecemeal nature rather than exercising design skills in a comprehensive manner. Then there was the promise held out by the achievements of science and technology in other fields, their ready acceptance by consumers and the potential of the computer. Last, but not least, the critique could fit, even bolster, a professional stance, as its central emphasis was on a neutral technical expertise.

Jim Amos, with his sociology degree and pioneering management style in Liverpool, seemed to personify the way ahead. He told the 1971 RTPI annual conference that:

planning is a process which may be applied to many sets of circumstances, and is characterized by its analytical techniques, its synoptic concern for the total environment, its decision systems and its orientation towards problem-solving action . . . planning may be described as the constantly evolving corpus of scientific methods used in the synoptic examination of man's environment and in making decisions affecting it. [40]

Later that year, in his presidential address, he argued that planning was 'not yet an exact science', and therefore individual planners would entertain different views about topics like public participation and land ownership. The Institute itself should not pronounce upon these topics, however; rather, it should seek to ensure that 'the processes of critical analysis are as exhaustive and unbiased as possible'. [41] Thus planning is defined as the exercise of a set of value-free scientific methods, while the social antagonisms that infuse issues like land ownership are transmuted into a pluralism of irrational beliefs, surviving only because the scientific method has not yet been adequately refined in such fields.

'Process' rather than 'product' was the new name of the game, and the profession's previous preoccupation with propounding ideal settlement forms was dismissed as speculative and utopian. Instead a spate of authors produced variants of an idealized decision-making process, with boxes, lines and circles intermeshing in ever more complicated fashions. Goal-setting was typically depicted as a key stage and a major weakness in past practice. However, part of the price for this incursion into the intellectual territory of public administration was that questions of the relation between expert planners and politicians had to be consciously faced. Chadwick in particular mused on some of the problems this posed. He concluded that the planner's public sector client was an ambiguous animal: it might be the politicians, chained to party dogma and looking only to the next election, or it could be the users of the environment now and in the future. In neither case was there any tradition of a clear elaboration of priorities on planning issues. His solution was that the onus lay with the professional planner, as guardian of the public interest, to identify the goals and he went on to discuss techniques which might facilitate the task. [42] Political choice was thus subsumed within technical expertise.

The models of the decision-making process, with their origins in public administration, management science and operations research, were derived from an analogy of the decision behaviour of an idealized, intelligent human mind, rather than from observations of the way that planning decisions were actually taken. [43] Thus, at the heart of the claim to replace a speculative utopia of urban form by an empirical science lay a speculative utopia of instrumental decision-making.

The most frequently acknowledged critique of the unreality of the model of the decision process, was that associated with Charles Lindblom. His criticisms and his alternative formulation of disjointed incrementalism are set out by Chadwick[44] and more fully by Faludi.[45] Lindblom dismissed the rational model as being impossible to apply in practice. He therefore described and justified existing decision-making procedures in the name of a neutral empiricism. In response, the advocates of the rational–comprehensive decision model argued that their models were intended to be inspirational rather than descriptive, establishing ideals of instrumental rationality to which practitioners should aspire, though might not necessarily attain.[46]

Faludi, drawing on the work of Mannheim and of Weber, through the writings of Friedmann, acknowledged the possibility of a more fundamental criticism of rational decision models. He recognized that 'functional rationality' and its associated form of 'functional planning', in seeking to fit rational means to predefined ends carried the risk of substantial irrationality. He contrasted this with normative planning, which 'is chiefly concerned with the ends of action of a social system'.[47] However, his discussion peters out as the choice between the two is ascribed to organizational structures and voluntaristic role perceptions of the planner as 'bureaucrat' or 'political'. Faludi sets 'human growth' as the end of planning. 'Human growth' is approached through the application of cybernetic principles to social and political theory, and is given a clean bill of positivist health by the fact that its components enjoy respectability in experimental psychology, can be analogously transferred from individuals to society and are susceptible to behavioural observation. Since Faludi sees the end of planning in this uncontroversial and 'scientific' manner, his discussion of functional versus normative planning is itself an exercise in functional rationality.

Therefore, after operating within local government for over half a century the British planning profession finally turned to the management sciences for intellectual nourishment, forsaking the mother's milk of the construction professions. 'Planning Theory' began to appear in the syllabuses of planning schools, taking over the slot previously filled by 'Principles and Practice', and strengthening claims to academic respectability. The claims to the generality of the planning process as a set of management techniques also constituted a legitimate intellectual base from which planners could lay claim to the new jobs opening in local government as the state wrestled with financial crises and deepening 'urban' problems by extending the application of management procedures.

By 1971 the RTPI could set a hesitant foot along the path of change that had provoked such bitter schisms in 1964–5. A discussion paper invited the membership to ponder five possible options for the Institute. These were: (1) no change; (2) a learned society rather than a profession; (3) an Institute of Planning which would embrace all types of planning (corporate, economic, social and environmental); (4) an Institute of Community Planning and (5) the eventual preferred option, an Institute of Environmental Planning. The final choice of the members thus amounted to an endorsement of the proposition rejected in the 1960s. The scope of planning was broadened slightly, while re-emphasizing the professional basis. The very fact that the Institute could credibly consider such a diversity of self-definitions testifies to the uncertainties about its own identity which planners were experiencing. Notably a very small minority of Institute members wanted to see no change in the focus and structure of the profession.

The continuing crises
Neither the reassertion of the traditional ideology with its emphasis on the creative individual designer, nor the scientism imported from North America in the 1960s, were sufficient to defuse the crises of motivation and legitimation experienced by planners. In particular the growing wave of public protests at the effects of planning decisions, shook the planning profession. The growth of community action directed against planning proposals in working-class areas particularly deepened the disillusion of younger planners who, drawn into planning out of a vague sense of social idealism, found themselves administering the destruction of communities. Amos, in his presidential address, made the point thus, 'In many instances, planners, aware of the side effects of their proposals, have become deeply concerned about their own conflict of loyalties to their client or employer, to society in general and to their personal integrity.'[48] Clearly then, individual planners faced problems of motivation as they were unable to control the social consequences of their own labour. However, the mushrooming action groups and the increasing awareness that planning decisions could have regressive effects threatened the legitimacy of the planning system. Practice had undermined civil privatism on planning issues. With the inspiration of the American model of advocacy planning, planners were even directly involving themselves in struggles against official proposals. At the height of the property boom, the RTPI President's solution to the deepening conflicts over the development and use of land was to call for a free planning aid service, along the lines of legal aid, to be set up to help 'those in need'. In a paper to the President's Committee on the Urban Environment, he was explicit about who the other beneficiaries of such a scheme would be:

Whatever the problem involved it is in the interests of local authorities and the professional institutes to begin thinking about how to solve them. If they don't, 'planning aid' will happen anyway and probably in a form they would not have chosen. Community groups will become angry and lash out in all directions, raising all sorts of confusions and political problems.[49]

The profession as a whole was deeply divided by the question of whether planners should set up free planning aid services, given the evident reluctance of government to fund anything equivalent to legal aid. The matter churned through an RTPI Working Party, and then the opinions of the branches were sought – tactics which were sufficient indications in themselves that the matter was viewed as being contentious. The most intemperate response came from the East of England Branch, who refused to have anything to do with planning aid, and argued instead for a stronger private sector within the profession. Faced with a very mixed response, the RTPI pragmatically decided to leave individual branches to take the initiative to establish a planning aid system in their area, though the Code of Professional Conduct was amended to permit members to give their services free of charge.

Not surprisingly the development of planning aid has been uneven across the country. More important, the term has embraced a practice involving at least four and possibly five different approaches. The Professional Advice Model is the one closest to the Institute's original intent and the one that creates least tensions with the orthodox role of a professional planner. Through surgeries, or a referral service operated with Citizen's Advice Bureaux, volunteers provide free information and advice on planning matters. Then there is Advocacy, where the planner directly promotes the client's interests on planning matters. Another form of Planning Aid has been primarily concerned with Adult Education, taking the message about how the planning system operates out to people, rather than waiting for the clients to present themselves. This is closely associated with a fourth model, where Planning Aid is seen as a part of Community Development, with the emphasis on working with groups rather than individuals to help them to learn by participating and thus building up self-help. Finally and less certain, there is Community Action, where planning aid is part of a wider political strategy of raising consciousness by organizing protest around issues.[50] These ambiguities in the meaning of 'Planning Aid' are not an accidental pluralism. They derive from the contradictions of interests that led to the formulation of the idea itself. In the process of urban development, class antagonisms have become fragmented among quasi-groups, identifying themselves as 'communities'. Their struggles have called into question the legitimacy of the planning and added to a motivational crisis within the body of professional planners. Planning Aid itself was propounded both as a means to assist in such struggles and as a mechanism of social control. It is no surprise then to find that planning aid is a deeply distorted language game, rich in reciprocal misunderstandings which derive from the false assumption of consensus.

Research suggests that planning aid is not, in fact, helping those in most need. Soon after the TCPA's service was set up, their Planning Aid Officer, David Lock, observed, 'We're seen as a good buy by the activist middle classes'.[51] Edgar and Bidwell, who have worked hard to establish a community development approach in Tayside, conceded, 'Analysis of the cases undertaken by the Dundee group suggests that those assisted were something of an elite.'[52] The research of Chree confirms this view.[53] The Professional Advice Model in particular discriminates in favour of those with the skills and ability to recognize that they have a planning problem, to know that planning aid exists and to have the time and courage to approach the service. This model therefore actually legitimates inequalities, in that the service appears to be equally available to all, even to benefit the poor, whereas the very nature of the provision predisposes it to use by the better off. In this way, the contradictions which made planning aid necessary and which resurfaced in the language itself break through also in the practice.

Paradigm change

So a major paradigm shift ocurred in British planning with the ascendancy of the systems approach. But that paradigm has failed to resolve the problems of the profession, indeed in some respects it has deepened them. It closely paralleled the systems revolution in geography, the advent of which Harvey described in terms of a model of the Keynesian revolution in economics, that was elaborated by Johnson.[54] A similar description is possible of the way the sociology of the planning profession helped the new ideas to take over. Johnson suggests, for example, that:

By far the most helpful circumstance for the rapid propagation of a new and revolutionary theory is the existence of an established orthodoxy which is clearly inconsistent with the most salient facts of reality, and yet is sufficiently confident of its intellectual power to attempt to explain those facts, and in its efforts to do so exposes its incompetence in a ludicrous fashion.[55]

The orthodoxy of British town planning in the 1960s was that planning was a design task which ought to be entrusted to the individual man of vision, who would design *in toto* the future environment at whatever spatial scale one cared to name. This simply did not fit the mundane reality of practice within the bureaucracy, nor could the polemics of the *Architectural Review* or Thomas Sharp really redirect that practice. So, as Johnson observes, the way was open for 'a new theory that offered a convincing explanation of the nature of the problem and a set of policy prescriptions based on that explanation'.[56] That explanation was that the problems planners faced were of their own making, deriving from an over-reliance on intuition, the anomalous persistence of a *beaux-arts* tradition in an age that was experiencing the white heat of the technological revolution. The prescription was a new scientific methodology, with better techniques. This new theory also exhibited the five characteristics which Johnson saw as necessary for acceptability. For example, 'First, it had to attack the central proposition of conservative orthodoxy . . . with a new but academically acceptable analysis that reversed the proposition.'[57]

The central proposition that planning was an intuitive design process, exercised by an individual, who produced a plan drawn out as a map, was replaced by the idea that planning was a general decision-making process, a team job, resulting in a flexible written strategy.

'Second, the theory had to appear to be new, yet absorb as much as possible of the valid or at least not readily disputable components of orthodox theory. In this process, it helps greatly to give old concepts new and confusing names, and to emphasise as crucial analytical steps that had previously been taken as platitudinous.'[58]

The continuities with the previous planning tradition remained strong: physical, or more trendily, environmental planning, could be acknowledged as a valid sub-system of the general planning process, functionalism remained unchallenged, and the expertise and neutrality of the professional were boosted. Goal setting, making explicit the intentions in the plan, was now projected as the lynchpin of the whole planning process. Similarly alternative plans would now have to be consciously evaluated.

'Third, the new theory would have to have the appropriate degree of difficulty to understand . . . so that senior academic colleagues would find it neither easy nor worthwhile to study, so that they would waste their efforts on peripheral theoretical issues, and so offer themselves as easy marks for criticism and dismissal by their younger and hungrier colleagues.'[59]

Armed with first edition copies of McLoughlin's book, and casually familiar with the writings in the *Journal of the American Institute of Planners*, students came through the planning schools in record numbers. They were the generation who had been drilled from the age of eleven in expectations of a meritocracy, piranahs who could devour the flabby intellectual flesh of lecturers and senior officers unschooled in the traditions of social science research.

'Fourth, the new theory had to offer to the more gifted and less opportunistic scholars a new methodology more appealing than those currently available.'[60]

People like Chadwick, McLoughlin, Amos and Faludi are ample testimony to the extent to which this desideratum was realized.

'Finally, [it had to offer] an important empirical relationship . . . to measure.'[61]

There were any number of relationships to observe and quantify – public attitudes, time-distance functions, environmental intrusion, etc.

Mike Cuthbert has suggested that the paradigm shift amounted to an attempt to reorganize the philosophical core of planning.[62] The earlier tradition was informed by design principles and the language of architectural form. It was concerned with the aesthetics of settlement form and structure. Despite the distortions overlaid by professional interests, it nevertheless had a connection with the British literary romantic culture that has been pre-eminently described by Raymond Williams.[63] It was a radical dissenting tradition, in which organic culture stood as a critique of the environment produced by freely competitive capitalism. Just at the time that popular protest was mounting, not least over the aesthetics of the city of late capitalism, the planning profession's self-understanding that derived from this open-ended social movement was truncated by the restructuring that the new paradigm ordained.

The 'new planning' was premised on a technical cognitive interest, that is the form of scientific knowledge it was striving to achieve was knowledge concerned with manipulation and control. Understanding of the city was displaced to the secondary status of theory for planning rather than of planning. Webber led the onslaught of those who affirmed the superiority of the urban form of American capitalism to any planner's dissenting alternative, a triumph for empirical reality over irrational beliefs. In the post-city age interaction was to be more important than place, despite the wails of those defending the accumulated meanings of places against new motorway plans. In the language games of systems planning the city was depicted as a milieu of objectified processes. The behaviour of atomistic decision-makers could be observed, their participation and interaction in the complex activity systems of urban realms could be codified and the physical environment could then be adapted to achieve the value-free aims of freedom of choice, flexibility and efficiency. Manipulation of the symbols would thus provide information allowing prediction and social control, just as in the more obvious areas of high technology production.

The planning profession has thus been engulfed in the wider processes of the scientization of production and of politics, in which the existing relations of production present themselves as the technically necessary organizational form of the good society, despite their central concern with the irrational domination of man and of nature. Planners have therefore become increasingly incapable of addressing the practical content of urban development issues, for questions of what ought to happen are projected as matters of technical explanation and control. The profession has thus sustained the attempts by the state itself to depoliticize such questions. Nevertheless, the contradictions still break through, leaving planners bewildered victims of their own self-image, which in turn has become increasingly blurred. Mathematical modelling of urban development is now out of fashion. Few have faith or interest in the elaborations of variants of rational decision theory, though it continues to occupy a prominent place in the planning theory syllabuses.[64] Planning aid can mean just about anything, except the actual practice of helping those in the most deprived conditions to control their own living environments. 'Men of Action', devoted to 'getting things done' are sidelined by a major recession. 'Planning and the Future', a discussion paper prepared by an RTPI working group, prescribed an extended planning role, full of co-ordination and sub-systems, community involvement and resource planning, left many of the 'old guard' totally bemused. It was published just as the IMF was pulling the rug from public spending, in the cause of monetarism and a more overtly repressive strategy to achieve social control.[65]

Despite everything, planners remain in thrall to the need to elevate the existing form of practice as the highest state of being to which they can aspire. The risks of doing otherwise in a hostile climate and with shaky egos are too much to contemplate. Yet emancipation, through a truly practical planning theory, can only be accomplished through a conscious struggle against the dominant ideology and the practice it sustains.

References and notes

1   C. E . B. Melville, 'Futures and Social Interests', mimeo (1976).

2   See in particular J. Habermas, *Theory and Practice* (Heinemann 1974), ch. 1 and also J. Habermas, ' On systematically distorted communication', *Inquiry*, vol. 13, (1970) pp. 205–18. An extract from the latter appears in P. Connerton (ed.), *Critical Sociology* (Penguin 1976), pp. 348–62.

3   R. Glass, 'The evaluation of planning: some sociological considerations', *International Social Science Journal*, vol . XI, no. 3 (1959), pp. 393–409.

4   H. Stilgoe , in the *Proceedings of the Institute of Municipal and County Engineers*, vol. XXXVII, no. 44 (1910–11).

5   Quoted in G. E. Cherry, *The Evolution of British Town Planning* (Leonard Hill 1974), p. 46.
6   G. E. Cherry (1974), p. 61.
7   E. R. Abbott, 'President's Address', *Town Planning Institute*, vol. IV, no. 1 (1917), p. 1. 'Practical' as used here does not carry the wider meaning of concern with ethics and politics.
8   G. E. Cherry (1974), p. 61.
9   Adshead's article appeared in an early issue of *Town Planning Review*, and is quoted in T. H. Mawson, 'Some of the larger problems of town planning', *Town Planning Institute*, vol. I, no. 8 (1915), p. 124.
10 T. H. Mawson (1915), p. 124.
11 See *Town Planning Institute*, vol. I, no. 8 (1915), p. 128.
12 T. Adams, 'Some recent developments in town planning', *Town Planning Institute*, vol. I, no. 10 (1915), p. 142.
13 G. L. Pepler, 'Economics of town planning in relation to land development', *Town Planning Institute*, vol. I, no. 5 (1915), pp. 63–77.
14 Ibid., p. 63.
15 Ibid., p. 63.
16 Ibid., p. 68.
17 Ibid., p. 70.
18 T. Sharp, *Town Planning* (Pelican 1940), p. 143. One might empirically question whether there were thousands of Englishmen in the Rhondda.
19 R. Glass (1959), pp. 393–409.
20 D. L. Foley, ' British town planning: one ideology or three?', *British Journal of Sociology*, vol. 11 (1960), pp. 211–31.
21 Films portraying the contribution that town and country planning would make to post-war Britain include *Proud City* (Ministry of Information, 1944, 1945), *Words and Actions* (Ministry of Information 1943) and *When We Build Again* (Bourneville Trust).
22 *Royal Town Planning Institute*, 1976, 'Memorandum of observations submitted to the Royal Commission on the distribution of income and wealth', para. 5.5 (vi).
23 Ibid., para. 3.2.
24 Ibid., para. 5.1 and 5.2.
25 For discussion of an example, see C. Hague and A. D. McCourt, 'Comprehensive planning, public participation and the public interest', *Urban Studies*, vol. 11 (1974), pp. 143–55, and especially p. 151.
26 See, for example, the Royal Town Planning Institute, *Examinations Handbook* (1976), p. 18.
27 L. Keeble, 'Principles and practice of town and country planning', *The Estates Gazette* (London 1969 fourth ed.) p. 10.
28 J. Habermas, *Legitimation Crisis* (Heinemann 1976), and in particular ch. 7, pp. 75–92.
29 *Report of the Committee on the Qualifications of Planners*, Cmnd. 8059, (HMSO 1950), para. 122.

30   Ibid., para. 122.

31   Ibid., para. 119.

32   Ibid., para. 71.

33   This is referred to in para. 105 of the Schuster Report.

34   L. Keeble, 'Planning at the crossroads', *Estates Gazette*, London (1961), p. 3.

35   *Architectural Review*, vol. 117, no. 702 (1955).

36   T. Sharp, 'Planning now', *Journal of the Town Planning Institute*, vol. XLIII, no. 6 (1957), pp. 133–41.

37   Of the architectural press *Building Design* has probably been the most vociferous critic. Planner-bashing in the name of creative architecture was honed to a fine art by Michael Mansor, an oft-quoted spokesman of the architectural profession. Dr Coleman's research and views are repeated in a number of papers. See, for example, 'Land use planning: success or failure?' *Architects' Journal* (19 Jan. 1977), pp. 94–134. In this she is well to the fore, with denunciations of trade unions and council housing.

38   For a blow-by-blow account of the EGM see the Special Supplement to the *Journal of the Town Planning Institute*, vol. LI, no. 3, (1965).

39   G. F. Chadwick, *A Systems View of Planning* (Pergamon 1971), p. 120.

40   F. J. C. Amos, 'The development of the planning process', *Journal of the Royal Town Planning Institute*, vol. 57, no. 7 (1971), p. 305.

41   F. J. C. Amos, 'Presidential address', *Journal of the Royal Town Planning Institute*, vol. 57, no. 9 (1971), p. 398.

42   G. F. Chadwick, pp. 120–3. See also J. B. McLoughlin, *Urban and Regional Planning: A systems approach* (Faber 1971), p. 106.

43   See, for example, A. Faludi, *Planning Theory* (Pergamon 1973), pp. 54–62, and J. B. McLoughlin, 95–103.

44   See G. F. Chadwick, p. 306, *et seq.*

45   See A. Faludi, ch. 8, pp. 150–70.

46   See, for example the preface to the Second Edition of Chadwick's book, published by Pergamon in 1978, pp. ix–x.

47   J. Friedman, 'Planning as a vocation', *Plan Canada*, vol. 6 (1966/7), pp. 99–124 and vol. 7, pp. 8–26, quoted in A. Faludi, p. 172.

48   F. J. C. Amos, 'Presidential address', *Journal of the Royal Town Planning Institute*, vol. 57, no. 9 (1971), p. 399.

49   F. J. C. Amos, 'Planning aid', paper to the *President's Committee on the Urban Environment*, Royal Town Planning Institute (1977), PC 72(16).

50   See D. West, 'Planning aid: theory and practice', unpublished BSc. Research Essay, Department of Town & Country Planning, Edinburgh College of Art/Heriot-Watt University (1980).

51   D. Lock, *The Surveyor*, no. 142 (1973), pp. 30–1.

52   L. Bidwell and W. Edgar, 'Planning aid, who gains?', *Planning Newspaper*, no. 7 (March 1980), p. 7.

53   G. Chree, 'Planning aid', unpublished MSc. thesis, Department of Town & Country Planning, Edinburgh College of Art/Heriot-Watt University (1981). See also D. Edwards and B. Curtis, 'Planning aid: an analysis based on the Planning Aid service of the Town and Country Planning Association', Reading University, School of Planning Studies, Occasional Paper 1 (1980).

54   D. Harvey, *Social Justice and the City* (Edward Arnold 1973), pp. 122–4. This draws on H. G. Johnson, 'The Keynesian revolution and monetarist counterrevolution', *American Economic Review*, vol. 16, no. 2 (1971), pp. 1–14.

55   Ibid., pp. 122–3.

56   Ibid., p. 123.

57   Ibid., p. 123.

58   Ibid., p. 123.

59   Ibid., p. 123.

60   Ibid., p. 123.

61   Ibid., p. 123.

62   M. Cuthbert, 'The role of theory in town planning', paper to Education for Planning Association, Planning Theory Working Group, Polytechnic of Central London, mimeo (1978).

63   R. Williams, *The Country and the City* (Chatto & Windus 1976).

64   G. Crispin and S. Hamnett, 'Planning theory: a collection of syllabuses', paper to *Conference on Planning Theory*, Oxford Polytechnic, (April 1981).

65   S. Law *et al.*, 'Planning and the future', The Royal Town Planning Institute, London (1976).

Part Two **Planning Practice**

Preface – A note on practice and case studies

'Practice' is a word uttered by planners in reverential tones. It is the *sine qua non* if academic activity is to have a justifiable use; a cudgel to beat dissent; the ultimate test of professional virility. The simulation of 'practice' has been the apex of planning education, the accumulation of 'practice' remains the key that unlocks the door to membership of the profession. Those seeking to understand cities, planning and their own roles as planners must therefore translate this notion of practice, explore the interests which fashion it at any particular time and probe the essence behind the appearances.

Part One sketched a theoretical framework within which town and country planning could be located. The city has been shaped by the developing logic of capitalism; contradictions endemic in producing the city have been advanced through class struggle, and are embedded in the system of state planning of land use, where they re-emerge as continuing crisis tendencies. The professionals' interpretation of these processes has been systematically distorted, reflective of a wider class domination, producing frustration and repression, not liberation. Part Two seeks to relate this body of ideas to the practice of planning, through studying Edinburgh as a case study in urban development and land use planning.

Case studies have been criticized as a research method by Lebas.[1] The cut-off dates which define the study period can be arbitrary, and can imply a coherence of explanation that cannot, in fact, be accomplished. In other words, the limitation of the case study to a relatively short time period carries the tendency to make the study ahistorical.

A related problem concerns the relation between theory and description in case study method. At one level this is a familiar criticism: the very empirical fertility of the method can suppress the theoretical interest, yet produce nothing more than a description of the uniqueness of the situation. The converse is the danger of over-generalizing from what is really a sample of one. Lebas points to the consequent trap of 'interpretation by implication', where the researcher recognizes the need for an organizing framework of theory to guide and illuminate the empirical work, yet never specifies the actual theory. In such circumstances the cognitive interests embedded within the methodology are obscured, and a false consistency is implied at the theoretical level. The theory is thus cocooned from criticism, and the problem of generalizing from a locationally specific account remains.

Despite these strictures, an argument can still be made for using case studies. Until the 1970s there were few case studies of planning; practice was to be simulated and idealized, not described and criticized. The suppression of such knowledge was a concomitant to the dominant professional ideology that was described in Chapter 3. The very appearance of a series of case studies was therefore, within this context, progressive. The American tradition of pluralist power analyses spawned the early works. This is no surprise given the symmetry between the pluralist thesis and the orientation of a case study method to local and periodized social relations. Thus Meyerson and Banfield explored decision-making in Chicago's housing programme in the early 1950s;[2] Gans recounted the devastation wreaked by urban renewal on Boston's West End;[3] Altshuler probed the gap between the ideal of comprehensive planning and its practice in the twin cities of Minneapolis–St. Pauls.[4] It was mainly American academics who imported the technique to Britain, as far as planning was concerned. Foley reviewed the classic Abercrombie plans for London.[5] In the mid-1960s Muchnick described the impotence of Liverpool's newly fledged Planning Department when they were confronted by the political muscle of their colleagues in the Housing Department.[6] Elkins came too, wrestling to fit Centre Point and the World's End housing scheme into a rational decision-making framework, marvelling en route at the centralization of power and lack of popular protest.[7]

Pahl's 'urban managerialist' thesis spurred sociologists to study planners as 'gatekeepers of the urban system', whose decisions, laden with professional ideology and 'middle class' values, could shape the distribution of resources between competing groups.[8] In this vein Dennis and Davies launched their polemics against the planners of Sunderland and Newcastle respectively,[9] while Hall and his co-authors provided a searching empirical account of the effects of planning in and around some of the major English conurbations.[10]

Lebas's criticisms of case studies can be levelled at many of these works. Similarly, the limitations of Pahl's original formulation of managerialism have been widely recognized, not least by Pahl himself.[11] Nevertheless, these studies made a real contribution to a more enlightened understanding of the nature of British planning practice. Their strength was that they exercised the tension between the declared intentions of planners and their actual practice, thus revealing a dimension which was at best latent in the professional literature. The resiliance of the orthodox professional interpretation of the nature of planning, and hence of the oppositional value of case studies, is shown by the fact that none of those listed above were written by British professional planners.

Such work within the broad traditions of community power studies has been attacked by Marxist authors, especially those associated with the writings of Castells. Lebas's strictures have already been outlined. Castells himself has been dismissive of any concern with space as an important variable, and with any notions of local power. Thus he observed, 'power is a relation between social classes ... what happens in a town does not relate to local power but to the specific expression of the class structure'.[12] However, as Biarez argued,[13] there is a need to consider the type of mediation of class power which *is* exercised by local actors. Furthermore, as Urry pointed out,[14] the 'national class structure' may not match up to anybody's specifically local class experience. Local patterns of income, occupational and class mobility, and the organization of local labour markets are thus matters of some importance. Urry suggested that important new local variations in class structures are now emerging, as capital becomes more sensitive to the local labour market rather than the overall region.

Thus, despite the reservations of some radical critics, there has been a growing interest in locally based analyses of the power behind urban development decisions. Much of the concern has drawn on the notion of the 'local state'. Cockburn, for example, looked at corporate planning and community participation in the London Borough of Lambeth. She stressed the role of the local state in reproducing both a labour force and also the relations of production. The actions of the local authority were thus interpreted in terms of a Marxist theory of the state in general: 'When I refer to the Lambeth Borough Council as 'local state' it is to say neither that it is something distinct from 'national state', nor that it alone represents the state locally. It is to indicate that it is a part of a whole.'[15]

Saunders's study of planning and urban development in Croydon also consciously opted to analyse the 'local state' rather than the 'local authorities'. However, unlike Cockburn, he did not directly equate the local state with the state at local level. He argued that though it was subordinate to central government, the local state was also autonomous in some ways. He saw the actual way the autonomy is realized in practice as being an empirical rather than a theoretical question.[16]

More recently Saunders has argued that the 'local state' concept should probably be abandoned, though the local political process remains a fertile area for analysis so as to gain a clearer picture of the degree of autonomy. His case is that British local government is primarily concerned with provision of social consumption, and thus that local political struggles are generally not constituted as class struggles.[17] Saunders therefore called for a dualistic approach, applying different theoretical perspectives to national and to local politics. At the national level, the interests of capital prevail; while, 'local political processes can to a large extent be explained . . . by a pluralist theoretical perspective which recognizes that political outcomes are likely to reflect the relative weight of effective preferences as articulated through shifting political alliances between different consumption sectors in the population.'[18]

A somewhat similar perspective on local power was reached by Simmie. He analysed development planning and development control in Oxford in yet another local case study. He described an 'imperfect pluralism'.

Within the changing context of central and local politics, power over development planning was exercised in different ways at different times by a limited number of different groups. The groups who exercised most power over development planning were those represented by formal organizations. Generally speaking, in order to exercise significant power over planning objectives, the main prerequisite was permanent, formal organization together with command over resources and some incorporation into the decision-making process of either local and/or central government. The main gains flowing from planning objectives consistently went to groups of this nature. Groups without these characteristics were not able to exert much influence over planning objectives and the gains accruing from them. Groups with none of these played little part in setting the objectives of development planning and sometimes suffered material and uncompensated losses as a result.[19]

Another contribution to this growing debate was made by Dunleavy. He drew attention to three non-local policy influences: the national nature of British local government; professionalism; and the extensive direct involvement of private firms in physical development and the provision of urban public services. Dunleavy also focussed on the growth of urban social movements, which he interpreted as reflecting 'both a fundamental collapse in the legitimacy of the operations of capital and state agencies in urban development, and the increasing displacement of social crises into consumption processes'.[20] Despite some empathy for the approach of Castells, Dunleavy concluded that local level research was necessary and could provide important, even unique, insights into the nature of social change and the precise mechanisms of policy development.

Thus a flourishing literature has developed in recent years in which local studies are an important element in urban studies in general, and in understanding the practice of town planning in particular. The kind of theoretical perspectives outlined in the first part of this book are themselves suggestive of the need to ask empirical questions at the level of a settlement or a region. The uneven nature of capitalist development prompted some contrasts in the development of the planning system within the United Kingdom – contrasts between Scotland and England, for example, a described in Chapter 2. Logically, then, one must probe the ways the locally specific form of development through time and the associated class structures, have impinged upon the practice of town planning. The second part of the book therefore tries to contribute to the debates outlined above.

The city selected for the local study is Edinburgh. In some respects the choice was fortuitious, as the author's adopted home provided a convenient basis for research. However, such coincidence should not obscure the fascination of Edinburgh for this type of research. Edinburgh's class structure is distinctly that of a capital city, a centre of administration and finance. It has a large middle class, dependent on the law, insurance, administration and education, rather than on manufacturing. Its working class has been similarly less significant than in a manufacturing city and has enjoyed correspondingly limited access to formal political power. The city's relations with the central state are mediated through the quasi-national role of the Scottish Office. Furthermore, Edinburgh is a place where the sheer topography and the physical environment (both natural and man-made) are important influences on the image of the place and on its town planning.

This factor warns against reductionisms, tempting at a national level or in less spectacular locales, to see urban development and town planning *solely* as a consequence of the mode of production.

The logic of the theories on which this book is structured point to a historically specific study of town planning. Edinburgh again provides fertile ground for such research. The aim of the next few chapters is therefore to gain a critical understanding of how this one settlement has been planned through time, and in whose interests.

References and notes

1   E. Lebas, *Movement of Capital and Locality: Issues raised by the Study of Local Power Structures,* paper to Centre for Environmental Studies Conference, 'Urban Change and Conflict', at York (1977).

2   M. Meyerson and E. Banfield, *Politics, Planning and the Public Interest* (The Free Press 1955).

3   H. J. Gans, *The Urban Villagers* (The Free Press 1962).

4   A. Altshuler, *The City Planning Process* (Cornell University Press 1965).

5   D. L. Foley, *Controlling London's Growth* (California University Press 1963).

6   D. Muchnick, 'Urban renewal in Liverpool', *LSE Occasional Papers in Social Administration,* no. 33 (G. Bell 1970).

7   S. L. Elkins, *Politics and Land Use Planning: the London experience*, (Cambridge University Press 1974).

8   R. E. Pahl, 'Urban social theory and research, *Environment and Planning*, (1969) vol. 1, pp. 143–53, reprinted in *Whose City?* (Longman 1970).

9   N. Dennis, *People and Planning* (Faber & Faber 1970) and *Public Participation and Planners' Blight* (Faber & Faber 1972), J. G. Davies, *The Evangelistic Bureaucrat* (Tavistock 1972).

10   P. Hall, R. Thomas, H. Gracey and R. Drewett, *The Containment of Urban England* (Allen & Unwin 1973).

11   For a discussion see P. Saunders, *Social Theory and the Urban Question*, (Hutchinson 1981). For Pahl's reformulation see the revised edition of *Whose City?*, published by Penguin in 1975.

12   M. Castells, 'Remarques sur l'article de P. Birnbaum. Controverse sur le pouvoir local', *Revue Française de Sociologie* (1974) vol. 15, p. 239.

13   S. Biarez, 'Ideological planning and contingency programming: the case of the Lille–Roubaix–Tourcoing conurbation, 1967–76', *International Journal of Urban & Regional Research,* vol. 5, no. 4 (1981), pp. 475–91.

14   J. Urry, 'Localities, regions, and social class', *International Journal of Urban and Regional Research,* vol. 5, no. 4 (1981), pp. 455–74.

15   C. Cockburn, *The Local State: management of cities & people* (Pluto Press 1977), pp. 46–7.

16   P. Saunders, *Urban Politics: a sociological interpretation* (Hutchinson 1979), p. 196.

17   P. Saunders, 'Notes on the specificity of the local state', in M. Boddy & C. Fudge (eds), 'The Local State: theory & practice', *School for Advanced Urban Studies Working Paper 20,* Bristol University, (1981), p. 25.
18   Ibid., pp. 35–6.
19   J. Simmie, *Power, Property and Corporatism* (Macmillan 1981), pp. 293–4.
20   P. Dunleavy, *Urban Political Analysis: the politics of collective consumption* (Macmillan 1980), p. 164.

4   The making of the historic city

Then all ye tourists, be advised by me,
Beautiful Edinburgh ye ought to go and see,
It's the only city I know where ye can while away the time,
By viewing its lovely scenery and statues fine.

Of all the cities in the world, Edinburgh for me;
For no matter where I look, some lovely spot I see,
And for picturesque scenery unrivalled you do stand.
Therefore I pronounce you to be the Pride of Fair Scotland.[1]

Edinburgh has a very distinct historical physical environment. It was the locus for important pre-twentieth century initiatives in town planning. The place, these initiatives and the long-established form of the local state have been important influences on subsequent planning practice. Town planning has been a way of manipulating urban change in an environment characterized by a rich legacy of historic buildings and a spectacular topography. However, as Geddes observed as long ago as 1910, 'Architecture and town planning in such a city, we plainly see, are not the mere products of the quiet drawing-office some would have them, they are the expressions of the local history, the civic and national changes of mood and contrasts of mind.'[2]

The historic image of Edinburgh has a contemporary importance both economically and ideologically. The logic of late capitalism – the conversion of idle capital into service capital and the simultaneous replacement of service capital with productive capital – is played out in the marketing of the city's environment to tourists. Cultural needs are thereby absorbed into the production process; a vision of a place becomes a commodity, whether as a picture postcard or a packaged holiday. The pursuit of the cultural experience of place by wage earners, a qualitative extension of cultural needs, is indeed one example of the civilizing influence of capital.[3] In the abstract the process holds a liberating potential, an interpretation of place as an historical entity, revealing the repressed possibilities of contemporary environments. In practice the image of place that is offered to consumers is neutralized, trivialized and packaged. The town planning system, through conservation and control policies, plays an important role in reproducing that image in a city like Edinburgh.

This image is also intimately associated with the form of the local state. The physical environment of Edinburgh records the social history over a long period, and it is the social history not just of a city but of a nation. A picture of continuity is therefore presented, the capital of Scotland, a symbol of nationhood and 'a corporate city represented all classes and all creeds'.[4] This is the city of culture – music, architecture, regal residences, capped by a castle and ending with the Georgian elegance of the New Town. It is a city not marred by industry nor by the associated conflicts between labour and capital. The image has derived directly from the experience of Edinburgh's large bourgeoisie, whose living has been made from finance, administration, the law, tourism and education, rather than directly from production. Equally the image serves their interests in reproducing the status quo of property and social relations. Furthermore, the image and the associated social milieux have a significant impact on planning practice, as later chapters will reveal.

This opening chapter of the case study therefore attempts a critique of this image through a historical analysis of the planning and production of the city in the period before the first planning legislation in 1909. Themes introduced in the preceding chapters can be directly developed. The early urban development of Edinburgh can be related to the development of the mode of production within that locality. The debates in Chapter 2 about the 'social origins' of British town planning and about the validity of an evolutionary interpretation can also be developed against specific practices in this city. Nineteenth-century Edinburgh likewise offers opportunities to explore the nature of local power structures, and their relation to urban development, a theme that is under-represented in the growing literature on planning history.

Three distinct aspects of the making of the historic city will now be discussed. The first is the planning and development of the famous New Town. The impact of the era of freely competitive capitalism will then be examined. Then, third, there is the practice of public health and planning reforms associated with the Improvement Acts during the latter part of the nineteenth century. Conclusions can then be drawn about development, the local state and planning in Edinburgh which formed the context for the statutory planning practice of the twentieth century.

From Old Town to New Town

In Edinburgh, as in other old capital cities the transition from feudalism to capitalism was strongly marked in the physical environment, as can be discerned from the map of Edinburgh in the 1820s, shown in Figure 1. The cramped Old Town of feudalism runs east from the Castle, while to the north is the spacious and geometrical lay-out of the New Town, fashioned by the rapid expansion of capitalism. Edinburgh's ascendancy as a settlement had been founded on the structure of feudalism. It was a fortress and a religious centre, with a tiny commercial area where the agricultural surplus product of the town's own burgh lands was marketed. The buildings which dominated the townscape were the castle and the churches. Until the latter half of the eighteenth century the city was

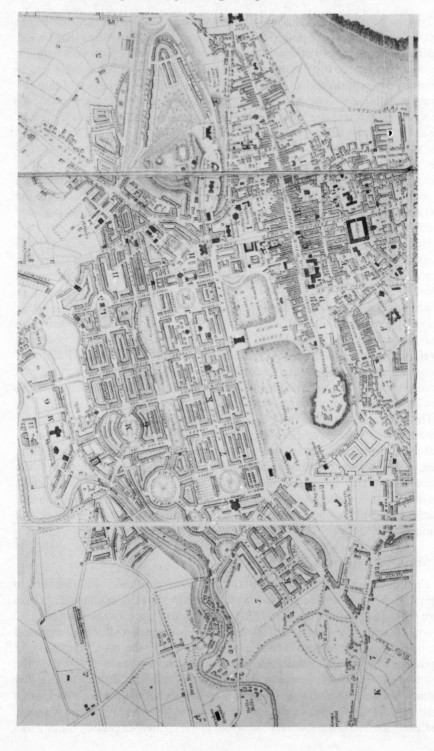

confined within a defensive wall, which had been built after the Scottish defeat at the battle of Flodden in 1513. Within this wall were crowded a cluster of multi-storey dwellings on the ridge sloping down to the east of the castle. This was the Old Town.

In the nascent capitalism of the seventeenth century land and property became important commodities and avenues for speculative investment. Perhaps surprisingly one of the leading investors was a charitable trust. George Heriot, jeweller, goldsmith and cashier to King James VI, had died in 1623, leaving the bulk of his £23,000 sterling fortune to a trust who were charged with creating a school for fatherless boys who were sons of the freemen of Edinburgh. The money had been made from precisely those activities where merchant capitalism was established at the very apex of the feudal pyramid; it was reinvested in land between 1623 and 1649.[5] The purchases were to reap a rich dividend when the New Town was built.

Wealthy citizens also began to invest in property during the last quarter of the seventeenth century.[6] Within the Old Town many of the medieval buildings were swept away. Those that replaced them displayed a new uniformity in elevations, as befitted business ventures. Parts of this phase of development can still be seen today, for example at Milne's Court, which was built in 1690, and extensively rehabilitated in the late 1960s.

The town council also began to ponder a more ambitious speculation. Edinburgh was probably the second largest city in Britain in terms of population. Some 30,000 lived crowded behind the Flodden Wall. The council's idea was to break out from behind the wall and build a new town. They faced problems in acquiring land from private owners and in financing the necessary infrastructure. In 1688 the Lord Provost visited the King in London, who agreed to provide funds and what amounted to powers of compulsory purchase.[7] However, the revolution of the same year meant that the scheme was taken no further.

The eventual development of the New Town was made possible and necessary by the economic advances and spread of capitalism in the mid-eighteenth century. The defeat of the 1745 rebellion ended political uncertainties and brought some of the benefits of England's colonialism to the Scottish economy. The *Scots Magazine* of August 1752 marvelled at the transformation:

Since 1746, when the Jacobite rebellion was suppressed, a most surprising revolution
has happened in the affairs of this country – the whole system of our trade,
husbandry and manufactures, which had hitherto proceeded only by slow degrees,
now began to advance with such a rapid and general progression as almost exceeds
bounds of probability.[8]

Lothian was already in the vanguard of the transition to a rationalized, capitalistic agriculture. The improvements were pioneered by a landowning aristocracy, who lived in Edinburgh. They were 'the most alert of their class who belonged to a coherent metropolitan society'.[9] Edinburgh provided them with a

Figure 1   *Edinburgh in 1835, showing the Old Town and the New Town. By Courtesy of Edinburgh City Libraries*

market and a link to London and the diffusion of new ideas. In 1722 the Burgh
Loch, just across the valley to the south of the walled town, was leased to one of
the leading local agricultural improvers. Thomas Hope of Rankeillor, the
President of the Honourable Society of Improvers in the Knowledge of
Agriculture, was to be charged a moderate rent, on the understanding that he
would drain the loch and make a walk around it with a narrow canal on each side.
An area of public open space was thus created, since known as the Meadows,
though the eastern section of the reclaimed land was feued for building. The new
technical control over nature was thus imported to the town, to create both
amenity, and a new outlet for capital investment.

Crucially Edinburgh was the locus for the financial and legal transactions
endemic to capital accumulation. The Bank of Scotland was formed in 1695, and
the Royal Bank of Scotland in 1727. The British Linen Company was founded in
1746 with its headquarters in the Old Town. It was originally a trading concern
distributing the linen that was produced by rural workers and their families in their
homes. Eventually the company's financial activities led to it becoming a bank.
The total assets of the Scottish banks escalated from £600,000 in 1750 to £3.7
million in 1770,[10] and they played a significant role in financing development in
the capital.

Edinburgh thus prospered as a centre of finance and for the distribution of raw
materials and the collection of finished goods. The rationalization endemic to the
Enlightenment also resulted in a rapid growth in education and the professions
within the city. This in turn fostered growth in associated industries such as paper
making, book binding and various service trades. Directly and indirectly this
surge of capital accumulation exerted pressures on the built environment. An
anonymous pamphlet appeared in 1752, apparently written by a local landowner,
Sir Gilbert Elliott of Minto, under the inspiration of George Drummond, the Lord
Provost. It so highlights the contradictions in settlement form between the city of
merchant capitalism and the spatial imperatives of capitalism as the all pervasive
mode of production and between Edinburgh's provincial and capital role, as to be
worth quoting at length. The economic and ideological virtues of a new type of
settlement, structured around the ordered, segregated consumption of space by
the emergent class, were exemplified by London:

We cannot fail to remark its healthful, unconfined situation . . . no less obvious are
the neatness and accommodation of its private houses; the beauty and convenience of
its numerous streets and open squares, of its buildings and bridges, its large parks and
extensive walks. . . . When we survey this mighty concourse of people, whom
business, ambition, curiosity or the love of pleasure has assembled within so narrow a
compass, we no longer need to be astonished at the spirit of industry and
improvement, which, taking its rise in the city of LONDON, has at length spread
over the greatest party of SOUTH BRITAIN, animating every art and profession, and
inspiring the whole people with the greatest ardour and inspiration.[11]

As for Edinburgh:

Placed upon a ridge of a hill, it admits of but one good street, running from east to west; and even this is tolerably accessible only from one quarter. The narrow lanes leading to the north and south, by reasons of their steepness, narrowness, and dirtiness, can only be considered as so many avoidable nuisances. Confined by the small compass of the walls, and the narrow limits of the royalty, which scarcely extends beyond the walls, the houses stand more crowded than in any other town in Europe, and are built to a height that is almost incredible. Hence necessarily follows a great want of free air, light, cleanliness, and every other comfortable accommodation. Hence also many families, sometimes no less than ten or a dozen, are obliged to live overhead of each other in the same building; where, to all the other inconveniences, is added that of a common stair, which is no other in effect than an upright street, constantly dark and dirty. It is owing to the same narrowness of situation, that the principal street is incumbered with the herb-market, the fruit-market, and several others; that the shambles are placed on the side of the North Loch, rendering what was originally an ornament to the town, a most insufferable nuisance. No less observable is the great deficiency of public buildings. If the parliament house, the churches and a few hospitals be excepted, what other have we to boast of? There is no exchange for our merchants; no safe repository for our public and private records; no place of meeting for our magistrates and town council; none for the convention of our burgh, which is intrusted with the inspection of trade. . . . To such reasons alone it must be imputed that EDINBURGH, which ought to have set the first example of industry and improvement, is the last of our trading cities that has shook off the unaccountable supineness which has so long and so fatally depressed the spirit of this nation. . . [12]

Proposals were therefore put forward by 'the magistrates and town council, the college of justice, and several persons of rank who happened to be in the neighbourhood of this place'.[13] These involved the building of an exchange and accommodation for law courts, the town council and an advocates' library. The plan was to obtain an Act of Parliament to extend the royalty, 'to enlarge and beautify the town, by opening new streets to the north and south, removing the markets and shambles, and turning the North Loch into a canal, with walks and terrasses on each side'.[14] The expense of the public works was to be defrayed by a national contribution.

In 1753 an Improvement Act was passed, aimed at public buildings, street widening and land purchase. City growth was directly equated with the new commerce, with possibilities for reinvesting surplus value. The *Scots Magazine* urged that the Act should be passed, for then the rest of Scotland would soon follow Edinburgh's example: 'The certain consequence is general wealth and prosperity: the number of useful people will increase, rents will rise and public revenue will improve; and, in room of sloth and poverty, will succeed industry and opulence.'[15] Work began on the Royal Exchange in 1753, with loans from the Bank of Scotland and the Royal Bank of Scotland. Drainage of the North Loch commenced in 1759, and in July 1763 tenders were invited for a bridge across it. However, the first expansion was in the opposite direction, to the south. James Brown, a speculative builder, acquired land on the Ross House policies and in 1766 began to build George Square. The £1200 he paid for the site was soon being reaped annually in feu duties.[16] This was housing for the city's elite, who in turn were the Scottish ruling class: early residents included the Countess of Sutherland, the Duchess of Gordon, Lord Braxfield (who became the effective head of the High Court), Viscount Duncan and Henry Dundas, first Viscount Melville, Lord Advocate 1775–83, and subsequently 'the most powerful man in Scotland'.[17] The title deeds of the George Square houses prohibited dealings in trade or merchandise, thus protecting its status as a high-class residential suburb through the exercise of the rights of the feudal superior.

The land holdings of the Heriot's Trust were the key to any northern expansion. The governors of the Trust agreed to feu land to the Town Council, subject to a proportion of the profit to the city from the feu being paid annually to the Trust, as an addition to the normal feu payment. The land was therefore sold to the city for what Sir Walter Scott described as 'a large sum of money'.[18] In 1766 the Town Council launched a competition for a plan for a new town. James Craig's entry, inspired by the development of Nancy in France, was universally approved by the adjudicators.[19] Consciously planned developments had been undertaken in England on private estates: the involvement of local government was the crucial new feature of the Edinburgh scheme. Despite the growing wealth of the local ruling class, this extra intervention was needed to force the attempts to catch up with the major centre of wealth, London.

Craig's plan was for a formal, regular and spacious development, giving physical expression to the Age of Reason. Its symmetry was nevertheless flawed, as the universalistic social norms expressed in a unified, planned design came into contradiction with the ethic of unrestrained individual liberty for the owners of property. In the east of the scheme an area where the main route from the south terminated could not be acquired. Thus Craig's eastern square could not be sited centrally at the end of that route and was shifted west. Furthermore, one of Edinburgh's wealthiest citizens, Sir Laurence Dundas, bought a plot fronting on to the eastern square, and had his palatial home built there, on a site where a church had been planned.

The New Town was a residential suburb for the class that ruled Edinburgh. It was populated by lawyers and landowners and redefined the pattern of social segregation over space. Though the *petit bourgeiousie* stayed in the old town, along with businesses and such industries as there were, the higher *bourgeoisie* made the short move north en masse after 1780, taking their servants with them.[20]

Craig's plan thoughtfully provided three rich streets, each 100 feet wide, and two poor ones of 30 feet width, with less noble architecture and rougher work. Craig's plan is simultaneously the emancipation of the *haute bourgeoisie* from the physical and economic shackles of tradition and their self-repression in the names of order and symmetry which they equated with prosperity and progress, their subjugation to a technological rationality hewn in the stern, gray stone. The contours of the ground were over-ridden, leaving a mannered cultivation of nature in enclosed gardens.

Further extensions to the New Town were planned and developed during the first quarter of the nineteenth century, though building was interrupted during the economic recession at the time of the Napoleonic wars.[21] These plans assumed a steadily increasing population of wealthy households, seemingly independent of any productive activity. Cheaper houses and industrial premises did not feature, though factories and workshops did intrude eventually on to vacant areas of land. The divided aesthetic of Edinburgh's built environment, the contrast between the rationalism of the Enlightenment New Town and the romanticism of the medieval Old Town, was deeply rooted in social practice. Writing in 1833, Chambers observed,

These fine gentlemen who daily exhibit their foreign dresses in Princes Street have no idea of a race of people who roost in the tall houses of the Lawnmarket and the West Bow, and retain about them many of the primitive modes of life and habits of thought that flourished amongst their grandfathers. . . . Edinburgh is, in fact, two towns more ways than one. It contains an upper and an under town – the one a sort of thoroughfare for the children of business and fashion, the other a den of retreat for the poor, the diseased and the ignorant.[22]

The New Town remains the most extensive area of Georgian architecture in Europe. It is hailed as a precursor of modern town planning, a counterpoint to the *laissez-faire* urban environments of the Victorian era. Such idealizations obscure the relation of the built form to the emergent socio-political structure. The Town Council played a key role in facilitating the development, but in a sense they were an obsolete body. The Council comprised thirty-three merchants and members of incorporated trades, who could only be elected by the retiring council. Just as the restrictive practices of the merchants and trades had become increasingly anachronistic in an age of freely competitive capitalism, so also had the local state form associated with those practices. Indeed, from 1772 onwards important functions of municipal management – lighting, cleansing, policing – had been removed from the Council, and vested in separate bodies of commissioners, who were at least partially elected by that part of the population who were ratepayers. When reform came in 1833 the Council was bankrupt, but it was precisely because the Council had acted as financiers in a 'modern' manner that the New Town was possible. Had the Council been consistent to its outdated composition and constitution, some different rupture to the development process would have been necessary.

The other part of the alliance that produced the New Town was the Scottish elite of landowners, gentry, lawyers and financiers who resided in the capital. Land development fit for a capital, and consistent with earning a return on investment, was the most logical expression of their endeavours domestically. Teachers were another important and growing part of this civil society, as the developing mode of production required a more educated labour force. Edinburgh University reached the height of its reputation between 1760 and 1820. Schools also proliferated and the progression for the male offspring of Edinburgh's lawyers and similar groups was established – elite school to university to professional practice and property ownership.

Hugo Arnot described Edinburgh in 1779 as depending 'chiefly upon the college of justice, the seminaries of education, and the inducement which as capital it affords to genteel people to reside in it'.[23] In 1805, Robert Forsyth noted that 'persons of title and rank abound in Edinburgh'.[24] He estimated there were between 2000 and 3000 lawyers living there, and some 1200 to 1500 people connected with the university. As the city had a population of 81,600 in 1801, these professional people and their dependents must have made up a substantial proportion of the residents. Forsyth noted: 'The trading part of the community consists chiefly of artists or shopkeepers, employed in supplying the wants or the luxuries of the numerous classes of wealthy inhabitants that have either a temporary or a permanent residence here.'[25]

The harmony of the New Town is thus the harmonious transition in the socio-political structure of the city; the coming together of merchant capital, finance capital and landed capital, without any revolutionary break precipitated by an ascendant industrialism or labourism. The Heriot's Trust is perhaps the most evident exemplar. Councillors, magistrates, financiers, lawyers and educationalists fused and were interlocked within it. Because of its landholdings the Trust played a major role in the development of the New Town and was a major beneficiary of it. It was in the vanguard of the drive both to education and to capital accumulation through speculation in land. Thus the Trust's annual income from rents, feus and similar services increased from £2169-17s-10d to £12,183-4s-4d between 1780 and 1820, the period which covered the main development of the New Town.[26]

In this process the role of the Town Council was crucial. Though Heriot's Trust owned land they could not themselves undertake the development of the New Town. As Sir Walter Scott observed:

to execute such a speculation as the erection of a New Town, was a task far beyond the duties and powers of the trustees of the Hospital. There was a chartered extension of the city's bounds, and of its rights to be procured, for the encouragement of settlers; there was property to be bought, roads to be made, levelling and other expensive operations to be undertaken, before there could be expected the least prospect of any valuable return. To have directed the funds of the Hospital to such a purpose would have been both unjust and criminal: and it was therefore clear, that while the ground continued the property of the Hospital, the proposed plan could not be executed at all, and the site for the intended New Town could not have been obtained. The transaction, thus considered, seems to have been fair and beneficial –as well to the Hospital, who obtained a price for their property much above what corresponded with any revenue they could themselves derive from it; – to the magistrates, as administrators of the city, who acquired the means of carrying through a most important train of improvements, and at the same time augmented the common good, or municipal property; – and to public, because the acquisition of that property by the magistrates, and its being included in the extended royalty, were indispensably necessary to the very existence of their splendid improvements, which have elevated Edinburgh into one of the most magnificent cities in Europe.[27]

The role of the Town Council was therefore crucial in absorbing the risk and in funding the unprofitable aspects of the development. It was a Council of merchants and traders, as Forsyth described:

The merchants and the trades hold the government between them, and are in some measure balanced against each other. As Edinburgh is not a manufacturing town, but is supported by the families of rank which resort to it, by the practicioners of the law, by the officers of the national government, and by the university established in it, the tradesmen or manufacturers of Edinburgh necessarily hold a place of very inferior importance in the community.[28]

While the lawyers, other professionals and persons who did not need to work for a living were excluded from the Council, they, like the Council, were part of a Scottish arm of central government which was based in Edinburgh and presided over from 1782 until 1805 by Lord Melville, a despot who was himself an Edinburgh man. As Henry (later Lord) Cockburn put it, in his classic description of the Edinburgh political scene at the start of the nineteenth century, 'Government was the master of nearly every individual in Scotland, but especially in Edinburgh, which was the chief seat of its influence. The pulpit, the bench, the bar, the colleges, the parliamentary electors, the press, the magistracy, the local institutions, were . . . completely at the service of the party in power'.[29]

There were certainly tensions then within this peculiar national/local state, just as one would expect at a time of major economic change. Whigs like Cockburn were bitterly critical of the way the Tories refused to sanction reform and there were jealousies between professionals and the Town Council. Nevertheless, in the planning and development of the New Town, the Town Council and the local legal, financial and landed interests came together in a way that signified not a plurality of groupings and a dispersal of power, but rather the extended nature of the local state, its symmetry with the centralized power of the national state and its class basis. Edinburgh's New Town was the product of the practice of a class. Those who owned land and capital controlled the development and were the most direct beneficiaries from it, notwithstanding the periods of economic slump which afflicted the actual development process. Those who had only their labour to sell did the building, might gaze admiringly on the 'improvements' thus bestowed on to the city, but generally resided elsewhere.

The New Town was planned: a coherent, regular, harmonious development pattern was achieved, with elegant proportions and a unified visual effect. It demonstrated in practice what could be achieved by the collaboration of local government, private enterprise and designers of taste and genius. It has thus doubly influenced subsequent planning in the city. On the one hand it constitutes a major environmental asset needing careful conservation, while simultaneously restricting the full functional development of a city centre in a more advanced stage of capitalism. On the other hand it has given planners an inspiring definition of an idealized set of relationships between local politics, the market and the professional planner; an idealization proved in the most appealing way in practice by results on the ground.

The conventional interpretation then is of a townscape manufactured single-handedly by the genius of the city's leaders. But where did the surplus come from to fuel such grandeur? Not merely from the place itself. Though technological advances and bouyant demand led to expansion in Edinburgh of sectors such as glass production, printing and coach and carriage building, these were consumer trades pliant on wealth already within the city, not prime generators of that wealth. For that wealth we have to look further afield. Forsyth described how Scots who had made their fortune in 'all quarters of the globe' returned to reside in their capital city. Similarly he noted English families whose fortunes were not quite sufficient to sustain a place in London society and who settled instead in the satellite of that metropolis.[30] The Athens of the North was paid for out of returns on investments elsewhere – in the exploitation of the colonies, from the agricultural improvements which drove landless labourers to emigration or to the new urban areas and from the nascent industrialization of other parts of Scotland. Edinburgh's population growth was spectacular between 1755 and 1821, increasing from 57,000 to 138,000, but it was outstripped by that of Glasgow, which increased from 31,700 to 147,000. As Scotland's industrial heartland developed on Clydeside, Edinburgh became ever more firmly the locus of administration, education and finance.

The city of freely competitive capitalism

The planned urban expansion into the New Town had been a direct result of the rise of a capitalist mode of production. Further planned development of the New Town was truncated by the full development of that mode of production. In the era of freely competitive capitalism urban development was structured by market forces rather than by any public plan. The results of this production of public place for private profit were expressed directly in the physical environment itself, though these contradictions were subsequently interpreted by the planning profession as 'muddle' or the results of industrialization rather than a specifically capitalist industrialism.

Edinburgh was in some respects remarkably little changed by local industrialization. The 'old' self-perpetuating council made up of merchants and members of incorporated trades had actively discouraged factory production within the city. In 1835 the reformed council gave way, but still incurred the wrath of some prominent citizens. Lord Cockburn, for example, was strongly opposed to the idea:

The town council approved of a report by a committee suggesting projects for the introduction of *manufactures* into Edinburgh! They are good enough to tell us that this would be quite easy. But all sane persons see that the idea of forcing such a thing is absurd, and that, if left to herself, Nature has too much sense to tolerate such an abomination in such a place. Weavers and calico printers, power looms and steam engines, sugar houses and foundaries in Edinburgh! These nuisances might increase our population and our pauperism, our wealth and our bankruptcies; but they would leave it Edinburgh no more. . . .

We must try to survive on better grounds, on our advantages as the metropolis, our adaptation for education, our literary fame, and especially on the glories of our external position and features, improved by the bluish smoke of human habitation, and undimmed by the black, dirty clouds from manufactures, the absence of which is one of the principal charms of our situation.[31]

The manufactures came despite Lord Cockburn's distaste. But they came in a form that reflected the peculiar structure of the capital's economy. Large-scale mechanized production developed in single firms rather than in concentrations of similar firms as in Birmingham or on Clydeside. Numbers engaged in large, heavily capitalized industries selling in national or international markets – engineering, rubber and printing – did increase more rapidly than the total occupied population. However, the small-scale craft industries catering to Edinburgh's local luxury market remained a prominent feature of the industrial structure. For the period 1841–1901 clothing was the largest industrial employer, apart from building, with furniture, leather, jewellery and coach-making all to the fore. Above all there was domestic service, a more significant employer than any industrial group, and a further testimony to the importance of the middle-class consumer market in the city.[32]

Nor did industrialization seriously erode the dominance of the professions. Edinburgh's banking and insurance serviced the industrial and commercial growth of Scotland: accountancy, originally a branch of the legal profession, flourished. Investment trusts grew in Edinburgh, financing overseas development. Thus the middle class of Edinburgh was remarkable both for its size and for its heterogeneity. It retained a group linked to the law, administration and landowners, but also developed a section associated with the economic changes of the Victorian period.

Transport was a bouyant sector of the Victorian urban economy. Its industrialization with the coming of the railways had a major impact on the urban structure. However, the impact of the railways was not solely due to the technology, but to the particular capitalist form in which the technology was implemented. The first Railway Act was passed in 1826 and it was under this legislation that Edinburgh's first railway was built. As with the New Town, an alliance of landowners and municipal enterprise were the moving forces behind the modernization. The company which promoted the 'Innocents Railway', which approached the city from the south-east, included the Duke of Buccleuch and the Marquis of Lothian and also the Lord Provost and Corporation of Edinburgh and the Magistrates of Musselburgh.

There followed a phase of intense competition between different railway companies. The Glasgow and Edinburgh Railway Company was formed in 1830 and opened in 1833. It was followed by the Edinburgh, Leith and Newhaven Railway, the North British Railway Company (formed 1842), the Edinburgh and Bathgate Railway (1847) and the Caledonian Railway (1848). As branch lines and stations followed the old horse-carrier roads and depots, conscious town planning was submerged while the companies competed for sites and profits.

The impact on the geometrical lay-outs planned for extensions of the New

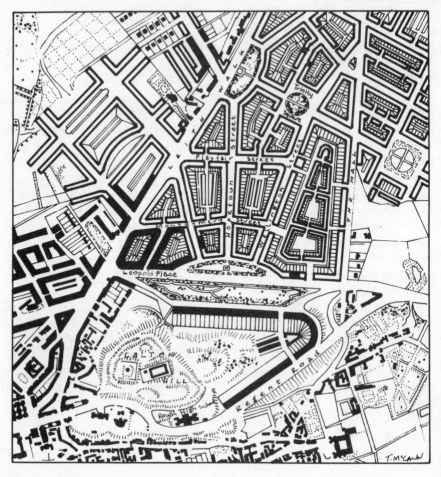

Figure 2   *The planned expansion of the New Town to the north-east, 1842*

Town was particularly abrupt. A plan for a further high-class residential suburb, extending the New Town to the north-east into the Pilrig area, was decimated by the swathes of railway lines. Figures 2 and 3 illustrate the way that industrial capitalism transcended the earlier plan.

The pursuit of profits by the railway companies thus threatened the existing patterns of enjoyment of amenity and environment by Edinburgh's large middle class. In 1836 the Edinburgh and Glasgow Railway Company sought to extend their lines east through Princes Street Gardens on the site of the old North Loch between the Old and New Towns. This excited great opposition from residents in Princes Street and elsewhere in the New Town, and the company shelved the scheme. However, four years later they resurrected their proposals. By then some of the leading opponents to the development had moved away; indeed, Princes Street was itself becoming more commercial than residential in character. The

Figure 3   *The actual development to the north-east of the New Town*

Lord Provost of the time divined that 'Providence has plainly designed the valley of Princes Street Gardens for a railway.'[33] The tunnels and cuttings soon followed, despite continued protests on environmental grounds led by Lord Cockburn.

In many ways the railway companies were the real planners of Victorian Edinburgh. Not only did the railways have a marked impact on the environment and on previously developed or planned areas, but they also facilitated and steered the pattern of suburbanization. The population of Edinburgh increased by 80 per cent between 1851 and 1901 and the city boundary was frequently extended. Building was thus an important sector of the local economy. Despite the industrial age the construction industry was not itself industrialized, rather it remained craft-based and conducted by a host of small local operators.

More significant than the small building firms in controlling the development process were the landowners. The structure of landholding was quite different to that of the building industry. The supply of building land was held by 'a comparatively limited number of superiors, all of whom were concerned to secure the maximum long-term income which their properties would yield'.[34] The largest ground landlords were probably the educational trusts, who administered the schools where Edinburgh's middle class educated their children. Certainly Heriot's Trust benefited from railway development on their land.[35] The trust also feued about 100 acres for housing and commercial development between 1858 and 1871, at which point they were about to feu a further seventeen acres for 'first class family housing', from which they anticipated an annual revenue of between £2000 and £3000.[36]

Another educational trust, George Watson's, benefited in a similar manner from the railways and the associated suburbanization. By the late nineteenth century both the main railways, the Caledonian and the North British, traversed their land, as well as the suburban railway and the Union Canal. The landowners are reported to have received 'large sums' for the land taken.[37] A major development of middle-class villas in the Merchiston area was on land also owned by this Trust. Feuing took place from 1853, at rates varying between £21 and £175 an acre. In general the Trust appears to have set feus at between £20 and £50 an acre for villa developments, but between £60 and £275 an acre where the development was to be tenement housing.[38] The pursuit of high feu duties by the landowners tended to increase densities as the builders juggled overall development costs against feasible rent-paying capabilities of possible occupants of the housing. Geddes caustically observed that the educational trusts were forcing high density living, 'with the best intentions, in the supposed interest of the upbringing of the child-life of Edinburgh!'[39] Even the Burgh Engineer recognized that by their refusal to release land more cheaply, the large suburban landowners were perpetuating overcrowding in the slums.[40]

The actual suburbanization process is neatly encapsulated in the development of the area between Merchiston and Morningside in the 1880s. The site lay on the urban–rural fringe, but within the extended city boundary and was serviced by the suburban railway and the city's tramway. The coming of the railway in particular transformed a village into a suburb. Old cottages which had straddled along the ancient routeway into the city were 'swept away, despite the protests of their inhabitants'.[41] A contemporary report by *The Scotsman's* property correspondent gives an insight into the part played by low labour costs in the suburban development of this area:

Although the property market has been comparatively sluggish during the past year, building operations have been carried out with considerable activity in various parts of the city, particularly in the southern and western suburbs. The cheapness of labour and the necessities of trade have, no doubt, contributed to this result, because the demand for property has at no time been brisk, capitalists finding more tempting outlets for their money in other directions. Workmen's wages have varied little from last year's rates, masons, joiners, and plasterers being paid at the rate of 6½d an hour; though the first mentioned class, in some exceptional circumstances, have been receiving 7d.[42]

In Morningside these men were building villas at five to the acre, on land feued at £30 per acre. The houses were then selling at £1200 each. In other words, the men building them would have to work a sixty-hour week for more than fourteen years before they would have been paid enough in wages to meet the purchase price, even if they had had no other living costs over that period!

Cheaper tenement housing was also being built in the same area, with flats valued at between £245 and £450 and feus at or over £2 per house per year. Flats were available for rent at between £20 and £30 a year.[43] The developers seem to have been small, mainly local builders. *The Scotsman* article named eight builders who were involved in the developments in Morningside, each doing a row of villas, or a terrace, or up to four tenements.

By their feuing decisions the landowners controlled the form and direction of urban growth. The result was a variety of developments matching the nuances of social status and extending the scale of social segregation over space. The higher ground in Merchiston, Morningside, Grange, Trinity and Newington was developed with grand detached villas set behind walled gardens, or with genteel stone terraces. Around the railway stations or the tramways were the rather anonymous, but utterly solid and respectable tenement flats for the clerks working up in the city. On the low ground favoured by the railway engineers and cheek by jowl with the factories were the working class tenements, in Gorgie, Dalry, Leith, Bonnington, Abbeyhill and Easter Road.[44] Figure 4 illustrates this development pattern.

Thus under freely competitive capitalism the uniformity and consciously imposed order that characterized the New Town planning was overwhelmed by the chaos of competition. The built form of this era of the development of Edinburgh embodied the more dispersed set of economic relations as the city became more extended and more differentiated. The class basis of the development remained, though the physical details were adjusted to the developing market demands of consumers. It was still the owners of capital and in particular landed capital, who as a class determined the form of the development. Notwithstanding this, there were evidently conflicts of interests, for example between competing railway companies, between these companies and those property owners whose amenity they threatened, or between landowners and builders; indeed such conflicts were intrinsic to the ethos of competitive capitalism, the real *non sequitur* was the notion that they would be best resolved through the operation of markets. In urban development in particular, important figures within the Edinburgh middle class came to realize that some measure of intervention by local government was necessary. Thus Edinburgh pioneered an early form of planned redevelopment, an experiment in physical planning which considerably influenced subsequent national legislation.[45]

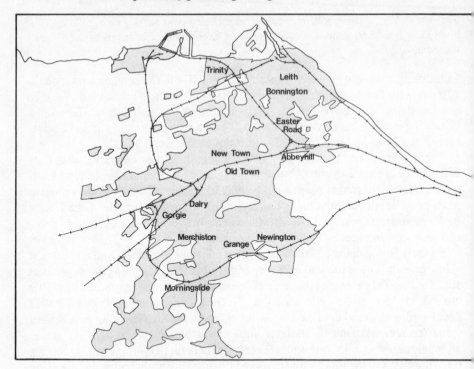

Figure 4   *The built up area and the railways, 1900*

The Improvement Act: social origins for town planning?

One consequence of urban development orchestrated by market forces was a calamitous housing situation for those unable to purchase adequate living conditions. Geographically this problem was concentrated in the Old Town. From 1801 to 1851 its population had grown from 20,000 to 30,000 by division and sub-division of existing houses. During these years there had also been some demolitions of working-class houses to make way for the railways and new roads associated with them. Thus in 1850 Blackfriars Wynd in the Old Town had a population of 1025 who lived in 142 dwellings which contained only 193 rooms. [46] Nearby was Middle Mealmarket Stair in the Cowgate, which before demolition in the 1860s housed fifty-six families, 248 people, on its five floors, with neither a sink nor a WC between them.

Geddes acidly claimed that throughout the century the squalor of slum life in the Old Town was 'mainly accepted by the middle and governing classes as a permanent supply of human material for its confused charities, for its vast schools of medicine and anatomy, and for its manifold religious endeavours'. [47] Nevertheless, a number of initiatives were mooted. Proposals were made in 1849 for the demolition of the worst housing by private enterprise, but no effective action followed. Edinburgh's extensive middle class also funded some 'philanthropy at 5 'per cent' solutions to the housing problem, though the rents were well above the means of the bulk of the working class.[48]

The Free Church of Scotland were prominent in the debates on the problem of working-class housing provision. They perceptively argued that mere clearance of the worst housing would be costly in compensation to the property owners and would not meet the need for rehousing. They advocated building new suburban houses, accessible to centres of employment but in 'open, airy situations'.[49] They recognized that landowners were the major obstacle, for they were reluctant to see their land used for working-class housing as it then deteriorated in value. The kirk therefore concluded that land reform was essential:

no great progress will be made in promoting the sanitary and social advancement of cities, until all the land within a certain radius of each town may be obtained, upon good cause shown before a proper court, and upon payment of a fair price for it, as sites for human dwellings. . . . Scarcity of land makes dear feus, and dear feus make dear houses and high rents.[50]

Such land reform would have posed a politically unacceptable challenge to landowners. All that was available to a local authority were powers of sanitary reform and during the 1850s Edinburgh Corporation became increasingly involved in such measures. However, the general statute, the Police and Improvement (Scotland) Act of 1850 proved not to be a very effective means of action. There was pressure for reform within the Scottish burghs, led by Provost Lindsay of Leith. This culminated in new legislation in 1862, which in many ways was the Scottish equivalent to the 1848 Public Health Act. The Burgh Police Act, also known as the Lindsay Act, was the first attempt in Scotland to use slum clearance as a means of sanitary improvement.

The major initiative that Edinburgh took under the 1862 Act was to appoint Dr Henry Duncan Littlejohn as Medical Officer of Health, the first such appointment in Scotland. The appointment may have been hastened by the concern caused by the collapse of a seven-storey tenement in the Old Town in November 1861, an incident in which thirty-five people were killed.[51] Littlejohn's 'Report on the Sanitary Condition of Edinburgh' appeared in August 1865. It made such an impact that a cheap edition was published in October. It catalogued the high rates of death and disease in the Old Town, but broke with the conventional wisdom of the city's middle class by attributing these to excessive densities and inadequate sanitation, rather than to the immorality and ignorance of the victims. Littlejohn recommended a number of public health improvements which required no new legislation – paving, draining, lighting and improvements to the sewers. Beyond these steps though he called for a planned redevelopment of the worst slums. His proposition was that roads could be constructed through the densely packed tenement blocks, thus providing space and light, 'opening them up'.

Littlejohn focussed on the planning of land uses and communications over quite an extensive area. As well as the roads he proposed the provision of children's play areas on vacant spaces freed by the clearances. There were also to be new tenements along the new streets where the displaced people could be rehoused. He also saw how designs could make use of the three dimensional form of the land, using slopes to create cellars which could be used as laundries. He also offered advice about the external appearance of any new houses, discouraging expensive designs.

The Littlejohn Report, then, was an exercise in town planning which clearly developed from and was directed towards sanitary reform. While paternalist in tone, it clearly sought to allieviate the very poor living conditions endured by a substantial section of the working class. To this extent then there is evidence for an interpretation of the origins of town planning in sanitary reform linked to social idealism and for an evolutionary and progressive path led by enlightened reformers from public health into housing and town planning.

However, that is only part of the story. To support his case, Littlejohn drew attention to the extreme visibility of 'pauperism and misery' in Edinburgh which was occasioned by the concentration of the poor in the Old Town. He argued that visitors to other cities such as London, Paris, Liverpool or Glasgow were less likely to have to pass through and therefore to see the poorer districts. Whether this argument stemmed from political convenience or personal belief matters not; the case for reform was directly connected to protecting the *bourgeoisie's* image of the city. Similarly, Littlejohn could not resolve the problems of land ownership and economics which created the working-class housing problem. The cheapest viable rent for a newly built small house would have been about £6 a year and that was much more than the labourers and unemployed living in their hovels in the Old Town could afford.

By revealing just how bad conditions were Littlejohn's report caused something of a scandal. In November 1865 the Council decided to seek parliamentary powers to put his recommendations into effect.[52] The election of William Chambers as Lord Provost added impetus to the reform idea. Chambers, a wealthy publisher, had himself written a 'Report on the Sanitary State of the Residences of the Poorer Classes in the Old Town of Edinburgh' in 1840, which urged sanitary reform. In the endeavours of Chambers we also have an individual figure who seems to fit the social reform interpretation of the origins of town planning.

Chambers campaigned hard to establish public and political support for the improvements. He took Littlejohn's proposals and modified them to give them a 'higher and more economic aim'. Littlejohn had sought to break up the packed tenement blocks by creating new streets running parallel to, or at right angles to, existing thoroughfares. Chambers, however, planned diagonal streets, running from corner to corner of a block. He argued that his pattern was more convenient and would avoid displacing industrial premises which were located in the blocks. He showed how a diagonal street rather than Littlejohn's scheme for one block could preserve two breweries, 'the purchase of which would involve heavy expenditure'.[53] Chambers's plan is shown in Figure 5.

The creation of 'convenient thoroughfares' appears to have been the primary objective of Chambers's scheme. He was also notably concerned to allay the fears of ratepayers about the costs and the problems of rehousing. He hoped to be able to acquire waste plots in the Old Town at a cheap price and believed that there would be a large demand for flats renting at between £6 and £15 annually, amounts that were well beyond the means of the worst housed. Indeed, Chambers explicitly wanted to prevent speculators putting up properties which would house 'the disorderly class of characters who prey on the weakness and vice of the community'.[54] Seen in this light the progressive aspects of the improvements appear more ambiguous.

Perhaps because they were contentious, the plans were put out to public consultation – over 100 years before the Skeffington Report! The responses to that exercise give an insight into the conflicting interests that shaped this early attempt at town planning. The Royal College of Physicians, the Chamber of Commerce, the Destitute Sick Society, the Senate of Edinburgh University, the City of Edinburgh Road Trust, the Parochial Board of the City Parish and the Association of Employers in the Building Trades of Edinburgh and Vicinity were all recorded as supporting the scheme.[55] This amalgam of professional, philanthropic and vested interest bodies resembled the lobby supporting town planning in Edinburgh in the 1930s, as described in Chapter 5. While these bodies are certainly varied, none could credibly be claimed to speak for the interests of labour. The main opposition came from ratepayers, who attended meetings held in their wards. Their main concern was with the costs that would be incurred and the New Town residents in particular resented any suggestion that they should pay to improve other people's housing conditions. This other component of the city's middle class thus helped to define the conditions on which sanitary reform might be acceptable. The gradual nature of the move from sanitary to social reform was in part attributable to such opposition.

The concern of the working class was that the improvements would actually exacerbate housing problems. The Parochial Board of St Cuthbert's, for example, had observed that the scheme would destroy cheap housing, a commodity already in short supply. Out of 11,130 houses rented at under £5 a year, only 133 were vacant, and there were only a further eighty-eight unoccupied in the £5 to £10 bracket.[56] Another housing reformer, the Reverend James Begg, argued that while the slums did indeed need clearing, clearance should not be undertaken until the more immediate need for additional cheap housing provision had been met.[57] One has to look to such sources for the expression of this alternative viewpoint, for the views of the actual slum residents themselves were never sought; the participation exercise focussed on middle-class organizations and the enfranchized ratepayers.

A further modification was made to the proposals before the Bill went to parliament. The City Architects, David Cousin and John Lessels, sought to trim what were deemed to be extravagances in Chamber's proposals. However, the architects also made additions, including one proposed by the Architectural Institute of Scotland. The total anticipated outlay for compulsory purchase of the slum properties was £306,995 and it was estimated that 3,257 households would be displaced. The sale of building areas was expected to recoup £111,071 and it

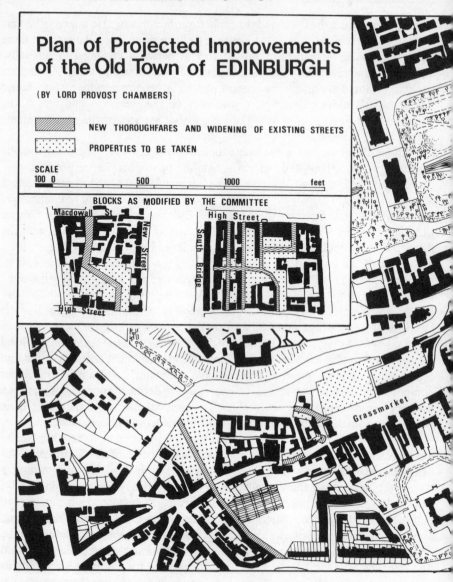

Figure 5   *Provost Chambers' Improvement proposals*

T. McCANN

was anticipated that new accommodation would be provided for between 2500 and 3000 households. The plan, which showed new roads, buildings and open space, is illustrated in Figure 6.

The streets and thirty-four clearance areas identified in the 1867 Act were almost exactly those of Cousin and Lessels, who became the architects to the Commissioners, who were the Town Council.[58] The Act thus authorized the Corporation to use some of the cleared areas for new streets, and to widen existing streets: the remaining cleared land could be developed as the Commissioners deemed fit and their intention was that this would be done in a profitable manner. Indeed, Chambers hoped all along that the Council's redevelopment endeavours would prompt private enterprise to follow suit.[59]

Thus there was no obligation on the Commissioners to rebuild housing, let alone to provide low rent accommodation, though they could spend up to £10,000 to acquire premises for displaced families if they evicted more than 500 persons in a six-month period, a threshold which could be exceeded if a certificate was acquired from a sheriff, stating that suitable alternative accommodation existed. Apart from that the only responsibility the Council had to the slum dwellers was to give them eight weeks' notice of impending eviction. The subsequent national legislation influenced by the Edinburgh Improvement Act, 1867 – the Artizans and Labourers Dwellings Acts of 1875 and 1880 – debarred improvement schemes unless the local authority could show that suitable alternative housing was locally available, though these provisions were again weakened in the housing legislation of 1890, which merely required a declaration that sufficient existing low rent houses were known to be vacant.

The progression from Littlejohn to Chambers to Cousin and Lessels to the Act and then to implementation completely confounds notions of a progressive enlightenment associated with the development of town planning. On the contrary, it demonstrates the way ideas and practice were shaped by the city's political economy. Only Littlejohn had expected clearance to result in new cheap houses for those displaced. As Smith noted, Chambers's advocacy and the eventual acceptance of the proposals, was mainly a manifestation of civic pride:

The slums had to be redeveloped because they were a disgrace to a city of Edinburgh's stature, at once undermining its contemporary reputation and its symbolic value as the repository of 800 years of Scottish history. The theme had powerful emotional appeal, and typically took the form that the old town of Edinburgh could not be restored to its proper place in the community until it was once again lived in by 'a superior class of people'.[60]

The Act amounted to a clearance plan rather than a redevelopment plan, the detailed planning being left to implementation and thus being incremental. It was in this implementation that the class-based economic interests behind the scheme were realized. While the area in most urgent need of sanitary improvement was at the heart of the Old Town around the High Street and between the Bridges and St John Street the Act was a way of remodelling a much wider area in the south of the city. The implementation did indeed begin in the centre, as 'a very narrow and stifling alley', St Mary's Wynd, was transformed to become a 'spacious thoroughfare'.[61] The nearby Blackfriars Wynd was treated in like manner, though the results were less satisfactory, the authorities being 'actuated by economical motives' and looking to the profitability of private enterprise in the realization.[62] A street planned between these two would have meant demolition of a printing works (Oliver and Boyd's) – it did not go ahead. Likewise another linking street planned between Blair Street and Old Fishmarket Close was not implemented; there would have been a strong case for it on sanitary grounds, but it had little justification in terms of commerce or communications.

Within the area of worst housing one of the streets which was developed was Jeffrey Street. This diagonal street led from the railway station to the Royal Mile. Tenements that were 'the haunt of the most abandoned characters'[63] were demolished and replaced by a school, shops, new tenements, but above all by a new and important thoroughfare between the New Town, the railway station and the expanding southern part of the city. This street was constructed on an arched masonry embankment, which is up to ten metres above true ground level. It is difficult to equate such a major and expensive engineering operation with an interpretation of the origins of town planning in a liberal reformist concern to improve living conditions for the badly housed.

All the new planned streets outside the area of worst housing conditions were implemented. Chambers Street is perhaps the most interesting. It did not figure in Littlejohn's original proposals. At £54,000 to acquire 327 dwellings it was the most expensive in terms of land assembly – for example, 381 dwellings had been bought on the east side of St Mary's Street for £28,480.[64] Indeed, there were few houses on the land acquired for the construction of Chambers Street. The main clearance of bad housing was in the adjacent Guthrie Street, which was conveniently included in the Chambers Street scheme. Cousin drew up a feuing plan for a thoroughfare eighty feet wide and 1000 feet long. This 'large and valuable area' was to be 'set apart for a superior class of buildings to those hitherto contemplated'.[65] The main users were to be a government department, the Department of Science and Art, for a Museum of Industry, Edinburgh University and the Watt Institute and School of Arts. Thus what had originally appeared to be an exercise in sanitary reform was in fact an expensive scheme for improving traffic movement and catering for institutional space requirements.

Other links in the South Side area also improved traffic flows without replacing houses, for example, at Marshall Street, Davie Street and Simon Square. In the west of the centre Lady Lawson Street was made from the demolition of seventy-five houses in Lady Lawson Wynd and provided an improved route between Lauriston Place and Castle Terrace. The effect of the improvements then was to remould the obsolete routes from the medieval Old Town to fit the standards and patterns of movement of the late nineteenth century.

The rents charged for the new houses provided under the Act were beyond the means of the poor, so that clearance merely shifted them on to the streets or into

Figure 6   *The revised plan for Improvements produced by Cousin and Lessels*

equally inadequate accommodation. The Inquiry into the Edinburgh Improvement Scheme held in 1893 noted:

one result of the Improvement Scheme of 1867 was the removal of a considerable proportion of the displaced people into the large and unsuitable houses standing on the areas now scheduled as unhealthy. They subdivided these houses, making the long, dark lobbies now objected to, and thus rendering them very much more insanitary than they had previously been.[66]

This type of analysis was constantly hammered home by Geddes, who argued that the chief beneficiaries of the 'improvements' were the landlords, while the poor were deprived of their homes and had their social ties ruptured. Others in authority, however, saw the recreation of new slums by the displaced poor as conclusive proof of their wanton habits.[67]

If the poor suffered the landowners did not. They were compensated at full market value for the loss of their land, with the going rate at around £12,500 per acre.[68] At these prices the improvements could not break even, despite the Trustees' commitment to getting the highest possible return on the land. Thus the 1867 Act schemes involved a subsidy of £400,000 from public funds, out of a gross cost of £500,000.[69]

Edinburgh continued to use improvement schemes until well into the twentieth century. In particular three more were promoted under the requirements of the 1890 housing legislation. These were in 1893, 1898 and 1900, and it was also under this Act that Geddes developed his alternative practice of rehabilitating some of the existing dwellings in the Old Town. Significantly these later schemes did not encounter the kind of opposition from ratepayers that had greeted the 1867 Act. The schemes were seen as important contributors to the overall sanitary improvement achieved in the last third of the century; the crude mortality rate for Edinburgh had been brought down from 30.4 per 1000 in 1869 to 16.1 per 1000 in 1894.[70]

In the Edinburgh improvement schemes we therefore see not just the extended involvement of the state in the reproduction of a labour force, but something of the political problems and commercial opportunities which that involvement posed. The details of the schemes were unique to Edinburgh, but their general features have parallels elsewhere. The refashioning of the commercial core of Birmingham by the local authority led by Joseph Chamberlain is a familiar story. The Glasgow Improvement Act of 1866 also led to the creation of thirty-nine new streets, and the development of shops, warehouses and artisans' housing and these endeavours had parallels in Leith and in London. Edinburgh's example is thus pertinent to the debates about the origins of British town planning by showing both a general experience and its specific local application. In the emergence of town planning from sanitary reform in the Edinburgh improvement schemes, 'social' aspirations were a rhetoric divorced from a practice which itself became increasingly technicized. Such social considerations as were put into effect are best understood as part of a wider attempt by the city's middle class to reproduce a fitter, more efficient and altogether more acceptable working class. The sector of the working class that could be construed as deriving a direct benefit from the improvements was those better off members who were also deemed sufficiently 'respectable' to gain a tenancy in one of the 601 local authority houses which had been built in the city by 1913.[71] Town planning in the Edinburgh improvement schemes was undertaken by professional men in local government, but by its structure and effects it was a practice for the benefit of the class who owned land or sought to accumulate capital from its development, and who had an interest in sustaining the local and national image of the historic city.

The local state and the historic city

The making of the historic city occurred before the introduction of statutory town planning, though it involved pioneering ventures in the practice of town planning. It entailed conflicts among diverse power interests which changed over time. Despite such plurality and dynamism, the dominance of the urban development process by a class has been the central theme of this chapter.

Not least significant of the conflicts has been the recurring tension between the imperatives of capital accumulation through development and the threats posed by that development to the inherited physical environment. The richness of that tension has derived from the social and cultural values associated with that environment – the sustained legitimation of elite power resting on a national historic and aesthetic legacy in a country stripped of nationality. The most vociferous critics of new developments were frequently leading citizens of taste and influence. The embodiment of that concern came with the formation of the Cockburn Association in 1875, honouring the name of Edinburgh's early 'environmentalist', Lord Cockburn. The Association was to be 'a popular association for preserving and increasing the attractions of the city and its neighbourhood'. The organizers wrote directly to the Lord Provost requiring him to call a public meeting to set up the society and 'the tone of the letter implies that the authors wrote as *inter pares*'.[72] At the inaugural meeting Lord Moncrieff spoke of the 'many leading and most valuable citizens' who shared the association's concerns.[73]

The Cockburn Association was therefore an active and influential environmental watchdog by the end of the century, just as Lord Cockburn had himself been in earlier years. Indeed the material in this chapter has shown that a variety of actors and institutions influenced the development and planning of Edinburgh before 1900. There were the councillors, themselves politically divided for most of the period, their officials, ratepayers, the kind of bodies consulted over the 1867 Act, landowners, builders, lawyers, banks, insurance companies and the railway companies, not to mention the central government with its special relationship with Edinburgh. On this basis it could be argued that power over development over this period was dispersed and shifting. A progression might be discerned from the central dominance of the Town Council as a creature of the national

government in creating the New Town, through to a phase when the major
entrepreneurs, railways magnates and small builders, took the key roles, to
greater Council intervention through the Improvement Acts, within which there
was a further shift in the fulcrum from the politicians to their professional officers.
The argument though has been that these shifts are entirely logical consequences
within the development of the mode of production itself – from merchant
capitalism, to freely competitive capitalism, to the first moves towards a state-
managed capitalism, within which, with the extension of the franchise, power was
itself shifted away from parliaments and elected bodies and towards non-elected
officials.

Thus the planning and development of Edinburgh was fundamentally controlled
by a class, an ascendant *bourgeoisie* who merged with the old Scottish ruling
class who retained their ties with the capital. The diversity of power centres was
diversity within a class, and the tensions were the tensions of this merger.
Throughout the period studied working-class citizens enjoyed no such power.

In terms of formal politics, the Liberals were predominant in the city for most of
the period from the reform of the Town Council until the last decade of the
nineteenth century. For some twenty years a number of ex-Chartists formed a
radical wing of the Liberal Party, a tenuous alliance in opposition to the landed
elite. The Trades Council formed a municipal committee in 1869 and unsuccess-
fully contested a handful of council seats in 1869 and 1870. However, in 1888 the
Labour Electoral Association was formed and in 1889, 1891 and 1892 a
candidate recognized by the Trades Council as a 'Labour representative' was
returned in the municipal elections.

The Trades Council had been an eminently 'respectable' body and an
important link in the alliance with the Liberals. The President of the Trades
Council had opposed municipal housing in his evidence to the 1884–5 Royal
Commission on the Housing of the Working Classes (Scotland). He argued that
such provision 'would strike at the industry and enterprise that lies at the very root
of our national existence'.[74] But by 1893 the Independent Labour Party had
municipal housing at low rents as part of its municipal programme, though Trades
Council support was still not forthcoming. Eventually in 1899 the Workers'
Municipal Committee was formed. They sponsored four candidates at the 1900
municipal election, campaigning for fuller use of local powers under the Housing
Acts and for the rehousing of tenants of demolished property. In the election
Dalry ward returned the city's first Labour councillor.

Thus for most of the period studied in this chapter the working-class movement
was denied the political power to influence the development of the city. When its
views on urban development were articulated its priorities were rents and housing
rights, rather than conservation or replanning. The extent to which these working
class priorities were outside the scope of early town planning, both in Edinburgh
and elsewhere, illustrates the extent to which such planning practice was a
practice by and for the *bourgeoisie*.

The thing that was distinctive about Edinburgh was just how dominant that
bourgeoisie was. The 1901 census revealed that Edinburgh had a much larger

professional and administrative labour force and a relatively much smaller industrial labour force than for example Glasgow or Dundee. The proportion of males and females in domestic service was more than double the figure for Glasgow. Furthermore a larger percentage of Edinburgh's working class was native to the city and hence more likely to be immersed in the hegemony of the capital, which the Socialist League's paper *Commonweal* described as 'the most bourgeois town perhaps in Britain'.[75] Females, and particularly spinsters, represented a higher proportion of the population than in any of the other Scottish cities. Domestic service and teaching provided them with major employment opportunities, but they did not – of course – have any direct voice in the urban development issues.

Much of the historic city endures. You live in it, walk through it and wonder at it. This historic environment, spectacular yet repressive, has been integral to all subsequent plans for Edinburgh. Its very anachronism has been a cultural prop to the dominant ideology, yet an impediment to the developing mode of production itself. The problems of restructuring yet conserving the historic city have been central to planning practice in twentieth-century Edinburgh. At the same time theorizing about the nature and potential of town planning has been shackled by idealistic interpretations of how the historic city was produced by a handful of far-sighted geniuses, guided by a classless sense of civic responsibility, social concern, national awareness and good taste. The rich and contrasting aesthetics of this special city are a constant siren to planners, luring them to suspend their critical faculties and to affirm the timeless truths of the positive face of this divided city.

References and notes

1   From 'Beautiful Edinburgh', in J. L. Smith (ed), *Last poetic gems: selected from the works of William McGonagall* (David Winter & Son 1971).

2   P. Geddes, 'The civic survey of Edinburgh', in the *Transactions of the Town Planning Conference,* Royal Institute of British Architects (1910), p. 551.

3   For a fuller discussion of the principles see E. Mandel, *Late Capitalism* (New Left Books 1975), p. 395.

4   J. Gray, *The Capital of Scotland: its precedence and status* (1980). This pamphlet was published by Councillor Gray in support of the restoration of Edinburgh as an all-purpose local authority, rather than the city being a District within the then Labour-controlled Lothian Region.

5   In this period, 'Scarcely an acre in the neighbourhood came into the market which [the Heriot's Trust] did not instantly acquire,' W. Steven, *History of George Heriot's Hospital*, (Bell & Bradfute 1872), third edition, pp. 64–5.

6   H. Armet, 'Notes on the rebuilding of Edinburgh in the last quarter of the seventeenth century', *The Book of the Old Edinburgh Club*, vol. 29 (1956), p. 137.

7   F. C. Mears and J. Russell, 'The New Town of Edinburgh – Part I', *The Book of the Old Edinburgh Club,* vol. 22 (1938), p. 171.

8   Quoted in F. C. Mears and J. Russell (1938), p. 178.
9   T. C. Smout, *A History of the Scottish People: 1560–1830,* (Collins 1969), p. 297.
10 Ibid., p. 245.
11 Quoted in A. J. Youngson, *The Making of Classical Edinburgh* (Edinburgh University Press 1966), p. 4.
12 Quoted in D. Daiches, *Edinburgh* (Hamish Hamilton 1978), pp. 123–4.
13 Ibid., p. 124.
14 Ibid., p. 124.
15 *The Scots Magazine,* 1752, quoted in F. C. Mears and J. Russell (1938), p. 180.
16 E. F. Catford, *Edinburgh: The story of a city* (Hutchinson 1975), p. 68. In Scotland feu duties were an annual payment in perpetuity to the original owner of the land.
17 D. Daiches (1978), p. 173.
18 Quoted in W. Steven, footnote, pp. 121–2. There was overlapping membership between the Trust and the Town Council. Several governors of the Trust opposed the scheme, arguing that it was improper for the Provost, magistrates and councillors among their number to be both vendors and purchasers. The feu of thirty-seven acres to the Council was finally approved by twenty-nine votes to eight, but law suits followed which were not resolved until 1766 when the Lords of Session upheld the sale.
19 The adjudicators were Lord Alemoore, Lord Kames, the Lord Advocate for Scotland, Commissioner Clerk and the architects, the Adams brothers.
20 T. C. Smout (1969), p. 372.
21 The first extension was designed by Robert Reid in 1802. In 1817 a competition was held to plan a further extension to the east. None of the four plans submitted satisfied the Town Council, who commissioned W. H. Playfair to produce a further plan. Part of this was built around Calton Hill, on land owned by Heriot's Trust. A further plan for the area to the west of Craig's New Town was drawn up by James Gillespie in 1822, which formed the basis for the development on the land owned by the Earl of Moray.
22 Quoted in T. C. Smout (1969), p. 371.
23 Quoted in T. C. Smout (1969), p. 379.
24 Quoted in D. Daiches (1978), p. 177.
25 Ibid., p. 178.
26 W. Steven, p. 228.
27 W. Scott, 'Provincial antiquities of Scotland', pp. 268–70, quoted in W. Steven, as footnote, pp. 121–2.
28 Quoted in D. Daiches (1978), p. 186.
29 Ibid., p. 180.
30 For a fuller discussion see D. Daiches (1978), p. 177.
31 Quoted in F. C. Mears, *A Regional Survey and Plan for Central and South-east Scotland* (Morrison & Gibb 1948), p. 12.

32   For a fuller discussion see R. Q. Gray, *The Labour Aristocracy in Victorian Edinburgh* (Clarendon Press 1976).

33   Quoted in P. Geddes (1910), p. 560.

34   P. J. Smith, 'Site selection in the Forth Basin', Ph.D. dissertation, University of Edinburgh (1964), p. 287.

35   W. Steven, p. 229.

36   Ibid., p. 230.

37   The Merchants' Company of the City of Edinburgh, 1891, 'The Merchants' Company Institutions: Landed Estates – Notes and Plans for the use of the Governors', Edinburgh, p. 11. Watson's Trust, like Heriot's, provided a basis for education from which important fee-paying schools developed and continue to prosper.

38   Ibid. The £60 figure was levied in the Gorgie development, and the £275 in nearby Merchiston. The Merchants' Company schools had very considerable investments in land in and around Edinburgh, and elsewhere in Scotland from Peterhead to Kelso.

39   P. Geddes (1910), p. 566.

40   *Report of the Burgh Engineer's Department* (1894), Edinburgh Corporation.

41   C. J. Smith, *Historic South Edinburgh*, vol. 1 (Charles Skilton 1978), p. 148.

42   *The Scotsman,* 25 April 1883.

43   Ibid.

44   For a full discussion of social spatial segregation in the city at this time, see G. Gordon, 'Status areas in Edinburgh', Ph.D. Dissertation, University of Edinburgh (1971).

45   See, for example, the debate on the second reading of the Artizans and Labourers' Dwellings Improvement Bill, 1875, *Hansard's Parliamentary Debates,* Third Series, 244 pp. 449–62.

46   R. F. Galloway, 'The Edinburgh Improvement Act, 1867', Fifth Year Thesis, Department of Architecture, Heriot-Watt University/Edinburgh College of Art (1975), para. 1.04.

47   P. Geddes (1910), p. 565.

48   For example, the Pilrig Model Dwellings, opened in 1851, housed forty-four families in three rows of two-storey housing, and paid a 5 per cent dividend. In 1862 the rents were between £5-12s-0d and £10-10s-0d a year. Another scheme, the Rosemount Buildings, provided ninety-six houses and five per cent.

49   Free Church of Scotland, *Report of the Committee on Houses for the Working Classes in connection with Social Morality, to the General Assembly of the Free Church of Scotland* (1862), p. 7.

50   Ibid., pp. 8–9. Pending such reforms the kirk preached self-help as the remedy, along with co-operation and abstinence. It was a strong supporter of the Edinburgh Co-operative Building Company Limited, which had been formed by masons during a lock-out in 1861. It built cottages rather than tenements, on land feued at £20 per acre. The price of the houses ranged

from £130 to £250. By 1875 the co-operative had built almost 1000 houses, and a further 400 were constructed during the next decade. By that stage, however, the co-operative was in effect a commercial comany. See *The Builder* (1861), vol. 19, p. 758, and also the Free Church of Scotland, p. 12.

51   The building at 101 High Street collapsed at 1 a.m. on Sunday 24 November 1861. It was then some 200 years old, and belonged to seven different owners. It had been occupied by twenty-five families, several of whom kept lodgers, and over 100 people were sleeping there when the tragedy occurred.

52   The decision to seek private legislation rather than use the general statute, in this case the Lindsay Act, in part reflected Edinburgh's traditional sense of independence and associated predilection for private legislation. However, it also probably represented an acknowledgement that the Lindsay Act was not really an effective vehicle for dealing with slum clearance areas as distinct to individual houses. See. P. J. Smith, 'Planning as environmental improvement: slum clearance in Victorian Edinburgh', in A. Sutcliffe (ed), *The Rise of Modern Urban Planning 1800–1914* (Mansell 1980), pp. 99–133.

53   Statement to the Town Council, 5 December 1865. This is reproduced in R. F. Galloway (1975), Appendix 6. This block was that between Niddry Street and St John's Street.

54   Ibid.

55   R. F. Galloway, para. 5.36.

56   Parochial Board of St. Cuthbert's *Report of the Chairman's Committee,* printed privately 19 March 1866.

57   J. Begg, 'The causes and probable remedies of pauperism in Scotland', *Chalmers Association for Diffusing Information on Important Social Questions* (1870), p. 21.

58   The Improvement Act was a well established procedure in Edinburgh. Chambers was adamant that the Town Council should be the Commissioners. He was possibly influenced by the scandal of the 1825 Improvement Scheme when the Commissioners, various nobility, were widely reputed to have been the major financial beneficiaries of the scheme.

59   W. Chambers, *Statement to the Town Council* (5 Dec. 1865), p. 10.

60   P. J. Smith, (1980), p. 113. Chambers had argued that the redevelopment would not affect the architecture of the historic High Street.

61   *The Builder*, vol. 36, no. 1860 (28 Sept. 1878).

62   Ibid.

63   Ibid.

64   R. F. Galloway, para 8.11.

65   *The Builder,* vol. 36, no. 1860 (28 Sept. 1878), p. 1004.

66   *Inquiry into the Edinburgh Improvement Scheme,* 1893, SRO DD 6/385.

67   See, for example, the comments of the Burgh Engineer in the Council Record for 6 Oct. 1885.

68 P. J. Smith, p. 124. The figure was for acquisitions in Leith, but Smith suggests that Edinburgh prices were about the same.
69 *Royal Commission on the Housing of the Working Classes (Scotland)*, (1885), q 18732. As Smith (1980) noted, 'At all times the Trust sought the highest financial return on its land. This is demonstrated in numerous ways, from its standard building conditions to the upset prices that it set at public auctions, and its reluctance to reduce either, even in the face of persistently weak demand. In the day-to-day administration of the Trust, fiscal responsibility was the ruling criterion, not social responsibility', p. 124.
70 P. J. Smith, p. 110.
71 *Royal Commission on Housing in Scotland,* (1917), q 387.
72 G. Bruce, *Some Practical good: The Cockburn Association – 100 years participating in planning*, (The Cockburn Association 1975), p. 22.
73 Ibid., p. 26.
74 *Royal Commission on the Housing of the Working Classes (Scotland)*, 1885, q 19188.
75 *Commonweal* 26 Feb. 1887.

5 The making of a planning ideology

This chapter traces the development of planning in Edinburgh from the lead up to the first town planning legislation in 1909, through until the outbreak of the Second World War. A critical approach to this practice can be built around the theoretical structure set out in Part One: the inter-related changes at the economic political and cultural levels need to be explored empirically in terms of their specific local impacts.

At a national level the key development in British capitalism in this period was the increasing international competition which it faced. That competition had been mounting during the latter decades of the nineteenth century, but the commercial and military struggles of the first quarter of this century were of an increased scale. The restoration of the gold standard in 1925 and the removal of almost all the protective tariffs imposed during the war, were attempts to reconstitute the old financial and trading networks in the forlorn hope that industrial profitability could be reconstituted. The international economic crisis of the 1930s saw the further decline of many traditional industries, but also ushered in the production of new consumer goods, one part of which was a speculative house building boom.

The political undercurrent during this period of unprecedented mass democracy was the rising influence of the working class and its containment. From a town planning interest, the most significant concession to working-class pressure was the improved provisions for housing. However, as Chapter 2 argued, the association between housing and town planning was complex; working-class agitation was largely directed towards housing, not town planning, while the Government was concerned in 1919 that stronger town planning powers might undermine the housing programme. The working-class 'victory' on housing was by no means complete and was followed by defeats on the industrial and political fronts in 1926 and 1931. As Chapter 2 argued, the main significance for town planning was the threat posed to the planning system of the events of 1931.

At the cultural level, the period was marked by the establishment of a planning profession and its development of a coherent ideology. In the 1930s in particular comprehensive planning was depicted as a rational middle ground between the extremes of *laissez-faire* and totalitarianism, a neutral and expert means of managing change that could protect democracy itself.

Edinburgh can now be used as a way of exploring how these developments over the period affected planning as an ideology and as a practice in one place. It is a particularly apt locus for such study. It was a city of finance and administration, within which there was nevertheless a substantial industrial presence and a numerically significant working class. In these respects the local state mirrored the structure and composition of the British state itself. The inter-war period saw major developments in both council housing and private housing, doubling the built-up area. The events of 1931 also had a direct impact as town planning was redefined to match the strident financial imperatives of the day. Last, but not least, some of the most influential members of the planning profession were associated with the city at this time. Thomas Adams, first President of the Town Planning Institute and an internationally renowned figure, was involved in important consultancy work. More especially, though, it was through Patrick Geddes and his distinguished son-in-law Frank Mears that Edinburgh became an important early centre for learning and ideas about town planning including its practice. The focus in this chapter is on the way that planning practice and ideology related to one another and to the class practices which controlled the development of the city. The central question is, What interests shaped planning in Edinburgh before 1939 and how?

Visions of town planning and housing reform

The debate about the 'social origins' of British town planning was introduced in Chapter 2 and developed in relation to the Improvement Act in Chapter 4. It can, however, be extended into the period of the early town planning Acts. Reformist origins cannot be disputed – town planning was part of that general process whereby existing structures and practices were adjusted within what remained a conservative social framework. The real debate then is on the interests which directed the path of reform and more particularly the relative roles of industrial capital and the labour movement. Their visions of the nature of town planning and its links to working-class housing and to the issue of landownership are of particular significance.

By the turn of the century Edinburgh's industry was suburbanizing, in an attempt to improve production and distribution. Breweries were prominent in the move from the centre to sites which were then at the edge of the city. The future role and location of industry began to concern Edinburgh's Town Council, not least because suburbanization across the city boundary could spell a loss of rateable value. In 1908 the council produced a Memorandum which looked at the problem and at ways of attracting new industries. The preamble of the Memorandum lauded Edinburgh's history, picturesque beauty, and status as a capital, and stressed the significance of these features to the further development of the tourist industry. The city's low rates were seen as an important attraction for new industries and the council identified sites where they ought to be located. These were in the growing south-western sector, but within the city boundary.

Patrick Geddes was dismissive of this official approach. He read the suburban trend as an opportunity to plan industrial development, so as to yield returns in 'energy and efficiency, in health and beauty, and therefore in money too'.[1] The task was to make 'Newer Edinburgh – an industrial city and a garden city in one, and this realisable within a reasonable period.'[2] The transformation would be achieved through pollution controls and the location of industry on the leeward side of the city, by the Innocents Railway and close to the Midlothian Coalfield.

Geddes was therefore advocating the adoption of an integrated town planning approach, covering not just new industrial attraction, but the future of existing industries, housing and living conditions and the natural environment. The mechanism for the planning was to be the civic survey, which by elucidating historical legacies, constraints and possibilities would provide the basis for practical action that was rooted in the place and its people. He claimed: 'City surveys are urgent, practicable, and useful, so useful that they must before long become for civic statesmanship and local administration what charts are now to Admiralty and to pilot.'[3] The surveys would lead to reports for action, informed by an ideal of unity between man and nature and man and man, a city design going beyond street lay-outs and the demarcation of sites for house building. The disorder of industrialism could be refashioned by a mixture of rational decisions and community involvement. The temporary agents for this new approach to urban development had to be those created by Geddes's own pioneering endeavours, the Outlook Tower and the Open Spaces Committee, whose members had created over a dozen small gardens on derelict plots in the Old Town through working in their spare time.

Around this time the city's labour movement was also urging the council to plan the town. The Trades Council and the Edinburgh Labour Party formed a joint committee to present evidence to the 1912 Royal Commission on Housing in Scotland. They saw town planning as a necessary link to working-class housing provision. They recommended that a local authority department should be set up to deal exclusively with housing and town planning: 'The duty of this department would be the systematic planning of the whole city, the necessary clearing and opening up of the congested areas, and the suitable provision of housing in the suburbs.'[4]

The notion of 'opening up' was an important aspect of the practice under the Improvement Schemes which was carried forward into this new vision of town planning. However, the committee were explicitly critical of the lack of 'methodical planning' in the Improvement Schemes and sought a much more comprehensive approach. The failings of the Improvement Schemes were not solely attributed to such technical considerations, however, for they had been '. . . severely handicapped by the dead weight of financial burden entailed by the excessive prices paid for slum properties, and for the sites on which they stood'.[5]

The power of landowners was a barrier to working-class housing aspirations not just in the slum areas but in the paucity of land available elsewhere for such housing. Edinburgh had been suburbanizing rapidly, with the main growth between 1891 and 1901 being in areas beyond the city boundary but served by the railway. Thus Colinton had experienced an 18 per cent population increase, Corstorphine 22 per cent and Duddingston 28 per cent. In the following decade these trends accelerated; though the population within the Edinburgh boundary only increased by 0.9 per cent, that in the suburban ring of Cramond, Corstorphine, Colinton, Liberton, Inveresk and the Burgh of Leith jumped up 12.1 per cent. This was overwhelmingly a middle-class suburbanization and indeed the building of working-class tenements dried up entirely after 1909.[6] The form of development in this period is indicated in Figure 7.

Snobbery seems an insufficient explanation as to why landowners were so niggardly in their release of land for working-class housing. The real answer lay in the form of the landownership. Under the system of feuing, the original owner and his heirs retained a permanent interest in the land through the receipt of feu duties Feuing was thus conducted with a view to long-term investment and the feu contracts were written so as to restrict the form of the development of the land so as to protect the long-term income and the value of any adjacent land held by the same owner. Not only was feuing for working-class housing a threat to the value of nearby sites, but it was perceived as involving an element of risk, since working-class housing provision was itself such a marginal economic proposition. The charitable trusts in particular, major landowners in Edinburgh, would need to ensure the long-term security of their investments.

Thus feus for working-class housing land reached up to £657 an acre[7] and were typically in the order of £230 an acre.[8] Landowners would reject lower bids for such land and wait until their asking price was met, even when land was being

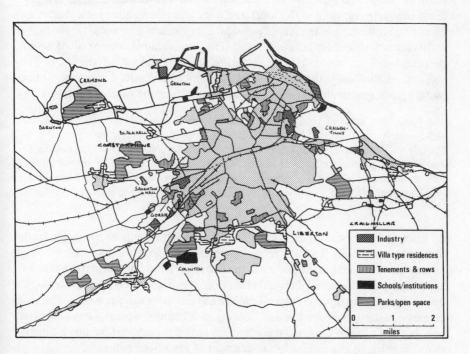

Figure 7   *The physical expansion of Edinburgh, 1893–1913*

priced beyond the reach of the builders. The builders either did not build, went bankrupt or built at very high densities.[9] Housing opportunities for the working class were correspondingly limited.

Not surprisingly then the joint committee of the Trades Council and the Labour Party saw the whole issue of land ownership and betterment as integral to any town planning strategy. Nevertheless, they stopped short of advocating land nationalization: instead they proposed legislation giving councils powers of first refusal, at existing use value, on any land sold or exchanged within their boundaries. Compulsory purchase powers were also suggested, again tied to existing use values and with the costs of clearing unfit areas being shared equally between central and local government. Betterment to adjacent properties resulting from local authority clearance schemes or open space provision should be recouped by the council. The committee's vision was that through such powers it would be possible to provide decent houses for workers and their families, cottages with gardens rather than tenements, where density and occupancy limits would be respected. Such houses would be rented at cost plus maintenance.

The labour movement in Edinburgh continued to advocate housing reform linked to more comprehensive town planning. In 1918 the Trades Council, Labour Party and Co-operative Guilds pressed the council to accept that the city urgently needed some 10,000 new houses.[10] A report on the city's housing problems by the Medical Officer of Health in 1921 showed the links once more between residential densities and mortality rates. The Trades Council criticized the inadequate response of the local authority and again called for a much more extensive replanning of the whole physical environment as a necessary means of satisfying working-class housing needs. They urged the clearance of all derelict property and the relocation of factories to the outskirts of the city. They recognized that only the better paid workers could afford the new council cottages, but saw in those planned housing areas the prototype of the future city:

The housing schemes at Gorgie, Wardie and Willowbrae are of the correct type, but unfortunately are at present beyond the means of those who suffer most from the housing shortage. Still, your Committee believes that a complete belt surrounding the whole city of houses similar in character is an object which should be striven after. This would ultimately become a healthy working-class suburbia, given a tramway system radiating from the city which would supply cheap and rapid transit.[11]

By the late 1920s and in the years that followed, the focus of the city's labour movement narrowed. The low rate of council house construction was criticized, as were the standards of the houses in the later years, but interest in town planning appears to have dwindled. Nevertheless a clear working-class perspective on the links between housing and town planning had been advanced. It was modest in its demands, asking only for cottage housing in a healthy working-class suburban belt, but it did make the crucial connection between ends and means, by linking town planning to the fundamental question of land ownership.

It might therefore appear that planning in Edinburgh in the twentieth century developed out of the preaching and practice of Geddes and his associates and the pressure exerted by an ascendant labour movement. That, however, is too one-dimensional a view. There is evidence that the city's landowners, industrialists and commercial concerns also had an interest in town planning, certainly in the special political and economic situation immediately after the end of the First World War. The Merchants' Company set up special committees on the Building Trade in the city, which reported in 1918, and on the development of Edinburgh, which reported a year later. The Merchants' Company was a major landowner, whose holdings at the time were valued at over £1 million and it also counted 560 of its members to be 'leading businessmen' in the city.[12] Their report on the development of the city was a fascinating attempt to promote town planning as a way of restoring industrial profitability, building a new relation between labour and capital, and also maintaining the benefits enjoyed by landowners – an ambitious prospectus by any standards.

The report strongly expounded the need to plan for an enlarged city (and to set up 'a Department for Town Planning and Civic Design, with a degree, as at Liverpool and London Universities'[13]). The suburban drift across the city's boundaries was seen as a drain on Edinburgh's rateable properties. The remedy lay in plans to ensure that this growth proceeded gradually and systematically. Attention was drawn to the experience of planning the New Town as an example of how advantages could be gained from planned extensions to the city.

The Committee therefore recommended that plans should be prepared that looked fifty years ahead and catered for a population of at least 1 million. The plans should take in an area within a six-mile radius of the city centre, thus extending well beyond the then boundary of the local authority. Such a swathe of land would be required to provide 'all necessary land for a choice of location for extensive schemes of village and garden suburbs to which people would be carried by high-speed tramways, and for new manufactories requiring large areas, as well as for a containing belt of open land to be permanently conserved'.[14]

As the plans would be long term they would not go into fine details, since the precise trends of development could not be predicted. Nor would the plans be rigid, but rather would 'preserve elasticity and adaptability to meet ever changing conditions and circumstances'.[15] The plans would show roads, railways and some buildings: 'Factories would be localised, and naturally placed convenient to transit by road, rail or water. The large houses would be distributed in residential districts, and artisans' houses, say 10 or 12 per acre, in garden suburbs and garden villages.'[16] Parks, open spaces, recreation grounds, allotments and play centres would also be shown; existing amenities would be preserved, long and interesting vistas would be created and war memorials planned. The whole design was to have a Scottish character and would use local building materials. A detailed regional survey was also called for.

The influence of ventures such as Port Sunlight and the more general campaigning for garden cities and suburbs was evident. The plan would reproduce social spatial segregation, but meet the pressures from the working class and sympathetic reformers for low density living and open space. Though the plan sought to re-create the form of class division in housing, the Merchants' Company explicitly claimed a vision of a larger, prosperous city, that served the general well-being rather than that of any particular class. 'We want a city that is self-contained and self-sufficing, a city with no soul-starving slums.'[17] And again, 'We want a transformation of urban life, and to foster in every way the health, vigour and contentment of the people.'[18]

Thus an important early elaboration of a need for town planning was applied to Edinburgh by one of the city's most prominent middle-class institutions. Behind the propositions for town planning was an attempt to construct a new alliance of industrial capital and the working class. As the report observed, 'If enlightened capital and enlightened labour will only work hand in hand for the common good, what vast potentialities lie slumbering in that combination.'[19] At a time of industrial unrest at home, and increasing international competition, a vigorous and contented labour force could be conjured, and the rates kept down, by a planned settlement form adaptable to market pressures. The 'self-sufficient' city would presumably continue to draw a return on capital invested elsewhere by its multiplicity of inter-connected financial interests.

In this vision, town planning was explicitly associated with an attempt to readjust the local economy in the light of changes which had been noticed even before the war. The report observed, 'A new world will require new methods. We can never return to the economic status quo.'[20] The trend already apparent to multi-national location of some Edinburgh industries was blamed on import duties abroad. The Merchants' Company therefore called for trade protection to prevent the drain of wages and rateable values. The proposition was that state intervention could boost economic performance, and so the report recommended that a local Ministry of Development should be set up, managed by successful businessmen. On the other hand, planning as control was not endorsed. 'Officialdom' was entreated to adopt a more permissive attitude to the extension of works and to treat new firms 'tenderly in the matter of rating'.[21]

The concessions being offered to the working class in an attempt to forge a new compromise presented some difficulties. Land and housing were central issues that had to be faced. The committee proposed new powers to permit local authorities to purchase whatever land they required at 1913 prices plus severance and 'worsenment' costs, but less betterment. This power would only run for a defined period. However, '... nothing should be done that would discourage enterprise, or tend to divert capital into more remunerative and less troublesome channels'.[22] Compensation should ensure that dispossessed landowners were as well off as before; and once acquired by the local authority, the land should be prepared by them for private development. Thus on the land questions, the conflicting interests of the businessmen seeking cheap land for factories and the housing for the labour force, and the Merchants' Company themselves as a major land holder, were resolved in calls for a local government planning system to effect the transfer of land from one private owner to another, all at a 'fair' price which protected the institution of private property, while preventing landowners from extracting extra rent by withholding their land from the market.

Land was integral to the housing strategy. The expectation in the national legislation – the 1919 Act – was that council houses would be provided at densities of no more than twelve houses to the acre. This was an alarming expectation given the feus normally imposed on land for working-class housing. Indeed, the corporation had already invested in fifty acres of land at Gorgie on the assumption that it would be building tenements, not cottages. The Merchants' Company were concerned that council housing built to these nationally imposed densities would saddle Edinburgh's ratepayers with a loss which would undermine the situation where the capital's rates were substantially lower than those in comparable urban areas.[23] More worrying still, there had recently been a rent strike in Coventry by tenants demanding even lower rents, and one in London for no rents at all. The Merchants' Company were strongly of the view that to charge anything less than 'economic' rents for the new council houses would be unsound. Indeed, the corporation had already invested in fifty acres of land at Gorgie on the housing a paying proposition, so that its provision could continue to be through the private sector. Thus in their attempt to meet the pressing need for improved working-class housing and thus usher in their new social order, the best that the Merchants' Company could propose was the freeing of property owners from their 'onerous burdens'. Drawing out the spatial form of the new city on a map was much easier than facing the political changes needed to realize it.

The first two decades of the twentieth century were marked by increased imperialist competition, the growth of the labour movement and heightened political struggles not just at the point of production, but also over housing issues. These definitive features were echoed in the seminal cases put forward in Edinburgh for town planning on an extensive scale. The Trades Council saw town planning as a step towards better working-class housing, at lower densities than would be possible under a market allocation process. Strengthened powers to acquire land were seen as essentials to achieve these aims. The beneficiaries would then be workers and their families, whose gains would be made at the expense of landowners and landlords. The Merchants' Company also looked to town planning for planned suburbanization, modernization of transport networks and slum clearance. However, they saw town planning as a way to revitalize the local economy and to forge a new relationship between the classes that would contain the aspirations of labour within existing capitalist forms and institutions. The vision of Patrick Geddes was more complex. He saw town planning as a way of harmonizing relations between people, and between man and nature. It offered an alternative to industrialism, that was still industrial, a challenge to capitalist structures that did not explicitly replace them. The actual statutory practice of town planning proved to be more limited and piecemeal than any of these three prescriptions.

Statutory planning

The 1909 Act provided for the preparation of planning schemes for undeveloped suburban land, rather than for a plan for a city as a whole. There were also problems in interpreting the legislation. These were compounded by the fact that the Scottish Board of Health provided less clarification and guidance than was available in England. Meetings were in fact held by the larger Scottish local authorities to try to decipher just what a planning scheme should entail under Scottish conditions.

Local government boundaries were a further impediment. Given that the planning schemes were intended to deal with expanding suburban areas, there was the likelihood that they would straddle the boundaries. The 1909 Act made provision for joint schemes involving more than one authority, or for one authority to have responsibility for a scheme which covered land in another authority's area. Edinburgh's early schemes tested out both these possibilities.

Edinburgh readily took on the planning powers conferred by the 1909 Act. In 1914 the Town Council set up a Town Council Planning Committee, which was rechristened the Housing and Town Planning Committee in 1918, as working class pressure on the housing question mounted. A Town Planning Scheme for thirty-six acres in the Belle Vue area was sanctioned by the Board of Health in 1912. This was followed a year later by a four and a half acre Scheme for Fountainbridge, close to the city centre, and by a much larger Scheme for 896 acres in the Craigentinny and Restalrig area on the north-eastern fringe. The Craigentinny Scheme was a joint endeavour between Edinburgh and Leith, with each local authority administering its own part. This meant that two different codes would operate within the same Scheme, for Edinburgh exercised controls through its own local statutes, while Leith used the Burgh Police (Scotland) Acts. By 1919 sanction had been given for four further Schemes in suburban areas, covering a total of 3014 acres. These were at Murrayfield and Ravelston, Murrayfield and Saughton, and Gorgie, all on the western edge of the then city, and at Abercorn/Duddingston/Niddrie on the east. In addition, sanction had been sought for a scheme covering a further 1299 acres at Granton, in the north. This scheme was contested by Leith where it applied to land within their boundary. Midlothian County Council had also promoted extensive schemes in the west at Corstorphine and at Blackhall, but they had also objected to attempts by Edinburgh to impose planning control across the boundary.[24] When local government boundaries were changed in 1920 there was a further recasting of the planning schemes.

The council then appears to have involved itself in a flurry of town planning activity, though one which was interrupted by the war, when no new Schemes were initiated. One reason may have been the long experience with the Improvement Schemes, but the intense pressures for middle-class suburbanization and the risks of losing ratepayers were probably more significant. Despite all the activity very little of consequence actually happened. By 1928 only one scheme, that for the small site at Fountainbridge, had been finally approved by the Scottish Board of Health. Indeed this was one of only two schemes that had received such approval in the whole of Scotland.

In the absence of suitable Scottish guidance, the early Edinburgh schemes drew upon the advice given to local authorities in England. The schemes were cast as Acts of Parliament and sought to prescribe layouts and future developments in a detailed manner. Reflecting on the experience the Burgh Engineer observed: 'There was an attempt to visualize the actual development of areas which might take several generations to mature. It left little or no room for "the changes that are sure to come", and it imposed on landowners detailed lay-out plans for which they had no need and less liking.'[25] Thus the limited nature of the planning powers under the 1909 Act meant that the designs were left as a set of ideas, divorced from implementation. It was the landowners and private builders who could effectively decide that pattern of suburbanization, and to be relevant a Planning Scheme had to conform with their priorities.

Ideas for a regional scheme involving Edinburgh, East, West and Midlothian Counties were discussed in 1924, but came to nothing. The intention had been to select the best lines for new arterial roads, but the counties were reluctant to commit themselves to the expenditure that the construction and upkeep of the roads would require.[26] Within the city, clearance and rebuilding continued in sporadic fashion through Improvement Schemes on the nineteenth-century model.[27]

By 1928 two Planning Schemes initiated before the war were ready for submission to the Scottish Board of Health for their final approval. These were for 896 acres at Craigentinny and 1700 acres at Duddingston. The proposals in them were 'as elastic as possible', so as to 'ensure the least disturbance and difficulty in the orderly development of the city'.[28]

The scheme for another suburban growth sector, Granton-Cramond on the north-west, was given over to Thomas Adams's firm of consultants for them to draft. Thus another prominent early planner became directly involved in planning in Edinburgh. The consultants' final report in 1930 was consistent with the stance the clients, Edinburgh Corporation, had adopted towards land use planning. Adams and his colleagues advised that the scheme needed to be flexible, broad-brush and agreed with the landowners. Such a scheme, they argued, would then directly benefit landowners by giving them security against changes in zoning. The main problems were to avoid liabilities for compensation, and to anticipate growth so as to impose reasonable restrictions. The report stated:

The main purpose is to obtain from a scheme the guidance and direction, rather than control, of growth, so that the joint interests of the public and the land proprietors will be equally protected, and so that wasteful expenditure will be avoided. The social and economic advantages of exercising foresight can be obtained without unreasonable cost or injury to private interests.[29]

Edinburgh's main response to development pressures in the city was the Edinburgh Corporation Act of 1926. This private Act gave the local authority powers to control building regulations, advertisement hoardings, amenity and elevations, so that amendments could be required to planned developments that were deemed to be injurious to amenity. The powers were very similar to the Model Clauses for the 1909 Act that had been produced in England, but which the Scottish Board of Health had failed to replicate. Within Edinburgh itself, detailed layouts could be required for new developments. The important corollary was that the council decided that the actual Planning Schemes could thereafter be less detailed, showing little more than the line and width of main roads, open spaces and areas for residential, industrial or 'indeterminate' development. Specification of the layout was therefore left to the initiative of the landowner or developer. This concession was welcomed by the convenor of the Housing and Town Planning Committee and by the Burgh Engineer as being likely to reduce opposition to planning.[30] The Edinburgh Corporation (Streets, Buildings and Sewers) Order, 1926, also allowed the corporation to impose standards for street widths and building heights in areas that were not included in a Planning Scheme, thus making such standards more uniform across the city.

So in the absence of action from the Scottish Office, Edinburgh produced its own legislation.[31] The content of the legislation was low-key, technical and uncontroversial, but the context and implications are important. Planning was being defined in practice as the steering of private initiatives, within a network of infrastructure and broad land uses defined by the local authority. It was a technical exercise, severed from issues of land ownership or working-class housing provision. The aesthetic was rooted in engineering, seeking little more than the avoidance of the 'disorder' of the urban structure created by *laissez-faire* industrial growth.

There was therefore a significant contrast between the actual practice of town planning in Edinburgh and the visions of those advocating town planning. The practice was tuned to the statutory framework, which had a limited and piecemeal character as the result of the conflicts at the level of the national state between industrial capital, landed capital and the labour movement. The local government professional officers in charge of the day-to-day (or rather more sporadic) operation of the legislation further emphasized the form of the practice. Those most involved appear to have been the Burgh Engineer and legal officers, people whose education and professional experience predisposed them to prefer continuity with past practice to innovation. However, in trying to elucidate why the practice developed in the way it did, one must also have regard to the wider character of the local state in Edinburgh. The labour movement never attained the political power to seriously challenge for the implementation of their vision. Indeed, the industrial unrest which gave their housing and planning ideals such impetus had been contained by the defeat of 1926. Nor was industrial capital in the city strong enough to carry through its vision of a local authority in partnership to promote industry. The vision propounded by the Merchants' Company was therefore sidelined also. The paradox is that the form of planning which they advocated (and which could never have led to the realization of their substantive prescriptions) was that which was practised by the local authority. The interests which defined the practice were fundamentally those of the landowning class.

Planning for modernization

The recurring dilemma in the planning of Edinburgh is how to reconcile the modernization of the city's structure and fabric with the preservation of the historic city. Many councillors, officials and members of the public have hoped that ignoring the problem would make it go away. However, one person who tried to put it squarely on the agenda was Frank Mears. In 1924 he urged the council to give thought to replanning the city. A committee was set up, but as Mears later observed,

while the ... committee was composed of people with expert knowledge, it broke down for two reasons; first because it was nobody's business to interpret and publish the data, and secondly because the officials took care that it should not interfere with their routine. They occupy their positions because they are instinctively administrators, not creators, and as good servants according to their lights they have no time for 'wild adventures'.[32]

Mears, however, was to have another opportunity to develop his proposals. It came indirectly but precisely from a conflict between the pressures for modernization and for the preservation of historic townscape. The issue created the first co-ordinated public protest over a development proposal in twentieth-century Edinburgh. A new Sheriff Court building was proposed for the prominent central site of the old Calton Hill jail. The site of the old Sheriff Court on George IV Bridge, just off the Royal Mile, would thereby have been freed to allow construction there of a new National Library of Scotland. Baillie Whitson, a leading councillor with a strong interest in town planning, in a newspaper article urged the public to respond before the plans were finalized.[33] The Cockburn Association joined the protests, calling for more time to consider the proposals and urging that the Royal Fine Arts Commission in Scotland should be consulted.

Over the months that followed it began to appear that the siting of the building at Calton Hill was a *fait accompli.* Opposition on amenity grounds built up both within the Town Council and in the Cockburn Association. A counter-proposal was prepared, with the support of the Royal Institute of British Architects. This was that a general survey was really required and that a design for building on the Calton Hill site should only be chosen after an architectural competition. A number of prominent professional bodies united around the Cockburn Association's position. These included the Scottish Society of Artists, the Faculty of Advocates, the Royal Scottish Academy, the Royal Incorporation of Architects in Scotland and the National Council of Women. When their initial lobbying was rebuffed the protestors took their case directly to the Prime Minister, Stanley Baldwin.[34] The result was that the proposals were reconsidered and eventually St Andrews House was built on the Calton Hill site, instead of the Sheriff Court. The environmentalists' victory was less than total, however, for the old Sheriff Court, whose architectural merits they had lauded, was demolished to make way for the National Library.

This first planning protest again illustrates the significance of the city's particular social structure in the process of physical change. The protestors explicitly campaigned as an expression of 'national' opinion on the matter, as befitted their status of association with the national elite resident within the capital. The links between the Cockburn Association and the Town Council were close, with the Lord Provost chairing the 1927 Annual General Meeting of the Association. The focus of their opposition was the central government administrative system and its development priorities which threatened the historic city.

This *cause célèbre* triggered further calls to plan the city in a more comprehensive manner. Lord Provost Whitson arranged a meeting of 'representative gentlemen' in November 1929, which set up a committee to consider the planning of the central area. Gentlemen they may have been (the National Council of Woman was not represented), but they were scarcely representative of the city as a whole, as Table 8 shows.

The representation was therefore drawn from the major institutional landowners in the central area, though the banks, insurance companies and retailing interests were not explicitly represented. These were complemented by the professionals with an interest in the environment – the Dean of Guild, City Architect and Burgh Engineer within the Corporation, the architectural bodies and the Cockburn Association as the 'unofficial' wing. A sub-committee of twenty was formed which included Frank Mears as the representative of the Edinburgh Architectural Association. Mears was again frustrated, and wrote to Provost Whitson as follows:

This new committee is not even composed of people with special knowledge of town planning – most of them are merely representative of elected or other administrative bodies – and they are there primarily to guard specific interests. So you have this hopeless condition of a working sub-committee of yourself, two architects, and a host of solid officials. Not only have these latter failed to produce, after all these months, a single idea, they have not provided a single element of information, either from their departments or from the Bodies which were circularised. . . . I must make the drastic move of writing out my views on the whole Town Planning project independently. This report may suffer from lack of data but the data are not to be forthcoming in any case.[35]

Mears did just that. He drafted a report and recommendations which amounted to the first thorough professional planning study of the central area. The ideas in it were to echo through strategies for the city for the next five decades. The plan is illustrated in Figure 8.

To Mears the crux of the problem was the large number of institutions, many of them educational bodies, who were seeking to expand *in situ* when their original location had not been consciously planned. In between them were 'patches of decaying buildings – breweries and workshops large and small, and badly arranged streets'.[36] Mear's solution was central reconstruction carried out to an overall plan, 'a great concerted scheme to cover perhaps 50 years – and to provide

Table 8   *Organizations at the 1929 Meeting on Planning the Central Area.*

Organization	Number of representatives
HM Office of Works	?
Edinburgh University	2
Royal College of Surgeons	2
Royal College of Physicians	2
The Royal Infirmary	3
Heriot's Trust	3
Heriot-Watt College	3
The Merchants' Company	3
The Lister Institution	1
The Faculty of Advocates	1
Royal Incorporation of Architects in Scotland	1
Edinburgh Architectural Association	1
The Church of Scotland	3
The Roman Catholic Church	2
The Cockburn Association	1
The Old Edinburgh Club	1
The Writers to the Signet Society	1
The SSC Society	2
The Royal Scottish Academy	2
Edinburgh Corporation	13
Sheriff Court House Commissioners	1
National Committee for Training of Teachers	1
Midlothian County Council	3
Edinburgh and District Trades and Labour Council	2

Source: F. C. Mears (1931), 'The City of Edinburgh: Preliminary suggestions for consideration by the representative committee in regard to the development and replanning of the central area of the city in relation to public buildings.'

in the end a renewed Historic Edinburgh rivalling any other famous city'.[37] To get the best of both worlds planned, orderly expansion had to be related to a conservation programme. The proposals were frankly idealistic so as to catch the imagination and so transcend the piecemeal planning efforts of the past.

Modernization of the road network was a key aspect of the strategy. Rationalization was proposed to improve traffic flows, but also to revitalize declining districts, a most indirect approach to the problems of poverty. Thus a by-pass was advocated around the eastern fringe of the central area, from Leith

Figure 8   *The plan prepared by F. C. Mears in 1931 for the central area of Edinburgh* (overleaf)

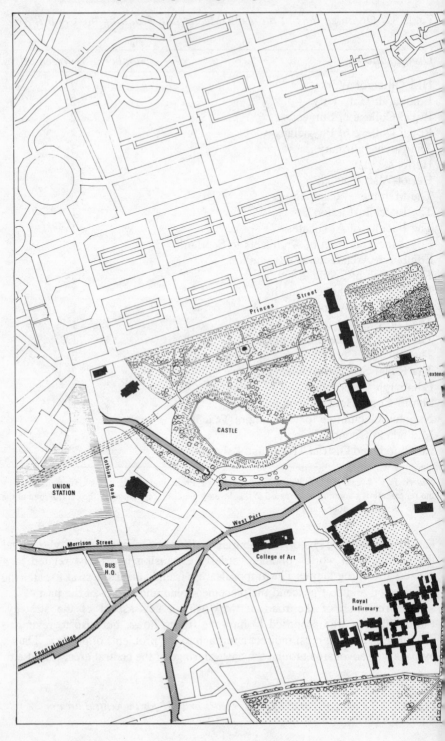

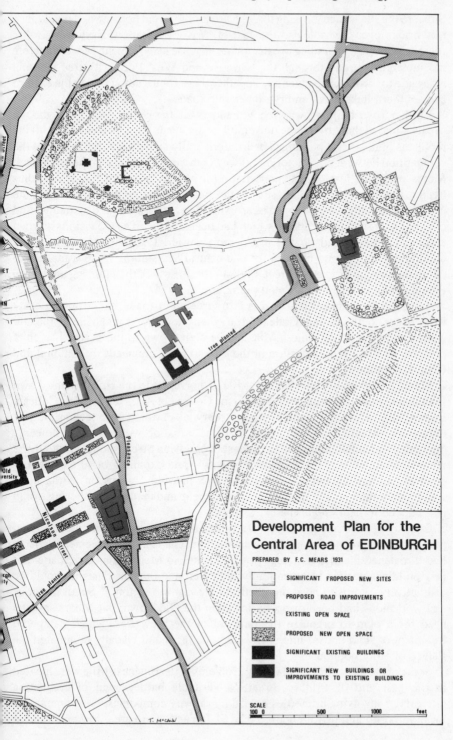

Development Plan for the Central Area of EDINBURGH

PREPARED BY F.C. MEARS 1931

- SIGNIFICANT PROPOSED NEW SITES
- PROPOSED ROAD IMPROVEMENTS
- EXISTING OPEN SPACE
- PROPOSED NEW OPEN SPACE
- SIGNIFICANT EXISTING BUILDINGS
- SIGNIFICANT NEW BUILDINGS OR IMPROVEMENTS TO EXISTING BUILDINGS

SCALE
100 0   500   1000   feet

Street to the Pleasance, passing through areas of low rent housing and involving a new bridge over the valley to the east of Waverley Station. East–west traffic routes also needed upgrading to cater for the increase in movement. Mears therefore recommended a road through the Cowgate and West Port, with tree planting alongside to increase the amenity. Together these routes amounted to the eastern and southern links of an embryo inner ring road.

Further road building was recommended for the South Side area, though Mears stressed that around the university traffic needs must be balanced with the problems of noise and parking. The irrational railway network, the legacy of the competition between the Victorian railway companies, was also to be replanned. Mears proposed just one 'Union' station at the west end of the centre, thus freeing the Waverley station site in the heart of the central area. This, he proposed, should be redeveloped as an exhibition hall, winter garden, market and offices, thus reviving a proposal which had been dismissed as too visionary when Mears and others had floated it a decade earlier. Likewise, Mears took the opportunity to reiterate his idea for one central bus station in the Canal Basin (Fountainbridge/Morrison Street/Lothian Road), which the Housing and Town Planning Committee had deemed premature in 1924.

The plan divided the central area into three main zones, each running east–west. In the south was the 'College Mile', then came the 'Royal Mile' in the Old Town, and then the 'Business Mile' of the New Town to the north. The chief problem was 'the reorganisation of the area to meet the needs of National and Civic Institutions'.[38]

Mears had identified the 'College Mile' in his report to the Housing and Town Planning Committee in 1924. It took in the College of Art, Heriot-Watt College, Edinburgh University and the Royal Infirmary, all of which were seeking land for expansion. Mears's solution was that the area of working-class housing, breweries and small industries to the east of Nicolson Street should gradually be reconstructed, so that Edinburgh University could expand around a system of quadrangles and gateways, with boulevards providing views on to the main university buildings. The inhabitants of the cheap and inadequate housing would be removed to help create the extra space.

The Royal Mile needed careful study and Mears proposed that a considered plan should be prepared to guide reconstruction. The 1927 Improvement Scheme had threatened historic buildings in Canongate, so Mears argued that sites for new buildings needed to be carefully identified and that the designs should be distinctively Scottish and sympathetic to the historic setting.[39] Small factories and workshops had been disappearing from the Old Town, but Mears saw the need for a plan to organize the removal of the breweries, which hampered treatment of slum houses interspersed among them and visually dominated the Palace of Holyroodhouse.

Some of the most difficult planning problems in the Business Mile were located at the east end of Princes Street, 'a veritable battleground of conflicting interests',[40] involving properties owned by railway companies, government, the local authority and private bodies. The St James Square area, low class and in poor condition, was 'an incomparable site for a great public building of national or civic character'.[41]

Behind the Mears proposals for the central area lay a complex of problems. Most evidently there were new functional space requirements to be met. The growing significance of motorized transport, the demands for a more healthy, trained and sophisticated labour force and the growth of state administration itself, all these reflected back in institutional pressures on land in central Edinburgh. But merely to let such pressures rip would be to threaten the historic image of the city and all the sentiments associated with it. Yet to fossilize that historic image indefinitely would be to create a cultural vacuum, to confess that modern capitalism was incapable of generating an urban form with which people could positively identify, and so was culturally bankrupt, parasitic on traditions which it had destroyed. The transition therefore had to be planned in such a way that traditional environments laden with meaning would be retained alongside new identities. The needs of the 'civic and national institutions' therefore had to be met, for, untrammelled by class, they were the very embodiment of this new yet continuous culture. Likewise planning, as a new, superior way of organizing the existing urban space, was a harbinger of the new cultural identity.

Mears was therefore quite prepared to accept amendment to details of his proposals. His overriding concern was to state the case for comprehensive planning in opposition to 'the haphazard methods of the last century'.[42] Such planning would be 'unifying in its general conception'[43] and would harmonize the demands on land, the historic heritage and the needs of the future.

In one sense the vision fitted Edinburgh's class structure extremely well; indeed, it was almost predicated by it. The small industries and occupants of cheap poor housing would have to move, the breweries could relocate to sites geared more to modern production and distribution, while the major beneficiaries would be the professional, educational and administrative bodies. Yet for all that the success of the strategy rested on a number of problematical conditions. First, those interests adversely affected had to accept that the changes were indeed for the greater good. Second, an act of faith was required in the skill of architects and planners to design a new environment that would indeed generate identity. Last but not least, it had to be accepted that the costs of delivering the future planned centre would be acceptable to ratepayers who regularly returned politicians seeking to keep Edinburgh's rates below those of comparable Scottish cities. Within this perspective the restructuring of the central area did not involve a class struggle, but an effort to persuade elected members to be brave and imaginative enough to plan on a large, long-term scale.

Planning to cut wasteful expenditures

Mears's proposals were instantly overtaken by the financial crisis of 1931. His report was discussed by the Adams team of consultants whose final report went to the council about a month after the height of the crisis. Adams and his colleagues tuned their ideas of town planning to fit the orthodox economic policies of the government and financiers. The consultants contrasted their approach with that in the Mears report which had been published six months earlier. They commented:

Mr. Mears approaches the problem along different lines than those we have followed. He presents ideas based on going to the 'limit of our imagination' and 'looking forward 50 years'. In our approach we are compelled to limit ourselves to the consideration of what is practicable in the immediate future. Both approaches have their value but their difference has to be recognised so that they may not be regarded as in any sense competitive. Under present economic conditions the question is what can be done at the least cost to prevent the evil consequences of haphazard growth, and to secure improvement of traffic conditions and regulation of land development. To carry out a limited programme in keeping with these conditions would not interfere with any more elaborate schemes to be developed later but, on the contrary, would result in providing the foundations necessary for more extended operations in the future. [44]

Adams and his colleagues therefore presented their ideas as a limited and pragmatic package. They even took account of the uncertainties surrounding the Parliamentary future of the Town and Country Planning Bill, arguing that their proposals were sufficiently robust to stand regardless of the fate of the planning legislation. The consultants presented town planning first and foremost as a means of promoting economies in public spending:

We have always taken the view that town planning should be carried out in such a way that it does not add to the normal expenditures of a community, that is to the amounts it will normally apply to making public improvements in any event. Secondly we believe it can be shown that an intelligently conceived plan will result in preventing wasteful expenditures, either those that are incurred in doing something wrong that comprehensive planning shows to be unnecessary, or doing something that might be right in itself, at the wrong time. [45]

The report continued in a similar vein. The consultants argued that zoning would protect property values from the consequences of an indiscriminate mixing of uses and that there were economic advantages in protecting amenities. Adams and his colleagues reviewed their proposals for the Granton–Cramond Scheme in the light of the financial crisis. They advised that each land acquisition should be carefully pondered by the council and should only be undertaken where a quick purchase would be profitable. The economic benefits of the scheme were stressed. It would, for example, lead to economies in unnecessary expenditures on road construction and give landowners a guide to the most profitable uses of their land. The Scheme would provide a basis for negotiating open space reservations with the landowners, thus avoiding costs of compensation. [46]

Nevertheless to really make savings on public expenditure something more than a planning scheme was required and to this end the consultants recommended that a general development plan should be prepared for the city. This would be a middle-range, non-statutory plan, more tactical and practical than Mears's fifty-year idealism, but more comprehensive and flexible than a planning scheme. It would be an advisory plan, approved by the Town Planning Committee. It would deal with both built and unbuilt areas and would be based on a civic survey. It should take in adjacent land in Midlothian County, if necessary, regardless of whether the county council agreed to collaborate. In essence though it would be an urban plan, not a regional plan: Edinburgh now had sufficient undeveloped land and needed more detailed planning of the urban area than a regional plan would provide. Such an advisory city plan would:

provide an intelligent guide to the withholding of expenditures, and this is where the emphasis must be placed now in making a plan. With the aid of an Advisory Plan, the Town Planning Committee will be able to recommend what can be done without. In the absence of such a plan, and a modest approach to implementation savings will be practised on uneconomical lines.[47]

The consultants reckoned that the plan could be produced for only £1000 and that once available, and with a modest approach to implementation, it would actually help to reduce the rates. As another benefit the plan would be a means for collaboration with the government and educational bodies in replanning the central area. It would also help in the attraction of more industries, while ensuring that such firms were located so as to do no harm to the economic value of Edinburgh's amenities and the city's tourist industry.

The consultants also suggested that the corporation's earlier planning schemes had covered areas that were too small. They noted that a further scheme had recently been prepared, for Craigentinny and Duddingston and they had themselves prepared the Granton–Cramond Scheme. They now proposed four further large-scale planning schemes. These were for Gogar–Corstorphine (5900 acres, including 1090 outside the city boundary) in the west; Colinton (5600 acres) in the south-west; Liberton–Gilmerton (5600 acres) in the south-east; and Newcraighall (4460 acres, including 3388 acres outside the boundary) in the east. Thus the built-up area should be swathed by six planning schemes in a horseshoe shape from the Forth shoreline. Successive planning committees and burgh engineers had agreed the need to plan these urban fringe areas. The consultants advised that work on these schemes should be deferred if the corporation opted to prepare the advisory plan, but otherwise early action should be taken to commence the planning of the remaining four schemes, without the co-operation of Midlothian County if need be.

Adams and his colleagues had observed that: 'Experience in Edinburgh shows that town planning operations may extend over very long periods, that they may be dealt with sporadically between other activities of the city.'[48] It can have been no surprise therefore that the council did not go ahead and commission an advisory plan for the city. Neither the ambition of the Mears proposals nor the pragmatism of Adams could shift the piecemeal and reactive style of planning that filled both the legislation and the political priorities of the council. The Craigentinny, Restalrig and Lochend Town Planning Scheme got final approval in 1931. In 1937 the Streets and Buildings Committee approved preparation of a Scheme for the south-east from Fairmilehead to Musselburgh, superseding the Abercorn Scheme and in 1938 the Granton–Cramond Scheme went to public inquiry.

One notable innovation had been the Scheme for Charlotte Square, which was approved in 1930. It essentially provided powers of negative control to protect a threatened Adam building and was the first scheme of its kind in Britain. For all that the change in name of the committee responsible for planning from Housing and Town Planning to Streets and Buildings says something about the shifting priorities associated with town planning in Edinburgh in the inter-war years.

The building boom

The built-up area of Edinburgh almost doubled in extent during the inter-war years. Abercrombie estimated that £38 million was put into development in the city over that time, with the peak in the middle 1930s when £3 million a year was being invested in the built environment by public and private bodies.[49] Given the permissive attitude to suburban planning controls, private builders and landowners were able to exert a major influence on the development pattern, just as they had in the nineteenth century. Building was one of the main growth sectors of the local economy in the decade from 1929 to 1939, and there were also substantial increases in employment in related sectors such as building engineering, trams and buses, and motor vehicle repairing. Building itself, with 10,600 employees in 1929 and 13,000 in 1939, was the major single employment category.[50] In some respects production of, rather than in, the city was more important as some of the traditional industries shed labour[51] and the increase in industrial employment lagged behind the average rate for Great Britain.[52]

Two key aspects of this Edinburgh building boom are worthy of comment. These are the dramatically increased availability of land for working-class housing and the strong links between the local authority and the private house builders.

The reluctance of landowners to feu sites for working-class housing development evaporated after the passing of the 1919 Act. Almost all the landowners around the city were contacted to see if they were prepared to sell their land to the corporation, and if so on what terms. Very few owners expressed reluctance or held out for high prices.[53] Smith suggested possible reasons for this abrupt change of attitude. There had been a long depression in the building industry which may eventually have driven down the expectations of the owners. Also valuation and acquisition were negotiated by the Valuation Office of the Board of Inland Revenue and the land had to be sold outright rather than feued. Smith suggests that the owners may have been reluctant to take on the government in these matters, and in effect settled for the best deal they could get.[54] The depressed state of agriculture and the wider investment opportunities becoming available may have been further influences, with landowners realizing the value of their assets and reinvesting elsewhere.

The corporation thus acquired considerable land reserves. Part of these were then feued to private builders for rented housing for lower to middle income groups. The builders also benefited from the reduced prices for development land. The increased availability of land also helped prominent building firms to assemble considerable land banks. Furthermore private building companies constructed the council houses on contract to the corporation.

During the 1930s a number of local building firms came to prominence. MacTaggart and Mickle Ltd were established in 1932, and developed in the Willowbrae area. In 1934 they bought sixteen acres at Pilton, which they fully developed over the next five years with housing for rent. In the same year they purchased ninety-four acres at Silverknowes, where they had sold 130 houses by 1939. A further fifty acres were bought at Blackhall, also in 1934, though only thirty houses had been sold there by 1939. Their major pre-war purchase was of 233 acres at Broomhouse in 1937, though this site was not developed until after the war.[55] This company explained their development strategy as follows: 'Our method of progressing with housing developments has always been to purchase farms on the perimeter of the built-up areas, and use the land according to public demand for the size and type of house suitable to each area.'[56]

James Miller and Partners Ltd were even more active. They were founded in 1934, though operations had in actual fact begun five years earlier through James Miller, the senior partner. By 1939 this firm had acquired seventy-two sites in Edinburgh, a total of 489 acres, their largest site being of fifty-one acres.[57] Both Miller's and MacTaggart and Mickle undertook work in association with Edinburgh Corporation.

Another local firm that started building houses in 1934 was A. Thain Ltd. They built bungalows in the Blackhall area with a local authority subsidy and then in Oxgangs. Edinburgh Corporation feued them land at Sighthill, where they built 500 flats. Though this latter scheme was not subsidized, the corporation financed the project, and laid down regulations about house types and rent levels.[58] Ford and Torrie, founded in 1928, built bungalows in the Craigentinny and Duddingston areas. For Edinburgh as a whole 43,471 dwellings were approved for construction by the Dean of Guild Court from 1918 to 1939.[59]

As well as encouraging private housing, Edinburgh Corporation had become landlord to around 15,000 council houses by the start of the war.[60] Over the same inter-war period Glasgow, a city with roughly twice the population of Edinburgh at that stage had built slightly over 50,000 council houses; Manchester and Liverpool had built 30,000 and 38,000 respectively.[61] Given the political situation within Edinburgh it is perhaps less relevant to ask why Edinburgh lagged behind the council house building rates for other cities, than to ask why it built so many. The sheer extent of housing need must have been a factor: Abercrombie's analysis after the war suggested that over a quarter of a million people were living in houses that were sanitarily sub-standard or unfit.[62]

The earliest council housing at Chesser and Northfield was in flats of two and three stories, using traditional Scottish building materials and providing gardens and open space. This was the housing praised by the Trades and Labour Council, though it was financially inaccessible to all but the better off workers. There was a considerable contrast in the quality of these early council estates built for the general needs of the working class and those later ones directed at slum clearance families. The Trades Council complained that the construction work was being skimped on these latter schemes[63] and the City Architect confessed that, '. . . owing to financial stress, some of the accessories like full community provisions and recreational areas proportional to the population were not available and all architectural treatment was starved.'[64]

Craigmillar, on the eastern periphery of the city, was one such scheme. The early tenancies were let to families relocated from the slum clearances in Leith and St Leonards. The development was planned for 8000 but by 1936 the population had reached 10,000. School provision fell behind targets;[65] the kirk fretted that in 1934 8000 souls existed there without a church or community facilities;[66] and there was criticism of the housing and general environment that resulted from attempts to economize on the development.[67] The Edinburgh Council of Social Service reported in 1936 that health facilities were totally inadequate; shops were too few, and expensive, and carried a limited range of goods; and that there was a dampness problem in the houses. The report put male unemployment in the area at 40 per cent. In addition, two classrooms detailed on plans for a Roman Catholic Primary School had been cut as an economy measure, so the school was instantly overcrowded and children had to travel out of the area for their schooling.

The inter-war building boom therefore extended and consolidated status divisions between housing areas. In particular the development of a stock of council houses brought fresh nuances of respectability and stigma within a working class who had previously shared more uniformly poor housing conditions within the private rented sector. Those rehoused from the slums on infill sites were still surrounded by industry and railways and lived at high densities. The more suburban rehousing schemes were usually close to the old tenement districts – Lochend, Prestonfield, Gorgie, Quarryholes, Piershill, Granton and Pilton. The exception was Niddrie in the Craigmillar area, a more truly peripheral location. Thus the low status council housing was predominantly in the north and east of the city, though most of the land purchased by the Edinburgh Corporation was in fact in the west and north-west. These western areas became the locations for the higher quality council estates, at Stenhouse, Saughton Mains, Chesser, Hutchinson, Saughtonhall and Sighthill. The 'aristocracy of labour', who could afford the higher rents and transport costs and who were perceived to be respectable and deserving tenants, moved to these areas. The only significant high status council development east of the centre was the early scheme at Willowbrae and Northfield, close to the amenity of Holyrood Park.

As the statement quoted earlier from MacTaggart and Mickle implied, the private builders also matched their perceptions of the amenity of the site to their house types and to the clients' means. Terraced houses or flats benefiting from the council subsidy and catering for the less well off end of the private market, were built mainly in the west, adjacent to the higher status council schemes. Further up the market the bungalows snaked out along the radial roads. The former villages that were swallowed in the urban spread became high status nodes, though the inter-war houses that fringed them were typically more modest than those of the pioneer Edwardian commuters. Colinton, Corstorphine and Duddingston are the most evident examples.

The building boom fundamentally altered the spatial scale of Edinburgh and also its texture. The high density city of 1918 was, by 1940, just the inner core, surrounded by commuter suburbs where the density rarely exceeded twelve houses to the acre in the owner-occupied areas. The extent and form of this inter-war development is shown in Figure 9. The building materials also changed: typically the new development was in bricks and harling, not stone, colouring the city a lighter grey. Thus the nascent environmental consumerism and the restructuring of production even in so tradition-bound an industry as building, began to make Edinburgh more amorphous, more standardized, more bland and less distinctively the Scottish capital. The production of the city thus threatened the ideology which sustained the relations of production within the city.

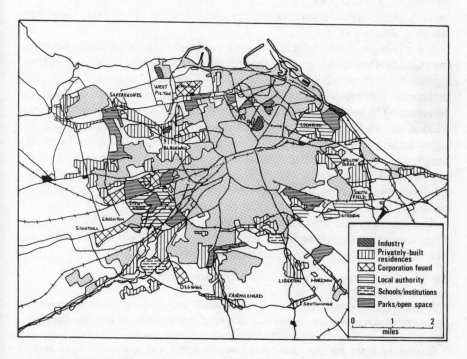

Figure 9   *The physical expansion of Edinburgh, 1919–1939*

The comprehensive planning ideology

The consequences of the suburban spread and the unresolved problems of the city centre created a chorus of calls for the preparation of a comprehensive city plan. A distinct body of public opinion developed around this theme in Edinburgh in the 1930s, in which professional architects and planners were to the fore. Thus Frank Mears was still reiterating his analysis and the proposals from his 1931 report to a luncheon of the Edinburgh City Business Club five years later.[68] John Begg, the President of the Royal Incorporation of Architects in Scotland, spoke of the possibilities for a new Edinburgh, with no slums, the railway out of Princes Street Gardens, the University coherently developed and an exhibition hall on the Waverley Station site.[69]

A major catalyst for the proponents of planning was the exhibition staged in the Edinburgh College of Art from 30 January until 6 March 1937, with the support of the Royal Scottish Society of Painters in Water-Colours. Drawings, diagrams and photographs were assembled by the post-graduates of the college who had worked on a survey of the city under the direction of W. T. Sutherland, R. H. Matthew, J. D. Carnegie and J. Galletly. The purpose of the exhibition was described by Matthew as being to draw public attention to the history and present condition of the city, and to: 'The urgent necessity for a comprehensive planning scheme, *prepared under expert guidance,* covering the whole area of the city, as the only method of safeguarding existing amenities, and of rectifying the serious planning blunders of the past.'[70]

The catalogue to the exhibition reiterated the critique consistently advanced from Geddes through Mears, that the ordered planning of the New Town marked a pinnacle from which *laissez-faire* industrialism had descended to create a haphazard and unsatisfactory environment, with the older areas degenerating into slums. The modern suburbs were mere 'building estates', unplanned in their relation to the whole and to one another and they had devoured valuable agricultural land and woodlands. The aesthetics of the bungaloid spread were also heavily criticized. The need for planning was urgent. The new suburbs needed to be connected by new roads, while the old town was still 'a hopeless muddle, with industry, slums and new working-class dwellings jostling and cramping the buildings, some of them new, of great public importance'.[71]

The catalogue also criticized the planning practice of Edinburgh Corporation. Their limited interpretation of the scope and nature of planning was contrasted with the possibilities of comprehensive planning:

Any planning schemes undertaken have been fragmentary, and therefore unsatisfactory.

A small area at Craigentinny has been 'planned' and planning has been interpreted as the laying down of main roadways and zoning certain areas for housing, but the imagination necessary for successful large-scale planning has been absent.

Charlotte Square has been preserved from vandalism and pious resolutions have been passed to plan large, unbuilt areas on the western fringes of the city.

Planning to be effective, must be comprehensive but no such plan for the whole
city has yet been proposed.
The basis of all sound planning is the preparation of a complete survey of the city.
This survey would cover the method of growth, scenery, topography, the nature and
direction of traffic, distribution of industry, housing, historical buildings etc., and in
fact the study of every aspect of present-day conditions and activities.
With this survey completed, and only on the basis of this information, can planning
be attempted, and only then under the guidance of the expert trained in this complicated
and highly specialized art of civic planning.
Planning without knowledge is useless and wasteful, but planning with knowledge
and inspiration, means order and beauty and may regain that pride of civic dignity
that was Edinburgh's and is surely worthy of this twentieth-century capital of
Scotland.[72]

These planners therefore saw that town planning could be something quite
different from the existing practice. Their critique drew its strength and credibility
from the fact that the production of the city was degrading the historic
environment and thereby denying the continuity of a classless symbol of national
identity fashioned by men of genius. Likewise the emergent urban form did represent
an irrational exploitation of natural resources. Yet the core of the planners' credo
was that change was possible without any political struggle; it did not even require
the public ownership of land. All that was necessary was a full civic survey and an
expert planner, a highly technocratic prescription.

Pending the introduction of comprehensive planning, the planners urged the
Town Council to use the Restriction of Ribbon Development Act and the 1932
Planning Act to effect control over development as quickly as possible. However,
John Begg was at pains to stress that their criticisms were not aimed solely at the
council, but at the people of Edinburgh as a whole.[73]

While the exhibition was running in the Art College, the Women Citizens'
Association and the local branch of the National Council of Women staged a
major public meeting on town planning. The public bodies present give some
insight into the constellation of interests involved in the debate about planning in
Edinburgh at that time. As well as the Department of Health for Scotland, there
were several professional bodies linked to town planning. These were the Town
Planning Institute's Scottish Branch, the Edinburgh Architectural Association,
the Royal Incoporation of Architects in Scotland and the Scottish Housing and
Town Planning Committee. There were also the environmental and amenity
pressure groups with strong ties to the planning profession, notably the Outlook
Tower, the National Trust for Scotland and the Cockburn Association. Other
pressure groups included national antiquarian bodies – the Society of Antiquaries
of Scotland, the St Andrews Society and the Old Edinburgh Club. Edinburgh
College of Art, Edinburgh University and the Educational Institute of Scotland
might be classed as educational bodies, though the College and the University
were also significant landowners in the central part of the city and the college was
also a part of the professional architecture and planning lobby. Other property

interests were also represented – the Scottish Land and Property Federation, the Scottish Estate Factors Society and the Edinburgh Merchants' Company. The Rotary Club and the Trades and Labour Council made up the list.[74] Of them all, only the last named might seriously be described as a working-class organization.

Lady Leslie Mackenzie, CBE, presided. Sir William Whyte, OBE, SSC, Secretary to the Scottish Housing and Town Planning Committee, explained the basis of town planning. It was about creating orderliness, amenity and convenience, securing proper sanitary arrangements, and protecting buildings of architectural and historic interest. He told the audience that proper planning could save money in the long run and protect property values. He also advocated the preparation of national and regional plans, though only ten planning schemes had been finally approved in Scotland by the time of the conference. Sir William attributed this paucity of statutory planning to the local authorities' involvement in providing houses.[75]

Speakers criticized Edinburgh Corporation for its failure to plan the city. However, the chairman of the Streets and Buildings Commitee, Councillor John Hay, defended their record. He explained the lack of planning by the demands made on the authority by council house provision. He claimed that the council 'kept an observant eye on the developments in Edinburgh', but he added that they had allowed the spread of the bungalows because there was clearly a public demand for that housing.[76]

The council's planning and development strategy was more forcibly defended by the Lord Provost, Sir Louis Gumley (the proprietor of a major estate agency in the city), at a speech to the Edinburgh and District Master Plumbers' Association. The Lord Provost said:

Some of our buildings are not, perhaps, beautiful, but if we had not had the bungalows we would have been short of very many happy households. People cannot afford to pay £1,000 to £1,500 for a house, whereas they are very happy in their £400 or £500 bungalows. I hope some more builders will come forward to build them.[77]

In the same speech the Lord Provost opposed the idea of an outer ring road on the grounds that it would divert custom from the city's shops.

Nevertheless the professionals continued their attacks. Robert Hurd castigated the 'architectural chaos' and the erosion of the unity of design in the New Town, in a speech to the Saltire Society and the Edinburgh University Fine Arts Society. He argued that a plan was needed for the city as a whole so as to harmonize development.[78] Even the Church entered the arguments. The Reverend Percival-Prescott told the Buccleuch Evangelical Church that it was folly to leave town planning to councillors whose one outstanding virtue was that they received a few more votes than anyone else. Give the job instead to the students of the Edinburgh College of Art, he urged![79]

There were also critics within the council. Councillor Thomas Murray (Labour) told the 1937 Women Citizens' Association conference on planning that 'conflicting private interests were so strong that it was completely impossible to conceive of a comprehensive planning scheme for Edinburgh'.[80] Another critic from a rather different perspective was Lord Nigel Douglas-Hamilton. On the floor of the council he attacked the complacency of the Streets and Buildings Committee, and their bankruptcy of ideas. Describing himself as 'an advocate of speed', he pressed for major new road building, including an outer by-pass in anticipation of an eventual Forth Road Bridge.[81]

Likewise the Edinburgh Chamber of Commerce favoured a more interventionist stance by the local authority as a means of modernization and industrial promotion. J. Graham Downes, their president, told a luncheon of the Edinburgh City Business Club that industry and commerce had not flourished in the city so well as they might have done. He complained that not enough effort was being made to attract and promote industry. He argued that not all municipal expenditure was bad, some should be viewed as an investment, whereas 'A timid, hesitating cheese-paring policy has been adopted'.[82]

The debate about planning was therefore essentially a debate among the city's *bourgeoisie*. On the one hand there stood those who saw planning as a means to promote the modernization of the city and to strengthen industrial capital. These included the Merchants' Company in their 1919 report, the Chamber of Commerce and individuals such as Lord Douglas-Hamilton. Their failure to make significant headway reflected the weakness of industrial capital within Edinburgh relative to other middle class interests. This group were aided by those professionals who had a direct interest in promoting planning, the architects and planners themselves, and by those organizations and individuals dedicated to preserving the historic, unifying and national image of the city, or whose aesthetic sensibilities were offended by the brash commercialism of the bungalows, a foreign building style in alien materials. Among this group were those who were or who believed themselves to be, in the Scottish national elite within the city. They did carry some influence, not least in their ability to sustain their propaganda through the press.

In opposition to stronger and more extensive planning stood the building contractors and landowners. They were supported by the city council, with which they enjoyed strong and direct links through prominent local politicians such as Sir Louis Gumley. In this period municipal politics were dominated by the Edinburgh Progressive Association, who described their members as being 'drawn from all walks of life, holding various political views, excepting Socialist and Communist'.[83] The Conservatives did not contest local elections and the Progressives also drew support from National Liberals. The Progressives' main policy was to keep down rates, a stance which they believed to be non-political. This then was the other face of *bourgeois* Edinburgh, whose calculating individual interest and commercially oriented sensibilities set them against the notions being peddled by the town planning lobby.

There is less evidence of any vibrant working-class involvement in the planning debate. After the Trades Council's early concerns for planning, energies were focussed on the narrower issue of council housing for much of the time. Nor do the city's major financial institutions appear to have been direct parties to the debate, though they must have played a role in funding the major investment in the built environment which characterized the inter-war years. Other prominent Edinburgh-based institutions such as the University were involved primarily as private landowners, protecting their own development interests.

The legislation passed by central government delimited the context within which town planning took place, and their manipulation of housing subsidies and direction of housing expenditures clearly had a very significant impact on the provision of council housing; and indeed, the boom in the private sector also. Throughout the inter-war years there appears to have been little difference of opinion on planning and urban development between the Edinburgh City Council and the government in London. Thus, when Edinburgh initiated local legislation to facilitate controls, it was in a form acceptable to parliament. The only controversies were generated not by the central state as arbitrator, but as developer.

The planning of inter-war Edinburgh thus reflected the broad national pattern, but with nuances and detail fashioned by the particular class structure of the city. The antagonisms latent in social production of the public place, the city, for the private expropriation of value, surfaced in issues which those calling for planning frequently addressed – the irrationality of the new environment, the destruction of agricultural land, the threats to historic buildings, and so on. Other manifestations of that same contradiction such as overcrowding, an acute shortage of good housing for most of the working population, the lack of facilities in the slum clearance schemes, were less frequently aired by the planning lobby.

Thus between 1900 and 1940 there developed in Edinburgh a significant gap between the practice and the ideology of town planning. It was the latter which commanded attention because its critique had some relevance, and was promoted by a powerful section of the civil society. The bulk of the enormous urban expansion and of the significant changes within the built-up areas, took place within 'flexible' and 'broad brush' planning controls. Planning was practised as a reactive means of avoiding the worst excesses of development decisions and as a way of more expeditiously servicing sites for new development by public and private agencies. Alongside, and as a critique of that practice, developed the idea of comprehensive planning as a means to orderly, harmonious development. This embodied both a forceful articulation of the technical nature of the planning process and a prescription of a particular urban form. Town planning was depicted as pre-eminently a technical and expert activity, dependent on exhaustive survey, which would then lead to a rational choice of plan. The rationality came from the information, not from any necessary change in social and property relationships. Such planning would subsequently sweep away the low-class bad housing around the city centre and the dirty, old-fashioned factories and workshops in such areas. Space would thus be freed for offices, tourists and civic splendour. A ring road would circumscribe the core. Beyond would be a residential area, close to, but sanitized by, a park belt from a factory zone where industry could produce on efficient, modern lines. The city would be girdled by an agricultural and horticultural belt, a source of fresh vegetables and a visual end to the urban area. Beyond would be properly functioning satellite towns.[84]

The advocates of planning were most frequently arguing their case against those interests favouring minimal local government activity and defending private property. This is probably the reason why the planners were so consistently insistent that their proposals in fact supported property rights and were a means to reduce public expenditure. The planning lobby never appears to have been pressed to defend this position against attacks from the Left. Issues such as the class nature of private land ownership, the segregation of housing areas, the equity of replacing low-rent housing by roads, the case for town planning to redistribute wealth rather than to create wealth, never entered the debate. The failure of the central demand, for an overall city plan, was interpreted as a failure of imagination among elected members, a piece of muddled thinking. That interpretation compounded the technocratic and class nature of the ideology. As Councillor Murray had noted, there was no comprehensive plan for Edinburgh because the conflicting private interests were so strong.

References and notes

1   P. Geddes, 'The Civic Survey of Edinburgh', in *The Transactions of the Town Planning Conference* (Royal Institute of British Architects 1910), p. 563.

2   Ibid.

3   Ibid., p. 574.

4   Edinburgh & District Trades and Labour Council, *47th Annual Report* (1914).

5   Ibid. At this time acquisition and demolition costs could amount to £20,000 an acre.

6   Edinburgh Merchant Company, *Report of a Special Committee on the Building Trade in Edinburgh* (1918), p. 3. The Merchants' Company, themselves major landowners, attributed this collapse to inflated building costs, but all the evidence points to the practice of landowners as being the crucial factor. See, for example, Scottish Land Enquiry Committee, 1914, *Scottish Land: Report of the Committee* and the *Report of the Royal Commission on the Housing of the Industrial Population of Scotland* (1917).

7   Edinburgh & District Trades and Labour Council, 1914.

8   P. J. Smith, 'Rural interests in the physical expansion of Edinburgh', in J. V. Minghi (ed.), *The Geographer and the Public Environment*, B. C. Geographical Series, No. 7, Occasional Papers in Geography (Tantalus Research Ltd 1966), p. 61.

9   Ibid.

10   Edinburgh & District Trades and Labour Council, *51st Annual Report* (1918), p. 16.

11   Edinburgh & District Trades and Labour Council, *Our Unseen City*

Revealed: A Tale of Housing Atrocities. Report on conditions revealed by the 1921 report of the Medical Officer of Health (undated), p. 7.

12   The Merchants' Company of the City of Edinburgh, *Report of a Select Committee of the Company on the Development of Edinburgh,* (Edinburgh 1919), p. 6. The committee was chaired by an architect, Mr T. P. Marwick.
13   Ibid., p. 10.
14   Ibid., p. 13.
15   Ibid., p. 13. This sentiment sounds very like some in the report of the Planning Advisory Group, which appeared almost half a century later.
16   Ibid., p. 14.
17   Ibid., p. 12.
18   Ibid., p. 14.
19   Ibid., p. 49.
20   Ibid., p. 39.
21   Ibid., pp. 27–8. Once again there are parallels between these ideas from 1919 and more recent 'innovations' such enterprise zones and urban development corporations.
22   Ibid., p. 37.
23   The figures quoted on page 55 of the Merchants' Company Report are: Edinburgh 71.85*d* in the £, Leith 79.45*d*, Dundee 90.6*d*, Greenock 91.31*d*, Aberdeen 92.31*d* and Glasgow 106.92*d*.
24   See A. Grierson, 'Reconstruction Problems', *Report by the Town Clerk to Edinburgh Corporation* (1919).
25   W. A. Macartney, 'Town planning in Edinburgh from the eighteenth to the twentieth century – and its lessons', *Journal of the Town Planning Institute,* vol. XV, no. 1 (1928), p. 37.
26   See T. B. Whitson, 'Discussion', *Journal of the Town Planning Institute,* vol. XV, no. 1 (1928), p. 25. Councillor Whitson was a former convenor of the Housing and Town Planning Committee.
27   One Improvement Scheme was prepared for part of the Canongate in 1922, another for an area in Leith in 1924, and these were followed in 1927 by schemes at the Canongate, Corstorphine and St Leonards. There was a further scheme in St Leonards in 1929, and over twenty small ones in the 1930s.
28   F. Harris, Address following F. Mears's paper to the Town Planning Institute meeting in Edinburgh, *Journal of the Town Planning Institute,* vol. XV, no. 1 (1928), p. 18. Councillor Harris was the convenor of the Housing and Town Planning Committee at the time.
29   T. Adams, L. Thompson and M. Fry, *Report on the plan for the development of the Granton–Cramond Area,* Report to Edinburgh Corporation (1930), p. 3.
30   See the comments of Harris and of Macartney, *Journal of the Town Planning Institute,* vol. XV, no. 1 (1928), p. 18 and p. 37 respectively.
31   Macartney suggested that the Town Clerk was the originator of the

legislation, and there seems no reason to dispute this. See Macartney, 1928, p. 37. In operating the legislation the corporation was assisted by an Advisory Committee of four, whose members were the appointees of the Secretary of State for Scotland, the Royal Scottish Academy, the Royal Incorporation of Architects in Scotland and the corporation itself.

32 Letter from Mears to Provost Whitson, 1930, in Mears Manuscripts, Edinburgh Room, Central Library, Edinburgh.

33 The article appeared in *The Scotsman*, 28 July 1928.

34 G Bruce, *Some practical good: The Cockburn Association – 100 years participation in planning*, (The Cockburn Association 1975), p. 45.

35 Letter from Mears to Provost Whitson.

36 F. C. Mears 'The City of Edinburgh: Preliminary suggestions for consideration by the representative committee in regard to the development and replanning of the central area of the city in relation to public buildings' (1931), p. 5.

37 Ibid., p. 4.

38 Ibid., p. 9.

39 Mears had himself been involved in restoring the sixteenth-century Huntley House on the Canongate a few years earlier.

40 F. C. Mears, (1931), p. 15.

41 Ibid., p. 16.

42 Ibid., p. 16.

43 Ibid., p. 16.

44 T. Adams, L. Thompson and M. Fry, *Final Report on Town Planning, City and Royal Burgh of Edinburgh* (1931), p. 6.

45 Ibid., p. 3.

46 Ibid., p. 5.

47 Ibid., p. 7.

48 Ibid., p. 8.

49 P. Abercrombie and D. Plumstead, *A Civic Survey & Plan for Edinburgh* (Oliver & Boyd 1949), Appendix I.

50 Ibid., p. 97.

51 Industries, recording a decline in insured workers from 1929 to 1939 were hosiery, footwear, general engineering, shipbuilding, stationery, printing, glass, contracting, railways, road transport, shipping and docks. The data is given in Abercrombie and Plumstead, (1949), p. 97.

52 P. Abercrombie and D. Plumstead (1949), p. 22.

53 P. J. Smith, (1966), p. 62.

54 Ibid., p. 62.

55 H. M. Bingham, 'Land Hoarding in Edinburgh', Unpublished MSc. Thesis, Heriot-Watt University/Edinburgh College of Art (1974), pp. 108–10.

56 Statement given to Bingham, and quoted on pp. 107–8.

57 H. M. Bingham, p. 115.

58   J. R. Kaucz, 'Residential Location: The application of the social physics model and the behavioural model to Edinburgh', Unpublished MSc. Thesis, Department of Town & Country Planning, Heriot-Watt University/Edinburgh College of Art (1976), para. 3.5.1.

59   P. Abercrombie and D. Plumstead (1949), p. 18.

60   Abercrombie and Plumstead put the figure at 15,142 (p. 18). D. Keir (ed). 'The City of Edinburgh', *The Third Statistical Account of Scotland,* vol. XV, (Collins 1966), gives a figure of 14,816 permanent houses, p. 384.

61   These figures are quoted in M. Broady and J. Mack, Administrative Problems and Social Development', unpublished manuscript (undated), p. 8.

62   P. Abercrombie and D. Plumstead (1949), p. 88.

63   See, for example, the Edinburgh and District Trades and Labour Council, *65th Annual Report* (1932).

64   E. J. Macrae, 'Historical Review', in P. Abercrombie and D. Plumstead (1949), p. 15.

65   Annual Report of the Edinburgh Education Committee, 1933.

66   *The Scotsman,* 11 April 1934.

67   *Edinburgh Evening News*, 18 January 1934. Also the Cockburn Association Annual Report, 1933.

68   Reported in *The Scotsman,* 2 Dec. 1936.

69   *The Scotsman*, 10 June 1933.

70   'Town Planning Exhibition: Explanatory and Historical Notes and Catalogue of Exhibits', Royal Scottish Society of Painters in Water-Colours (1937), p. 1.

71   Ibid., p. 3.

72   Ibid., pp. 3–4.

73   *The Scotsman*, 13 Feb. 1937.

74   The participating organizations of the Conference were listed in *The Scotsman,* 24 Feb. 1937. The paper carried two reports of the Conference: a brief one by a woman journalist, and a long one by a male.

75   *The Scotsman,* 24 Feb. 1937.

76   Ibid.

77   *Edinburgh Dispatch,* 8 Jan. 1938.

78   *Scottish Daily Express*, 15 Feb. 1939. The Saltire Society is a body concerned with Scottish artistic and cultural life, thus again expressing a Scottish national identity, a theme with which Hurd himself sympathised.

79   *Evening Dispatch*, 13 Jan., 1938. The college began a planning course in 1932. Frank Mears was prominently involved. For an account of the course in the late 1930s see J. Walkden, 'Notes on the work of the Department of Town Planning, Edinburgh School of Architecture, Edinburgh College of Art', *Journal of the Town Planning Institute* (March-April 1940), pp. 85–91.

80   *The Scotsman,* 24 Feb. 1937.

81   *The Scotsman,* 7 Jan. 1938.

82   *Edinburgh Evening News,* 3 Nov. 1937.
83   J. P. Mackintosh, 'The city's politics', in D. Keir (ed.) (1966). p. 313.
84   Probably the fullest articulation of this vision was given in a letter from 'Zar', published in *The Scotsman,* 1 Nov. 1933.

6 The arrival (and departure) of the expert planner

The years during and immediately after the Second World War are often seen as the 'golden age' of British town planning. Planning as the regulation of private initiatives in suburban expansion was seemingly transformed into planning for national reconstruction. For the first time town planning seemed to be a major arm of a new, more egalitarian approach to social policy. Town planners became charismatic figures, men of vision whose expert designs would usher in the New Jerusalem. Then the early 1950s saw these hopes dashed. Planning was just an appendage of the local government bureaucracy, presiding over the spread of subtopia and wirescape. The planner had been reduced to a mere administrator.

Part One of this book tried to interpret the adoption of the planning ideology by the state during war time as a reflection of a changed balance of inter- and intra-class forces. However, it was argued that the extended state intervention in urban development was in a form that could not resolve the contradictions; rather, it predicated their re-emergence in a distorted form within the planning system. The consequent gap between the rhetoric and practice of town planning created both public antagonism and also an incipient crisis of motivation within the profession itself.

The working out of these national tendencies within Edinburgh was particularly fascinating. On the one hand, there was already a well-developed, articulate and influential lobby within the city before the war urging the practice of comprehensive planning. On the other hand, the city did not suffer the bomb damage which hastened planned reconstruction in other cities and facilitated the associated modernization. Furthermore, town planning in Edinburgh continued to be administered by the same officials whose attitudes had so frustrated Frank Mears in the 1920s and 1930s. Similarly the political scene continued to be controlled by the Progressives, in whose eyes the passing of town planning legislation by a socialist government in London might be seen as an irrelevance if not as something to be treated with suspicion.

This then was the cauldron in which Edinburgh's planning practice was stirred. The changing balance of class power and the associated concern to reimpose social control led to a new flirtation with comprehensive planning. In this endeavour the corporation were prodded by central government. Sir Patrick Abercrombie, the archetypal planning figure of the age, came to express the ideology of comprehensive planning through one of his great master plans, but, in the specific conditions of the time and place the ideology floundered. Instead, statutory planning practice was reasserted on the reactive and incremental model of the past.

Once again the case study can reveal something of the empirical detail behind broad national developments. In reviewing the period from the war to the approval of the first Development Plan, this chapter reveals how and why the ideology of planning was contradicted by the practice. It notes the origins of the problems of rationality and legitimacy which were later to so dominate town planning and are themselves the focus of the following chapter.

Reassertion of social control: the new acceptance of planning

Before the Second World War the Edinburgh Town Council had consistently set their face against any comprehensive planning of the city. Not even the entreaties of Thomas Adams, that such planning would be a way of cutting spending in a rational manner, were sufficiently enticing. However, once an allied victory began to appear likely the council began to face up to the uncertainties of the peace. On 6 May 1943 they set up an Advisory Committee on City Development. A motion that there should be three councillors on the committee received only eight votes.[1] Instead it was made up of a trio of distinguished citizens. Its chairman was J. L. Clyde, KC (later Lord Clyde), with the other two members Sir Thomas Whitson, the former Lord Provost who had been prominently associated with town planning from the 1920s and Sir Donald Pollock, the rector of Edinburgh University.

Their task was to prepare the ground for a plan, rather than to actually produce one. Their brief implied a recognition of the inevitability of post-war redevelopment and a concern with the threat thereby posed to the historic city. Their terms of reference were:

To report upon the general considerations governing the development and redevelopment of the City as the Capital of Scotland and the preparation of planning schemes in relation thereto. In particular to survey the influences which have tended to the creation of the existing character of the City and its place in the national and local administration, the extent to which these influences are still operative and the circumstances and considerations which now exist and which may be anticipated to arise; to consult with persons and bodies whose activities and interests may be associated with the development and redevelopment of the City; and to make recommendations thereanent.[2]

Some impression of the reasons why planning had gained a new acceptability, and of the interests pressing for planning, can be gained by studying those who responded to the committee's invitation to put forward views and by analysing the report itself. Over 150 individuals wrote to the committee and Clyde and his colleagues considered that the response was representative and revealed a large measure of agreement on what should be done.[3] A crude measure of the representativeness of the respondents can be gained from their addresses, as shown in Table 9.

Table 9   *Addresses of letters to the Advisory Committee on City Development, 1943*

Address by area	Number of responses
New Town	25
Middle-class suburb	57
Working-class areas	30
House of Commons (MPs)	6
Other	25

Source: Report of the Advisory Committee, Appendix I, pp. 39–41.

Note: The author has assigned addresses to areas in the following manner:
'Middle-class suburbs' are defined as addresses in Cramond, Trinity, Merchiston, Morningside, Colinton, Liberton, Blacket, Bruntsfield, Marchmont, Corstorphine, Joppa, and Ravelston.
'Working-class areas' are defined as addresses in Wardie, Inch, Stenhouse, South Side, Saughton, Dalry and Leith.
'Other' are mainly addresses outside Edinburgh, or no address, and also include servicemen.
There was also one more address within Edinburgh which could not be traced.

This analysis of the individual respondents is clearly rough and ready and probably overestimates some categories. Nevertheless it does show both the relative significance of the expression of opinion from the New Town and also that there was pressure from working-class areas for planning.

As well as individuals various organizations put in views and these have been grouped in Table 10.

Table 10   *Organizations making representation to the Advisory Committee on City Development, 1943*

Group	Organization
Finance, industry and landowners	Barnton, Sauchie and Bannockburn Estates. Committee of Scottish Bank General Managers. Company of Merchants of Edinburgh*. Edinburgh Chamber of Commerce and Manufacturers. Edinburgh and District Master Builders Association. Granton Harbour Ltd. Leith Chamber of Commerce. Leith Dock Commission. Multiple Shops Federation. National Federation of Business and Professional Women's Clubs.

* This body could also be included under the 'educational' grouping.

Group	Organization
The legal profession	Faculty of Advocates. Society of Solicitors in the Supreme Courts of Scotland. Society of Writers to His Majesty's Signet.
Artistic bodies	Edinburgh Film Guild. Edinburgh School of Speech Training and Dramatic Art. National Galleries of Scotland. Royal Scottish Academy. Royal Scottish Society of Arts. Royal Scottish Society of Painters in Water-Colours. Scottish Community Drama Association, South-East Division. Scottish Modern Arts Association. Scottish Society of Women Artists.
Educational bodies	Edinburgh College of Art. Educational Institute of Scotland. Heriot-Watt College. Royal College of Surgeons. Royal Society of Edinburgh. Society for Teaching the Blind to Read. Students of Edinburgh College of Art. University of Edinburgh.
Amenity interests	Cockburn Association. Colinton Amenity Association. Edinburgh Architectural Association. Light Railway Transport League. National Trust for Scotland. Outlook Tower. Old Edinburgh Club. Scottish Youth Hostel Association. Society of Antiquaries of Scotland.
Working-class interests	Edinburgh and District Trades and Labour Council. Electrical Association of Women. Scottish Council of National Labour Organization. St Leonards Flower and Allotment Association. Saughtonhall Social and Athletic Association.
Other	Blackhall Ratepayers Association. Edinburgh Council of Social Service. Edinburgh Women Citizens' Association. The Guildery of Edinburgh. Presbytery of Edinburgh. The Scottish Convention. Scottish National Party. Society of Friends. Women's Pension League.

Source: The organizations are listed in Appendix II in the report of the committee, pp. 42–3.

The persistence of the pre-war planning lobby, comprising professional, artistic and amenity interests was therefore evident. However, the representation of finance and industry was stronger, and there continued to be a notable number of women's groups involved in the discussions about planning.

Exhibitions were held during the summer of 1943, under the auspices of the corporation, College of Art and Edinburgh Architectural Association. Thus the local authority was directly co-operating with those bodies that had been so critical of its pre-war planning performance, though they still did not necessarily share the same perspective. Opening the exhibition at the National Galleries, Frank Mears expressed the view that Edinburgh was on the threshold of a great adventure. There should be no more complacency. He prophesied, 'a noble ring road bounding the city on the south and west, a real green belt, not yards, but miles wide, with cornfields, market gardens and dairy farming', and the agricultural villages could be revived. The Lord Provost, Sir William Darling, put a rather different emphasis on the choice to be made. He drew attention to the prospect of major coal mining development close to the city; this was unlikely to create 'a graceful attribute'. He urged that Edinburgh's citizens should consider what kind of city they wanted; 'one developed on the industrial plan or on the plan of a great capital city'.[4]

While anxiety about industrial development was to the forefront of the Lord Provost's mind, the views of the city's existing industrialists were very fully articulated by the Edinburgh Chamber of Commerce and Manufacturers. They pressed for a more positive strategy towards industrial development. At the same time they argued that everything possible should be done to keep Edinburgh's reputation as a historic and romantic city. They therefore called for a planned industrial estate on the edge of the city. They identified possible sites at Corstorphine/Gorgie/Slateford in the west, the Abbeyhill/Portobello area in the north-east and at Granton/Craigleith in the north. They wanted houses for workers to be provided close to these estates, but opposed 'colonies of workers employed in the same factory being closely associated', citing the example of the 'general culture' of mining communities as the reason for their embargo.[5]

The Chamber favoured a green belt around Edinburgh and redevelopment of the slum areas, including the removal of traffic bottlenecks. They wanted new roads, in particular an east–west link from Haymarket through the Grassmarket and Cowgate to Holyrood Park. They supported strict planning control on the urban fringe and in the city centre, but opposed the development of satellite towns while there was still land available within the city. The Chamber also recognized the need for action on housing, not least to help those afflicted by one of the curses of the age, the shortage of servants:

In view of the shortage of domestic assistance which may possibly still exist after the war, serious consideration should be given to the provision of suites of apartments for the middle classes, where there would be a common dining room, and domestic assistance readily available under supervision of trained and efficient staff.[6]

A review of the Advisory Committee's report casts further light on the interests pushing the local authority towards a greater intervention in the process of urban development. The three men had met with the Secretary of State for Scotland and decided that, for Edinburgh, 1943 was nothing less than 'a rendez-vous with destiny'.[7] They sought to 'preserve the essential unity of the city', while tackling the housing and industrial problems that were caused by 'unregulated expansion in all directions'.[8]

The suspension of the building programme since 1939 meant there would be a 'formidable housing problem to be tackled' after the war. Early adoption of a definite policy could save time and money.[9] They estimated that there was an absolute shortage of some 10,000 houses, and it was 'unthinkable' that men should return from the front to find themselves homeless in their own city.[10] Fortunately the corporation owned sufficient land within the boundaries to meet this scale of need. Over and above this, however, was the need to replace overcrowded and slum housing. Even though Edinburgh had the lowest proportion of overcrowded houses of the four Scottish cities redevelopment and modernization of obsolete houses would need to be planned.

New industries would also be needed to insure against 'booms and slumps in trade'.[11] The Advisory Committee repeated the views put by the Chamber of Commerce and recommended that the local authority should provide industrial estates: 'the principal attraction of an industrial estate lies in the relief which it affords from the capital expenditure in erecting a factory, which is so serious a deterrent to an new venture'.[12] The success of the industrial estates was central to the committee's whole development strategy and the class compromise that underpinned it. They were opposed to the compulsory purchase of existing industrial premises, on the grounds that it was costly and against the interests of industry. They therefore sought to encourage the voluntary relocation of firms to the suburbs, so that redevelopment could be effectively carried through in the old areas where housing and industry were intermixed. Furthermore, the clearance of unfit housing would in any case reduce the pool of locally available labour in the old industrial areas, while also leaving the relocated workers without local employment, unless jobs could also be suburbanized. Planned and subsidized decentralization of housing and industry was therefore thought to be essential both to secure efficient production and to maintain social harmony.

One sector where growth was anticipated was tourism. The committee recommended that hotels and restaurants should be developed and the historic areas of the city preserved. They also floated the idea that the staging of good class concerts could draw in more tourists. Realization of the city's culture as a commodity therefore again required town planning.

Modernization of the road system was another essential. To improve the economic viability of the Leith Docks, a new western and a south-eastern approach was approved. The road from the south-east was to follow, in part, the route from Leith Walk to the Pleasance that Mears had advocated in his report in 1931. It was suggested that this road might run in tunnels through the ridges of the city centre, thus concealing the road and saving on the costs of land acquisition.[13] An outer ring road was also proposed.

Mears's three Miles were also given special attention. The Advisory Committee strongly favoured redevelopment of the south side area, so that the whole of Edinburgh University could be developed on a unified site. For the 'business mile' of the New Town, tighter planning controls were urged, together with the conversion of large houses into flats because of the 'servant problem'.[14] For Princes Street they recommended a competition to prepare a design guide for the frontages. Likewise a complete survey of the Old Town was called for to safeguard the historic buildings. To ensure the continued vitality of that mile, Clyde and his colleagues recommended that all local government offices should be concentrated around the City Chambers and that other buildings should be used for the headquarters of various historical, antiquarian and professional societies.

Over the city as a whole great emphasis was given to the creation of 'communities', self-contained in areas bounded by major transport routes. Each would have its own shops, industry, open space and recreation facilities. Wherever possible, nursery schools, child welfare clinics and gymnasia would be provided and accommodation for youth organizations. Above all there would be a hall and a community centre, to encourage community spirit. Here was the antidote to the haphazard dormitory growth. Similar considerations prompted Clyde, Whitson and Pollock to recommend a ceiling of half a million on the growth of the city as a whole. They felt that beyond that threshold it would cease to be 'a unity' and that the scale would mean that control would pass from elected members to technical officers.[15] They therefore argued against satellite towns, favouring instead the creation of self-contained communities adjacent to existing settlements beyond the green belt. A contemporary commentator suggested that the experience of the big peripheral housing schemes built by the council in the 1930s turned the committee against the fashionable idea of satellites: 'Welfare workers in new housing schemes have discovered there, among the artificially created communities, the lack of a sense of social responsibility that the same people had formerly retained although living in deplorable housing conditions'.[16] Considerations of social control and the reproduction of existing social relations within a context that threatened rapid change were therefore integral to the new role which the rulers of the city were according to town planning.

There can also be no doubt that the report was precipitated to some extent by central government's developing acceptance of planning. The report notes:

there is much talk in these days of Planning, and of Planning Experts. Some say that nothing is to be gained by Edinburgh considering its own development, since the Planner will lay down and determine where development is to go, that the Government will fix where industry is to be established and where housing is needed, and that, if Edinburgh will just wait, it will get its proper share in the general scheme.[17]

The committee opposed such passivity and said there was no need to wait for decisions on Barlow, Scott and Uthwatt before planning Edinburgh. Significantly they were anxious that the style of planning adopted in the city should stop short of the ideals of the evangelists: 'Fired with enthusiasm for the new science of planning they lay aside all financial considerations, they urge the adoption of "the broad view", they talk of "aiming high", and they recommend the approval of idealistic and often revolutionary proposals, which they fondly hope can be realised fifty or a hundred years hence.'[18]

Revolution was not on Edinburgh's agenda. Clyde and his colleagues divined that planning could never control the future, 'unless we are to become a country of robots'.[19] Instead they put forward a pragmatic middle course – acceptance of the need for planning but that planning to be firmly the result of deliberations by the trusted City Council, not any Planning Expert of central government. To this end almost all the recommendations of their report could be achieved through the existing legislation. However, the report advised the corporation to act quickly and to monitor progress every three years.

The report was well received. Clyde, Pollock and Whitson were rewarded with silver quaichs from the council, and the Lord Provost praised them for bringing planning down to earth.[20] The adjustment of the ideology of comprehensive planning to fit the more cautious development ambitions of the council was their real success. One dissenting note was struck by T. Forbes MacLennan of the Edinburgh Architectural Association. In a letter published in *The Scotsman*, he argued in favour of high flats and against the redesign of the Princes Street frontages.[21]

Central government at this stage was urging local authorities to undertake surveys as a way of preparing for post-war reconstruction. Officials in the Scottish Office were unhappy about Edinburgh's track record in town planning: the key figure remained William Macartney, the City Engineer, who had only one qualified town planner on his staff. A Scottish Office official went to see Edinburgh's deputy engineer, Mr Haldane, to inspect the city's planning work. He reported that Mr. Haldane

seemed to regard surveys as of minor importance, particularly having in view Mr Macartney's extensive knowledge of the details of the whole city. . . . It is clear that Mr Macartney and Mr Haldane are well satisfied with the present position of planning for the city, which position from our standpoint is extremely unsatisfactory.[22]

Though the Clyde Report had edged the corporation towards acceptance of the need for a plan for the city as a whole, it did not allay the anxieties of the Scottish Office. Implementation of the report was left in the hands of Mr Macartney, an arrangement which prompted the Scottish Office to note: 'The corporation do not appear to be considering any new arrangements for planning in spite of suggestions from the public and letters in the press criticising their present attitude to planning.'[23]

A letter was drafted for the Secretary of State, Tom Johnston, to send to the Lord Provost, Sir William Darling, asking him to use his influence to get a preliminary planning survey carried out 'with all possible speed'. There were clearly differences of opinion between the central government and the local authority on the appropriate form for town planning practice. These differences were certainly influenced by the personalities of the officials most directly involved and also by the character of municipal politics in Edinburgh. But the differences also reflected the wider balance of class forces, especially as these related to urban development. In essence the formula being urged by central government was more aligned to the interests of industrial capital, those seeking to improve working-class living conditions and the priorities of the central state itself in planning and managing the emergent post-war economy. The position of the corporation favoured landowners and builders, the ratepayers' lobby and the priorities of the authority itself in ensuring the continuities of its past practices as far as possible.

Meanwhile the central government moved to set up a regional plan for the area that included Edinburgh. The Secretary of State for Scotland brought the various planning authorities together to set up the South East of Scotland Regional Planning Advisory Committee. This body then appointed Frank Mears as their consultant and aided by a small professional team he started his task of preparing a regional plan for an area that stretched from Loch Lomond to Berwick and covered 3600 square miles.

Mears's report, published in 1947, was the first significant regional planning study to take in Edinburgh. It combined a vibrant awareness of the unfolding political economy of Scotland's development, with a nostalgia for a way of life and an associated settlement structure which modern capitalism had destroyed. Above all it sought to perpetuate the historic character of Edinburgh expressed in the settlement form and the associated social structure.

Thus Mears related the problems of this vast region to what he called 'industrial and financial methods' that favoured massive concentrations of industry and manpower.[24] These had resulted in the decline of rural areas as their populations moved to the urban settlements which consequently sprawled into the surrounding countryside. Mears saw this rural decline as a mirror of the declining prosperity of the whole of Central Scotland *vis-à-vis* the growing south-east of England. His analysis anticipated more recent debates about relations between metropolitan centres and dependent peripheral regions. Thus he interpreted mid-Scotland's dependence on heavy industry as putting it on a par with 'certain colonial dependencies which have been exploited to their disadvantage as sources of raw materials'.[25]

One problem which the study had to grapple with was the major post-war expansion of coal mining which was anticipated by central government for the area around Edinburgh.[26] Some 40,000 miners were expected to move from the Clyde Basin to the fields in East and Midlothian, with a further 7000 going to West Lothian. To Mears this raised the spectre of a further phase of haphazard industrial growth, the kind of urban development of which he and his mentor Geddes had been so unremittingly critical. The prospect of one-industry, one-class settlements, overshadowed by waste tips was unacceptable, economically, socially and environmentally. The prospect of such settlements merging into

Edinburgh of all places threatened the historical character of the city. The alarm was not restricted to Mears; on this matter concerning town planning, the Edinburgh Corporation was in agreement with him, if not in others. Their attitude remained: 'Edinburgh is a capital city, it is not a competitor of any other city. It does not seek to model itself on any other city. It wants to be what it has been, but only more so.'[27]

Mear's solution was to accommodate the coalfield growth in the existing distinct settlements outside Edinburgh. He had always held the Scotland of small East Coast burghs in high regard, while being antipathetic to the industrial Scotland of the giant Clydeside conurbation. He now suggested therefore that the New Towns Act might be used to plan the economic and social requirements of these 'constellations', which were seen as federal groups of settlements co-operating to produce a gracious development. The consultants therefore advised their clients to rigorously prohibit the unplanned coalescence of settlements. To this end no Edinburgh overspill was to be directed to the east and south-east of the city, where all the available development land would be needed to house the immigrant miners and their families. Likewise development to the west would need to be strictly controlled. The stop-line for city spread was to be an outer ring road leading to a road bridge over the Forth Estuary. Further development would need to be channelled to the constellations beyond the road. In many respects, then, the prescribed regional strategy was in tune with the development proposals advanced by the Clyde committee.

The strategic planning of Edinburgh as a whole had been persistently advocated before the war, but never practised. During the war the idea came somewhat grudgingly to be accepted in Edinburgh and was even put into practice at a regional scale within which Edinburgh was included. The documents of the time indicate a number of factors which prompted this rethink. Central government were urging Edinburgh Corporation to at least carry out a form of civic survey, to gather the information needed for any planned reconstruction. There was even the fear that the government might step in and impose its own plans on the city. In part this changing attitude within Edinburgh represented the subservience of the local authority to central government, their perceptions of town planning having become misallied for the first time.

It was the government's attitude, rather than the corporation's that had changed to produce this discord. This change derived from an altered balance of class forces within the national state. Nuances of this altered balance were also evident within Edinburgh and paved the way for the new acceptance of a more comprehensive form of town planning at the local level. There were disconcerting prospects facing the city's *bourgeoisie* – of soldiers returning to embittered homelessness, of workers congregating in housing estates which before the war had been seen to breed a sense of 'social irresponsibility', of the city being engulfed by large, rapidly expanding working-class housing areas in which lived miners with their proud working-class culture and tradition of militancy, and there was the fear that as peace returned so industry would lapse back into the slumps of the pre-war years. Any formula which could assuage such anxieties was at least worth exploring. Town planning held the promise of protecting the status quo, identified as the 'unity' of the city, through a new and not too demanding class compromise. With a bit of luck town planning might even overcome the nagging problem posed by the shortage of domestic servants.

The new acceptance of town planning was riddled with contradictions. On the one hand, Edinburgh, as the capital, was a cultural expression of the unity of a nation which was suffering a semi-colonial exploitation of its resources and whose nationhood was denied. On the other hand, that 'unity' filtered through the physical environment of the place, projected a classless symbol, a settlement unstained by relations of production. Critique and ideology were impossibly interwoven. Similarly the continuity of the symbol was threatened by developments within the mode of production, the 'industrial and financial methods' which Mears referred to, which were eroding what he perceived to be the traditional way of Scottish life. Yet the city was itself both the product of those same forces and interests, and the locus from which significant aspects of them were still directed. Moreover the form of strategic planning that was now accepted and even practised sought simultaneously to effect social control, protect historic symbols and ensure efficient modernization without in any fundamental sense extending control over those very same 'industrial and financial methods'. Such planning could rework the contradictions, but not resolve them. The success of these plans and reports was that they helped to defer and deflect the crises: their failure was that they could only defer them and deflect them into the practice of planning itself.

Putting the ideology into practice

The regional plan did not attempt to plan the internal structure of Edinburgh. For that task Edinburgh Corporation had hired one of the world's most eminent planning consultants, Patrick Abercrombie. The Burgh Engineer, Mr Macartney, had opposed such an appointment. In January 1944 he told the Streets and Buildings Committee,

It would be a relatively simple matter to prepare, or to get some outside person to prepare, elaborate drawings of city improvements where cost and inconvenience to certain citizens were of no concern. But such schemes would possibly in the end find themselves pigeonholed and forgotten. It is considered, therefore, that the small technical staff available can be more usefully employed.[28]

For once, however, Macartney's concern to protect the material interests of 'certain citizens' and his own control of planning in the city, was not successful. He was invited to assist Abercrombie in preparing a civic survey and plan, a role he fulfilled for a few months before departing to take the chair in Municipal Engineering and Town Planning at Alexandria in Egypt. Abercrombie's chief aide was instead Derek Plumstead, who had collaborated with him twice in the past.

Abercrombie acknowledged the help given by corporation officials in preparing his plan. He was also keen to stress the continuity of his work with the report prepared by the Clyde committee. Their 1943 report had provided a coherent programme; the task of the consultants now was to translate that into a plan. Abercrombie therefore reaffirmed the disadvantage of further urban growth. Town planning at this time was an important ideology seeking to consolidate the class compromise of the war years and reproduce it and the associated social control in the new and uncertain peace. It is interesting to note then that Abercrombie's plan argued that further urban growth would lead to social disintegration. This danger was sensed to be particularly acute in Edinburgh, not because of the city's famous snobbery, still less because of the more fundamental cleavages within the social structure, but because of the topography. The hills on which the city had been built were perceived as dividing people, and lessening the sense of partnership.[29]

Control of the spread of the city was thus a means to achieve greater social integration. In advancing this policy Abercrombie and his colleagues also appealed directly to the form of *bourgeois* interest in the city which was represented by the dominance of the Progressives in local politics. It was argued that further growth would impose a burden on municipal services and therefore put up the rates. Above all, the report shunned the prospect of the capital being fused with a 'Black Country' development of industry associated with the growth of the coalfield settlements.[30] Agreement had therefore been reached with the regional planning team under Mears, and with the Scottish Office, to hold the population of Edinburgh at 453,000 permanent residents.[31]

The extent of the inter-war development gave an indication of the rate of change which the city might experience in the future. Abercrombie and his colleagues insisted that such change had to be planned if the mistakes of the past were not to be repeated. The plan set out to regulate the growth of new housing areas and the clearance of obsolete areas, both to meet functional needs and to foster a sense of social cohesion among the citizens. 'Community planning' was specifically posed as a counter to the mere housing schemes of the inter-war years.[32] To this end the city was divided into seven 'community units', each of around 60,000 people, and these units were sub-divided into neighbourhoods accommodating about 10,000. The size of a community was primarily determined by functional considerations such as the distance between homes and workplaces, the economic provision of a complete range of schools and the population needed to support an attractive and convenient shopping centre.[33] The plan was structured around 'precincts' where a single land use would dominate and which traffic would skirt rather than penetrate. The outcome of the planned redistribution of the population would then be a series of 'socially self-supporting communities'.[34]

Density zoning was the mechanism to achieve population redistribution without overspill or the coalescence of settlements on the urban fringe. Fixed densities also facilitated the planning of neighbourhood units and guarded against over-development of sites. The controls of the plan were fixed in net residential densities, closing the loopholes that gross densities offered to the 'nimble witted'.[35] Four zones were specified as can be seen in Figure 10. The residential

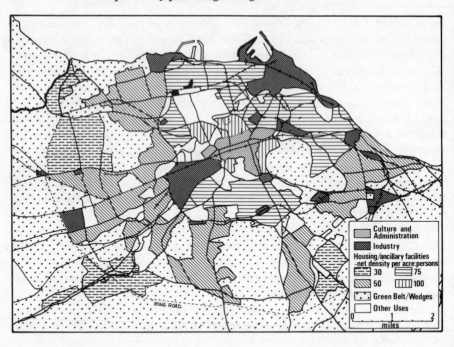

Figure 10   *Sir Patrick Abercrombie's plan for the city, 1949*

areas closest to the centre of town were to be at a net 100 persons per acre. Around these was a swathe, mainly in the north, east and west, at seventy-five persons per acre. Then to the west, south and east was a zone at fifty persons per acre. Finally a few outer suburbs on the north-west, south-west and south-east would be at thirty persons per acre. The net densities were for the zone as a whole, and thus allowed for flexible interpretation on individual sites, with the proviso that no plot should be developed at above 100 persons per acre.

The programming of redevelopment might be determined by the housing conditions, but the future use was decided by the location. Industrial zones were proposed for the redevelopment areas at Leith and Gorgie/Dalry. At St James Square, close to Princes Street, unfit housing would make way for commercial uses. The idea of a University precinct around George Square that had been canvassed by Mears in 1931 and endorsed by Clyde, Whitson and Pollock, was reiterated in the plan. Clearance of working-class housing and the movement of the residents was not a particularly controversial proposition; after all it had been practised since the Improvement Act of 1867. Similarly, a ceiling on city growth was seen as desirable to promote social control. However, the social geography of the city made the translation of the generalities into specific proposals deeply problematic. In particular the belt of middle-class Victorian villas stretching from Grange to Merchiston did not meet the required density and the deficiency threatened both service provision in the area and the wider aims of the integrated plan. As the plan noted,

these neighbourhoods should be redeveloped to the higher density of 75, in order to avoid the mal-distribution of population caused by excessively low density persisting so near the centre of the city. Furthermore, if the Dalry and Gorgie industrial zone is to be depopulated in accordance with the zoning principles of industry and home separation, the Merchiston area at least will require to be redeveloped to house a proportion of the workers in this industrial zone.[36]

The plan went on to suggest that the Grange area might then be redeveloped with flats to house the refugees from the new workers' Merchiston.

Restructuring of the city to improve conditions of production, to provide an adequate local labour force and to maintain social harmony was entirely consistent with the interests of local capital. Indeed, back in 1943, that 'rendez-vous with destiny', such moves had seemed essential to the city's *bourgeoisie.* Within the Abercrombie Plan, however, it now appeared that these objectives to be fully realized required the invasion of one of Edinburgh's 'better' areas by working-class households. Unity was, of course, desired in the abstract. In reality the banishment of slum clearance families to Pilton or Craigmillar was one thing, their elevation into Merchiston quite another. The fundamental contradiction between labour and capital thus resurfaced as a struggle about status and the rationality of the plan itself, a struggle between a fragment of the city's middle class defending their property interests as householders and a team of planning consultants.

Modernization of communications provoked similar problems, threatening private property, the city's tradition of low municipal spending and even the unifying historical fabric itself. The plan noted that pre-war traffic flows would double once petrol restrictions were lifted. Accidents were already increasing and congestion was imposing an 'uneconomic burden on the operating costs of commercial traffic'.[37] Abercrombie therefore came out for a set of road proposals which were considerably more extensive than those urged by Mears in 1931, or by Mr Clyde and his colleagues. The proposals are shown in Figure 11.

The Bridges By-pass was to be a dual carriageway sweeping round the eastern fringe of the central area. It would slice through the volcanic plug of Calton Hill in a tunnel and would be buried likewise under the High Street, before crossing the Cowgate and heading south to the Pleasance. From there an eastern fork would run parallel to the Innocents Railway and out to Duddingston and the A1 for London. The western fork was to run along Melville Drive, between the public open spaces of the Meadows and Bruntsfield Links. Its continuation was planned south-west to Colinton, then on to Fairmilehead, thus by-passing the narrow and steep Morningside Road. The west link of what was really an inner ring road was a short length from the West End to join this new road.

The problem that remained was how to close the ring on the north side of the centre. A route along Queen Street, through the New Town, was discounted on

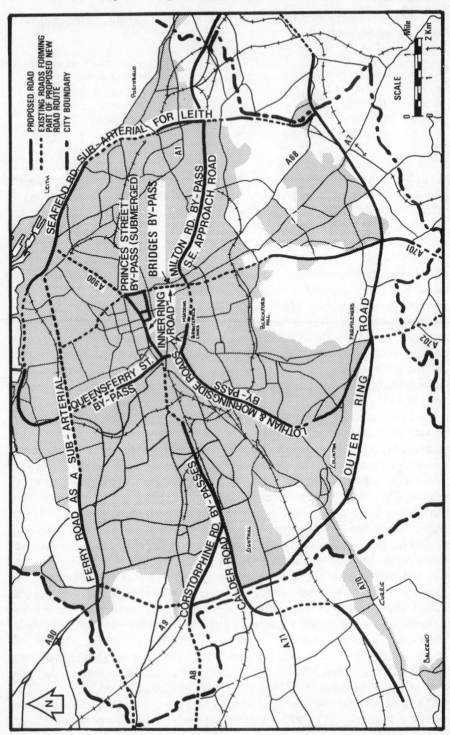

the grounds that it would entail the extensive demolition of valuable properties and would destroy much of the splendid Georgian architecture. Princes Street Gardens was about the only area north of the central ridge where there were no valuable properties, but to run a road above the railway there raised major amenity objections and there would still need to be extensive demolitions at either end of the link. The Cowgate, a low-class area, was an 'attractive alternative', but when examined in detail it was rejected. There would be engineering problems in road widening below George IV Bridge and the South Bridge; the new route would run right through the historic Grassmarket; and 'the precinctal quietude in the vicinity of Holyrood Palace would be shattered'.[38] There would also be more problems of engineering and demolition further east. Faced with this conundrum, Abercrombie opted for a daring solution, a route along the famous Princes Street itself. The plan proposed a new road beneath Princes Street itself, but open on the south side where the land slopes steeply down to the gardens. The only property affected was already ripe for redevelopment – the St James Square area in the east and slum property behind Lothian Road in the west. The great merit of the solution was that it isolated the only northern route that avoided substantial demolition of good property and historic buildings.

The plan proposed other roads as well. Access to Leith Docks was to be improved. An outer by-pass should be constructed when the coalfield developments generated traffic flows sufficient to justify the expenditure. Improvement of radial routes to dual carriageway standards was also recommended. Abercrombie defended his 'bold approach' to road building by referring to the similar phase of road construction carried through in the city during the nineteenth century under the Improvement Schemes. While the Ministry of Transport could not give official approval to the proposals in the advisory plan, the report noted that they were 'not antagonistic' to them.[39]

Transport planning included the railway system. A restructured freight network was put forward, including new goods yards. The plan recommended that all long-distance passenger traffic should be concentrated at a two-level station at Morrison Street, on the western fringe of the central area. Waverley Station could then be downgraded and the routes into it could be electrified, allowing the line through the garden to be tunnelled over, thus hiding the blemish bequeathed by the Victorian railway companies. Development would also be possible above the covered railway station at Waverley.

The Abercrombie Plan was the ideology of comprehensive planning put into practice. A man of international repute, an eminent member of the new breed of Planning Experts, was invited to draw up the plan for the city as a whole that would be the only sure antidote to the muddle of the nineteenth century which had been repeated rather than remedied in the piecemeal planning before 1940. The plan was derived from extensive civic survey in the Geddesian tradition, though, 'his method was different from the fact finding science leading to a Plan that has developed in recent years'.[40] The plan was the result of applying planning

Figure 11 *Sir Patrick Abercrombie's road proposals, 1949*

principles and standards to the information collected in the civic survey: 'From the mass of data obtained and illustrated in the form of maps, the Planning Scheme may emerge as a logical sequel marrying what is best from the old with what is considered best for the future.'[41] Rational technical expertise would thus produce social as well as physical integration and efficient expenditure. The interest of all would be served.

Maps and supporting visual illustrations packed the report and filled the walls of the council chamber when Abercrombie explained his proposals to his clients. The elaborate emphasis on presentation was more than the mere whim of an architect–planner. The presentation was central to the technocratic interest that fashioned the plan. The visual synthesis of the displayed facts was the way the expert remorselessly derived the solutions to the problems of the city. The presentation itself thus emphasized the neutral and objective nature of the plan.

The claims of comprehensive planning could not be achieved in practice. By the time the final report was being put together it was already a dead letter. Political opposition had surfaced when the consultants made their interim report in 1947. The first reaction of the chairman of the Planning Committee was distinctly lukewarm. Councillor Douglas, the chairman, was quoted as saying, 'The plans are so revolutionary they will require long and careful study before the Town Council come to a decision.'[42] Within the language games of Edinburgh Corporation this amounted to polite damnation. At the press conference for the launch of the Interim Report, Abercrombie acknowledged that he had anticipated some controversy. He confessed that his proposals to remove all housing from the Leith industrial area might be 'a bit on the drastic side'.[43] The Lord Provost, Sir John Falconer, attempted to paper over some of the cracks between the advantages of a planned modernization of the city and the threats which that posed:

you may be a little surprised and perhaps disappointed that [the proposals] seem to be so radical and so far reaching, and that they apparently involve much expenditure. You will keep in view, however, that some of the suggestions are concerned with very large alterations, which call for attention in any event, where the growth of the city requires immediate regulation. If that regulation is not made, the requirements of the future may be handicapped by the buildings which we must now erect. Our planning may be a hindrance instead of a help. The greatest advantage of planning is to ensure that we mould operations so as to attain the correct objective.[44]

A public exhibition was mounted to display the proposals. A few days elapsed before the major onslaught on the report was launched in a letter to *The Scotsman* from Dr A. Melville Clark, FRSE, of the Cockburn Association. He described the report as 'an outrage', which embodied 'sacrilegious proposals' for a 'streamlined necropolis'. The extensive road network and the comprehensive redevelopment of Leith were especially criticized. Throughout the letter Dr Clark attacked Abercrombie and Plumstead for being foreigners, whose experience was in planning the reconstruction of blitzed cities: they were not Edinburgh men, and

'Edinburgh is an unblitzed city – as yet'.[45] Two days later a further letter was published, from 'Surveyor', dismissing the plan as 'visionary and impossible of execution'.[46]

There were some letters in support of the plan, notably one from 'Biologist', who pointed out the Dr Clark's calls for organic growth of the city amounted to an endorsement of 'a continuous monotony of bungaloid suburb'.[47] However, there can be no doubt that some of those who had come to accept the need for planning as a way to orderly, efficient and harmonious development were forced to rethink their ideas by the Abercrombie Plan. The fact that it was the work of somebody outside the city's own elite compounded their doubts. As the study progressed towards the Final Report, the sniping increased. Mr D. Webster Robertson wrote to *The Scotsman* expressing concern that the corporation might yet proceed with the plan when very few of the city's businessmen had seen and studied it. He observed that: 'The call for a wholesale replanning applies admirably to war-devastated cities but Edinburgh is unique in having come scatheless out of the war, and we have no excuse for this scandalous expense and disorganisation.'[48] Criticisms of the plan by Professor A. H. Campbell were published a day later.

Not surprisingly then, the Preamble to the Final Plan began with these words:

A Plan for Edinburgh must needs be a hazardous undertaking: there can be few cities towards which the inhabitants display a fiercer loyalty or deeper affection, feelings which have existed in the past and which persist today. Even its blemishes are venerated . . . The planner who dares to propose improvements must go warily, and whatever he proposes he must expect sharp and informed criticism and even abuse.[49]

Abercrombie sought to turn his status as an alien to advantage, arguing that it allowed fresh thoughts to be brought to bear on the city's problems.[50] When presenting the plan to the council, he sought to reassure the clients. He explained that many of the proposed developments would not be implemented within twenty years, they were merely included so as to remind the council not to initiate other developments that might prejudice long-term needs. The consultants sought to allay anxieties about the financial implications of their proposals. Abercrombie emphasized that the controversial suggestion for a redesign of the Princes Street frontages need not cost the ratepayers money. Similarly Plumstead dangled the carrot of the construction of luxury flats at Holyrood, which could be let at rents of £200 a year, thus bringing income to the municipal coffers.[51]

The critics were not assuaged. Dr Melville Clark again described the plan as 'a desecration and a sacrilege', which advocated change for the sake of change. While calling for the area around Holyrood House to be made worthy of a Royal Palace, he was dismissive of planning: 'The whole tendency of planning is not towards life and its diversity, but towards monotony, uniformity, regularity, and the dead hand of officialdom.'[52]

The Planning Committee reviewed Abercrombie's Plan. Baillie Romanes (Labour) opposed the limit on the growth of population in the city and argued for the provision of more industrial land. He was opposed by the City Treasurer, James Miller (Progressive), who argued against changing Edinburgh into an industrial town.[53] Eventually the committee agreed to fix a limit of 500,000 on the growth of the city. The Lord Provost stressed that to exceed that ceiling would threaten the character of the city, and pointed to the example of Glasgow which, at one million, was 'far too big an organization to control'. Councillor Johnson-Gilbert (Progressive) also made comparisons with Glasgow and expressed fears that the development of the coalfields would spoil Edinburgh, which, he believed, should be preserved as the capital city.[54]

There were difficulties, however, when getting down to details and sites. For example the Planning Committee discussed the provision of housing for the people who would be relocated from Leith. Mr Plumstead pointed out to the committee that there was an acute shortage of undeveloped land close to Leith and recommended that the playing fields of George Heriot's School, at Goldenacre, could be used for this purpose. The school could then relocate its playing fields to the suburbs. The Lord Provost, Sir Andrew Murray, protested, pointing out that he and several other members of the committee were Governors of Heriot's Trust. The committee instructed Mr Plumstead to think again.[55]

The scepticism of the Planning Committee towards town planning after Abercrombie was indicated by their decision to offer Mr Plumstead only a short two-year contract as their Town Planning Officer. He wrote them a long letter of protest, stressing the impracticalities of such a temporary arrangement. After due consideration the committee relented and voted by eight to six to give him the job for three years! To help in the task of producing the Development Plan for 1 August 1951, he had four planning assistants.[56]

As the months went by the political system asserted more and more clearly the need for the Development Plan to be much less disruptive to existing activities and property owners than Abercrombie's blueprint. By the middle of 1951 work on the Development Plan had made little progress and the Lord Provost, James Miller, gave this advice to his Town Planning Officer: 'I think the plan should cover just the minimum requirements which the [Scottish Health] Department wants.' Baillie Bell supported these sentiments: 'It would be far better if we made our plan as simple and as flexible as possible, which, after all, would make it capable of adjustments as time goes on.' Mr Plumstead assured his political masters that he had no intention of recommending an elaborate and detailed plan.[57]

The Chamber of Commerce had also pared back their support for comprehensive planning. They produced a report advising the council against over-ambitious projects, a sentiment that was endorsed in a leader article in *The Scotsman*.[58] By 1952 the planning staff numbered about twenty, but the tone of the Planning Committee remained low key. Councillor Bell, presenting the Committee's Annual Report for 1952, was quoted as saying, 'We shall not be able to afford for a considerable time many of the Utopian schemes that are envisaged in the report. Edinburgh does not require drastic alteration. Nature has provided us with wonderful material and we should not allow our city to be messed about by enthusiastic planners.'[59] When the Development Plan was eventually approved by the council, in March 1953, Councillor Johnson-Gilbert spoke of 'the end of a tedious journey in town planning'.[60]

Planning in Edinburgh in the decade between the Clyde Report and the first Development Plan was thus characterized by a double inevitability; first, that comprehensive planning ideology would be put into practice and second, that the practice would result in disillusionment. Planned modernization of the city was both necessary and politically unacceptable. Clyde and his two colleagues had pointed the way to a comprehensive plan for Edinburgh that derived from the interests of the city's middle class at a time when the peculiar conditions of war time made their continued domination problematic. Abercrombie saw himself as the inheritor and guardian of that tradition. The appeal of comprehensive planning was therefore that the state through local intervention could provide the new infrastructure needed both directly and indirectly for production. Through engineering 'community', planning would also generate a new class compromise. The historic image of the city as a symbol of classless unity would be preserved and, equally important, planning would prevent the fusion of the city with major concentrations of coal miners and their families, a transition that would have directly challenged the basis of local political power.

In practice preservation and modernization could not be mutually achieved in the 1940s, even by one of the most respected and imaginative of the new Planning Experts. Nor could the package be delivered without imposing substantial costs on the ratepayers, without directly threatening the interests of some of the city's disproportionately large number of middle-class property owners. Thus the plan would directly menace just those sections of the *bourgeoisie* which had the strongest stake in the local political structures that operated through formal democracy. This inability of the ideology of comprehensive planning to realize its claims in practice constituted a crisis of rationality within the adimistrative system. However, by the early 1950s changes had occurred which made avoidance of the crisis easier. The threat of a major national shift in political power towards the working class had been averted. The need to plan 'community' was thus less strident and the risk of central government imposing an unacceptable plan on to Edinburgh had vanished. Planning practice in the city thus reverted to the model of 'flexibility', modest proposals and adaptation to the initiatives of developers that had characterized the pre-war years, though central government did now require the preparation of a Development Plan for the whole city. Furthermore the crisis of rationality was attributed to the more ludicrous and peripheral aspects of the ideology, notably the overblown claims made by the planning experts for their own expertise. The superstar planning consultant was replaced by the more anonymous local government official, with a skeleton planning staff. The crisis was thus resolved by deferring it.

Workable planning or Hitlerism? The Development Plan

It might be argued that the failings of the Abercrombie Plan should not be ascribed to any systematic crisis of rationality of the kind described above.

Rather, it could just be that Abercrombie, prominent planner that he was, simply got it all wrong on this occasion. Again it might be said that fashions changed, so that the proposals came too late to be acceptable. The first Development Plan provides a basis for judging such interpretations. Comparisons can be made between it and Abercrombie's Plan to see whether any clear pattern was evident in the changes between them and the factors relating to such a pattern.

The Development Plan endorsed the aim of containing the growth of the city. However, the form of the containment policy was notably more permissive than that proposed by Abercrombie. The 1951 census had revealed a population of 473,684, an increase of 30,642 on the 1931 figure. Abercrombie had advocated a limit of 453,000 permanent residents. The Development Plan plumped for 500,000 as the target figure for 1973, thus offering both growth and containment at the same time. Edinburgh's population could continue to increase at around the inter-war rate, while assuring those fretful of a reincarnation of Glasgow that the magic half-a-million threshold would not be crossed. The plan therefore intended that Edinburgh would be girdled by a green belt, with protected fingers of open space protruding into the urban area. For all that, the plan envisaged the conversion of 1425.2 acres from agricultural to urban uses in the first five years, with a further 1307.4 acres being lost to agriculture in Phase Two, the five- to twenty-year period. These were from a base figure of 10,200 agricultural acres. Even on those areas still zoned for agriculture, 'consideration may be given, according to individual circumstances, to the approval of proposals for other uses such as institutions and small areas of low density development'.[61]

Though the enthusiasm of the Scottish Office for planning had waned by this stage, nevertheless they did not share Edinburgh Corporation's predilection for suburban spread. It was the Department of Health for Scotland who insisted that Abercrombie's green belt be given statutory effect in the Development Plan. Edinburgh's council had not wanted to restrict peripheral expansion, but had been overruled by the government's desire to protect agricultural land.[62]

The willingness to pragmatically sift the initiatives of developers in the green belt was characteristic of the tone of the whole plan. 'Use zones' were identified where a particular land use would be dominant. However, these were less exclusive than Abercrombie's precincts; other uses might be acceptable within them and applications would be judged on their merits.[63] Nor were non-conforming uses necessarily to be removed wholesale from the zones. Thus Abercrombie's zoning of Leith for industry was considered to be, 'almost too drastic to be acceptable in any form'.[64] Instead, Leith was zoned for a mixture of industrial, residential and commercial uses.

The main redevelopment proposals from Abercrombie that were endorsed by the Development Plan were those which most directly benefited prominent city institutions and commercial interests. Thus the idea of an educational precinct, Mears's old 'College Mile', survived. Redevelopment of the north side of George Square, that early suburb of the ridge settlement of the eighteenth century, was proposed to allow Edinburgh University to erect a medical school. The area of cheap, old and poor housing between the Art College and the West Port was proposed for redevelopment for 'cultural, university and public buildings'. Both these developments were scheduled for Phase Two of the plan. In addition a further area of almost sixty acres around the university in the South Side area was also demarcated for eventual conversion to university and cultural use, though no phasing was indicated.

Another area earmarked for redevelopment in both the Abercrombie Plan and the Development Plan was St James Square, the area of cheap housing, small shops and businesses just north-east of Princes Street. This key central site was zoned for commercial uses and programmed for Phase Two. Abercrombie's speculations that this might be the site for a civic theatre or major concert hall were not reiterated.

The road proposals in the Development Plan are shown in Figure 12. They were less extensive and less likely to cause controversy than those in Abercrombie's. The statutory plan still sought to modernize the road network, so as to provide 'rapid and safe access to and from the city centre'.[65] As in Abercrombie, this meant a tunnelled route around the east of the centre, a southern link along Melville Drive and major road developments on the western fringe of the city centre. The real difference then was the northern link, which had even taxed the ingenuity of Abercrombie. His ambitious scheme for a triple-decker Princes Street was abandoned, but no replacement was suggested through the belt of high-value property in the historic New Town. Abercrombie's aspirations to restructure the railways similarly disappeared.

In a similar fashion the industrial land allocations sought to match the provisions of the Abercrombie Plan, but to reduce the disruptive effects. Abercrombie had recommended a net gain of 400.2 acres for industry, made up of the difference between a gain of 643.8 acres and a loss of 243.6 acres. The Development Plan allocated 478.5 acres of undeveloped land for industry, including 124 acres that would not be developed during the twenty-year period. Redevelopment for industrial use from other uses would yield a further 127.7 acres, though again this included 58.7 acres that would only be affected after the first twenty years. Redevelopment of existing industrial sites added a further 6.3 acres.

The other notable feature of the Development Plan is the extent to which it pared back the scale of concessions to working-class interests which were implicit in Abercrombie's plan. The fixing of residential densities in the Development Plan was more attributable to likely tenure than to the abstract notion of distance from the city centre which Abercrombie and his colleagues had operated. The idea of redeveloping Merchiston and Grange to increase the densities was predictably dropped. Housing redevelopment was concentrated on Leith and the area around Holyrood and St Leonards. The redevelopment was also to be at substantially higher densities than the consultant had envisaged. The Civic Survey and Plan had set a threshold of 100 persons per acre as a maximum density. The rationale was explicitly derived from the experience of the pre-war council housing schemes, notably at Niddrie and Pilton, where densities of eighty persons per acre coincided with a lack of recreational space and a degraded environment.[66]

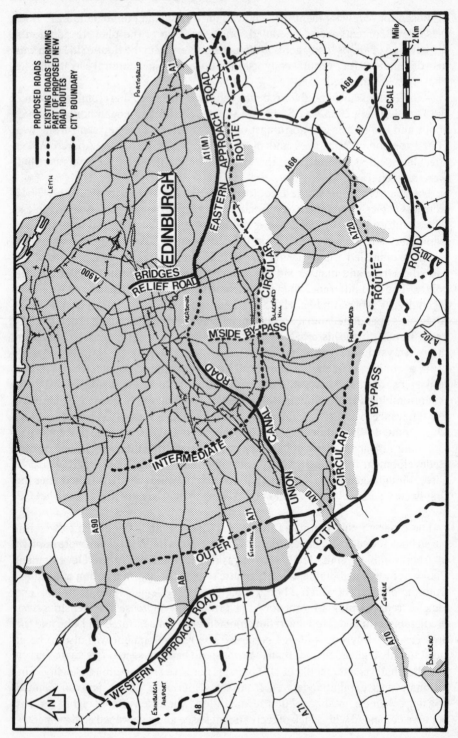

In contrast, the redevelopment densities put forward in the Development Plan were at or above 100 persons per acre in most areas, as Table 11 indicates.

Table 11 *Proposed densities in housing redevelopments*

Site	Area (acres)	Density (ppa)
Dumbiedykes Road	3.1	140
Arthur Street	4.2	140
Kirkgate	3.8	140
Canongate	6.5	100
Cables Wynd	2.0	100
Sheriff Brae	2.2	100
Spey Street	1.6	100
Lapicide Place	0.7	100
Abbeyhill	1.4	50
Williamsfield (Portobello)	0.7	50
Slateford	0.5	50

Source: City and Royal Burgh of Edinburgh, Development Plan, 1953 Written Statement, p. 23.

Further development was also proposed in the large council estate at Pilton. In Phase One 32.5 acres were to be built up for housing at 140 persons per acre. Likewise extra houses were to be built in Craigmillar around the Niddrie area, albeit at densities of less than 100 to the acre.[67] The scale of playing field provision recommended by Abercrombie for the local authority schools was also cut back drastically in the Development Plan. The Civic Survey catalogued the total area of local authority school playing fields in the city as 145 acres, or 0.3 acres per 1000 population. The proposition was that the ration should be increased to 1.8 acres per 1000, so that the plan scheduled an extra 660.3 acres for this purpose.[68] The Development Plan proposed the retention of 137.5 acres then in use for local authority school playing fields. However, the further provisions contained in the plan only brought the total up 310.1 acres.[69] Meanwhile, Abercrombie's proposal to rehouse slum residents from Leith on the George Heriot's playing field at Goldenacre had disappeared.

The Development Plan was consistently presented as being more pragmatic and politically acceptable than Abercrombie's. An *Evening News* leading article noted how the frills from the consultants' plan had been trimmed:

The present plan concerns itself with laying down the scope and location of industry and housing development during the next twenty years, together with hard-headed and fairly ambitious schemes for the improvement of road communications. . . . The Plan as a whole does provide the framework, the co-ordination, the broad conspectus so essential if piecemeal, uncontrolled haphazard development is to be avoided. It is a workable and business-like proposition.[70]

Figure 12 *The road proposals in the 1957 Development Plan*

Similarly a 'Planning Official' was quoted as saying that some of Abercrombie's ideas could not have been implemented in a 100-year programme; in a twenty-year plan a lot of them had to be jettisoned.[71]

The pragmatism largely succeeded in defusing the hostilities that Abercrombie's plan had stirred. Sixty-three objections were lodged against the new plan, covering 115 properties, However, by the time the public inquiry started in April 1954 only twelve remained, affecting around twenty properties. The twelve were a disparate collection of landowners whose interests were adversely affected. The British Transport Commission opposed the closure of the Costorphine branch railway, while Scottish Omnibuses Ltd were unhappy about the planned disposition of bus stations. Allotment holders objected to the loss of their plots for housing. Edinburgh University fought the suggested density of 140 persons per acre on a twenty-two acre site at Salisbury Green beneath Arthur's Seat, which they wanted to develop as student residences at forty to fifty persons per acre. The strongest criticisms came against the redevelopment at St Leonards, where the managing director of a firm of brewing engineers described the impending compulsory purchase of his factory as 'Hitlerism'.[72]

The underlying principles of minimal change were enunciated by the corporation's spokesmen at the inquiry. The Planning Officer, Mr Hewitson, stressed that the plan aimed above all to preserve the city's existing character. There was consequently no desire to develop a large amount of industry in the city. The corporation's QC, Mr Guest, made the same fundamental point – Edinburgh's future was as a commercial, administrative and cultural centre, devoid of heavy, noxious industry. He promised that the zonings would not be rigidly applied. The roads were seen as being necessary to reduce traffic congestion and thus improve links between home and work.

The style of presentation of the plan and the format of the inquiry, were determined by the statutory requirements. The whole style was thus technical rather than popular. The Plan was backed by a written statement which was a laborious catalogue of sites, acreages and zonings, the myriad of property parcels blurring any overall conception of urban structure. The accompanying texts were dull descriptions, whereas Abercrombie's had been laced with photographs, sketches and quotations from Stevenson and Scott. Discussions at the inquiry hinged around the technical specifics of particular sites and properties, rather than the aims of the plan as a whole.

No major critique appears to have been launched against the Development Plan. Its considerable achievement was to re-establish civil privatism on urban development issues, legitimizing an extended state involvement in producing and managing the urban fabric. A number of factors made this new legitimacy attainable. The soldiers had returned to poor housing conditions and, contrary to the fears of 1943, had tolerated them. Rising living standards and a new surge of commodity production had made a class compromise of a form few had anticipated. Political acceptability of the plan was now possible because the only bourgeois interests in the city which it now seriously threatened were marginal fragments, notably small industrialists and the private landlords whose properties would be compulsorily acquired: for such unremunerative investments the prospect of being compensated for the loss of the asset could scarcely have been a total disaster. Even where change was proposed that would affect the image of the historic city, or property interests within it, a question mark must still have hung over the likelihood of the change actually occurring. Plans had been churned out vaunting changes in Edinburgh for around a quarter of a century, but precious little had really altered, so why should this time be any different?

The price to be paid for securing the acceptability of the proposals was again in terms of their rationality. To prevent the widely deplored growth of the past, there was to be a flexible plan. The urban containment would be achieved within a growth programme, where Edinburgh Corporation were in fact reluctant to restrict expansion, but were being pressed to do so by central government in its desire to protect agricultural land, and by the surrounding county councils, most notably East Lothian, which was the only local equivalent to the rural shire counties round most of the big English cities.[73] In like manner the plan included an inner ring road where the northern link was missing. The zonings in the plan sought to provide some assurances to property owners about the future value and use of their property. However, the very flexibility of the plan and the blighting effect of proposals that stretched beyond twenty years undermined the notion of certainty. Slum clearance rehousing was planned at a high density despite the perceived problems which such practices had generated in the past. If the scale and pace of modernization that the plan implied was insufficient to keep the city's industry competitive, that deficiency was muted and would not be instantly apparent, for there was no symbolic litmus test around which the competing companies could unite. While change remained nothing more than drab tables of statistics, prepared by bureaucrats and vetted by councillors who could be trusted to keep the rates down and oppose 'Socialism', crisis could be contained. Once the development pressures ripped, it would be a different story. The Development Plan, slightly amended, was approved by the Secretary of State for Scotland in September 1957.[74]

References and notes

1   *The Scotsman,* 7 May 1943. The mover of the resolution was the Rev. Dr W. A. Guthrie.
2   City and Royal Burgh of Edinburgh, 'The future of Edinburgh', *The report of the Advisory Committee on City Development* (1943), p. 3.
3   Ibid., p. 4.
4   *The Scotsman,* 23 July 1943. Other speakers at the opening of the exhibition were the President of the Royal Incorporation of Architects in Scotland, Mr J. R. Mackay, FRIBA, and the Marquess of Bute.
5   Edinburgh Chamber of Commerce and Manufacturers, 'Memorandum to the Advisory Committee on City Development' (1943), p. 5.
6   Ibid., pp. 6–7.
7   City and Royal Burgh of Edinburgh (1943), p. 10.

8   Ibid., p. 10.
9   Ibid., p. 11.
10   Ibid., p. 12.
11   Ibid., p. 19.
12   Ibid., p. 20.
13   Ibid., p. 22.
14   Ibid., p. 30.
15   Ibid., p. 17.
16   G. Scott-Moncrieff, 'Plan for Edinburgh', *The Scottish Field*, no. 42, vol. IXL (1943).
17   City and Royal Burgh of Edinburgh (1943), p. 5–6.
18   Ibid., p. 6.
19   Ibid., p. 6.
20   *The Scotsman,* 15 Feb. 1944.
21   *The Scotsman,* 3 Jan. 1944.
22   'Surveys: Edinburgh Town Planning', File DD 12/1429, Scottish Records Office.
23   Ibid.
24   F. C. Mears, *A Regional Survey and Plan for Central & South-East Scotland* (Morrison & Gibb 1948), p. 1.
25   Ibid., p. 14.
26   *Report on the Scottish Coalfields,* Cmnd. 6575, HMSO (1944).
27   Minutes of the South-East of Scotland Regional Planning Advisory Committee, File DD 12/36, Scottish Records Office.
28   Minutes of Edinburgh Corporation Streets & Buildings Committee, Jan. 1944.
29   P. Abercrombie and D. Plumstead, *A Civic Survey and Plan for the City and Royal Burgh of Edinburgh* (Oliver and Boyd 1949), p. 29.
30   Ibid., p. 29.
31   Ibid., p. 30.
32   Ibid., p. vii.
33   Ibid., p. 35.
34   Ibid., p. 35.
35   Ibid., p. 32.
36   Ibid., p. 36.
37   Ibid., p. 39.
38   Ibid., p. 42.
39   Ibid., p. 39.
40   Ibid., p. vii.
41   Ibid., p. 4.
42   *Edinburgh Evening Dispatch,* 3 Oct. 1947.
43   *The Scotsman,* 3 Oct. 1947.
44   *The Scotsman,* 3 Oct. 1947.
45   *The Scotsman,* 16 Oct. 1947.
46   *The Scotsman,* 18 Oct. 1947.

47 *The Scotsman,* 21 Oct. 1947.
48 *The Scotsman,* 8 Dec. 1948.
49 P. Abercrombie and D. Plumstead (1949), p. 1.
50 Ibid., p. vii.
51 *Edinburgh Evening Dispatch,* 9 July 1949.
52 *Edinburgh Evening Dispatch,* 19 Jan. 1950.
53 *The Scotsman,* 22 July 1949.
54 *The Scotsman,* 1 Sept. 1949.
55 *The Scotsman,* 14 July 1949.
56 City and Royal Burgh of Edinburgh, Minutes of the Planning Committee, 28 Nov. 1948. Mr Plumstead eventually resigned in June 1951, and his deputy, Mr. Hewitson, succeeded him in Feb. 1952, but with a permanent post.
57 *Edinburgh Evening Dispatch,* 5 June 1951. Mr Plumstead blamed alterations to the City Chambers for the delays in producing the plan. These had disrupted the day-to-day working conditions of his assistants.
58 *The Scotsman,* 21 March 1952.
59 *The Scotsman,* 5 Dec. 1952.
60 *The Scotsman,* 20 March 1953.
61 City and Royal Burgh of Edinburgh, *Development Plan*, (1953), Written Statement p. 67.
62 T. Hewitson, personal communication, quoted in P. J. Smith, 'Rural interests in the physical expansion of Edinburgh', in J. V. Minghi and E. C. Higbee, (eds), *The Geographer and the Public Environment*, British Columbia Geographical Series no. 7 (1966), Occasional Papers in Geography, Tantalus Research Ltd., Vancouver, p. 65.
63 City and Royal Burgh of Edinburgh, *Development Plan*, (1953), See 'Use Zone Table' in the Appendix.
64 Mr Hewitson, the Town Planning Officer, expressed this view when addressing the Leith Rotary Club, as reported in the *Edinburgh Evening News,* 8 March 1956.
65 City and Royal Burgh of Edinburgh (1953), p. 10.
66 P. Abercrombie and D. Plumstead, (1949) state the following in Appendix 1, pp. 87–8: 'no one can reasonably claim, for example, that the Corporation's pre-war housing schemes at either is [sic] happy where the ground is overbuilt, with too little ground left for the amount of demand for communal use the occupied flats have created. The ground is downtrodden and derelict in appearance and incapable, except perhaps by strict estate supervision, of being maintained as a green open space. These dwellings are found to represent a density of 80 persons per acre (net residential density). The condition would be allieviated if these flats had been built in 10 storey blocks instead of three or four storeys for the same number of people, thus reducing the number of building blocks and the amount of ground built upon. More ground would have been added to the environment of the place for communal recreation and gardens. Taking these

examples into account it is not thought that the maximum density as a criterion should exceed 100 persons per acre. The standard of living conditions so far as they are affected by the density of development is considered to be unsatisfactory where it is in excess of 100 persons per net residential acre.'

67   City and Royal Burgh of Edinburgh (1953), p. 22.

68   P. Abercrombie and D. Plumstead (1949), Appendix 4.

69   City and Royal Burgh of Edinburgh (1953), pp. 52–3.

70   *Edinburgh Evening News,* 5 Sept. 1957.

71   *The Scotsman,* 5 Sept. 1957.

72   *The Scotsman,* 8 April 1954. The corporation added a Comprehensive Development Area at St Leonards in the years that elapsed before the Plan was finally approved by the Secretary of State.

73   The attitude of the counties was most fully evident in the East Lothian County Council Development Plan, 1955.

74   He called for more consideration to be given to the road improvements at Tollcross, and to the Holyrood Section of the eastern approach road, and also required the deletion of the road proposed between Roseburn and Maybury in the west of the city.

7 The erosion of legitimacy

By the early 1950s the antagonisms and protests sparked by Abercrombie's visionary designs for Edinburgh had been damped down. The 1953 Development Plan provoked no widespread public opposition. By the late 1960s, however, town planning was probably the most contentious issue in the city and the local political parties were split internally about what should be done. Such events confound any notions that the development of planning has been a steady and inevitable progression towards acceptability. How then can the shift from disinterested tolerance to hostile protest be interpreted?

Precisely such protests over planning proposals were the stimulus behind the early case studies of planning in local situations. The literature on urban social movements was also inspired by such conflicts. The drift in the writing has been to recognize that struggles over urban planning have been fought by interest groups defined on the basis of consumption rather than production. Major debates continue, however, about the nature of local power structures, the links between local and national power and the character of the local state; also the extent to which a class analysis can be applied to conflicts which are neither fought in the name of a class, nor united with struggles in the workplace. Study of local practice has proved an important adjunct to theorizing.

In approaching these questions in Edinburgh and for this period one has to take cognizance of the analysis of the local political structure written at the time by Mackintosh. He unambiguously defined a pluralist pattern of power: 'there is no one body which expresses civic opinion, nor is it possible to point to a single institution or group of people and say that they hold the reins of power'.[1] Similarly, as this chapter will show in some detail, the predominant form of conflict over town planning involved more than one protest group and was usually between middle-class or even upper-middle class residents and the local authority or the university.

For all that, an interpretation of the events solely in terms of locally based power structures appears inadequate. At a very basic level, the mounting controversy and loss of public confidence in planning in Edinburgh over this period was by no means unique. The very generality of such protests should make one cautious of overly local emphases. Furthermore, the planning in Edinburgh was conducted within a statutory system developed through the national state, where ultimate power of decision resided with the Secretary of State for Scotland and the officials of the Scottish Office. However, to fully sense the wider constraints on local power and their class nature, town planning needs to be related to the developing character of British capitalism during the period under study. As will be described, planning practice in Edinburgh was centrally concerned with urban renewal. As such it was an important part of that drive to modernization, through extended state intervention, that was characteristic of Britain as a whole and especially of Scotland, during the period. The state increasingly intervened in the economy and in the cities so as to increase productivity and the rate of profit.

Within this perspective the work of Habermas on the crisis tendencies in advanced capitalism has a particular relevance.[2] Chapter 6 has already applied the notion of a rationality crisis to the preparation of Edinburgh's first Development Plan. Following that theory the development of such a crisis might be expected to predicate a crisis of legitimation. The extended intervention of the state, while in the interests of capital, undermined the market as the traditional and accepted means of allocating resources, or more specifically for our purposes, of producing the city. Failures to meet the demands placed upon that intervention, and/or the expectations of it, thus threatened public perceptions of the fairness, efficiency and credibility of the actions of the state. The very involvement of the state repoliticizes conflicts which had been depoliticized by appearing through a market form to be no more than the exchange of equivalents. Hence the state itself has to struggle to maintain civil privatism and to secure mass loyalty through the system of formal democracy.

In seeking to apply this theoretical framework to the development of town planning within Edinburgh, there is a need to focus on the form of the modernization imperatives in a city with a non-industrial economic base; the interplay of local and national states; the way in which the intervention of the administrative system threatened cultural traditions and symbols; and the nature of the ensuing politicization and its management. In Chapter 1 the modernization of cities in advanced capitalism was related to the problems of over-accummulation and the associated need to create new commodities and to increase the productivity of labour. From this, three important aspects of such urban development were identified – suburban expansion, central area reconstruction and the restructuring of transport. It is to the specific manifestations of these aspects that we now turn to probe the developing legitimation crisis within town planning in Edinburgh.

Suburban expansion and the modernization of housing

As noted in the previous chapter, improved working-class housing conditions were seen as a necessary step to avert a deeper post-war crisis. Thus the quantitative and qualitative problems of housing were a crucial factor in persuading Clyde and his colleagues of the need for comprehensive planning in Edinburgh. Likewise, Abercrombie's plan sought a transformation in the housing conditions for a substantial proportion of the city's households. Not surprisingly then local authority house building dominated the decade immediately after the war.

House building was an industry in need of modernization. The construction process was still dominated by craft skills and was labour intensive. In the years after the war these problems were compounded by the acute shortages of houses, building materials and labour. The state therefore pioneered prefabrication of components in an attempt to gain the benefits of increased labour productivity associated with industrialized production methods in other sectors. Within Edinburgh the result was the development of about 4000 prefabricated houses, largely on suburban land. These houses had a life expectancy of ten years, though a further 150 'pre-fabs' were built which were intended to be permanent. Despite the attempt to industrialize the houses were relatively expensive to provide. There was the additional disadvantage that the form of the construction necessitated low-density development, with difficulties in developing at over nine houses to the acre, so no more temporary houses were built after 1949.[3]

Provision of permanent council houses followed. The development pattern followed the land acquisitions made by the council in the inter-war period. New sites were also purchased on the edge of the city, typically those spaces between the earlier council developments that had flanked the radial roads.[4] This extension of state intervention posed both economic and political problems, which had impacts on the practice of town planning.

The financing of council housing worried both central government and the local council, especially as labour and materials costs were inflating and interest rates were also rising. One local response, which did not directly affect statutory town planning, was to put up the rents. Thus in 1953 the corporation narrowed the gap between the rents charged for pre-war council houses and the dearer rents paid by tenants of post-war dwellings. A further increase in 1957 sought to tune rents more finely to variations in amenities and standards of the houses and surrounding environment. In this way the finanicial problem posed by housing the workers was met by increasing the charges and redistributing those charges around among the tenants themselves. Again the balance of class power within the local political system is indicated by the fact that council house rents within Edinburgh were notably higher than in the other Scottish cities.[5]

The changes which had a more direct impact on town planning and the design of housing areas originated with central rather than local government. The funding of the council house building programme posed problems and thus from 1952 onwards the Scottish Office began to urge local authorities to economize. Semi-detached cottages were discouraged, in favour of terraced houses and blocks of flats three or four storeys high. Further economies were required in the internal space standards and fittings. In 1956 the Department of Health for Scotland again reviewed its regulations for public housing, reducing the standards recommended at the end of the war.[6] The basis of subsidies was also changed. From 1952 government had provided local authorities with £39/15/0d for each three apartment council house, £42/5/0d for a four apartment and £46/15/0d for a five apartment. The Housing and Town Development (Scotland) Act of 1957 reduced the subsidy to a flat rate of £24 for a sixty-year period, regardless of the size of house. However, the same act increased the subsidy given for building flats in blocks of more than six storeys. This had the desired effect in Edinburgh as elsewhere. The first block of multi-storey council flats had been built in Gorgie in 1952. By 1961, Councillor Tom Morgan (Progressive), the convenor of the Housing Committee, was saying, 'There is no doubt that it is desirable to develop at a high density in the central area and the most desirable development is multi-storey flats.'[7] However, the 'multis' were by no means being confined to the central area; they were also being built, or on the drawing boards, for Leith redevelopment sites and for the more peripheral council housing estates such as Gracemount and Muirhouse.

The switch to high-rise council housing did owe something to local factors as well as to the pressures from central government. As noted above, influential local councillors endorsed the concept. In addition, the pattern of land ownership within the city was a further stimulus to high rise development. By 1961 the council had only a two-year supply of building land left and the rezoning of areas from open space was being considered.[8] Meanwhile extensive tracts of land with potential for residential development were being held by the major local building companies.

The attempt to produce a new stock of housing for members of the working class was not an exercise in comprehensive town planning. The divorce of town planning from land ownership ensured an *ad hoc* approach: the council houses were built where sites were available. One consequence was that such developments became contentious when they infringed on owner-occupied areas. The first of these conflicts occurred in the late 1950s, in the Clermiston area. The residents of the high status suburbs of Corstorphine and Davidson's Mains were affronted by plans to build over 2000 council houses on adjacent land. They organized and protested and managed to force some modifications to the original plans.[9] What had previously been mere plans now became tangible threats to the perceived interests of the city's large middle class. The visible and immediate cause of the problems was the corporation; the administration's role as developer thus compromised the proclaimed neutrality of the administrative system. The Progressives, with their ideological distaste for politics and intervention, were therefore caught in the classic cleft stick of at least the nominal responsibility of administering an intervention that was germinating a political backlash. One of the achievements of the administration was to contain the extent of these conflicts by concentrating council house development in and around the existing peripheral council schemes.

Nevertheless on some sites implementation of planning proposals posed peculiar difficulties. One particular example was a twenty-one acre site in the St Leonards area that had been zoned in the Development Plan for redevelopment in the first five-year phase. Lay-outs were prepared by the corporation's Architect's Department and approved by the Planning Committee. However, the proposal to build five 25-storey blocks of council flats on a site which stood in front of the scenic splendour of the Salisbury Crags did not attract universal acclaim. There was a protracted wrangle with the Royal Fine Arts Commission and the Ministry of Works. Some observers suggested that the root of the concern was the prospect of council tenants peering down into the royal residence at Holyrood Palace.[10] It took several years before an acceptable design could be agreed.

The development of private housing also depended on an interplay between local and national influences. In the immediate post-war years the level of activity was sharply constrained by central government controls. Building licences had to be obtained and even when a licence was granted the size of the house and the selling price were still restricted. In 1945, for example, the overall area could not exceed 1000 square feet for a two-storey house, or 930 square feet for a bungalow or flat and the selling price was pegged at £1200 (£1300 from 1947). After 1948 the local authorities were left to fix the price in relation to local conditions. These attempts by central government to restrain consumption at a time of shortages did not extinguish private building in Edinburgh, but it did remain at a low level until the controls were removed in 1954.[11]

Once building licences were abandoned, local factors became more significant influences on the development pattern. The biggest problem for private sector house building was the shortage of development land and the ownership of that land. In part the supply was restricted by physical constraints – the estuary to the north, the Pentland Hills to the south and areas subject to mining subsidence to the east. Zonings in the Development Plan further restricted the potential supply. Similarly, the local authority housing programme took land which might otherwise have been used by the private sector. The remaining development land was largely controlled by those private building companies that had grown in Edinburgh in the 1930s, most notably James Miller and Partners and MacTaggart and Mickle.[12] The early pattern of private post-war development therefore tended to be dominated by these two firms and was characterized by the development of relatively small sites. An analysis of planning permissions shows something of the relative significance of different building companies in Edinburgh in this period, as is shown in Table 12.

In all from 1949 to 1953 planning permissions were given for 4094 private houses and for a further 4550 in 1953–8. Edinburgh's house-building industry thus remained locally based and dispersed among a variety of operators, but with two dominant firms. The pattern was, however, changing with the arrival of national companies such as Wimpey, who built their first houses in Edinburgh in 1955, at Redford. The pattern of private development was largely suburban infill.[13] By the early 1960s there were complaints from the builders of a shortage of land. These came particularly, and not surprisingly, from those national companies trying to expand into the Edinburgh market. Wimpey claimed in 1961 that they had no development land left in the city and were having problems getting more. They stated that much of the land zoned for new housing was unsuitable for their type of low-density development, or was held by owners who would not sell.[14] Mowlem (Scotland) Ltd made similar claims.[15] Smaller local firms such as Fred Ford Ltd were similarly short of land.[16]

Table 12   *Number of private houses granted planning permission for the main building companies in Edinburgh, 1949–58*

Company	1949–53	1953–58	Total 1949–58
James Miller	2152	911	3063
MacTaggart & Mickle	310	969	1279
Boland	54	220	274
Wimpey	0	599	599
Ford & Torrie	57	210	267
A. Thain	4	73	77

Source: J. R. Kaucz, 1976, 'Residential Location: The application of the social physics model and the behavioural model to Edinburgh', Unpublished MSc. Thesis, Department of Town & Country Planning, Heriot-Watt University/Edinburgh College of Art, Figs. 7.4, 7.14, 7.16, 7.18, 7.20, 7.22, 7.24.

Thus the issues of housing alone made some update of the Development Plan administratively desirable. What was notionally the Quinquennial Review was completed in 1965, eight years after the approval of the Development Plan and twelve years after that plan had first been published. Meanwhile there had been considerable housing development at the edge of the city, as can be seen from Figure 13. Since the designation of the green belt in the 1957 Development Plan, there had been continual pressure from the housebuilders for release of land within the belt. However, retention of the green belt was an emotive cause; the image of the coherent, unified, historic capital was wedded to the containment of the settlement and to the amenity and visual character provided by the extensive reservations of open space within the city. Development proposals for greenfield sites were always likely to precipitate residents' action groups protesting against loss of amenity and the deleterious effects on the value of their property. In addition there was the background pressure from the agricultural interests within central government to protect good agricultural land.

There were also those aspects of housing provision where the corporation was more directly involved. By the early 1960s the emergency prefabs had passed their designed life span. The 1961 census also revealed that despite improvements during the 1950s, one Edinburgh household in four still had no fixed bath. Though no full survey had been undertaken since 1946, it was estimated that there were 28,000 substandard houses in the city at the time of the Review.[17] The economics and politics of rising consumer expectations and the relative labour shortage of the time, meant that a labour force had to be retained in the city in superior accommodation than had been the case in the past. The only way that this could be done was through a programme of redevelopment and council house building and to be efficiently carried through that programme needed to be planned.

Figure 13   *The physical expansion of Edinburgh, 1945–1964*

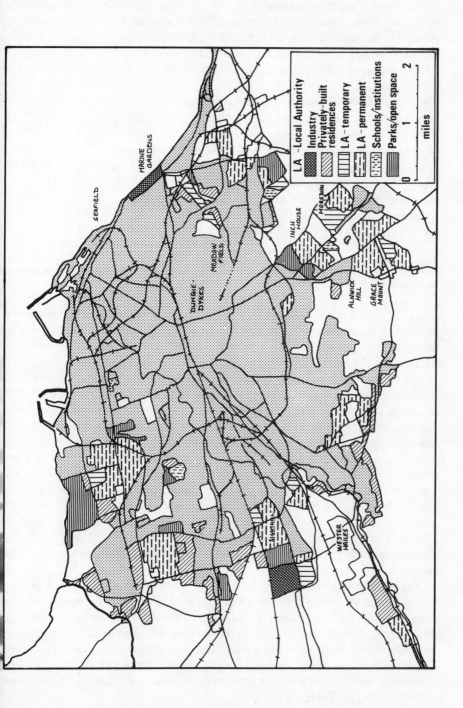

The Review attempted to assess the city's housing requirements and to allocate land accordingly. There were technical difficulties in the exercise, particularly in relation to the uncertainties over migration patterns and future occupancy rates. Notwithstanding these difficulties, the Plan proposed that 33,500 local authority houses should be built. The land for them would be found as shown in Table 13.

Table 13   *Local authority housing proposals*

Sites	Houses	Acres
New houses in clearance areas, and present and future areas of comprehensive development	10,700	138.5
Redevelopment of temporary housing sites	5,500	322.6
New houses on sites in new and expanded local authority housing areas zoned in the Development Plan	7,700	380.6
New houses on sites to be determined	9,600	?
	33,500	841.7

Source: City and Royal Burgh of Edinburgh, 1965, Development Plan Review, Written Statement, pp. 7 and 24–6.

The plan therefore recognized the need for a major programme of council house building, but the land for a substantial proportion of those houses could not be identified, as questions about possible overspill had not been resolved. The densities in the public sector housing areas were planned to be considerably higher on average than those on land reserved for private housing. On new sites public housing densities were scheduled from fifty to 140 persons per acre, while the range for equivalent private housing sites was between ten and seventy-five persons per acre. In redevelopment areas new council houses were planned at densities up to 190 persons per acre.[18] Public housing provision was to be concentrated in the redevelopment areas, the prefab sites, which in general were already adjacent to local authority schemes, and on two major peripheral sites. These latter were at the old mining village of Newcraighall on the eastern edge of the city, beyond the Craigmillar housing estate, and at Wester Hailes on the west, near the corporation scheme at Sighthill. Newcraighall amounted to 110.2 acres, Wester Hailes to 189 acres. The new council housing areas were therefore largely planned to conform to pre-existing patterns of residential status areas within the city.

The Review sought to provide land for the construction of 10,800 new private houses within the city. Though this was only around a third of the number of new council houses that were planned, the land area allocated for new private housing, 840.1 acres, was almost the same as for the local authority housing. In addition redevelopment for private housing was planned for another 37.1 acres at Colinton and Portobello. Much of this land was, of course, owned by the two building companies who had held such a prominent position in the city for the previous three decades, as Table 14 shows.

Table 14 *Ownership of land zoned for residential use (private) in the 1965 Quinquennial Review*

Owner	Already zoned residential in 1957 Development Plan (acres)	Additional zoning for private res. in 1965 QR (acres)	Total (acres)	Per cent
Estates and farms	38.7	266.0	304.7	43
MacTaggart & Mickle	123.4	—	123.4	17
J. Miller & Partners	98.2	9.2	107.4	15
Other developers	4.0	38.5	42.5	6
Secretary of State	—	82.6	82.6	12
Miscellaneous	8.6	39.8	48.4	7
	272.9	436.1	709.0	100

Source: H. M. Bingham, 1974, 'Land Hoarding in Edinburgh', Unpublished MSc. Thesis, Department of Town and Country Planning, Heriot–Watt University/Edinburgh College of Art, p. 88.

Note: The Secretary of State deleted 131.1 of the 840.1 acres that were zoned for private residential development. Bingham's analysis was based on the 709 acres that were approved.

Thus the Quinquennial Review sought to make more land available for private builders, though it clearly did not fully satisfy their aspirations. However, as the tabulation implies, any shortfall was much more damaging to the interests of building firms trying to break into the Edinburgh market from the outside than it was to the two largest firms in the city. The shortage of development land and the consequent inflation of land prices was beneficial to the firms that already held building land within the city.

The Review therefore released a considerable area of land for development. It also sought to consolidate and extend the green belt. The practice that followed saw the conversion of land within the green belt and of private open space for residential uses. Table 15 shows the change in private open space provisions.

Table 15 *Changing provisions of private open space*

	1957 Development Plan (acres)	1965 QR (acres)	1969 Proposal (acres)
Private amenity open space	1634.7	1522.8	1445.3
Private recreation open space	337.0	327.2	321.8
	1971.7	1850.0	1767.1

Source: City and Royal Burgh of Edinburgh, 1969, 'Open Space Report'.

Bingham calculates that between 1957 and 1973 about 300 acres of green belt were released for private housing and a further 240 acres for local authority housing, usually after a public inquiry.[19] The main areas zoned for private housing in the plan of 1965 were in the south and south-west suburbs, at Hunter's Tryst, Woodhall, Dreghorn, Baberton (separated from Wester Hailes by the line of the outer by-pass) and at Southfield and Cammo House.

Landowners and developers pressed their case for a more permissive policy towards private housing developments at the Public Inquiry into the Review. The extent of land zoned for public housing was also attacked. Wimpey's representatives complained of an acute land shortage and rocketing land prices. Sir James Miller himself bemoaned the fact that nobody was looking after the interests of the owner-occupiers and predicted that the proposals in the plan would mean an annual rates increase of $4d$ in the £ for the next twenty years. He urged a more vigorous overspill programme, to give council tenants the opportunity of living outside Edinburgh. In reply the Town Planning Officer, Mr Hewitson, argued that on past trends between 800 and 1000 private houses were being built in the city each year. The proposition in the plan, therefore, was that this building rate should continue for around ten years, after which time new private houses would have to be built beyond the city boundary. Thus the aim of containing the city ran counter to the interests of those builders who did not already have a land bank in the urban area, though the policy was supported by the adjoining county authorities. Indeed, Midlothian County Council objected to the zoning of the land at Baberton and Woodhall, claiming that since the sites were outside the line of the outer by-pass, such development constituted sprawl.

The public inquiry revealed deficiencies in the technical basis of the proposals. The Secretary of State for Scotland took the view that the corporation simply did not have adequate information to produce a population figure for 1985. There were also discrepancies between different parts of the written statement in the data for housing provision. Furthermore, the Inquiry had elucidated the fact that the estimated densities, particularly the higher ones, were not being realized in practice. The Labour Secretary of State, Mr William Ross, therefore reduced the estimated local authority housing provision from 16,057 to 14,806, because he considered that planned densities were excessive 'to permit a well-ordered development with the necessary amenities for modern urban life'.[20]

In contrast, the Secretary of State increased the allocation for private houses from 10,800 to 11,823.[21] The Reporter had carefully sifted the arguments of the developers and of property owners who had contested the zonings for twenty-four sites. His recommendations were generally accepted by the Secretary of State, often with relatively minor amendments. No discernible pattern of political priority emerges in these decisions; densities, phasing, and zoning are juggled between the plan, the objectors, the Reporter and the Secretary of State, within an agreed set of technical criteria. Despite the political priority accorded to housing in the 1960s and despite the potential divisions between a Labour Secretary of State and a Progressive City Council, the housing aspects of the Development

Plan Review remained depoliticized. There was no co-ordinated campaign against the proposals and conflicts were a mere haggling between developers and local property interests.

Planners have persistently claimed to be neutral experts, whose arbitration of land use conflicts protects the public interest. This ideology is consistent with the proclaimed impartiality of the state itself. The way the private housing land question was progressed through Development Plan Review, public inquiry, Reporter's recommendations and Secretary of State's decisions, might seem to make this interpretation credible. However, it begs a number of considerations. The Review sought to manage rather than redirect the restructuring of housing provision that was already occurring. The plan was for regulated suburbanization consistent with the conservation of key landscape elements that were integral to the image of the city and with the protection of the best agricultural land, as required by central government officials. The density of the new housing was to vary markedly between private and public sectors – those who could afford to do so would live on the ground, while the council tenants would be in flats. The locations assigned to the two sectors were also different – social spatial segregation was an implicit aim in the Development Plan Review.

The Development Plan Review minimized but did not eliminate the situations where council housing was to be developed close to owner-occupied estates. Where such aberrations did occur there was controversy. The main opposition came at Alnwickhill and at Wester Hailes, but each case was fought by isolated groups of objectors. Likewise the homeless, the badly housed and the 11,000 or so households then on the waiting list were disparate, unorganized individuals, and were not party to the public inquiry on the statutory review of the Development Plan. Indeed, the technical style of the plan and the associated statutory procedures, imposed extra barriers between decisions within the administrative system and political challenge. It was on these circumstances that the ideology of the profession and the state was anchored.

The legitimacy of the local authority's town planning was threatened by the housing question, but not substantially eroded. Indeed, that legitimacy was bolstered not just by notions of fairness associated with the waiting list, but also by the mediation which the planning process entailed between developers and objectors. Nevertheless a major problem remained. It was in the interests of local employers to have a well-housed local labour force and the provision of new housing boosted both the construction industry and commodity consumption in general. On the other hand, the provision of such housing at a price lower-income households could afford was not a market proposition. When undertaken through the local authority there were problems of land availability and political hostility from ratepayers. These contradictions took the form of deficiencies of rationality in the plan: the planned densities for council housing were too high to attain in practice (let alone in terms of providing an acceptable living environment), the scale and location of overspill could not be determined and the legacy of unfit housing could not be expeditiously eradicated.

Reconstruction and the property boom

As was the case in the UK as a whole during the 1950s, service sector employment in Edinburgh grew both relatively and absolutely. The only new industrial area of any size that was developed within the city during this period was the 126-acre Sighthill Industrial Estate, located on the western edge of the city. The estate had been on the drawing boards from 1939, but development did not commence until 1952. Sighthill then attracted firms engaged in food processing, light engineering and the production of precast concrete and other building materials. Despite this, manufacturing employment in the city as a whole declined markedly between the censuses of 1951 and 1961, as Table 16 shows.

Table 16   *Employment change in Edinburgh, 1951-61*

	1951		1961	
	'000	%	'000	%
Primary	4.51	2.1	3.81	1.6
Agriculture, forestry and fishing	2.30	1.1	1.20	0.5
Mining and quarrying	2.21	1.0	2.61	1.1
Manufacturing	68.81	31.3	58.94	25.2
Food, drink and tobacco	17.59	8.0	16.93	7.3
Chemicals	3.12	1.4	2.81	1.2
Metals and engineering	21.54	9.8	18.20	7.8
Textiles, leather and clothing	6.01	2.7	3.50	1.5
Bricks, pottery and glass	1.79	0.8	1.26	0.5
Timber, furniture	3.80	1.7	2.48	1.1
Paper, printing and publishing	10.19	4.6	11.02	4.7
Other manufacturing	4.77	2.2	2.74	1.2
Construction	15.81	7.2	17.95	7.7
Services	130.58	59.4	152.07	65.2
Gas, water and electricity	3.58	1.6	3.73	1.6
Transport and communications	22.03	10.0	22.14	9.5
Commerce and finance	38.61	17.6	49.11	21.0
Professional services	24.70	11.2	28.50	12.2
Public administration and defence	19.46	8.9	17.53	7.5
Unclassified	—	—	0.56	0.2
	219.73	100	233.33	100

Source: Census of Scotland, GRO, Edinburgh.

Though manufacturing employment declined, Edinburgh's unemployment rate remained substantially below the Scottish average. As can be seen from Table 16, the major growth was in commerce and finance and professional services. The employment trends thus re-emphasized the city's disproportionately middle-class social structure. However, the same trends also generated development pressures, as the financial, administrative and educational institutions sought to satisfy their growing demands for space within the central parts of the city. As was shown in the Calton Hill development in the 1930s, and over Abercrombie's plan to restructure the city, such pressures within Edinburgh were bound to be deeply problematic.

Nationally this early post-war period was characterized by deficiencies in labour supply that were both quantitative and qualitative. One response by the state was to substantially expand higher education. A planned physical expansion of Edinburgh University was already an established and recurring motif in plans for the city. The university also had a development plan of its own, which had been drawn up by Sir Charles Holden in 1945. This included proposals for redevelopment of George Square with new university buildings. Apart from one intrusion on the north side, the square had remained substantially unaltered architecturally since its construction as the first southern suburb in 1776. Moves to implement the plan provoked a controversy described by a contemporary writer as 'one of the most prolonged and violent in Edinburgh's history'.[22]

The proposals in the Holden Plan had been worked-up by Basil Spence and Professor Robert Matthew. The plan was to demolish the eighteenth-century buildings and replace them by modern buildings tailored to meet the university's requirements for growth. The intention was to create a new arts building and a library, as well as extending the medical school. Only the houses on the west side of the square were to be retained, as these could meet the functional requirements of some smaller departments. After some delay, the Town Council gave planning permission in 1956.

Opposition to the plan mushroomed, essentially on amenity grounds. After all, the square was still almost complete, it was the predecessor of the New Town and, as Keir observed, it 'was associated with successive generations of notable citizens'.[23] Thus the continuity of the historic image, even a part of the heritage of the Scottish ruling class, was threatened by an institution that was closely associated with that class and by the logic of instrumental rationality on which that class had prospered. The historic square was defended by the National Trust for Scotland, affronted citizens writing from high-status addresses and many of the university's own staff and students. Interestingly, the Cockburn Association did not join the protests. However, an Edinburgh Georgian Group (which later became the Scottish Georgian Society) was formed to fight the demolition.

In 1959 the protestors appealed to the Secretary of State for Scotland to set up an inquiry into the scheme. The Secretary of State rejected this call, but took the most unusual step of convening a working group made up of four members from the university and four of the protestors. His hope was that a compromise could be worked out in this way: after all, the protestors accepted the validity of the university using the square and much of the surrounding area, their case was that the historic buildings could be adapted for university purposes. The Amenity

Societies Study Group met on six occasions, with the brief to find an alternative solution, provided that such a solution offered advantages at least comparable to those in the university's own plan. Having failed to achieve this, the Group referred the matter back to the Secretary of State, inviting him to decide between three alternatives. These were, either to accept the university's proposals, or to amend them by adapting the houses to university purposes, or to prepare a new scheme.

The Secretary of State ruled in favour of the university. He argued that the expansion of higher education was a key part of public policy, and therefore the growth of Edinburgh University should not be delayed. He supported his decision by referring to the views of the Historic Buildings Council. They had suggested that while the architecture of George Square was interesting, it was second class when compared with Charlotte Square. The Secretary of State's own technical advisers had also indicated that the buildings were dilapidated and unsuited to conversion to the standards required by modern university buildings. The fourteen-storey David Hume Tower began to rise above the Meadows from the south-eastern corner of the square. In aesthetic terms it did nothing to persuade the objectors that their criticisms had been ill-founded, nor did it restore their confidence in the local authority's planning decisions.

The configuration of interests present in the George Square controversy strained beyond endurance the capabilities of both the council and the planning system to achieve the proclaimed mediation between development pressures and the 'public interest'. Though the issues were never politicized in class or even party terms, the legitimacy of the state itself was undermined. The Secretary of State, for example, clearly felt the need to treat the objectors very seriously and to be seen to go as far as was possible to accommodate their ideas. The Amenities Societies Study Group and the technical support from the Historic Buildings Council were means by which the state sought to restore legitimacy, while ensuring that its development priorities could still be satisfied. The rupture of Edinburgh's classic skyline by the erection of David Hume Tower expressed the forced marriage between the historic capital and the interventionist state, so as to reproduce a labour force.

The drive to restructure the fabric of the city came directly from the state itself, as in George Square, and from the construction industry and the developing branch of capital involved in commercial property investment. Unfamiliar physical forms were integral to these new opportunities for capital accumulation, but the same forms were likely to provoke public antipathy, especially as to be most profitable they would have to be located within Edinburgh's cherished historical environment. The case for adapting the city to accommodate these strange edifices was frequently articulated by prominent planners and architects associated with the city. The professionals used their neutral, technical expertise to legitimize the developmental desiderata of property capital. By arguing that modernization could be made acceptable with proper planning they obscured the interests at play. The result was a protracted, often heated debate about planning, in the course of which planning became discredited with large sections of the public, because of its association with development.

In 1958 Alan Reiach was arguing strongly in favour of high-rise buildings in the New Town at George Street. Mr Reiach was one of Edinburgh's most respected architect–planners and a member of the Princes Street Panel, which advised the local authority on design matters affecting the premier shopping street. He spoke in support of major redevelopment proposals for a site on George Street, arguing that the ridge there would be the proper place to locate high buildings, though he suggested that the towers should be restricted to 120 feet in height. He advocated the demolition of Rose Street and Thistle Street, the streets designed in Craig's original plan for lower rent properties and their replacement by car parks. If such a plan were implemented, he prophesied, George Street could be transformed to become one of the finest commercial streets in Europe.[24]

The case for high buildings in the centre of Edinburgh was also pressed in the September 1958 issue of *Architectural Review*. An article by 'M. L.' criticized the restrictions on high buildings which the Planning Committee imposed. Instead the author called for the creation of a new townscape, unshackled by the rigidities of an inflexible plan. The architectural profession persistently argued that they should be given a stronger say on aesthetic matters in the city. Basil Spence, when President of the RIBA and masterminding the development proposals of Edinburgh University in George Square and the South Side, called on the Town Council to consult expert advisers on aesthetic matters.[25] In this he was supported by the Cockburn Association and by the Earl of Haddington as President of the Georgian Group.[26] The Edinburgh Architectural Association took a deputation to the Lord Provost, to urge that the Corporation should employ private architects, rather than just give work out to contractors.[27] They were supported by Nicholas Fairbairn, who argued that such a move would be an antidote to the environmental deterioration which the city was experiencing.[28]

Architects and planners were also represented on the sub-committee set up by the Edinburgh Chamber of Commerce in 1962, to prepare their evidence for the Development Plan Review. The Committee included Percy Johnson-Marshall, Mr Lawrie Nisbet from the College of Art and two more architects with private practices in the city, as well as Councillor Robert Smith (Liberal), who was a Chartered Surveyor. Their report endorsed a development-led approach to planning, so as to adjust the city to 'the increasing tempo of social and technical advancement'.[29]

Edinburgh was sucked into the national 'property boom' in the early 1960s. Within a few years several central sites had been earmarked for schemes valued at millions of pounds. One of the early proposals was for a 178-feet high tower block extension to the George Hotel in George Street. The case for the developer was put by Mr McIndoe, probably Scotland's leading planning appeals consultant. He argued that there was an urgent need for extra first-class hotel accommodation in Edinburgh and that restriction of growth in the city centre was a bad thing. A spokesman for the National Commercial Bank threatened that unless controls were relaxed, George Street would become a mere museum piece, sans banks and insurance companies. In contrast, Percy Johnson-Marshall described the designs as 'urban barbarism'.[30] The Secretary of State turned down the appeal against the refusal of planning permission.

Highland Engineering Ltd were more fortunate, getting permission for a £400,000 office block of eight storeys in Jeffrey Street early in 1963. The site was one where an earlier plan for a five-storey block, priced at £120,000, had been abandoned in 1958 for financial reasons. The tenants for the new building, as for several others, were the government, seeking extra floorspace to accommodate their extended administration. The Argyle House development at the West Port was another block where central government agreed in advance to take out a long-term lease.

Inevitably the development boom impinged on Princes Street's prime but archaic frontages. The Princes Street Panel had acknowledged that the street had become a jumble of styles and sought therefore to steer new developments to conform to a uniform type of facade. The annual report of the Planning Committee for 1963 noted the demolition of four listed buildings in Princes Street. The report claimed that progress was being made in modernizing the commercial activities within the city, while observing that there had been some opposition. The most controversial development had, in fact, been the demolition of the Scottish Life Association building, which was replaced by a chain store. The Scottish Georgian Society led the protestors, though the Cockburn Association was not among them. Ex-Provost Sir J. G. Dunbar was particularly upset at the way that local firms were being squeezed out of Princes Street because it had become so expensive.[31]

On the other side of Princes Street the corporation and British Rail agreed a scheme to redevelop Waverley Station and the adjoining Waverley Market. The £10 million project was to have involved the construction of a platform over the station. A pavilion was to be built on the platform, rising fifteen feet above the level of Princes Street. The Royal Fine Arts Commission were heavily critical.[32]

A major redevelopment had been designed for the other station close to the city centre, Haymarket, just months earlier. In 1964 planning permission was granted for a twenty-storey office block, and two ten-storey office blocks, together with shops, parking and a petrol filling station, in what added up to a £2 million project. In all 256,280 square feet of office floorspace and 16,608 square feet of retailing were to be created. In the same meeting of the committee, planning permission was also given for a 102,000 square feet office development by Lloyds and Scottish Finance at Orchard Brae, to the north west of the city centre.[33]

Major commercial redevelopment was also planned for the Tollcross area, which *The Scotsman's* property correspondent described as being 'certain to attract leading developers'.[34] A London-based firm of planning consultants, Jellicoe and Coleridge, were appointed to submit plans, as the corporation's own Planning Department did not have sufficient staff to do the job. It was envisaged that the corporation would spend £4.2 million on the acquisition and demolition of property. They would build a huge raised traffic roundabout, with an inner ring road passing twenty-six feet over a traffic free shopping centre below. The centre was to be developed by City Wall Properties (Scotland) Ltd, at an estimated cost of £2 million.[35] The company had been formed in Spring 1965 as a Scottish subsidiary of City Wall and was closely tied to the Edinburgh-based Standard Life for its finance.[36]

Near to Tollcross the corporation was also involved in plans for a £4 million conference centre and cultural complex at Castle Terrace. This scheme, as part of a plan to provide an opera house for the Festival City, involved two theatres, a 100-bedroom hotel, a conference suite, restaurants and exhibition areas.[37]

Development proposals were also well advanced for the St James Square area, at the eastern end of Princes Street. The Development Plan had zoned the area for commercial redevelopment and a Comprehensive Development Area plan was drawn up in 1960. A Public Inquiry was held in June 1961 to hear the few objections to the scheme: though Georgian buildings were involved, they were not of the best and the vast bulk of the houses were substandard or unfit. No less than eighteen developers tendered to be involved in the redevelopment and in October 1963 the corporation drew up a short list of three candidates. One withdrew, leaving the choice between the Murrayfield Property Company and Hammerson's. The Town Planning Officer recommended that Hammerson's proposals should be accepted, as they were superior on planning and architectural grounds. However, the councillors opted for Murrayfield. Throughout the choices were strongly geared to strict commercial criteria, as indeed the central government advice on city centre planning suggested they ought to be.[38] A £10 million partnership scheme was being talked of, involving shops, offices, a hotel and parking with improvements to the roads. The tenants of the offices were again to be the government.

The other area where major commercial development was expected was in the South Side. Edinburgh University became concerned that piecemeal commercial redevelopments of low architectural standards would undermine their hopes for a unified and dignified in-town campus. Their planning consultant, Professor Johnson-Marshall, came up with the idea that a Comprehensive Development Area should be designated. The redevelopment was to have three aspects. Alongside the university's own development programme, the corporation was to oversee the renewal of housing and the construction of new roads, while the Nicolson Street area would be redeveloped for commercial purposes by the Murrayfield Real Estate Company. The scheme was backed by the Corporation's Planning Committee in 1962 and the three parties formed a Joint Co-ordinating Committee. Eventually a CDA plan was approved by the Town Council in 1968, though it was never to be submitted to the Secretary of State, as it was overtaken by events.

The importance of the university itself as a property developer should not be underestimated. Between 1963 and 1968 eight major university buildings were completed in the South Side. Indeed, during the period from 1962 to 1966 the university received grants totalling £5.7 million for seventeen building projects.[39] Heriot-Watt was also expanding and in 1966 was responsible for the building of the Mountbatten Building in the Grassmarket. In addition, the Royal Infirmary aspired to undertake a £15 million building programme close to the two universities.[40]

Edinburgh in the early 1960s offered rich pickings. As the city was tied firmly to administration and finance the demand for office accommodation was considerable. Furthermore the main office area, the New Town, was subject to planning restrictions, thus augmenting the scarcity of purpose-built modern offices. The booming logic of property speculation was irresistible to a Council which prided itself on its financial acumen and which had traditionally sought to reach a concordat with development interests in the city. Thus the Town Planning Officer felt that, 'future developments can be permitted without disadvantage and sometimes with advantages to the exceptional amenities of the city – if the developments are suitably located and designed'.[41] To help him steer this wave of property development around the city's enormous stock of listed buildings, Mr Hewitson had, in early 1962, just six other professionally qualified planners. This ratio of planners to population was notably lower than in comparable British cities at the time,[42] just as Edinburgh's rates were also lower.

The local authority's planning capacity was not solely limited by its reluctance to adequately staff its Planning Department. The planners had no control over the movements of capital that initiated the property boom, nor could they do much about the temporary collapse of the market that came in the later 1960s. They did not influence the decision of central government to try to cut back public expenditure, which meant reductions in the planned building programme of the University Grants Committee for the quinquennium 1967–72 and which created mounting problems of delays and uncertainties in the South Side area.

Fundamentally the planning endeavours of the council were encompassed within the workings of market processes. The development at the St James Centre illustrated their dilemmas most fully. In the early stages of the project there was a bitter row, albeit a private one, between the corporation and the Royal Fine Arts Commission. The commission's views on the competing designs were not sought and when they discovered that the plan chosen involved a tower block some 274 feet high and a massive high-rise slab that blocked the view at the end of George Street, the commission expressed their deep concern. The local authority were themselves both financially involved in the scheme and beholden for its success to their development partners, Ravenseft Properties, who took over Murrayfield. Their bargaining position was weak. Under the terms of the deal the corporation acquired and cleared the site, were beholden to complete major road works adjacent to the site by the opening day and to provide a pedestrian approach bridge from the east across the roads and were effectively debarred from charging rates on empty properties within the completed complex. The developers then took a 125-year lease on the land, at a basic ground rent of £100,000. The net income over £386,000 on initial letting was to be halved, though the benefits of increases in rental after the initial letting would be split 60/40 in favour of the developer. This more favourable division for Ravenseft was agreed as an amendment to the original deal, which had specified a 50/50 split once Ravenseft had taken an 11 per cent return on their investment. It was thus compensated for the introduction of Corporation Tax and the slowing down of the economy in the period after the property boom. It is estimated that the corporation invested £4 million in acquiring and servicing the site and compensating the property owners. The roadworks associated with this part of the inner ring road were costed at £7.1 million in the Quinquennial Review.[43] In 1975–6 the return to the ratepayers after their receipt of ground rent was £5117. The local authority was thus more effective in securing a profitable investment for the developers than for the ratepayers.

The property boom thus reactivated the persistent and deep contradiction between the modernizing imperatives of the drive to capital accumulation and the ideological investment in the culture expressed by the historical townscape. Property development *par excellence* constituted the 'unearned' appropriation of value through the provision of 'unwanted' commodities, the unacceptable face of capitalism. The commodities were unwanted in that the aesthetics of the developments expressed nothing more than the functional requirements of administration, and the maximization of capital and its concentration. This triumph of accountancy they expressed so fully as to foster public alienation not identity. Further there was the illogicality of the competitive generation of schemes for vast developments which would be mutually incompatible in strictly commercial terms if they all went ahead.

The planning system then sought to manage these contradictions so that through the intervention of the administrative system, the proclaimed rationality and impartiality of the urban development process could be reasserted. Such an exercise was to prove almost impossible to achieve in practice. Of course some applications were refused and not all the appeals were sustained, but nevertheless the capacity of the planning system was fundamentally constrained both by the priorities of the local political system and by its wider subservience to the market. Furthermore a rational plan had to resolve the competition between the differing schemes coming forward and had to integrate and resolve the total impacts on the physical environment created by the drive to capital accumulation reflected in the modernization of the processes of production and distribution and by the conversion of unprofitable activities into commodities. In Edinburgh during the 1960s the thread that tied all this endeavour together, and which prompted a crisis of legitimacy, was the inner ring road.

Restructuring the transport system

Increased car ownership and usage was central to the consumer boom of the 1950s and 1960s. It was both a direct and an indirect creator of new commodities. However, the consequent increases in traffic congestion amounted to a considerable indirect cost to the production system itself. Reducing these costs therefore became a central concern of urban planners at this time. In Edinburgh, as Abercrombie had realized, the problem was complicated by the environmental heritage and the associated patterns of social spatial segregation. In particular the standard prescription of an inner ring road could not be fitted easily through 'soft' areas of decaying and substandard working-class housing. The expanse of the New Town to the north of the centre posed extreme difficulties.

The problems first came to prominence at Randolph Crescent, on the north-western edge of the central area. The corporation proposed to build a traffic roundabout, which the New Town residents perceived as threatening the Georgian architecture and their own property interests. This conflict came hard on the heels of the controversy at George Square, further eroding public confidence in the local authority's capability to manage urban change.

Proposals for a traffic roundabout at Randolph Crescent had been drafted by the City Engineer some years earlier. They had not been included in the twenty-year phasing of the Development Plan, however, because officials of the Ministry of Transport had indicated that the scheme was unlikely to be given financial aid from central government within that time, so the unprogrammed proposal in the 1953 Plan had not been contentious. However, in 1957 the Ministry indicated that finance would now be available. The corporation therefore drew up an amendment to the Development Plan to incorporate the roundabout into the first five-year phase of the Plan. Compared with the later road plans for the city, very little property was threatened. To make the roundabout the corporation reckoned that some basements would have to be filled in, street levels would have to be altered and the granite setts would be replaced by a modern asphalt surface. In addition, seventy-three trees would have to be demolished. Such disruption was seen to be justified by the relief to traffic congestion that the roundabout would afford on a major route into the city centre at a time when car ownership was increasing rapidly. Without the roundabout, the officials feared that further traffic would transfer to Princes Street itself, leading to a further deterioration of the showpiece shopping parade. With the discrete freeing of finance by central government the corporation was launched on a collision course with some of its most prominent citizens.

A vigorous protest rapidly developed. This time the Cockburn Association did involve themselves, as, again, did the Georgian Group. More local protestors included the Lord Moray's Feuars and the Randolph Crescent Proprietors. The activists included eminent men, notably Sir Compton Mackenzie, Moray McLaren and the Earl of Haddington, who were supported by Sir John Betjeman. Through the support of the Edinburgh Architectural Association they had the backing of professional planners and architects, whose letters to *The Scotsman* queried the technical competence of the corporation's proposals.

A recurring strand of criticism concerned the cost and value for money of the scheme. Official estimates put the cost of the roundabout at £80,000 or £100,000. The question then was whether such expenditure could be justified for what was supposedly a purely local traffic improvement, saving rush-hour motorists a mere thirty seconds' delay. The suspicion prevailed that the roundabout was but the precursor of some more extensive remodelling of traffic movements in the central area, a plan hitherto unrevealed and quite possibly not fully worked out. The EAA argued that the corporation's ultimate intention was to establish a northern by-pass of the central area, running from the Forth Bridge in the west, round the centre via Randolph Crescent and Queen Street on to London Road and then east to the A1. The concomitant was that corporation buses would be routed through the New Town, degrading its amenity and, implicitly, its social exclusiveness.[44] Such criticisms had a twofold significance. First, they appealed to the traditional desire of the city's *bourgeoisie* for low rates and limited local authority expenditure. Second, they called into question the good faith of the corporation. By alleging that the roundabout was but the thin end of a concealed wedge, the prominent protestors were eroding the legitimacy of the administrative system. This is not to suggest they acted out of malice or in a conspiratorial manner. As professionals they would presumably have been aware that the search for an acceptable northern line for an inner ring road had defeated Abercrombie and that the Development Plan had discretely omitted a northern link, while planning the road improvements required to handle the mounting traffic volumes in other parts of the city. The challenge to legitimacy would therefore have been predicated by the crisis avoidance strategies of the Development Plan itself.

The row that developed around the proposals of BBC Television to broadcast a feature in the *Panorama* programme shows both the depth of the distrust of the corporation that the Randolph Crescent scheme generated and the influential connections of the various protagonists. The mere fact that the BBC decided that a row about a traffic roundabout in Edinburgh was a matter worth a national airing is itself significant. While it is not unusual for local London issues to be so elevated, the decision can only be explained by two factors. On the one hand public protest over planning proposals must still have been something of a novelty in 1958. On the other hand, and probably more important, were the personalities who were protesting. The BBC intended to stage a debate, with Betjeman, Compton-Mackenzie and Hubert Fenwick, RIBA, putting the protestors' case. However, Edinburgh Corporation declined to take part, on the grounds that the impending public inquiry made the matter *sub judice*. The feature was cancelled at short notice, with the protestors alleging that the local authority had used their connections to bring behind-the-scenes pressures to bear. The BBC said that the Randolph Crescent feature was taken out because there were other international news items that had to be covered instead. A ten-minute feature was eventually transmitted in *Panorama* on 20 April 1959, several months later.

The attacks on the integrity of themselves and their officials stung local councillors. In response they attempted to re-establish the neutrality and technical basis of their actions and to discredit their critics. Thus in a bitter council debate on the scheme, Councillor Bruce Russell said, 'It is our plain and bounden duty as a road authority to provide proper facilities for the passage of traffic.' Treasurer J. G. Dunbar argued that change was inevitable and that the New Town could not be exempted. Several councillors queried the good faith of the objectors. After all, the roundabout had appeared in the 1953 Development Plan Town Map, albeit not very distinctly, and as something that would not come to pass in the next twenty years at least. Nobody had protested then. Furthermore, when the Cockburn Association were first shown the scheme in 1957, they had said they were

244   *The development of planning thought*

impressed by it, while reserving their position on the details. Why the sudden hostility? Councillor Russell suspected some 'sinister influence' was at work in the minds of the Cockburn Association, while Baillie Ingham castigated the association as comprising a few people distinguished in walks of life which gave them no experience in a matter of this sort, together with others who were jumping on a bandwagon.[45] In a report to the council, the chief officers dismissed their critics as ill-informed, a view that could probably be sustained in the light of the limited information which the officials had made public about their plans.[46]

Nevertheless the local political system was destabilized by the issue. A senior Progressive Councillor, Tom Curr, publicly associated himself with the Cockburn Association's criticisms.[47] Councillor McLoughlin, whose ward included the site, at first supported the plans, then changed his mind. One of the residents of the Crescent was himself a former Baillie, Mr J. B. Mackenzie, who proposed a southern by-pass through the Cowgate as an alternative, while admitting that it would pose problems around Holyrood Palace.[48] When they were first presented, the proposals drawn up by the technical officers had been approved unanimously by all relevant committees and also by the full council. In the light of the public criticisms the council decided to reconsider the matter. When they did so, the scheme was re-approved by 43–13.

The saga brought into question not just the good faith of the authorities, but also the technical rationality of their proposals. Critics argued that instead of deriving the proposals out of a comprehensive analysis of the interplay of transport, land use and environment, the officials were merely engaged in a piece of road engineering. This theme was hammered home in letters to *The Scotsman* signed by authors appending ARIBA, AMTPI after their names.[49] Such professionals argued that at the very least expert traffic surveys were required, whereas even the corporation did not claim that their proposals were based on anything more than a one-day traffic census; when a further census was taken in the adjoining streets on 21 August 1958, the police refused to say whether it was in any way connected with the impending public inquiry! Throughout the corporation fought a running battle to paper over the deficiencies in their initial proposals. Faced with the outcry over the proposed destruction of the Randolph Crescent gardens and their mature trees, the corporation ingeniously suggested that since the gardens were essentially Victorian they were out of character with the Georgian architecture around them. Just five days before the public inquiry was to start, the Planning Committee amended their proposals, so as to belatedly include tree planting along the verges between the roads, together with an unspecified monumental feature in the middle of the roundabout.[50]

The Inquiry was contested by the Cockburn Association, the Moray Place Feuars, the Scottish Georgian Society, the EAA and the Randolph Crescent proprietors. Their expert witnesses included D. S. Wishart, who presented an alternative, cheaper road line, albeit one involving some demolitions, A. T. McIndoe and Robert Hurd. The corporation countered with their own officials, the Lord Provost and prominent planners, including Rendel Govan (who suggested that the business life of Edinburgh needed a proper 'inner circle ring road'), William

Kinnimouth (who felt the scheme would become a *tour de force* of town planning, if the roundabout were designed as a piazza with a fountain), Joseph Gleave (head of the Edinburgh College of Art architecture school 1939–49) and John Wilson Paterson, a former President of the EAA. The Inquiry began in June 1959, ran for three weeks, then was adjourned and completed in October. It cost the objectors £6000, an awful lot of money for 1959. The corporation's case was not helped by their failure to consider what impact the introduction of a new set of traffic lights at the West End of Princes Street would have on traffic movements in the area. On 24 November 1960 the Secretary of State for Scotland rejected the Randolph Crescent scheme, on the grounds that the corporation had not demonstrated that the traffic roundabout was the only practicable form of control: the scheme was premature; an overall plan was needed for city centre traffic.

Thus central government, having teased the scheme into existence, eventually vetoed it. The Secretary of State's solution was that advocated by most of the professional critics of the proposals. Faced by conflicts between modernizing the traffic system and preserving the historic environment, the hope was that an expert survey and plan could produce a rational solution, harmonizing all the interests. The application of the right technical expertise would allow traffic to be diverted to some usually unspecified, but surely uncontentious location, so facilitating the eternal preservation of the Georgian splendours of the New Town. The planning ideology shaped in the inter-war period but discredited when put into practice by Abercrombie was given a new lease of life as a means of resolving the crisis situation. It gained a new credibility because the technical case put forward by the corporation was so weak. Paradoxically, then, this deficit of technical rationality obscured the more fundamental limits on the corporation's planning capacity, notably its inability to reconcile the complicated and intermeshed middle class interests in the modernization and preservation of the city.

The confrontation between affluent and articulate property owners and the administration, with elected members nodding or shaking their heads on the side, left the city's traditional political structures in some disarray. As a contemporary letter to *The Scotsman* put it,

Important though the question of Randolph Crescent gardens is, it raises the much larger question of the relationship between the Town Council and the general body of citizens. Why is it so difficult for the ordinary citizen to take a practical interest in the affairs of his city: why is it so difficult for him to obtain information on what is going on and what is proposed for the future of his city? And why, when prominent citizens like Sir Compton Mackenzie and Mr Moray McLaren raise in public queries as to future policy which are of interest to all, are their queries left unanswered by the Town Council?[51]

Though the mechanism of the public inquiry, and its outcome, may have done something to ease the worries of those who could raise sufficient funds to subject the administration's priorities to scrutiny, the seeds of doubt and disaffection had been sown.

The inner ring road

The first official mention of an inner ring road came on 7 May 1963, when the City Engineer, Mr Dinnis, submitted a report to the council in connection with the redevelopment of St James Square. The first protest letter was published in *The Scotsman* five days later. The gestation of the proposals took place in a technical working party which met several times over the 1964–5 period. Its members were the City Engineer, Town Planning Officer, Chief Constable, Transport Manager and representatives from the Town Clerk's and City Chamberlain's departments. They were assisted by the corporation's planning and highways consultants and representatives of the Scottish Development Department, British Railways, Edinburgh University and the Princes Street Panel. The personnel included Professor T. E. H. Williams, Professor of Engineering at Newcastle University, D. S. Wishart, Professor Johnson-Marshall, and Sir William Kinnimouth. The group set out to establish the best highway plan for Edinburgh.

Staff from the City Engineer's department toured six European cities and reported positively on their systems of ring route urban motorways.[52] The experts deliberated and their proposals were passed by the relevant committees and the full council with scarcely a ripple, though the only Liberal on the Council, Robert Smith, did record his opposition when the Quinquennial Review of the Development Plan, which included the ring road, was approved in February 1965.

By 1964 the number of vehicles in Edinburgh had more than doubled from the 1951 figure and even showed a 35 per cent increase from 1960. The Development Plan Review therefore projected substantial traffic growth up to the end of the century at least. It also appeared that only a small percentage of the traffic could be syphoned off by an outer by-pass. The Plan noted the problems this scenario created in terms of costs and the preservation of areas of architectural and historic interest and concluded that major new roadworks were a necessity, together with parking controls and traffic management.

The proposals, illustrated in Figure 14, were built upon the road network scheduled in the 1957 Development Plan, though the details were altered. A number of routes included in the earlier plan were deleted. These were the Western Approach Road, Union Canal Road, Bridges Relief Road and Tollcross to St Leonards Link Road. They were replaced by:

1 An inner ring road – complete with grade separated junctions and designed for high traffic capacities. The line led from St James Square, under Waterloo Place, over the eastern end of Waverley Station, and under the Canongate to St Leonards. This eastern link was scheduled for Phase One. Phase Two was to run west to Tollcross and Haymarket. From there the western leg ran under Donaldson's Hospital grounds, over the Water of Leith and on to Comely Bank. Phase Three, the northern link, went along the Water of Leith to Canonmills and on through Broughton.

Figure 14   *The road proposals in the 1965 Development Plan Review*

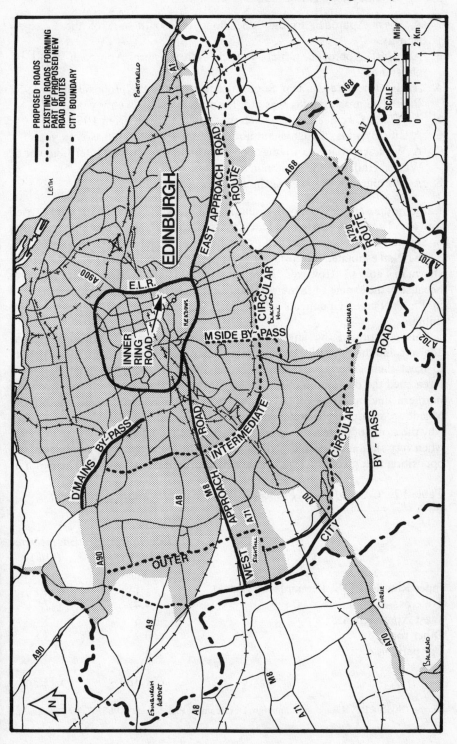

2   A West Approach to the M8, along the south side of the Glasgow railway.
3   An East Approach, which was the old Eastern Approach Road rechristened.
4   An Intermediate Circular Route, which repeated the proposal of the 1957 Plan. The programming was still for a period after twenty years.
5   An Outer Circular Route, which was again a legacy from 1957.
6   A City By-pass, though again not programmed until after twenty years.
7   A West Approach to Livingston link, running from the Outer Circular at Wester Hailes to the city boundary.
8   A Morningside By-pass, again not programmed.

Earlier proposals for Cramond, Granton, Tollcross and Haymarket were carried forward. There was also to be a Davidson's Mains By-pass, a new suburban road at Straiton-Burdiehouse, as well as improved approaches to Leith Docks.

The Plan estimated the costs of the proposals for the first ten years. These are shown in Table 17. However, the full costs would have been considerably more, because of the expense in acquiring land for the northern link of the inner ring road in Phase Three. Opponents of the plan frequently quoted figures of £100 million.

This constituted the attempt of the technical officers, their professional advisers and the Scottish Development Department to restructure the city so as to meet their criteria of technical rationality. However, the inner ring road threatened the demolition of sound, owner-occupied housing, especially on the northern link, and was routed through some high-amenity areas, notably the Meadows, where an elevated highway was envisaged. This still does not explain why the storm of protest that erupted was so much more vehement than in 1953, when very similar proposals were included in the Development Plan, or even the opposition that greeted Abercrombie's road proposals in 1947–9. The depth of

Table 17   *Costs of Road Proposals in the First 10 Years of the Plan*

	Acquisition and demolition (£m.)	Engineering (£m.)
Inner Ring Road (St Leonards–St James)	1.1	6
Tollcross–Haymarket	4.4	7.5
West Approach–M8	1.6	5
Other roads	0.2	3.8
Car parking	4	1
	£11.3m	£23.3m

Source: City and Royal Burgh of Edinburgh, Development Plan Review, 1965, Written Statement, p. 16.

the hostility might be explained by two related points. First, the proposals could no longer be dismissed as mere utopian doodling. Development pressures on the city at this stage were evidently intense and the credibility of the implementation of the plans was correspondingly increased. Furthermore, similar schemes were already being put into effect in other cities. The second factor was the growing loss of public confidence in the local authority's ability to manage change in the urban environment in an acceptable manner. For example, the long concordat between the Cockburn Association and the council had splintered at Randolph Crescent. In 1955 the council had mused that East Princes Street Gardens might make a good car park, a scheme that was hastily withdrawn after an angry public meeting organized by the Cockburn Association. Then in 1963 the Dean of Guild had the inspiring idea that six multi-storey car parks might be built in Queen Street Gardens in the New Town, before again beating a retreat. George Square was also still remembered and lamented as the new tower blocks soared over the skyline of the Meadows.

The city's political system that was dedicated to maintaining the *status quo*, or even reliving the glories and privileges of an earlier age, was hoist with a situation where the weight of technical evidence, and the pressure of developers, told them that the *status quo* was no longer an option. Yet Edinburgh's peculiar social geography, and the functional and locational requirements of the city of late capitalism, meant that the disbenefits of the process of change could not easily be deflected entirely on to the working class and their 'soft' living areas.

The problems were compounded by the particular nature of the city's administration. The historic antipathy of the Progressives towards planning as anything more than the piecemeal prevention of the worst excesses of development forces, had created a Planning Department that was short of staff and widely reputed to be ranked in low esteem within the bureaucracy. Certainly it was thought to carry less conviction and influence than the City Engineer's Department. Thus, despite the involvement of planners on the technical working party, the road proposals in the Quinquennial Review appeared to have been derived without any overall consideration of the inter-relation between land use and traffic, let alone any thorough examination of public transport-based strategies. The Review proposed to keep environmental standards 'flexible' until after the effects of the ring road were known. A parking plan was not produced as part of the Development Plan. That came some time later, as the controversy was moving to a crescendo. Then the City Engineer proposed two- and three-deck underground car parks beneath Princes Street and Queen Street Gardens and under St Andrew's and Charlotte Squares, a proposition that did little to restore confidence in the ability of the planners to make their professional colleagues responsive to environmental considerations.[53]

One consequence was that some of the most vociferous critics of the ring road were themselves planners, who were stung by the way the plan humiliated the expertise of their profession. Brian Parnell, a lecturer at Glasgow School of Art and a planning consultant, condemned it as a road engineer's plan which would destroy amenity, without solving the traffic problems because its analysis was so blinkered.[54] Tony Travis, from the Edinburgh College of Art Planning School, called for a more comprehensive planning approach, including the creation of a capital planning commission to lift Edinburgh planning out of the slough of competing interests, together with better public relations and more public participation.[55] Even Professor Johnson-Marshall eventually dissociated himself from aspects of the roads plan.

The plans were publicized in November 1965, with a lull before the opposition became vocal and organized. Predictably the most heated controversy flared around the northern line of the ring road. Faced with the extensive stock of expensive and historic buildings to the north of the centre, Abercrombie had sought to burrow a road beneath Princes Street. The row at Randolph Crescent was about an implicit attempt to steal a route through the New Town. Now the line was flung further north, keeping quite clear of the most prestigious streets, but still threatening swathes of owner-occupied properties, whose residents reliably returned Progressives to the Council and Conservatives to Westminster. Among their ranks were the solicitors, journalists, doctors, architects and civil servants who both made Edinburgh what it is and who constituted a potent opposition.

The Belle Vue Community Association were one of the first protest groups to form. By November 1966 they had 130 members and had dispatched two petitions to the Secretary of State. Hard on their heels came the Warriston Crescent Residents Association, defending their Georgian homes. The Comely Bank residents began to organize too, as did those of Gayfield Square. As the groups mushroomed along the northern link, they significantly strengthened their position by pooling their efforts into the North Edinburgh Joint Committee, which coordinated the opposition and raised £6000 to fight the inquiry.

Opposition in the south was not long delayed. In December 1966, the Meadows and South Edinburgh Group was formed at the meeting held in the flat of an art college architecture lecturer, Paul Newman. His colleague, David Skinner, was also on the committee. The Meadows Group distributed 10,000 notices seeking support and collected signatures on a petition. They worked closely with the Cockburn Association.

These groups staged packed public meetings. There was a unanimous vote of no confidence in the council's abilities to handle the city's future without the participation of the citizens.[56] Increasingly the critics pitched their case at the process by which the plan had been derived, rather than at the minutiae of the particular alignment. This built solidarity among the protestors, who could not then be divided by propositions that the route might be shifted to avoid particular properties. Just before the inquiry the Chairman of the Planning Committee, Councillor Millar, indicated that the route might be altered to avoid Warriston Crescent,[57] but the resolve of the objectors was undented. Nevertheless the opposition remained primarily directed at the northern and southern links. The eastern link, through areas of sub-standard working-class housing, excited little controversy. Again the main opposition to the proposals at Tollcross, another working-class area, was directed at the constraints which the elevated junction there forced on the design of the route through the Meadows.

The officials had sought to establish the principle of an inner ring road through the Development Plan Review, while leaving the actual details to be determined at a later stage of implementation. Thus the brochure publicizing the Plan only illustrated the route in diagrammatic form as a dotted line on an eye-level panoramic photograph of the city from the Salisbury Crags.[58] The logic, clearly reflecting the recommendations of the Planning Advisory Group, may have been sound in an ideal administrative world, but in reality it created problems. As with the Abercrombie Plan twenty years earlier, the practice confounded the ideology. Of course everyone supported the idea that a ring road was needed to take traffic away from the historic core, to ease congestion and to afford ready access to and through the centre. Indeed, the critics of the Randolph Crescent scheme had demanded an overall plan for city traffic. Here at last was that plan, looking to the year 2000, when each household might have two or three cars. But support was translated into vehement opposition once the ideas were specified into a six-lane highway with a ninety feet carriageway, grade separated junctions, and tunnels, running through seven miles of Edinburgh. The blandness and generality of the earlier propositions appeared to critics to signify both incompetence and deceit. Cynicism deepened when this tentative line, that merely illustrated the principle of a ring road, was suddenly pronounced to be the actual line, subject only to 'minor changes'.[59]

The loss of public confidence in the good faith and technical capabilities of the administration substantially destabilized the political system. Support for the road proposals within the Progressive Party was sapped as their councillors were assailed at hostile meetings of their constituents. After one such meeting in Corstorphine, Treasurer James MacKay asserted that while the Progressives supported the need for a new road, they did not endorse the actual northern route in the plan.[60] The most notable Pauline conversion was achieved by a Progressive councillor for Merchiston, Maurice Heggie. He had been on the Highways Committee from 1963 and was its chairman in 1965. In May 1965 he became a member of the Planning Committee and became its deputy chairman as the Plan moved towards the inquiry. He had thus overseen the preparation and approval of the ring road proposals and had been an outspoken supporter of them against early critics. By January 1967 he was leading the Progressives who were opposed to the roads. As Secretary of the Progressive group, he was calling for the complete withdrawal of the entire ring road. The city's four Conservative MPs also came out in opposition. The most outspoken right-wing supporter of the Plan remained Councillor John Millar, the Chairman of the Planning Committee.

The issue was also dividing the Labour Party. The leader of the Labour group of councillors, Jack Kane, was deeply sceptical of the proposals by January 1967, feeling that he, like the general public, had not had sufficient information to make a decision, despite one to approve the plan having been taken a year before. Tom Oswald, MP for Central Edinburgh, was a leading Labour critic of the plan. Among the councillors, the most prominent Labour opponent of the road proposals was significantly a relative newcomer, Sheila King Murray, who argued that the Labour members had endorsed the plan from totally inadequate information made available by the Progressives.[61] She was reprimanded by a more experienced colleague, Councillor Tom McGregor, who stressed that the proposals had been drawn up by the working party of accredited experts and had in no way been influenced by the Progressives.[62] It was presumably because they had such confidence in the neutrality and expertise of their officials that the majority of Labour members backed the plan. However, the General Management Committee of the City Labour Party came out against the roads, though only after setting up their own working party on the matter which was itself deeply divided. Labour members of the Planning Committee consistently backed their officials, while much of the agitation against the scheme came from party activists in some of the more middle-class areas that were directly threatened. The changing political awareness that the conflict brought about thus raised questions about the accountability of Labour councillors and the representativeness of the activists, which have become themes in Labour politics nationally in the 1980s.

The actions of the council illustrate the fragmentation of traditional political loyalties and the bewilderment of the politicians squeezed between their resolute officials and hostile constituents. First Councillor Heggie failed by ten votes to two to persuade the Planning Committee to delete the northern section of the ring road. Then the council decided to convene a special meeting just four days before the public inquiry was due to begin. The extraordinary meeting was to consider whether to amend the plan and the parties decided to give members a free vote on the issue.

The meeting was addressed by the officials and consultants who all spoke in favour of the ring road. Mr Hewitson conceded that some 1500 houses outside the redevelopment areas would have to be demolished, but reiterated his belief that an eighty to ninety feet wide ring road could be built without seriously damaging Edinburgh's special environmental qualities. The City Engineer stressed the need to build the ring road to protect the city centre from being flooded with traffic. Professor Williams assured the elected members that an elevated motorway through the Meadows would retain the amenity of the area, as there would still be pedestrian access to the open space. Mr Wishart stressed the need to cater for cars to keep the city's businesses viable. The £100 million cost attributed to the scheme was dismissed as exaggerated; Mr Dinnis put the figure at £50 million, Mr Hewitson at £44 million. The only note of expert doubt was the confession that two members of the working party, Professor Johnson-Marshall and Mr Kinnimouth, had not been 'entirely satisfied' with the final proposals.

After a long debate the chairman of the Planning Committee, Councillor Millar, moved to retain the existing plan. He was seconded by Councillor Crichton (Labour). Thirty-two members voted for the motion, seventeen of them Labour, fifteen Progressive. They were opposed by twenty-six votes, nine from Labour members, seventeen from the Progressives. Councillor Smith abstained, and seven others were absent. A relieved Councillor Millar concluded that the city definitely needed to appoint a public relations officer to answer the public's questions on planning.[63] In other words, the new politics of environment had to be countered by the new techniques of depoliticizing public discourse. Just weeks earlier the same Councillor Millar had been saying that it would be wrong to disclose details of the proposals to the public, as that was the true function of the public inquiry.

The inquiry

The public inquiry on the Development Plan Review was convened on 17 January 1967 and then adjourned pending the decision of the extraordinary Council Meeting two days later. It reopened on 30 January and ran for forty-one days, accumulating 6000 pages of evidence. The ring road was the first issue considered and discussions on it ran for six weeks.

In the course of the inquiry, Mr Hewitson revealed that his Department had prepared two inner ring road plans. Two inexperienced planners had been given a year to study the problems of the central area and had come up with a northern route through Queen Street Gardens, tunnelled beneath Moray Place and Wemyss Place, a prospect which the Town Planning Officer described as 'appalling'. Nevertheless this proposal for a tight ring round the commercial core, and running through the New Town, had been studied by the technical working party in April 1964. The second plan, drafted in November 1964, was substantially the one in the Development Plan, though that had actually been prepared by the City Engineer's Department on the basis of ideas originated by the working party.

Mr Dinnis now costed the inner ring road at £54 million, with the other road proposals at a further £38 million. The costs of land acquisition for the inner ring were put at £20,775,000. Mr Dinnis admitted that officials from the Scottish Development Department had been critical of the extent to which the figures exceeded the £40 million they had earmarked for road development in Edinburgh, but he said the job of the working party had been to produce the right scheme. No cost-benefit analysis of the roads had been attempted. The City Engineer asserted that subsidized bus fares were no answer to the city's escalating traffic problems.

Professor Arthur Ling was the most prominent expert witness for the objectors. He attacked the whole basis of the roads proposals, which he described as 'premature, preconceived and wrongly based on inadequate preliminary investigation'. They were not integrated with the land use planning, public transport or parking. Professor Ling held up Abercrombie's proposals as being a much more balanced approach which merited re-examination.

Mr McIndoe linked the public outcry over the Edinburgh proposals to a growing unease with planning everywhere. He particularly highlighted the ambiguity about whether the proposals were merely illustrative of a principle, or site-specific. The inquiry was apparently examining a fluid line near which a ring road was to be built. Once approved, the corporation would have the power to build the road anywhere they wanted, provided it was reasonably close to the line. Mr McIndoe said that this showed the deficiency of the planning machinery and the Reporter interrupted to concur with him.

Willie Ross, Secretary of State for Scotland, gave his decision in a thirty-three-page report in January 1968. He described the concept of a ring road as 'pre-conceived'. Nevertheless, he approved the eastern link, subject to adjustment of the interchanges. He also approved the East and West Approach Roads, together with the by-passes for Davidson's Mains and Morningside and the Cramond foreshore road. However, he did not approve the northern link, on the grounds that it would do great damage to amenity and could not be routed through redevelopment areas. The Secretary of State called on the corporation to appoint a consultant 'of the highest calibre' to prepare a plan and transport study for the central area. The southern link of the inner ring, from St Leonards to Haymarket through the Meadows, was approved, subject to further examination by the consultants.

Central government therefore constrained the development ambitions of the local authority, despite the prior involvement of representatives of the Scottish Development Department on the working party which had fashioned the ring road. The Secretary of State followed his Reporter and responded to the technical deficiencies in the corporation's case (notably the inadequacy of the data base, and the lack of integration of the land use and transport planning) and to the public hostility that the plan had generated. Nevertheless, the solution which central government imposed fundamentally reasserted the primacy of technical analysis on urban development decisions. A consultant of the highest calibre would come up with the correct answers and thus either make the conflicts go away, or expose those dissenters as ignorant and motivated by self-interest in the face of the public good.

Much of the road plan was indeed endorsed. The Reporter's findings of fact stated,

At the Inquiry there was ultimately no serious dispute about the need for primary dis-tributor roads or motorways of expressway standard near the centre of the city. The real issue became confined to the form *and* location of the new primary distributor roads, and, in particular, whether the Corporation had discharged the onus upon them of showing that the correct solution was a motorway in the form of a complete ring along the line they now propose.[64]

The imperative of modernizing the road system was therefore accepted. However, the Reporter had criticized the lack of communication both within the local authority and towards the public. A respected outside consultant would be the mechanism to redress these impending crises of rationality and legitimacy within the administrative system.

A physical development plan for a city, in which the transport strategy for the central area was unresolved, would probably be failed if submitted as a 'practical' project by a planning student. In practice that is what Edinburgh was left with in 1968. The credibility of the plan was further undermined by a procedural hiccup. The Review had been prepared in the wake of the Planning Advisory Group Report, but ahead of the consequent change in the planning legislation, which came in 1969 in Scotland. Flushed with enthusiasm for PAG's ideas, the corporation had delineated Action Areas on their maps, where future proposals for change would be brought forward. The Reporter ruled that it was out of order to do so, since the statement of intent to produce proposals did not amount to proposals *per se*. The Secretary of State endorsed this view, and ruled that the 1957 Development Plan zonings should be restored in those areas and that references to Action Areas should be deleted from the Written Statement. Thus areas where planned change was seen to be imminent were left with zonings first derived some fifteen years earlier.

The plan was left as a moth-eaten blanket, creating substantial areas of planning blight. The central area traffic proposal and the areas for redevelopment had largely been declared then shelved. Some major industrial zonings had been deleted[65] and the record with the implementation of the 1957 Plan must have raised doubts about just how rigorously the Green Belt would be protected. The issue of overspill was unresolved, the whole question of housing provision and future population remaining sketchy. Yet the plan was pre-eminently the product of officials, exercising a technical rationality; it had been nodded through by councillors of both the main parties before they became aware of the public disaffection that the proposals triggered. The manifest deficiencies in rationality at the end of the exercise are therefore somewhat ironic. Just as the elected members had found themselves squeezed between resolute officials and an implacable opposition from constituents, so the officials were squeezed between irresolute councillors vulnerable to political whims, the same self-interested public opposition and the ambiguous backing of central government. The planners among them had to also contend with the other priorities of the other corporation departments. Such tensions must have strained the professional planners' self-image as the expert protectors of the public interest in land and physical development through the mechanism of a comprehensive plan.

At one level these dilemmas might be ascribed to mistakes, misunderstandings and changes of fashion. After all, the plan could have shown Comprehensive Development Areas rather than Action Areas, just as more thorough origin and destination traffic surveys might have been conducted to strengthen the case for the roads. Such an interpretation would be consistent with the new planning theory that was being forged at the same time, with its calls to planners to be more 'scientific', to adopt a corporate approach and to be more informed of responses within the 'community system'. It was also, as we saw, the interpretation favoured by Councillor Millar (with his calls for better public relations from the planners) and by central government with its prescription for an expert of the highest calibre to solve the problems.

The robustness of that interpretation when put into practice will be analysed in the next chapter. At a theoretical level it can be criticized here. The forces promoting change in the physical fabric of Edinburgh in the 1960s did not arise by chance; they were integral to developments in the mode of production itself. They threatened, but could not replace, the identity with the meanings embedded in the historic physical environment. They likewise threatened the property interests of substantial sections of the city's disproportionately large and centrally located *bourgeoisie*. The planning endeavours floundered so massively because the contradictions they were attempting to manage could neither be systematically elucidated within the limited statutory powers of town planning and within the political structure of local power within the city, nor could they be so suppressed and managed within that framework as to prevent them erupting into public struggles.

This is not to romanticize the conflicts which developed. The struggles were directed against the local administrative and political systems and were predominantly fought by people who in no sense saw themselves aligned with the labour movement. They were not connected with struggles at the point of production, nor did they challenge the central state itself. Indeed, devices such as public inquiries helped re-establish the legitimacy of that state for those who could afford to participate in them. The political demands raised in the struggles remained vague, and susceptible to incorporation within the language and techniques of politicians and administrators who could learn from the lack of sophistication in their earlier mistakes. Mr Drummond Hunter, as Secretary of the North Edinburgh Joint Committee, was the leader of the most prominent and successful group of campaigners against the ring road. He was a solicitor and hospital administrator. In his hour of victory he stressed that their actions had not been a revolution, but a revulsion by ordinary citizens against bureaucracy and the party political system. He called for a whole new language of politics, concerned with quality in human terms and citizen participation.[66] The local state could adapt to such a call, though not without incurring casualties. What it could not do was match the language and practice.

References and notes

1   J. P. Mackintosh, in D. Keir (ed.), 'The City of Edinburgh', *The Third Statistical Account of Scotland*, vol. XV (Collins 1966), p. 310.
2   J. Habermas, *Legitimation Crisis*, (Heinemann 1976).
3   D. Keir (1966), p. 375. In 1946 there were 31,021 one-apartment 'single end' tenement flats and two-apartment 'room and kitchen' homes within the city. A total of 43,583 Edinburgh households were overcrowded at the standards set down in the 1944 Department of Health Circular 149. These standards also revealed considerable overcrowding at the time of the 1951 Census, particularly in Craigmillar and Pilton where the main slum-clearance council housing had been built in the pre-war years. For details see D. Keir, pp. 377–8.
4   The estates at Colinton Mains, Hyvot's Bank, Muirhouse and Silverknowes were built up on these purchases.
5   D. Keir (1966), pp. 386–7.
6   For details see D. Keir (1966), pp. 375–6.
7   *The Scotsman*, 17 Aug. 1961.
8   Ibid.

9   For details see the Clermiston Housing file, at the Edinburgh Room of the Central Library, George IV Bridge, Edinburgh.

10   *The New Statesman*, 9 Feb. 1962.

11   Warrants issued by the Dean of Guild Court give an indication of the resurgence of private house building after 1954:

1946 – 156	1953 – 290
1947 – 148	1954 – 431
1948 – 185	1955 – 812
1949 – 161	1956 – 782
1950 – 105	1957 – 641
1951 – 89	1958 – 636
1952 – 182	1959 – 630

Warrants issued by the Dean of Guild Court to private enterprise builders. *Source:* D. Keir (1966), p. 388.

12   J. R. Kaucz, 'Residential location: The application of the social physics model and the behavioural model to Edinburgh'. Unpublished MSc. Thesis, Department of Town and Country Planning, Edinburgh College of Art/Heriot-Watt University (1976), described the situation as an oligopoly. See Ch. 9, para. 4.1.0.

13   The main private developments of this period were at Southfield, Mountcastle, Inverleith, Corstorphine, Oxgangs and Colinton.

14   *The Scotsman*, 15 Feb. 1961.

15   *The Scotsman*, 29 Oct. 1963. Mowlem were seeking to build fifty houses on an eight-acre site to be purchased from the College of Domestic Science for £38,500 subject to planning permission. This development was opposed by a local residents' committee.

16   *Edinburgh Evening News*, 15 July 1960.

17   City and Royal Burgh of Edinburgh, *Development Plan Review, Report of Survey* (1965), p. 9.3.

18   City and Royal Burgh of Edinburgh, *Development Plan Review, Written Statement* (1965), pp. 24–5.

19   H. M. Bingham, 'Land hoarding in Edinburgh', Unpublished MSc. Thesis, Department of Town and Country Planning, Edinburgh College of Art/Heriot–Watt University (1974), pp. 73–4.

20   Letter from the Secretary of State for Scotland to the Town Clerk of Edinburgh, dated 9 May 1968, p. 10.

21   Ibid. The letter describes the issues and recommendations for each site.

22   D. Keir (1966), p. 392.

23   Ibid. p. 392.

24   *The Scotsman*, 24 Jan. 1958.

25   *The Scotsman*, 29 Jan. 1959.

26   *The Scotsman*, 30 Jan. 1959.

27   *The Scotsman*, 22 Oct. 1960.

28   *The Scotsman*, 10 Sept. 1960. Mr Fairbairn was a prominent figure on the Edinburgh cultural scene, and later became a Conservative MP.

29   Edinburgh Chamber of Commerce, *Quinquennial Review Committee's Report* (1963), p. 4.

30   *Edinburgh Evening Dispatch*, 19 Feb. 1963. The developers were Grand Metropolitan Hotels Ltd. The Lord Provost, Sir J. G. Dunbar, spoke strongly against the proposed development at the Public Inquiry. He argued that control was essential to protect the New Town, and that the corporation was deeply attached to the history and traditions of Edinburgh, its culture and its attraction to tourists. See G. Bruce, *Some Practical Good*, (The Cockburn Association 1975), pp. 47–8.

31   *The Scotsman*, 6 June 1963.

32   *The Scotsman*, 12 June 1964.

33   *Edinburgh Evening News*, 19 April 1963.

34   *The Scotsman*, 28 June 1961.

35   *The Scotsman*, 8 Dec. 1966.

36   *The Sunday Times*, 15 Jan. 1967.

37   *The Scotsman*, 8 Dec. 1966.

38   See 'Town centres, approach to renewal', *Planning Bulletin* 1 (HMSO 1962), and 'Town centres – cost and control of redevelopment', *Planning Bulletin* 3, (HMSO 1963).

39   University Grants Committee, *Review of University Development, 1962–66* (HMSO 1966), Appendix 6.

40   *The Scotsman*, 8 Dec. 1966.

41   *The Scotsman*, 24 Aug. 1960.

42   *Edinburgh Evening Dispatch*, 8 March 1962.

43   See G. Hume, 'St. James Centre: finance and development', in H. Peacock (ed.) *The Unmaking of Edinburgh*, Edinburgh University Students Publications Board (undated), pp. 31–2. See also the City and Royal Burgh of Edinburgh, *Development Plan Review, Written Statement* (1965), p. 16.

44   *The Scotsman*, 5 June 1958.

45   *The Scotsman*, 6 June 1958.

46   *Edinburgh Evening News*, 28 April 1958.

47   *The Scotsman*, 16 Jan. 1958.

48   *Edinburgh Evening News*, 30 July 1958.

49   See, for example, the letters published from Ian Fyfe, *The Scotsman*, 28 Feb. 1957; R. J. Naismith, *The Scotsman*, 31 Dec. 1957; R. S. Ferguson, *The Scotsman*, 31 Dec. 1957; and C. A. Hope, *The Scotsman*, 9 May 1958.

50   *The Scotsman*, 28 May 1959.

51   Letter from Sinclair Shaw, *The Scotsman*, 30 Dec. 1957.

52   City and Royal Burgh of Edinburgh, *Major Highway Planning*, City Engineer's Department (1964).

53   Seven car parks were proposed to provide 38,000 parking spaces in the

central area, 24,900 of which were to be off-street. The costs of the scheme were put at £15 million.

54   *The Scotsman*, 16 Jan. 1967.
55   *Edinburgh Evening News*, 18 Jan. 1967.
56   *The Scotsman*, 16 Jan. 1967.
57   *Edinburgh Evening News*, 13 Jan. 1967.
58   City and Royal Burgh of Edinburgh, *Town Planning Brochure Development Plan Review* (1966).
59   *The Scotsman*, 23 Dec. 1966.
60   *The Scotsman*, 14 Dec. 1966.
61   Letter published in *The Scotsman*, 9 Feb. 1967.
62   *The Scotsman*, 14 Feb. 1967.
63   *Edinburgh Evening News*, 24 Jan. 1967.
64   Quoted in J. G. Gray, *Streets Ahead: A brief study of highway planning in Edinburgh since 1945* (The Edina Press 1975), p. 21.
65   The main new industrial zoning in the Development Plan Review was a site of just under 200 acres at South Gyle, in the west of the city. The Secretary of State deleted the site, and restored the zoning as agricultural land within the green belt. His case was that there were problems of access to the site which could not be resolved ahead of decisions on the line of an outer by-pass. A proposal to reclaim estuarial land for industrial uses was also deleted as being premature. See the letter from the Secretary of State to the Town Clerk, dated 8 May 1968, Annex 2.
66   *Edinburgh Evening News*, 15 Jan. 1968.

8 Control or cleavage – the struggle for the city

The demise of the Development Plan Review heralded the end of an era. The Review had been prepared for a city beset with the problems of projected growth. The temporary economic and political relationships that underpinned the long wave of post-war affluence were ascribed an eternal status. The claim of the planners was to produce an objective assessment of that growth and to harmoniously translate it into a pattern of phased physical development. The opposition directed at that pattern manifested the need for better techniques of prediction and planning. However, such technical modification could not contain the consequences of recession and fiscal crisis.

The Review had also been pre-eminently the product of the administrative system, with minimal inputs from the public or elected members until the plan had been finalized. The ensuing hostility showed the need for more sophisticated publicity and consultation procedures. Likewise, the Review was produced by an administrative system in which there were tight boundaries around the different departments; indeed, substantial credibility had been won by objectors who claimed that the Review failed to integrate the planning of land use and traffic. To meet such criticisms and to give better value for money, reorganized management structures were needed, able to operate in a corporate manner.

The problems of planning practice in Edinburgh thus fitted with the new initiatives being forged by central government, such as the Civic Amenities Act and the Housing Act of 1969, together with the recommendations of the Planning Advisory Group, the Skeffington Committee and the Paterson Committee. This final chapter of the case study therefore examines the shifting styles, policies and organizational structures of planning in the 1970s in Edinburgh.

The recurring question which has prevailed throughout the case study remains what interests defined the basis of planning practice? Again the central concern are with the interplay of the central state, local government, professionalism and other local sources of power. However, the crisis management strategies of the local state should be seen in relation to the developments in the mode of production as a whole. There was the onset of a deep and prolonged economic crisis which entailed extensive devaluation of exchange value locked in the built environment, the creation of mass unemployment and the new spatial division of labour.

As a free-standing capital city in an attractive physical environment, a city rooted in finance and administration and boosted by the exploitation of

Scotland's off-shore oil resources, Edinburgh in the 1970s did not suffer the economic collapse experienced by the traditional manufacturing cities of the advanced capitalist countries. The 'inner city problem' could be glimpsed in the run-down of old industrial and shipping areas like Leith, but the scale did not compare with the major English cities. Within Scotland Clydeside inevitably dominated national thinking about deprivation. Nevertheless, by the early 1980s the Jeckyll and Hyde city of Edinburgh was a locus of great inequality; life in the affluent suburbs or gentrified central locales was very different from in the stigmatized peripheral council estates where few school leavers could seriously contemplate the prospect of employment, let alone a career.

The struggle for the city was still locally fought. In a period of sharpened class conflict one would expect local consumption-based struggles to become increasingly politicized and for the state, in its attempts to re-establish civil privatism to be pressed into adopting new measures. Similarly one might anticipate that the centrist ideology of the professionals would become ever more difficult to sustain in practice, thus deepening their crises of identity and motivation. These hypotheses now need to be explored empirically, to grasp how the local class relationships, political structures and the unique physical environment inter-related to create this most recent phase of town planning practice within Edinburgh.

The return of the expert planner

The prime urban planning questions in Edinburgh at the start of the 1970s were about transport. The Secretary of State had ruled on the transport aspects of the Development Plan Review in January 1968. The proposed Inner Ring Road had provoked bitter public controversies, as the previous chapter described. In response the Secretary of State had called on the corporation to appoint an expert consultant to undertake a planning and transport study of the central area. Implicitly then the hope was that more and 'better' information would reveal a technical solution that would re-establish civil privatism and restore public confidence in the capability of the administration to manage the modernization of the city.

Freeman Fox, Wilbur Smith and Associates were already engaged on a transport study of the Greater Edinburgh area. It was no surprise then that they were asked by Edinburgh Corporation in July 1968 to take on the traffic aspects of the central area study. The planning consultants were not appointed until February 1969. Colin Buchanan and Partners were chosen for the job from a short list of three. Thus Sir Colin Buchanan joined the list of distinguished professional planners who had grappled with the problems of reconciling change and conservation within Edinburgh.

This mediation of locally based social conflicts by the appointment of expert consultants was willed, even directed by, central government. The Scottish Office also provided a financial contribution of £110,000 towards the £260,000 costs of the study. Nevertheless it would be misleading to depict the

262   *The development of planning thought*

consultants as mere ciphers of the central state; they were independent professionals. Indeed Buchanan's earlier work on 'Traffic in Towns' had been widely
and approvingly quoted by the campaigners against the inner ring road. These
appointments then were well received locally and accorded well with dominant
professional views of the period about the need to integrate the planning of traffic
and land use. For all that, the germination of new conflicts was discernible.
Though working jointly, the consultants remained two separately appointed teams
of planners and transport engineers. In July 1968 test borings had begun around
the routes of the eastern and southern links of the inner ring road, for the Secretary
of State had basically endorsed these lines in his response to the Development
Plan Review. Furthermore the City Engineer, Mr Dinnis, had visited Tokyo and
had returned from the Orient more convinced than ever that Edinburgh needed an
inner ring road.

The consultants' study was launched in October 1969, with assurances that
there would be an extensive programme of public consultation. In part this reflected
ideas current in the profession at that time, but here it also related directly to the
local crisis of legitimacy prompted by the proposed inner ring road. Meanwhile
the City Engineer went ahead with the detailed design work for the approved
eastern link of the ring road. It was to have the widest road tunnels in Britain, with
a capacity to carry 2000 vehicles an hour in one direction, at a probable speed of
50 m.p.h. This contradiction between the rhetoric of participation and the *fait
accompli* of the eastern link now prompted further controversies.

Just a few years earlier the eastern link, aligned through the 'soft' areas of St
Leonards and the Pleasance had provoked few antagonisms. The Secretary of
State's blessing for the link had passed almost unnoticed by the euphoric objectors who had thwarted the northern link. Now, however, criticisms began to
mount. Councillor Smith (Liberal), the earliest elected member to express unease
at the whole ring road strategy, voiced his concern at the fact that the designs suggested the road would pass within fifty feet of a hospital. Another veteran doubter,
the Conservative MP for Edinburgh South, Michael Clark Hutchinson, unsuc-
cessfully tried to amend the Roads (Scotland) Bill, to prohibit buildings, exca-
vations and tunnelling in Princes Street Gardens, Calton Hill, the Meadows,
Bruntsfield Links and Leith Links. Nevertheless the corporation met on 2
October 1969, and agreed to the construction of the Eastern Link Road, despite
expressions of unease by some councillors.

Opposition began to mount as the contracts were given for site offices to be
used for the construction of the road. As the legislation required, the scheme was
advertised and objections were invited. However, the contrast between the public
participation invited for the Eastern Link Road and that promised in the consultants' study was abrupt. The public were invited to submit objections to the
Final Order for the road: to help them make up their mind they could see a small
scale drawing, a set of chainage tables and the Order itself, all of which were
available on request in the Town Clerk's office. Those ardent enough to make
such requests found that the tables could not be read with the drawing because the
chainage points were not marked on it.[1] Belatedly a public exhibition of the road

designs was opened in the Planning Department on 6 April 1970. Far from re-storing public confidence it fermented more vehement opposition. The sheer scale of the six-lane motorway, its slip roads and 'trumpet' interchanges seemed to pre-empt all transport planning in the central area. Furthermore, spokesmen for both the planning and transport consultants explained that the Eastern Link Road was a 'given' within their brief.[2] The designs appeared just months before the consultants' interim report was expected, so that the actual proposals, their timing and the minimal scope for participation together constituted a major prob-lem of legitimacy for the work of the consultants.

It was therefore impossible for the consultants to maintain their credibility and to stay silent on the question of the Eastern Link Road. Thus in July 1970 Colin Buchanan endorsed the need for the road 'in principle', but expressed his team's unease at the extent to which the designs constrained planning for the central area as a whole. The intersections in particular begged questions about the rest of the network upon which the consultants were still working. Buchanan's comments undermined the technical rationality of the City Engineer's designs in two further respects. He was reported as saying that his team were not yet sure whether a six-lane motorway was the scale of road required; and he also noted that the drawings implied heavy flows of traffic on the eastern section of Princes Street in perpetuity, whereas the consultants were seeking to reduce traffic along the prime shopping parade. Buchanan also directly confronted the problems of legitimation. In deference to those sceptical of the need for new roads the consultants were testing a 'minimum road investment' option: the good faith of that exercise could not be squared with endorsement and expeditious construction of a six-lane motor-way.[3]

The opposition that developed was widespread, encompassing institutions, pressure groups and individuals. Edinburgh University and British Rail both had property interests in the area affected by the road plans and lodged objections. The Royal Fine Arts Commission, addressed by Buchanan on 9 July, concluded that the projected road was totally unacceptable and broke all the rules of planning.[4] The Edinburgh Liberal Party were vocal opponents of the road. The Scottish Trades Union Congress carried a resolution attacking the road and the paucity of participation, in what was seen as a straightforward issue of cars versus people.[5] The veterans of the campaign against the inner ring road united behind a city-wide anti-roads pressure group, the Edinburgh Amenity and Transport Association. Their honorary vice-presidents were Sir Compton Mackenzie, Lady Ritchie Calder and Professor Tony Travis, the Head of the Art College Planning School. EATA had contacts with a similar body who were opposing London's motorway box proposals. Their arguments were pitched at a technical level, suggesting that the Eastern Link Road was not the product of integrated planning and could be the precursor of substantial changes elsewhere in the city.[6] Despite their seeming diversity the bulk of the opposition was held together by their property interests and by a belief that town planning founded on the 'right' expertise and technical procedures could ensure the harmonious reproduction of the historic city.

Elected members began to respond to this public pressure. The four Liberals on the Council came out against the road and the twenty-eight-strong Labour group decided to put the whip on, thus obliging the doubters within their midst to oppose the road. In addition the nine-member Conservative group, then emerging from the Progressives, also opposed the scheme. Thus the beleagured corporation asked the Scottish Development Department not to fix a date for the public inquiry until the corporation could hold discussions with their consultants. Design work on the road was stopped.

The discussions took place late in 1970 and revealed deep splits between the planners and the highway engineers, undermining the notion of a single technically correct solution discernible through the application of neutral expertise. Buchanan was urging the investigation of a watered-down version of the Eastern Link Road, cutting its size and eliminating two major intersections and a tunnel under Calton Hill. He argued that this would be sufficient until the need for a more ambitious road might be established at a later date. He was supported by Edinburgh's Town Planning Officer, Mr Hewitson. However, the City Engineer, Mr Dinnis, dismissed the idea as 'inadequate', saying that it would only make the environment worse. The transport consultants backed this view, telling the Planning Committee that they were in 'fundamental disagreement' with the Buchanan team on this matter. The Planning Committee sided with the planners.[7] The Highways Committee stayed loyal to their officials and required the planners to produce firm proposals on the link road within six months, a task which the planners estimated would take a year to accomplish.[8] There had been prolonged and articulate debate on the issue within the city, led by pressure groups from middle-class areas and with professionals well to the fore. It appears that the issues and the form of the debate cut across the traditional political perspectives of the elected members, leaving them disorientated and in the thrall of their officials.

For all that, political judgements were being made, not least by the experts themselves. The consultants had submitted an Interim Report to their clients in July 1970. An edited version was made available to the public in February 1971. The public version excluded a detailed description of the transport system being tested, on the grounds that disclosure would result in unnecessary blight. The report set up and then knocked down two 'extreme' solutions, 'full motorization' and 'no new road'. The former was rejected because it would create enormous environmental damage; the latter because it was judged by the consultants to be not 'feasible politically'.[9] They anticipated a growth in car ownership in Edinburgh and Musselburgh from 70,000 in 1968 to 175,000 in 1991. Thus the technical experts exercised an overt political judgement to focus their evaluation work on high, medium and low investment in roads solutions.

The report was the end of the honeymoon. Despite the carefully nurtured programme of public participation, the confidence of the anti-roads protestors in the objectivity of the study was shattered when it became clear that a strategy based on public transport and tight controls on car usage was not even judged worth testing. The Meadows and South Edinburgh Group bitterly rejected the report. They condemned one of the fundamental assumptions in the analysis, the idea that traffic should be channelled along the 'cracks' between the 'urban rooms' that were the areas of cohesive environments. They argued that the report had simply extrapolated trends in car ownership and declining public transport and had failed to rigorously develop an alternative land use strategy to that in the Development Plan. The Group also challenged the decision not to disclose the actual routes being tested; they saw such confidentiality as undermining the notion of public participation.[10] EATA were also critical.

The limitations of the consultants' brief now became evident. The planners could only look at the central area; the question of a transport strategy for the rest of the city rested with the Freeman Fox team. An eastern link road, and even a southern link, was really a 'given'. The brief also required the consultants to plan for the 'continuance of the Central Area as a flourishing commercial centre' and to promote the 'highest standard of accessibility' to the centre that was compatible with environmental objectives.[11] The Secretary of State's decision of January 1968, on the Public Inquiry into the Development Plan Review, could be construed as an attempt to defuse controversy by deferring a decision on the roads strategy. The pragmatic attempt at crisis avoidance now began to run into the same problems that had beset the original ring road plan. The aspirations to legitimate an efficiently planned modernization of the city's road system were being pursued by bolstering two of the most criticized deficiencies of the earlier ring road planning. These were the lack of public participation and the inadequacies of the technical analysis.

The consultants' Second Interim report[12] appeared in October 1971. It exemplified the scientization of planning which characterized the period. A formidable amount of data was analysed. There was extensive use of computer programs with cryptic and beguiling names like STEP (Synthetic Trip-End Estimating Process) and TRANSITNET. Four alternative schemes were evaluated with robotlike code names, A2, B1, C and E. They represented respectively 'low' investment in roads, 'moderate' investment, the ring road and radials as they were in the Development Plan Review, together with a grid of primary roads. The alternatives were then put through the rigours of a cost-benefit analysis, which revealed the superiority of B1. Social and environmental analyses were also conducted, measuring visual impact and noise impact and quantifying an 'environmental deficiency index'. The findings pointed to strengths in A2, which could be improved by further modifications. Most conclusively, the tests demonstrated the desirability of a new ingredient in the mix, an Intermediate Circular Route. The ICR could run as a ring through the Victorian suburbs, possibly along abandoned or underused railway lines, taking the traffic moving around the town which previous plans had directed at the Inner Ring Road.

The consultants therefore drew up a further, preferred set of proposals and gave it the brand name 'Scheme X'. This took the progression towards moderation a stage further; it was a compromise synthesizing the successful aspects of the previous options. The technical expertise thus worked remorselessly towards what was thought to be a consensus solution as a basis for a further round of public participation. The key features of Scheme X were a tunnel under the West End of Princes Street and an ICR. The notorious and abused Eastern Link Road was rechristened the Bridges Relief Road, and slimmed to a mere four lanes. The scheme proposed to take all major traffic off Princes Street, diverting it to Queen Street, at the heart of the New Town. In this way west or east-bound traffic could be routed around the north of the centre. In effect then the idea of a ring road around the central area was endorsed. However, the ring was now termed a 'central area distributor loop' and its role was seen as being the handling of the local traffic of the centre, since the ICR would absorb the other trips. Thus the scale of the CADL could be less than that envisaged for the ring road in the Development Plan Review.

The prescription was premised on the assumption that real per capita incomes would increase by 2½ per cent per annum and that the extra wealth would result in increased car ownership and use. The projections suggested that by 1991 only 29 per cent of all Edinburgh households would be without the use of a car, with one household in four running two or more cars. The compromise nature of the scheme meant that some account was taken of those citizens who would still rely on public transport. Scheme X proposed the creation of busways along congested sections of central roads and earmarked £3.7 million for this. However, this sum should be seen in relation to the £64 million costing for the new roads in the scheme. A further investment of £11 million in off-street parking provision was recommended. Evidently the proposals were intended to achieve net environmental gains in the city as a whole, but the broad distributional implications of Scheme X were that considerable sums of public money should be invested so as to retain the competitiveness of the central area for retailing and office activities and to reduce travel times to the most direct benefit of what was seen as the majority of the citizens, who were or would become car users.

The study was of unprecedented technical sophistication within Edinburgh, yet it did not probe the likelihood of an energy crisis, or a deep and extended economic recession. Affluence for all, and its conversion into mobility, were seen as reasonable and uncontentious assumptions for practical men to make; all that followed could then be handled by the computer. In fact the prescription of an Intermediate Circular Route followed the pattern that was discernible from Abercrombie onwards, as major road proposals were advanced, criticized and then moved further out. The result was that properties immune from blight at earlier stages of the saga were now threatened and their previously acquiescent residents were recruited to the ranks of the protestors. Scheme X ensured that yet more pressure groups were spawned by aggrieved owner-occupiers, this time in more suburban locations. At last the consultants, who had previously complained of the apathy of suburban residents to their work, began to receive invitations to address meetings at venues not totally disconnected with the line of the ICR. The Morningside Amenity Group formed in reaction to the report. The suburban railway line earmarked for the ICR ran at the bottom of the gardens of the plush villas of the area. Further round the ICR to the north-west, a meeting organized by the Blackhall Co-ordinating Committee was described by the consultants as 'very hot'.[13] While the platform speakers spoke the language of 'primary distributors' and a 'hierarchy of roads', their audience fretted about whether *their* house would be demolished, or merely overlooked by a new road. The equity issue of the whole roads plan was raised by the Craigmillar Festival Society. Every plan from Abercrombie onwards had included a south-eastern approach to the St Leonards road, cutting through the stigmatized council estate and blighting land along the line. The Festival Society, the pioneering community group in the area, began to ask why their area, with probably the lowest car ownership rate in the city, should play host to a road for more affluent commuters, which would attract traffic from existing routes in better-off parts of the city.

Craigmillar Festival Society were the exception, as a working-class organization protesting at the plans. It was not their voices which presented the consultants with their fundamental headache, rather, like Mears, Abercrombie and the city's technical officers before them, they were hoist on the petard of the city's social geography. It was impossible to find any continuous line of 'soft' areas, which could channel a relevant new road system. Wherever the line was pushed, it sooner or later ran into high-income owner-occupied areas and drew protests. Even the old railway lines were being defended. EATA called for more investment to be put into public transport and dismissed the proposals for a channelling of traffic along Queen Street as being quite unacceptable.[14] The North Edinburgh Joint Committee also attacked the impending desecration of Queen Street and expressed a preference for Abercrombie's solution of a by-pass beneath Princes Street as a better solution.[15]

As controversy mounted, Mr Dinnis re-entered the fray to ignite any oil that might have been poured on the troubled waters. The City Engineer produced a report suggesting that Scheme X should be rejected and that an inner ring road should be built instead.[16] This inspiration brought predictable protests from EATA, the Cockburn Association and the North Edinburgh Joint Committee. Nevertheless the Planning Committee resolved by seven votes to four to submit Mr Dinnis's report, along with those of other officials, to the consultants for consideration. This decision did little to repair relationships between the administration and the growing body of public opinion that doubted the feasibility of building new roads and protecting the environment and property interests.

Like Abercrombie before him, Buchanan must have sensed even before it appeared that his final report would not prove acceptable. When 'The Recommended Plan', shown here as Figure 15, was published in November 1972,[17] Professor Buchanan was quoted as being 'slightly pessimistic' about its implementation, unless it was backed with 'absolute determination' by elected members.[18] The consultants stressed that their plan was a package of interdependent proposals and advised against the temptation to select elements from it to implement in isolation from the scheme as a whole. The plan retained all the essential elements of Scheme X. It was priced at £104 million, at 1970 prices, and entailed a possible loss of 2700 houses. EATA immediately condemned the proposed 100 per cent increase in private car use and the 16 per cent reduction of travel by public transport. They called for all major road schemes to be deferred until a regional structure plan was produced.[19] The Cockburn Association expressed similar sentiments. Support for the plan was, however, forthcoming

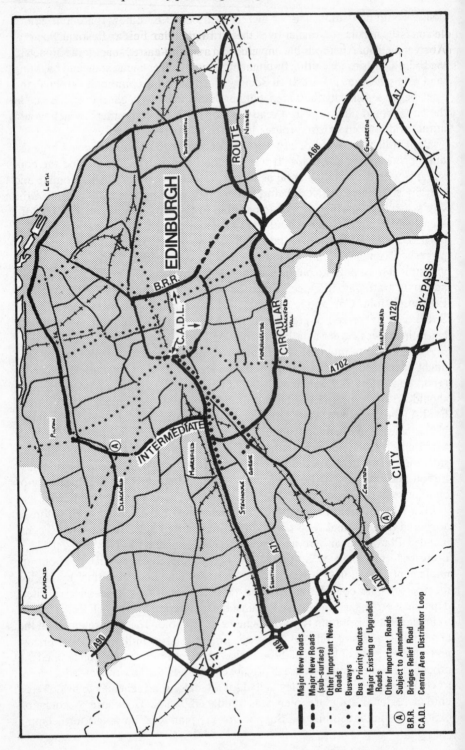

from the Corstorphine Trust, a residents' group in a area not threatened by new roads, but suffering intense traffic intrusion already.[20]

The *coup de grâce* came swiftly. About a week before the 1973 municipal elections, and with an eye clearly on the polling booths, the Labour Party in Edinburgh called a press conference. They alleged that the right wing parties (the Conservatives and the Progressives) were nurturing a secret plan to build an inner ring road after all! The evidence of this clandestine intent was the 200 houses which the corporation had purchased since mid-1971, which happened to lie along the line of the Inner Ring Road. Furthermore, the councillor who had most fiercely defended the ring road in the traumatic days of 1966–7, Councillor John Millar, was now the Chairman of the Highways Committee. Labour assured the voters that they, in contrast, were unequivocally against building such a road.[21]

The Conservatives upped the stakes at their press conference. They discounted Labour's allegations and made it plain that they too were against an inner ring road. Better still, they also rejected the proposals advanced by the Buchanan and Freeman Fox team! Instead Conservative policy favoured a rail system and they deplored the appalling prospect of thousands of good homes being affected by road building. Their planning spokesman, Councillor MacLennan, triumphantly observed, 'The fact that the Conservatives have rejected the Buchanan Report shows up the Labour Party's rumour about the inner ring road to be an election gimmick.'[22]

Away in Bristol, Professor Buchanan sighed, 'If this group of people care to chuck out a carefully considered report just like that, without investigating the alternatives they suggest, then that is their responsibility.'[23]

The Labour Party, their bluff having been called, similarly rejected the Buchanan Report before election day, while the Liberals stood on a platform of only implementing the non-controversial aspects of it.

A few weeks before this hectic decision-making the Planning Committee had set up a technical working party to advise them on the Recommended Plan and, significantly, on the public reaction to it. The key personnel in the working party were the City Engineer, the City Planning Officer, the Transport Manager and the Chief Constable. In two reports, in July 1973 and January 1974, they basically endorsed the proposals of the consultants.[24] They urged that the less controversial aspects should be proceeded with, but also pressed for early action on the Central Area Distributor Loop. Thus the corporation began to implement stronger parking controls and to plan short stretches of bus lane. A further team of consultants, De Leuw, Chadwick, Oh'Eocha, were commissioned in April 1974 to review the public transport elements of the Recommended Plan. In particular they were asked to re-examine the potential of a rail-based public transport system, with an integration with feeder bus services. The idea of a light rapid transit solution had been consistently urged by Professor A. W. Hendry, Professor of Civil Engineering at Edinburgh University, and had been strongly supported by

Figure 15   *'The Recommended Plan' of the Buchanan/Freeman Fox Study, 1972*

EATA. The consultants reported in February 1975 and concluded that a light rapid transit or minitram system might be feasible, but that an all-bus option would be a lower cost alternative to either a rail-based system or to the Recommended Plan. Their report was presented in February 1975, just weeks before the demise of the Edinburgh Corporation in local government reorganization. The decision was thus left for the new Lothian Regional Council and so the lines of the various road proposals continued to be safeguarded.

Thus, to the end, the Corporation of the City and Royal Burgh of Edinburgh was unable to reconcile the contradictory imperatives of modernization and conservation. Any notion of strategic planning remained deeply flawed in practice because of the lack of an acceptable transport strategy. In the Buchanan study, a model of scientific technical progress fashioned by professional planners of high integrity and calibre, took on the functions of legitimating political power. The plethora of techniques were used to show the inevitability of a particular social process – increasing affluence and mobility – and to fashion the adaptation of the environment accordingly. In Edinburgh and on this specific issue, the scientization of politics failed to depoliticize the public. 'Participation' failed to contain discourse to the level of public relations. Similarly the testing of public opinion to provide more sensitive information of consumer preferences in fact unearthed such antipathy to the professional image of the needs of the future city, that it had to be discounted on the grounds that the protestors might well be unrepresentative.[25]

The participation thus reworked the contradiction between the imperatives of technical progress which the professionals perceived as being expressed in a rationally planned road system and the property interests of Edinburgh's large middle class. The more the controversy developed, the more the road lines were shifted around, the more antagonisms were created. The image of the motorway city, and its realization elsewhere and especially in Glasgow, increasingly contradicted the meanings within the physical environment of Edinburgh – continuity, history, identity, excellence were to be sacrificed to function and mass production and consumption. For all that the opposition remained tied to the single issue and fragmented from other political struggles. It is even doubtful whether the unifying of the opposition on a city-wide basis through EATA could have overcome the localism of the diffuse opponents but for the sheer extent to which different areas had been affected by plans over more than a decade. The politicians, torn between electoral responsiveness and loyalty to their officials, suffered similar fragmentations behind the unifying facade of the party whip. The conflicts were waged on environmental rather than class grounds. However, the environmental case was rooted in the protection of property rights and the image of the city. The protagonists were those members of Edinburgh's middle class whose livelihoods were not dependent on increasing accessibility within the city for producers or shoppers. The conflicts therefore related directly to the economic base of the city and its associated social structure and physical environment. They were rooted in the practices if not of an entire class, then of significant fractions within a class. Similarly pluralist interpretations would presume that power was locally based, but this case shows the crucial, albeit 'hidden', role played by central government in shaping the conflicts through the Secretary of State's decision on the Development Plan Review.

For all that the struggles were locally fought, with the corporation and the consultants in the firing line, rather than the Scottish Office. Some cross-class alliances were formed and the objectors more and more moved to a position of advocating increased investment in public transport as the alternative to road building. There was a growing realization that urban development entailed the redistribution of costs and benefits. This politicization did not result in a substantial change in the balance of class power locally, or *vis-à-vis* the central state, but it was sufficient to destabilize the previous practices of professionals and of elected members. The state, in seeking to plan the modernization of the urban structure to adjust it to the emergent patterns of production, distribution and consumption of commodities, threatened property and the meanings associated with the physical environment. The result was the politicization of fragments within the class structure, withdrawal of legitimation from the local state and a discrediting of professional ideology with a consequent loss of motivation and identity for the professionals.

From redevelopment to conservation

The uncertainties about the road plans had a most marked impact on the trio of major commercial redevelopment areas that were strung around the line of the inner ring road. Substantial road works were carried through adjacent to the St James Centre development, as the developers had required. Alongside the massive roundabout, the Centre itself was rising monstrously on the skyline, confirming all the anxieties that the Royal Fine Arts Commission for Scotland had expressed about its aesthetics. Its sheer mass and box-like structure and its drab concrete facades drew extensive expressions of distaste. Whatever its commercial merits, the St James development did little to foster public identity with the city of property capital and consumerism. Ironically, at a time when the packaging and marketing of commodities was achieving new scales of sophistication, permitting an unparalleled manipulation of consumers, the physical environment associated with those same dynamics was, in this case, scorned and rejected. Shoppers patronized the air-conditioned mall, but reviled the development as a whole.

The development of St James Centre sealed the fate of major commercial proposals at the other two redevelopment areas at Tollcross and the South Side. It was never likely that three massive new shopping developments were a viable proposition in and around a central area which already boasted one of the foremost shopping parades in Europe, on Princes Street. The years of blight caused by the unresolved road plans took most of the gloss off the prospect anyway.

The Joint Co-ordinating Committee for the University/Nicolson Street Comprehensive Development Area did not meet between 1970 and 1973. Murrayfield Real Estate, the property interest in the committee, had been taken over by Ravenseft, who were the developers at the St James Centre, a mere mile away. Their interest in the South Side was effectively dead. Edinburgh University had suffered financial uncertainties in its building programme from 1966 onwards, due to national government attempts to cut back on the growth of public expenditure. Nevertheless, the university proved a more durable property developer in the area than the property companies, remaining committed to large-scale redevelopment despite the financial problems, and in the face of mounting public calls for conservation. Their position was set out in a report prepared jointly by the Factorial Secretary and their Planning Consultant, Professor Johnson-Marshall, in January 1969:

> Before any policy changes are made with regard to the future of areas such as Buccleuch Place and the other buildings owned by the University, the consequences of abandoning the hard won right to expand the University in a restricted area must be closely examined. It should be noted that in the past, predictions of the future size of the University have always been overtaken by events. A change in the present policy to one which includes the long term conservation of a larger number of buildings may create a precedent and lead to demands for the preservation of further buildings not on the draft list.
>
> In terms of the city as a whole, the main conservation effort is bound to be concentrated in the Royal Mile and the New Town. The University/Nicolson Street area is typical of . . . obsolete areas where the opportunity exists to create new environments on the scale of the original New Town.[26]

Thus, again, the image of the New Town was conjured up to sustain the idea that imaginative large-scale planning of urban areas could be successfully undertaken. That which was revered from the past was used to legitimize the destruction of historic environments that were depicted as merely 'obsolete'. The meanings in the physical environment, and the language used to describe them, were shaped by the interests of the interpreters. The corporation therefore assembled and acquired large tracts of the South Side and earmarked them for university development. The Housing Acts were used for the clearance and purchase, since the CDA had no statutory status.

Conservationist pressure continued to mount. It focussed particularly on Buccleuch Place, a wide street of listed five-storey Georgian tenements. By October 1971 the university was involved in studying the feasibility of conserving the block which it had earlier expected to demolish. Two months earlier amenity societies had fiercely opposed a planning application from the university to demolish a church and two Georgian tenements on the adjoining Buccleuch Street. Eventually this application was withdrawn.

In March 1973 the university held a public exhibition. It revealed their more limited development ambitions and proposals for the conservation of Buccleuch Place. Restrictions on finance for university development were explicitly identified as one reason for the change in development strategy. Thus by 1973 the university, like the Murrayfield Real Estate Company, was unable to carry through redevelopment of the South Side on a scale like that envisaged in the late

1960s. Likewise the prospects of major road building in the area were receding. The Joint Co-ordinating Committee met in April 1973 to decide what might be done. On 12 July they recommended that the City Planning Officer should review and revise plans for the CDA and should designate part of the South Side as a Conservation Area. The proposals were accepted by the Planning Committee.

This shift towards conservation obviously owed something to the campaigning of the local amenity groups. However, it would not have come about without the combined influence of market forces, central government constraints on university finance and the local authority's inability to steer through its road building aspirations.

A move from redevelopment to rehabilitation was also occurring in housing policy in the city. In the mid-1960s the corporation had commissioned a consultant's report on unfit housing. The Jones Report[27] focussed on amenity deficiency, which meant houses lacking at least one facility, or where the kitchen sink, wash-hand basin, bath/shower or WC were in non-ventilated spaces. The consultant visited 36,000 houses in areas where sub-standard housing was known to exist, though he excluded those properties that were already on the 1967–70 Clearance Schedule. Of those visited, 28,506 were found to be deficient in at least one facility. The scale of unfitness was subsequently confirmed by the 1971 Census, which used a more restricted assessment of amenity deficiency, as shown in Table 18.

Table 18   *Households by Tenure and Amenity, 1971*

Tenure	No hot water		No bath/shower		No exclusive use of flush WC	
	Number	Per cent	Number	Per cent	Number	Per cent
Owner-occupied	2800	3.8	7945	10.7	1975	1.5
Public rented	845	1.7	1245	2.5	370	0.7
Private rented (unfurnished)	6245	25.5	11790	48.2	1815	7.4
Private rented (furnished)	675	7.1	1550	16.4	3445	36.5

Source: General Register Office, 1973, Census, 1971, Scotland, County Report, Edinburgh City, Edinburgh, HMSO, Table 25.

Such data on the backlog of unfit housing must be set in the context of the clearance rates which the city had achieved, its increasing shortage of land for local authority housing and the political antipathy of right-wing councillors to council housing. From 1950 to 1973 a total of 7352 houses had been dealt with through Clearance Area and Housing Treatment Area procedures and a further 2735 houses had been cleared through CDA procedures. In addition 5806 individual unfit houses had been the subject of Closing Orders or Demolition Orders under the Housing Acts.[28] In other words, even if house clearance proceeded at the high rates of the 1950s and 1960s, the prospect was that unfit housing would persist for another generation.

The policies that had been followed for the past twenty years were therefore demonstrably incapable of meeting their declared intentions. The problem in part derived from the deferred contradictions of earlier periods. The dwellings built to house the burgeoning labour force of the nineteenth-century city and the environment associated with those houses were obsolete within an economy tied economically and ideologically to rising expectations. The original building standards, coupled with the chronic squeeze on the ability of the owners to maintain the properties, meant that a substantial part of the housing stock was now in a bad physical condition. This 'misfortune' was compounded by the limited planning capacity of the local authority, most noticeably expressed in the shortage of land for council houses and the financial restrictions of the housing cost yardsticks and the housing revenue account. The class contradictions were thus complex and extended both historically and spatially. They mirrored the factors behind the change in policy nationally that the 1969 Housing Act introduced.

In April 1973 the Housing Committee revised its demolition programme for 1974–8, so that only 2399 of the 5821 houses in it would be demolished, while the rest were now to be improved.[29] Even so, the 1971–3 programme, which mainly involved demolition, was allowed to proceed largely intact. By the end of 1974, forty-five Housing Treatment Areas for improvement had been put forward, involving almost 2000 houses. The change in policy was supported by both the main parties though there was a polarization over the agency. Labour councillors argued for municipal purchase of properties and direction of the programme, but the Conservatives favoured housing associations and private initiatives. By the mid-1970s some half a dozen housing associations were engaged in tenement rehabilitation.

Individuals and property companies benefited from this improvement boom which peaked in the early 1970s. The award of grants to the latter was a further source of party political controversy, with Labour members opposing the giving of public money to 'speculators'.[30] By checking the lists of Closing Orders in Council minutes, companies were able to buy flats quickly and cheaply and then get grants to bring them up to standard, before re-selling or re-letting at a higher price. Applications for improvement grants ran at around 400 per month before the change in legislation in June 1974, after which the average dropped to 120 a month.[31]

The shift in policy from redevelopment and new building to conservation and rehabilitation must also be seen in relation to the evident working-class dissatisfaction with the new council housing of the period. This was significant both directly in mobilizing action groups and indirectly in terms of the housing management problems posed by the unpopular estates for the administration. The exemplar of such disaffection in the early 1970s was Wester Hailes. This new development for 17,500 people on the western edge of the city was the last large council housing scheme to be built in Edinburgh. Its planning and implementation reveals some of the reasons for the change in planning style away from the design of large new developments, towards participation, co-ordination and management.

In the mid-1960s, Edinburgh Corporation faced an acute problem in meeting the housing expectations and needs of that substantial section of its citizens who were unable to purchase reasonable housing in the private market. Faced with seemingly inexhaustible pressures for new housing and a shortage of land for residential development, the Housing Committee sought to build as many houses as possible as quickly as possible through using high densities and large sites.[32] To this end they resolved to acquire 287 acres at Wester Hailes and a further 235 acres at another peripheral site, Alnwickhill.[33] Both sites were in the Green Belt; both were close to middle-class owner-occupied estates, which quickly spawned pressure groups to oppose the plans at public inquiry, which was duly held in the summer of 1964.

At the inquiry the corporation argued that the scale of unmet housing needs in the city justified development in the Green Belt. Mr Hewitson countered criticisms on amenity grounds by suggesting that 'There could be a good architectural effect along . . . the ring road which would run along Wester Hailes by carefully placing one or two multi-storey blocks in the development.'[34]

The main objectors were the Liberton Association (to the Alnwickhill development) and the Wester Hailes Amenity Association. They were supported by the Cockburn Association and the Edinburgh Architectural Association. They managed to employ an advocate and to hire a consultant, Mr McIndoe, to present their evidence. Their case was two-pronged: they attempted to show that the corporation had over-estimated the scale of housing need and to defend the amenity value of the Green Belt sites. Mr McIndoe argued that the 1985 Edinburgh population was likely to total 472,000, not the 500,000 projected by the corporation. He proposed redevelopment of temporary housing sites, inner city house building and the reconstruction of older council housing as alternatives to the proposed development.[35] The residents of Juniper Green voiced fears that if Wester Hailes went ahead they might be 'swamped by a council scheme',[36] and that the values of properties in the area would be depressed.[37]

The Reporter decided that the corporation had not adequately sustained their case. However, the Secretary of State, Mr Ross, gave permission for development at Wester Hailes, while rejecting the proposals for Alnwickhill. His decision rested on the priority of ensuring an adequate supply of land for the housing programme. Within that constraint he concluded that there was no other alternative large site that could be developed with less objection than Wester Hailes. Again, the decision of the Secretary of State crucially influenced the local urban development. The Chairman of the Planning Committee, Councillor Millar, suggested that as Alnwickhill was not available for housing, densities in the Wester Hailes scheme could be increased on those originally planned.[38] Wester Hailes was hence to be planned at a density of 100 persons per acre. In marked contrast, a site at Baberton, just across the line of the proposed ring road from Wester Hailes, was zoned in the Development Plan Review for private housing at a density of twenty persons per acre.

Thus the corporation began to acquire the land in which to build. The transaction was not wholly to the disadvantage of the land owners; for example, Wester Hailes Farm, forty-five acres in extent, was bought by the local authority for £149,340, whereas in 1954 it had changed hands for only £4750.[39] Landownership carried the political power to negotiate terms in a way that was quite beyond the tenants who were to move into the scheme. An illustration is the involvement of Wimpey, the large building company. In June 1965 the Planning Committee refused them permission to develop a 156-acre site for housing, as part of it was covered by the proposed Wester Hailes development and part was in the Green Belt. After negotiations the firm agreed not to obstruct the corporation's acquisition of sixty-eight acres of the land, while indicating that they hoped they would be allowed to develop at least twenty-five acres for private housing.[40] They also hoped to have an opportunity to build part of the Wester Hailes housing for the corporation through a negotiated contract.[41] Eventually Wimpey developed Baberton for private housing and won the contract for the building of 226 houses in the West Burn area of Wester Hailes.

The Housing Committee was undoubtedly the main force behind the scheme within the corporation. The Planning Committee played a subservient role. Once the Secretary of State had given approval for the development, the next stage of the planning was not undertaken by the Planning Department. Instead the Housing Committee hired a firm of planning consultants, Sir Frank Mears & Partners, to produce a lay-out.[42] The consultants' report was presented six months later. They tried to plan Wester Hailes like a New Town, though the unified and extended planning powers of a Development Corporation were not available. Ideas of seeking special parliamentary powers were entertained, but dropped, because 'time was the enemy', as one of the consultants later observed.[43]

Physical features exacerbated the difficulties of a brief seeking a high density development. The site was traversed by a canal, a railway track and overhead electricity cables. It sloped some 220 feet from south to north, across a series of rolling mounds running east–west. The steep slopes necessitated considerable areas of embankment to achieve satisfactory engineering standards for the roads. Pressures on the land were compounded by the expectation of a remorseless progression to affluence and mobility. Car parking was provided at one space per house, with further provision for decking if the need arose. Roads were planned on the principles propounded in 'Traffic in Towns', so the estate instantly became the second largest area of vehicle/pedestrian segregation in Scotland, after Cumbernauld. In presenting their plan the consultants recommended that 'the basic idea of urban enclosure should be all pervasive'[44] – given the constraints it could scarcely have been otherwise.

The original designs were modified during the implementation phase; indeed a

Development Plan Amendment was drawn up in 1973 because of the extent of the changes. As with the earlier planning the changes reflected the dominance of the interests of capital in planning the scheme, remote from the concerns of the tenants. The consultants had planned for clusters of shops, schools and play areas to be developed within the housing areas and along the main pedestrian route, as the need arose. However, their proposals to leave some plots vacant, to preserve flexibility for the future, were rejected as wasteful. The whole shopping structure was reassessed. After discussions between the corporation's Estates Department and Woolco, the corporation decided that Wester Hailes should have one large shopping centre that would serve a wide catchment on the west of the city and beyond. By June 1968 a short list of three possible developers had been drawn up, namely Rank City Wall, Samuel Properties and Arndale Developments. Rank City Wall were eventually given the contract, despite the fact that their scheme omitted provision for a Woolworths store (one of the requirements of the brief) and despite their financial proposals being less favourable to the city than those of Samuel Properties.[45] The scheme as eventually accepted gave the corporation a ground rent of £36,000 and a one-third equity participation. The centre was eventually opened in 1974. The local authority was therefore not just planning the development, but directly involved as a partner in a commercial scheme and thus in the direct implementation of the logic of the market. When the first tenants moved into Wester Hailes they found only two local shops, and there was no bus service to the nearest district shopping centre at Sighthill.

Thus the planning and implementation of shopping facilities stretched over nine years and directly involved property capital, while the then and future residents of the area could only participate as a statistical aggregate of consumers. Many of the decisions were arrived at in private to preserve commercial confidentiality. The dispersed and more accessible shopping clusters were abandoned. Similarly the provision of social facilities, originally intended to create a 'town centre' rather than just a commercial centre, lagged far behind the development of the profitable aspects of the scheme.

Implementation coincided with sharply rising costs in the construction industry. This created major difficulties in meeting the housing cost yardsticks of the Scottish Development Department. Economies were made in the details of designs, laying the basis for a stream of subsequent complaints by tenants about their dwellings. Thus a report by a tenants' group in 1977 commented,

There are perhaps two fundamental reasons for the poor quality of construction – the cash limits imposed by central Government which meant that, with inflation, standards were continually dropped to keep within the limits; and the use of designs by different contractors, some of which seem to have been 'off the shelf' and not suited to the needs of the site or the people.[46]

Among the problems which the report attributed to design faults were: the attraction of rodents by the high cellulose content of many of the building materials; dampness; lack of sound insulation between flats; and unsatisfactory gas and electric heating systems.

Wester Hailes quickly became unpopular. The first families, who moved to the estate in 1968, faced all the problems of living on what was, in effect, a large building site. The first of the twenty-two multi-storey blocks planned for the scheme was in use by 1971, by which time the general unpopularity of multi-storey blocks was causing difficulties for the local authority. In 1969 when plans for the Wester Hailes Park and Drive area of the scheme were being considered, the City Chamberlain reported to the Housing Committee that multi-storey flats were becoming difficult to let.[47] By 1970 the City Chamberlain and the Finance Committee were urging the Housing Committee to eliminate multi-storey blocks from future contracts, but the Housing Committee was of the view that pressure on the waiting list was so intense that people had to go into multi-storey blocks.[48] The committee eventually turned against multi-storey blocks in late 1972.

So Wester Hailes quickly became a 'difficult to let' peripheral estate, with few community facilities. The Housing Committee, seeking to get some income from flats which were otherwise empty, made a block of eighty-five flats available to Edinburgh University for student accommodation.[49] The bulk of the rest of the new residents were young families with young children,[50] so the lack of local health and pre-school facilities was particularly marked. In 1973 the Social Work Department's Special Projects Team analysed the problems of the estate. They reported that over 86 per cent of the children in Wester Hailes were from families at or below the poverty level.[51] The all-electric houses in the estate built for an age of affluence and mobility were simply too expensive to operate for many of the low-income families.

To depict the planning and development of Wester Hailes as a series of 'mistakes' by the local authority, in which the Housing Committee was dominant, would be reductionist. Nor can the estate's problems be ascribed unequivocally to the machinations of capitalists. It would be even more absurd to present Wester Hailes as the simple result of working-class political pressure for more council housing, the vindication of the fears expressed at the outset by the Wester Hailes Amenity Association. Rather the development was the result of the struggle between these interests. To the local authority in the mid-1960s, within that long wave of post-war affluence, Wester Hailes was an administrative necessity, to avoid a major housing crisis, a perspective endorsed by central government at the inquiry. Though council housing was not popular with the local *bourgeoisie,* the scheme opened financial opportunities for developers. In this situation, the working-class interest in getting better housing was geographically dispersed within a city where the labour movement had never held controlling political power, or that interest was represented by the few pioneering settlers in the new estate: this constituted a weak bargaining position. Thus the constraints under which the planning and development took place were predominantly those of capital and the state, both locally and centrally, and these constraints ensured that the crisis avoidance strategy would generate further crises.

In its early years Wester Hailes therefore symbolized a growing awareness among working-class residents in the older parts of the city that the long struggle for better housing conditions could not be won unconditionally. They came to a recognition similar to that reached by the city's *bourgeoisie* in its struggles against the roads proposals. The modernization of the city, so ardently desired to match the physical fabric to the expectations of the consumers of proliferating commodities, also entailed a process of deprivation. The local authority, and more particularly 'the planners', were the visible agents of that deprivation, just as market forces were the spontaneous bearers of commodities for individual consumption. The *angst* was thus translated into a withdrawal of legitimation from the planning system. The administration, faced with this developing crisis tendency, sought to modify its style of planning. Redevelopment and the design of large-scale new housing areas gave way to rehabilitation, conservation, and a new emphasis on participation and co-ordination.

Participation and co-ordination

The development of public participation in planning in Edinburgh reflected the pattern of national legislation and guidance. However, the specific local problems of containing disaffection over planning matters were also significant. The practice of public participation fostered by the local authority was riddled with mutual misunderstandings. Planners and the public alike were torn between their intentions and the limited room for manoeuvre which existed between the conflicting priorities of the state and local 'communities'. The contradictions, dispersed among the mushrooming though fragmented quasi-groups, were therefore imported into the language and practice of participation, rather than resolved. New games were being played, the rules only becoming clear as you played. When they found they could not win, some players gave up, while others began to forge new alliances which would alter the rules.

Edinburgh Corporation's first formal participation exercise on a development plan was staged in Leith in 1971. An exhibition, 'Tomorrow's Leith', was held in the old fire station building and a public meeting was held. The intention was to provide information and hear the views of residents on the preparation of a local plan. Since Abercrombie's drastic proposals to make central Leith a purely industrial zone, plans had given more emphasis to residential redevelopment, in the light of the continuing housing problems of both the area and the city. However, mounting unemployment and the loss of Development Area status in the late 1960s had reopened the case for industrial uses.

The central issue at the exhibition was therefore the relative allocations of land uses. Visitors were asked to deliberate on the merits of five alternative plans, one of which constituted a 'balance' between the others. The choice was to be made in a vacuum, hermetically sealed by the statutory responsibilities of the planning authority. There was no information on rehousing procedures and prospects for those whose houses might be redeveloped. Still less was there any indication of the type and likely availability of the jobs that were equated with the purple columns in the land use budgets. The plans were neither costed nor programmed. These deficiencies were compounded by shortfalls in the actual presentation of the material.[52] In part these difficulties derived from inexperience and from the working practices of the administrative system itself, where departmental barriers remained strong and the Planning Department weak. More fundamentally the deficiencies were also related to the forces and interests producing the structural decline in employment in the dock-related and other industries of what is, in effect if not in geography, an inner city area. Similarly the housing problems were rooted in the economics and politics of providing adequate housing for people on low incomes. It was these relationships which were reduced to a 'choice' of land use budgets. 'Tomorrow's Leith' could not be defined on the basis of the exhibition – even the mere preparation of the local plan dragged on through most of the 1970s.

One might argue that the corporation's approach in Leith was less sophisticated than that attempted by the Buchanan/Freeman Fox team on the roads issue in the city. But even that exercise had conspicuously failed to create the desired sympathy and consensus around the consultants' proposals.[53] It was against these failures that the Planning Department embarked on its next major foray into public involvement, in the long blighted South Side area. There a vigorous local pressure group had grown up, the South Side Association, vocally critical of past policies for the area.

The review of the University/Nicolson Street CDA began in 1973 and one of the corporation's first decisions was to appoint a team of consultants to expedite the work. Professor Johnson-Marshall's firm were appointed. To the officials this appeared a logical and pragmatic step, the professor had an international reputation, and as consultant to the university had a vast experience in planning the South Side. Activists in the South Side Association saw the move as something more sinister – the main author of the grandiose redevelopment plan which the association had formed to fight was to be centrally involved in preparing a new plan. The university, their *bête noire*, had its man doing the planning, while the association could only look to the openings offered by public participation.

The participation exercise was first considered by the Planning Committee on 15 November 1973, some months after the work on the review had commenced. The committee decided that a public meeting would be premature without proposals to consider. Rather, as an experiment, participation would be focussed through an advisory panel and a local Planning Workshop, which would give out information. The panel idea clearly owed something to Skeffington's Community Forum. In addition, meetings, talks and exhibitions were anticipated.

The Convenor of the Planning Committee at the time was Councillor Smith, who, almost a decade earlier, had been the sole opponent of the Inner Ring Road when the plan first came before the Council. Councillor Smith, a Liberal, was sympathetic to the idea of 'community planning'. He saw the workshop and panel arrangement as an experiment that was justified by the shortcomings revealed in earlier initiatives. He commented:

The Planning Officer and I discussed the situation as to how best we could get *reaction* from local people and we came to the conclusion that we had never tried a workshop system. There had never been an Advisory Panel in Edinburgh. We'd tried a variety of other ways which hadn't been terribly successful so we decided, let's try this.[54]

A meeting was convened in a local hall by the Planning Department on 4 February 1974. The department had distributed a leaflet two months before, indicating that a panel was to be formed. Those returning the questionnaire on the leaflet were then invited to the meeting from which the panel was to be constituted. The Planning Department hoped that people in the South Side would form street associations, representatives from which could then combine with those from other groups to form the panel. The idea of street associations was derived from the New Town, where such groups flourished; little thought appears to have been given to whether the very different social structure of the South Side would really generate such bodies.

The role of the South Side Association in the panel was clearly a critical issue. The City Planning Officer explained the relationship he foresaw: 'I thought in fact the SSA would form the basis of the Advisory Panel, because they had been very active in the area, ... I had hoped, in fact, that the SSA would have been *absorbed* by the Advisory Panel.'[55] He saw the panel as channelling the views of all the interests in the area to his department: 'The result of such composite representation may be that when the final plan was submitted to the Secretary of State no party would then come forward with objections, since all parties had had opportunities to express their views via the panel when the plan was being formulated.'[56]

Thus the interest of the Planning Department in establishing public participation was to incorporate their most vociferous critics alongside other more 'representative' groups within a dialogue, which would confirm the legitimacy of the decisions that were to be made.

In practice the panel became frustrated with their seeming inability to influence policy, especially policies of other departments within the corporation. These failings confirmed the suspicions of the local authority which had been nurtured in some panel members by the years of blight. Some had very direct, personal grievances: the corporation had compulsorily purchased the shops of two of the small traders on the panel; another member had been forced to move from the area when his house was demolished; while the panel was in being one member was served with a Closing Order on his house, another trader had his shop demolished and a second was served with notice to quit pending demolition.[57] The Secretary of the Nicolson Street Traders' Association remarked, 'At the start, I regarded all Corporation officials as my enemies.'[58]

During 1974 the panel met, passed resolutions, minuted them and the minutes went off to the corporation. However, the demolitions and closures continued under the Housing Acts as the planners pieced together their draft proposals for conservation in the area. The inability of the administrative system to switch policy quickly and consistently further undermined the attempts of the planners to restore legitimacy to their actions and to re-establish civil privatism over policy for the area. Thus on 9 September 1974 the panel carried a resolution condemning the activities of the Housing and Highways Committees, observing, 'The Corporation's recent actions have further deepened the cynicism felt throughout the area after years of neglect and lack of communication.'[59]

282   *The development of planning thought*

As the panel became more openly disaffected, so official doubts began to grow about their 'representativeness'. From its inauguration until April 1975 the panel included among its numbers traders (many of whom lived locally), old age pensioners, students, a planner, an architect, a local vicar and other assorted local residents. One could certainly argue, though the Planning Department did not, that women were under-represented. In other respects the panel reflected the fragmented social groupings in the area. The high turnover among its membership (the composition changed by around 50 per cent in the first eighteen months) was also representative of an area of students, private renting, demolitions and closures. In all the circumstances the panel represented a remarkably coherent coalition, held together by a perceived common enemy.[60]

If the early experience of participation confirmed the scepticism of some of the panel, it also disenchanted the officials. When interviewed in early 1975 the Chief Planning Officer commented,

I was hoping that at very early meetings they'd have set down and said, 'Well what should be the planning objectives of the whole of this area?', and tried to list, quite a simple listing of items such as the rehabilitation of derelict property, stabilization of the population of the area and things of that sort, rather than the problems they did get involved with.[61]

Thus the panel, by articulating local concerns on matters beyond the limits of statutory planning, were seen to have strayed beyond their remit. They had also expressed views on 'planning objectives', but in sporadic resolutions scattered through the minutes of meetings and not in a conventional survey report. The Planning Officer concluded that the experience had taught him to get more directly involved in the appointment of members to any future panel, so as to ensure that what he perceived to be all interests were adequately represented.[62]

Although one local councillor was on the panel, elected members played a relatively insignificant role throughout. This may have been due to the quirks of ward boundaries, for the South Side was carved up between four wards, with its fragments a small, peripheral part of each. More fundamentally the alliance of interests that made up the South Side Association only politicized the issues to the extent of counterposing institutional interests (the university and the corporation) against local interests. The class basis of the transformation of a working-class housing area by a tripartite agreement between a property company, a major middle-class institution within the city and a right-wing dominated council was never seriously thematized. The contrast in participation through the economic power of land ownership and access to finance, with the more limited countervailing political power of a coalition of diverse local social groupings brought together in a panel was not a rallying point. Indeed, to have organized on that basis would have been to have risked splintering the coalition and having the limited opportunities opened for participation withdrawn.

The South Side participation exercise therefore remained dominated by the local state's priorities to steer change in the face of an economic crisis which had made a nonsense of earlier plans for the area. The mutual mistrust and recrimi-nations reflected in a distorted fashion the contradictions, containing them to the level of individuals and the corporation as an administrative entity. Participation and the appearance of the South Side Local Plan geared to conservation deflected the crisis tendencies, though they could not, *per se*, carry through the speedy regeneration of the area. Still less could the planning system give the rump of old, poor residents who constituted the South Side 'community' the power to deter-mine their own living conditions.

Just a couple of miles from the South Side there was developing a remarkable community-led initiative in public participation. The development of the Craigmillar housing areas has been sketched in earlier chapters. The overcrowding and lack of facilities were criticized in the earlier years of the estate before the Second World War and again by Abercrombie. Further houses were added in the 1950s, then came the multi-storey blocks. By 1962 Craigmillar still had no library, sixth-year school or community centre, though its population was over 20,000. A local mother, stung by the lack of opportunity for her son to learn the violin at school, decided that Craigmillar should put on its own 'Festival', to release the talents of its people which were being repressed. The festival became an annual event, organized by the Craigmillar Festival Society, with the mother, Helen Crummy, at the helm. As a network of local contacts developed, CFS became involved in a range of caring activities. After seven years they obtained token funds under the Urban Aid scheme to operate a team of neighbourhood workers who helped local residents. With it came £1000 for a community projects fund.

From the outset the society had had very close links with its elected members. In the early 1970s it began to build contacts with professional 'advisers' living outside the area, but sympathetic to their aspirations. Two issues in particular drew them towards architects and planners. One of the old mining villages within the ward was threatened with demolition and its residents campaigned to be rehoused back in the village and for some rehabilitation.[63] The second con-troversy concerned the location for a secondary school in Craigmillar. A site to the north of the estate, with a catchment taking in middle-class areas, was turned down after a planning public inquiry, which had been vigorously contested by the residents living close to the site.

The society's contacts were greatly strengthened when one of their local coun-cillors became the first and only Labour Lord Provost of Edinburgh in the early 1970s. In 1972 the Lord Provost's Committee Pilot Project was initiated. It stemmed from a motion proposed by another Labour councillor: 'That the Cor-poration set up a Joint Committee to examine the needs of a selected area of the city in need of rehabilitation, with a view to instituting a pilot scheme in that area to improve amenities, restore community life, and encourage self-help projects.'[64] Craigmillar, with some of the most severe indicators of multiple deprivation in Britain, was to be the area. It is interesting to note how the language used in the motion, so as to secure support for the project, pays homage to the *bourgeois* view of Craigmillar's problems. The matrons of Morningside could agree that the area had once been perfectly all right; it now needed rehabilitating because of the reluctance of tenants to help themselves and to show the proper 'community spirit'.

The administrators also saw the idea of an experimental inter-departmental project as useful, coming as it did while local government reorganization was pending. In addition there was the hope that the initiative would lead to a reduction in those aspects of life in Craigmillar which were a problem to the administrators. When the City Planning Officer attended the Planning Workshop Conference organized by CFS in June 1973, he declared that the area's problems stemmed from the fact that it was a one-class community. He expressed the hope that the pilot project would lead to more community initiative in caring for the environment.

For the CFS the project meant extra funding, more staff and new projects. The Festival got bigger and better, children were taken for holidays and into play schemes, old age pensioners' lunch clubs prospered and the disabled were helped. The society coined the term 'liaison government', to express the idea of more effective official action being achieved by bringing people and officials together. There were whole day conferences and numerous working parties. The planners dutifully attended, though the Housing Department, landlord to the area, showed scant inclination to get involved.

As a follow-up to the Pilot Project, the CFS pulled off an even bigger coup, winning major funding from the EEC's anti-poverty programme, with matching contributions from Lothian Region and central government. The award, the only one made directly to a community group, was for an action-research project on the contribution that liaison government could make to relieving poverty.

A full and systematic review of the Craigmillar experience is a topic worth a book in itself. However, a few relevant points can be made. The local state and the social practices it constitutes, played a crucial role in planning and developing Craigmillar. The empty, damp and difficult to let houses and the perennial problems of vandalism and lack of facilities were the visible symbols of the failure of the administrative system to fulfil its declared intentions. That failure, and the political resource afforded by local councillors, spawned the flourishing community group, which identified the local authority as the most evident and logical focus for its demands, and consequently sought professional advisers to strengthen the society's technical case. The society therefore won bargaining rights over certain aspects of social life in the area.

Some of the results of the exercise exemplify the limits on even this form of locally-led participation. Craigmillar now has community centres and even a sports centre; however, the latter is a resource for the whole of the east side of the city and the level of charges are beyond the pockets of many of the local residents; as the fiscal crisis in local government deepens there are plans to cut back its opening hours. There is a sixth-year school, though not on the site the CFS wanted and the employment prospects for its pupils are bleak. Some of the older houses have been improved, though it has been a protracted exercise, much disrupted by spending cuts. Industrial estates have been established, though by no means all the jobs in them have gone to local people and unemployment has soared so that it now probably exceeds the levels of the 1930s. A resolution to prepare a comprehensive local plan, genuinely integrating the range of local authority inputs to the area, was carried at the council, but no action was taken because of staff shortages in the Planning Department. The society itself became a major employer in the area, but the ending of the EEC experiment and the mounting crisis of expenditure within local government meant that by the early 1980s the scale of employment and activities was running down. Participation and co-ordination, as means of social control, were too costly and had failed to overcome the problems of rationality and legitimacy which had predicated them.

The Craigmillar Festival Society has frequently been held up as an exemplar to other groups. Certainly its experiences and its model of a wide-ranging community development strategy begun in the community itself, and anchored in the arts and social welfare, has been built upon elsewhere in Scotland. Despite its strong links with the Labour Party, the CFS remained fundamentally an area-based organization in its campaigning, rather than the standard bearer for a co-ordinated struggle by working-class groups throughout the city.

The experience in Craigmillar and the work of the Social Work Department's Special Projects Team in Wester Hailes began to influence Edinburgh Corporation in the years just before local government reorganization. A Labour councillor, in October 1973, successfully moved that the corporation should adopt a Social and Community Development Programme. This would run in parallel with the Lord Provost's Pilot Project in Craigmillar, but would focus on other deprived areas in the city. Like the project in Craigmillar, it eventually received funding from the EEC's anti-poverty programme. Census data were analysed to identify the areas of deprivation where the SCDP would operate. Four were selected, the old tenemental and industrial areas of Central Leith and Gorgie Dalry and the large council estates at Pilton and Wester Hailes.

The objectives of the programme were approved by the corporation in June 1974. They were,

1   To define areas of multiple deprivation within the city, analysing the problems of these areas and creating and implementing policies on an inter-departmental basis in order to eliminate deprivation.
2   To provide a comprehensive picture of problem areas in order to determine priorities in a meaningful way.
3   To make local government more effective and accessible to local communities.
4   To assist local people in deciding, planning and taking action to meet their own needs with the help of outside resources.
5   To help local communities to adapt to the pressures of social, economic and physical change.[65]

Deprivation was thus ascribed to inadequate service delivery, which could be eliminated by co-ordination and participation. Communities were to be helped to adapt to the pressures of change, not to be given the power to analyse, still less control those pressures. Although the project was laced with research and monitoring, these underlying assumptions about the nature of inequality were not subjected to either theoretical or empirical testing.

To eliminate deprivation in four areas of the city housing some 74,000 people, a small Central Research Unit, staffed by relatively junior officers, was set up in the Planning Department and gradually area co-ordinators were appointed to each area. The planting of the project in the areas was less rational than their identification. Wester Hailes got priority because it was a new area, and there was a case for acting quickly before things became worse. Central Leith and Gorgie Dalry vied with each other as Local Plan work progressed for them elsewhere in the Planning Department. Pilton, arguably the most deprived of the four, came last, as there was no administrative imperative to put it anywhere else.

Relatively little had happened by local government reorganization in 1975. The two-tier split of functions complicated the management structures of the project, so much so that by 1977 the official report confessed, 'The mechanism for the response to the requests made from local areas is now cumbersome.'[66] The area co-ordinators fostered self-help schemes and participation in the areas. A Programme Advisory Group, staffed by personnel from the main departments in the Region and the District, managed the project, and sought to infuse the rest of their departments with its principles and recommendations. They reported to a Joint Committee made of an equal number of elected members from the two authorities. This committee met on a six-week cycle on Friday afternoons, 'a time which reflects the newness of the Committee and the prior commitments of the members' time'.[67]

Within the local authorities different departments responded in different ways to the SCDP, as Table 19 indicates. It did not take long for the people from the estates who got involved in the SCDP to realize that participation came with strings attached: 'We only make suggestions; if they fit in with the Local Authority's existing plans, that's OK, but if not they don't necessarily take any notice.'[68]

One of the community workers in Wester Hailes, Colin Gillain, observed in 1976 that much of the time at meetings was spent by officials explaining the problems of the administration to tenants – the different time scales, budgeting arrangements, committee structures and so on. Tenants, suitably instructed in the difficulties of meeting their needs, were expected to retire wiser and more contented.[69] A District Council planner commented in 1979 that participation in SCDP was most likely to achieve results where participants could match their claims with the legal obligations of a department.[70] One consequence was that in the SCDP areas groups formed around concerns reflecting the internal structure of local government. In a sense then the practices under SCDP conjured a pluralist local structure. Similarly, the area co-ordinators were seen by some politicians as competitors for the role of local representative.[71]

The whole SCDP was structured around the ideology that a consensus was possible around the optimum technical approach to eliminating deprivation in the four areas. The fact that after local government reorganization the two authorities involved had differing political complexions was not therefore seen as a stumbling block. As a senior member of the Programme Advisory Group put it when interviewed, 'Everybody expected the Joint Committee members to debate without their party political badges on.'[72] Thus the contradictions which the programme was structured to contain re-emerged in the role dilemmas of the elected members and in the problems those dilemmas created for the officials. As the head of Lothian Region's Policy Planning Department commented, 'I was always staggered that [the consensus requirement] was considered politically very bad. [Coming out of a Committee meeting] politicians would say, "Do you know who you were agreeing with?" . . . Even small issues were politicized and . . . the Joint Committee members never retained their SCDP badges in standard service committees.'[73] The politicization eventually led the Conservative-controlled Edinburgh District Council to withdraw from the project in 1978. Opposition was led by one of their members on the Joint Committee, Councillor Aidan McLernan, who depicted the project as no more than a social work exercise that was generating 'mountains of paperwork' and 'repetitive and incomprehensible reports' in pursuit of 'increasingly unrealistic objectives'.[74] The tide had turned against the phase of extended technical administration as the Butskellite solution to the problems of deprived areas.

Reorganization and recession

Changes in planning practice have their roots in changes in the economic system. Statutory town planning practice is the practice of the state, an activity infused with the dynamism of the continuing, though changing, class struggle. The shift from an extended technical planning process seeking to incorporate the management of deprivation and the process of public involvement to a more limited and politicized planning hinged on the changed economic conditions as the recession of the 1970s deepened. The impact of these changes on planning and development in Edinburgh can be traced from the first major reports produced after local government reorganization.

The old Edinburgh Corporation ceased to be in April 1975. The new Edinburgh District Council administered the same area, as well as the suburbs of Currie and South Queensferry. The extensions of the old boundaries were modest, with contiguous suburbs such as Musselburgh remaining in other authorities. Crucially though Edinburgh after reorganization was just one of four Districts in Lothian Region, albeit much the largest, with some 472,000 of the estimated regional population of 754,000.[75] The Labour Party, while short of an overall majority, were the largest group on the region.

Like the other Scottish regions Lothian produced a Regional Report in May 1976. This policy document, unique to Scotland, was intended to provide a basis for corporate policy making. In Lothian the report was prepared by the new Department of Policy Planning. Much of it was a mundane statement of existing policies and commitments inherited from the constituent authorities. However, the report also made clear the changed economic climate within which the new

Table 19   *Some departmental responses to SCDP*

Authority	Department	Nature of involvement	Relevance to department	Departmental view of participation
District	Administration	Administrative aspects of programme	As for any other administrative matter	
	Director of Finance	Minor and peripheral		
	Recreation	Have learned through local contact	Has not influenced departmental policy. Finance is not available	Useful for consultation
	Housing	Observation, no commitment	None, area focus is not relevant to housing policy as laid down by statute. Department considers itself answerable to Housing Committee only.	In local areas housing department have their own ways of consulting local people. SCDP become an additional participant among others
	Cleansing		The approach reveals possibilities for developing better service	Useful for consultation
	Local planning	Not central, but important	SCDP develop the views of local residents, one interest among many others in the area	As laid down by Acts of Parliament

authority was to operate, with central government seeking to limit local government spending through the issue of financial guidelines.

The effects of the ending of the long wave of post-war affluence could also be detected from many of the statistics in the report. Male employment in Lothian had declined by 12 per cent from 1964 to 1974, a loss of 23,247 jobs. More women had been taken into the labour force, as female employment increased by 7.5 per cent, a rise of 9044 jobs. Edinburgh had the lowest unemployment rate of the four Districts and a rate below the Scottish average. Nevertheless, the greatest absolute number of unemployed were to be found in Edinburgh, and in areas like Leith, Pilton and Craigmillar the unemployment rates were acknowledged to be very high. The report proposed, though it did not elaborate, an area-based strategy to tackle the problems of multiple deprivation.

Table 19 cont.

Authority	Department	Nature of involvement	Relevance to department	Departmental view of participation
Region	Strategic planning	Central, encourages area focus through regional policy	In favour of positive discrimination and inner city revitalization. Sees SCDP as complementary	As laid down by Acts of Parliament
	Social work	Central, department already has area focus	Better co-ordination and coverage of needs. (Notes that certain problems are solved locally through workshop (SCDP) instead of through department)	Important
	Education	Central	Much the same as social work.	

Source: Internal evaluation and interviews. The classification of answers is by P. Wiberg (1980).

The report sought central government clarification on the future of Livingston New Town, a notably less prescriptive stance than Strathclyde adopted in relation to the proposals for Stonehouse. Continued development at Livingston would make major demands on the region's resources, but unlike at Stonehouse much of the money would have to be spent anyway because of the existing scale of development in the new town. Livingston's relatively successful record at attracting employment was also noted approvingly. In response the Minister of State at the Scottish Office, Mr Gregor Mackenzie, argued that Livingston was a good investment:

Livingston has cost about £110 million, of which £50 million has come from central government, £37 million from the private sector, £15 million from public utilities and £8.5 million from local authorities in Lothian. This is the substance of co-operation and we are glad that Lothian has obtained from it jobs [over 300 a year, the overwhelming majority in industrial enterprises attracted from outside the region], housing for its people, a commercial centre of major significance and an asset from which it can not only take pride but a not insignificant revenue.[76]

Thus the broad pattern of previous policy was reasserted on the new town. However, there were growing signs that continuing past policies would be an insufficient response to changes that were occurring. The District Report produced by Edinburgh District's Planning Department in 1977 charted some of these trends. It revealed that the population of the district had declined from 483,967 in 1961 to 468,861 in 1976.[77] The population structure was also aging, as a result of the out-migration of younger people. The main loss of population was from the inner tenement areas, while new growth had occurred at and beyond the periphery of the city.

The report revealed that employment in manufacturing in the city had contracted by 30 per cent between 1964 and 1974, a loss of 18,593 jobs.[78] This rate considerably exceeded the overall Scottish rate. Even faster rates of decline were noted in the primary and construction sectors, though they were numerically less significant. The city had been excluded from Development Area status until August 1974 and this was thought to be a factor in the decline of manufacturing. Even after 1974 it was difficult to compete with Livingston, which enjoyed Special Development Area status. However, the problems could not be entirely attributed to the workings of regional policy, for the structure of Edinburgh's manufacturing industry had exacerbated the rundown. The mainstays of local manufacturing – food and drink, (particularly brewing), paper, printing and publishing and engineering – were all sectors undergoing severe rationalizations and technological change nationally and shedding labour in the process. The report anticipated that male unemployment could exceed 10 per cent by 1981; with hindsight, a conservative estimate.

The District Report also showed some of the changes that had been occurring in housing. The volume and overall quality of the housing stock had indeed been improved since 1961, but problems were again looming. Though the housing stock had been increased by almost 1 per cent per annum between 1961 and 1976, 6.4 per cent of all households in the city still had their names on the council's house waiting list, over 11,000 households in all.[79] Shifts in tenure were also recorded.

The report suggested that in June 1976 there were 714 acres of land readily available for private sector housing development, but only 295 acres for public housing. Extrapolating past rates of development the land supply would be

Table 20   *Edinburgh dwellings by tenure, 1961, 1971 and 1976*

	1961		1971		1976 (est)	
	Number	*Per cent*	*Number*	*Per cent*	*Number*	*Per cent*
Owner occupied	70,350	43.8	81,000	46.7	85,759	47.2
Private rented	48,639	30.3	36,598	21.1	34,574	19.0
Public rented	41,482	25.9	55,849	32.2	61,460	33.8
Total	160,471	100.00	173,447	100.00	181,793	100.00

Source: City of Edinburgh District Council, District Planning Report (1977), p. 27.

adequate for private builders until 1983–4; the real shortage was land for council housing.[80] Pressure for development in the green belt had mainly been in the west of the city and, in all, planning consent had been granted for the development of 900 acres for non-green belt use. The conversion of green belt land was most evident along the major radial roads, with the result that the green belt had become in effect a series of green wedges.

The question of central area office development had inevitably been embroiled in the city's protracted deliberations over a transport strategy. Eventually in March 1974 the Edinburgh Corporation had adopted a policy of restricting new central area office development, except for offices with a special need to be there, extensions to existing premises up to 10 per cent of the gross floor area and the rehabilitation of buildings of special architectural or historic interest which involved extraordinary costs. Other new offices were to be directed to South Gyle, Leith, Nether Liberton and other district centres.[81] The policy was first adopted on an interim basis in July 1973. However, as with the constraint policy of the green belt, monitoring cast doubts on the effectiveness of the implementation of the policy. From 1970 to 1973 permission was given for 1 million square feet of central area offices and from 1973 to 1976 for 1.02 million square feet.[82] Again, from 1970 to 1973 approvals were given for 2.23 million square feet of offices in the district centres, but in 1973–6 this dropped to 1.72 million square feet.[83] The market pressure for offices was not in places like Leith, but at sites on the edge of the central area and adjacent to main traffic routes and often on sites that were previously in industrial use.

As this and previous chapters have argued, Edinburgh Corporation practised a limited and reactive style of planning for many years. The epitaph for that practice might be taken from one paragraph of the District Report, which read: 'The basic planning issue which has been identified in this review of the City District is the continuing uncontrolled dispersal of activities – of people, houses, employment, shops and community facilities – from the city into the suburban areas and beyond the boundaries of the District.'[84] Clearly central government and the surrounding local authorities had played their part in the 'uncontrolled dispersal'. However, the underlying dynamic was that of the market. Among the consequences were a decline in environment and jobs in the inner city areas, unmet needs for community facilities in the peripheral areas, the loss of good agricultural land and an escalating transport problem. The topography and the legacy of historic buildings still made Edinburgh a distinctive city, but, physically, more extensive areas than ever before had become just like any other city.

The Structure Plan and the politics of transport

By the late 1970s the economic situation was changing so fundamentally that continuity of previous policies (the strategy usually favoured by most administrators) was fraught with problems. It was more transparent than ever before that such policies were unlikely to achieve their declared ends and the political climate was changing in a way that threatened the consensus assumptions around which many of the policies had been constructed. This was the context within which Lothian Region was preparing its Structure Plan. The mere fact that there was no previous Structure Plan did not mean that there were no prior commitments and preconceptions. Above all else there still hung the unresolved issue of a transport strategy, the issue which more than any other had undermined the credibility of the officials over the previous twenty years at least.

The Structure Plan was published in May 1978. It followed a consultation document on the 'Considerations' behind the Plan (March 1977), an Interim Statement (November 1977) and Report of Survey (also November 1977). The plan explicitly set out to be a 'realistic' document, focussing strongly on the next five years, while establishing a land-use strategy for the 1980s. Not surprisingly, its central concerns were the problems posed by the deteriorating economy and by the associated cuts in public expenditure, a marked contrast to the problems faced during the review of Edinburgh's Development Plan in the early 1960s.

The plan set out four major aims:

1   To improve Lothian's performance and ability to compete for economic development.
2   To direct resources to areas of social need and to strengthen existing communities.
3   To conserve all resources including farmland and minerals, and to utilize wisely infrastructure and vacant urban land.
4   To protect and enhance the physical environment of the city, towns, villages, countryside and coastline of Lothian.[85]

There were latent contradictions between these aims. The ability to compete for economic development did not imply directing resources to areas of social need and would probably mean the conversion not conservation of farmland. In the event the plan opted to steer development away from greenfield sites and towards the inner areas of Edinburgh, while also accepting the need to promote development at Livingston. The region's employment problems were to be addressed by providing more industrial sites and advanced factories, allocating extra land for office development in the centre of Edinburgh (thus modifying the stated policy of the old corporation) and by supporting the retention and expansion of existing firms.

Within Edinburgh the plan sought to stem out-migration by directing development to vacant land and by emphasizing rehabilitation. The shrinking jobs in manufacturing were to be retained and diversified. The city's cultural heritage was to be protected as an important asset of the tourist industry and a greater emphasis was to be given to the development of suburban centres for shops and offices. The plan thus exhumed many previous strategies and pressed them into service once again despite the changed situation; one might argue that in view of the statutory constraints within which structure plans operate, the authors had little scope to do otherwise.

One of the original intentions of structure plans had been to integrate the planning of land use and transport. This the Lothian Structure Plan conspicuously failed to do. Not surprisingly, the development of a transport policy had been proceeding in parallel to the preparation of the structure plan, and with some difficulty.

The first Transport Policies and Programme statement had been approved by the council in September 1975. It expressed the intention of urgently resolving the years of planning blight resulting from indecision over road plans. A 'Green Paper', prepared by a technical working group of officials including the Chief Constable and the Directors of Highways, Public Transport and Physical Planning, quickly followed. This discussion paper was carefully non-committal and invited public comment on what might be done. It did not put forward a transport plan for the city. Rather it sought to consider 'the minimum new road and public transport network which should continue to be safeguarded by the Regional Council pending the more thorough review foreshadowed in the first TPP'.[86]

The Green Paper proposed that the council cease to safeguard the line of the Eastern Link Road, the Southern Link Road, the Intermediate Circular Route, the South East Spur and the London Road busway. This meant that three of the most contentious of previous proposals were to be abandoned – the Eastern and Southern Links and the southern route of the ICR. With them Buchanan's strategy was to be buried. Nevertheless the paper suggested that a 'minimum network of new roads' would still be needed to create a better environment, and to reduce delays to buses. Happily such roads now needed to be no more than dual carriageways, with intersections at one level. These roads included the Outer City By-Pass (which had never been contentious), West and East Approach Roads and a Leith Docks Approach Road. However, a Central Area Distributory Loop was also proposed to facilitate traffic management and to maximize pedestrianization. Thus the idea of an inner ring still remained, its scale and function redefined as in Buchanan, but without the ICR which Buchanan had used to justify that redefinition. Possible problems of coping with increased traffic flows in the inner southern suburbs were noted. The report therefore did not propose a network, but just the safeguarding of routes which the authors considered essential to a network. In part these contortions reflected the imperatives of a participation programme in which decisions were not supposed to be pre-empted. More fundamentally they derived from tensions between the views of the officials and the way that opinion was developing among elected members of the new authority and in particular among the Labour group on the council.

Labour opposition to the building of new roads had been spearheaded by councillors whose wards lay in their path. Councillor Rutherford (Labour, Holyrood) and Councillor Cairns (Labour, Meadows) proposed and seconded a motion calling for the abandonment of the Bridges Relief Road and the Central Area Distributor Loop at the Edinburgh District Planning and Development Committee. It was carried by a majority of one, having been opposed by Councillor Kean, who was the Conservative Chairman of the Committee, and by Councillor Smith (Liberal), the former Chairman of the Edinburgh Corporation Planning Committee.[87] The full District Council endorsed the decision to oppose the safeguarding of these roads on 29 July 1976, against the advice of their Director of Planning.

At the Regional Council Councillor Foulkes (Labour, Holyrood/Meadows) was a prominent opponent of the safeguarding. Two more Labour Councillors, Milligan and Mulvey, whose wards were threatened by the Western Approach Road, were also to the fore. The Labour MP for Central Edinburgh, Robin Cook, campaigned consistently for investment in public transport and house improvements instead of roads.

Labour opposition to road plans was sustained from two further sources. Groups from working-class areas became more involved than previously in protests against road proposals. The Craigmillar Festival Society had long contested the safeguarded route through their area, a route first drafted by Abercrombie. CFS stepped up their campaign, and their local Labour councillors were involved in it. Elsewhere an umbrella group, SCRAP, united nine groups from the South Side, St Leonards and Tollcross areas, as well as the Meadows and South Edinburgh Group, in the campaign against the Bridges Relief Road. In the west the Stenhouse–Whitson Action Group developed in a council estate, and with links into the local Labour Party. Helped by community workers from the Edinburgh Council for Social Service, they fought the West Approach Road both without and within the Labour Party.

The second influence on Labour councillors was the Regional Labour Party, the delegates to which are elected from the General Management Committees of the constituency parties. More particularly, there was the Planning and Transport Working Party. This group of rank and file party members, nominated through the branches and constituencies, insistently hammered out the theme of 'maximum investment in public transport and minimum investment in new roads'. They argued that the advice from the officials amounted to a political stance, albeit an unconscious one. It favoured car users, who were a larger part of the population in middle-class areas than in working-class parts of the city. It diverted resources from public transport, which the majority of the people were reliant upon, and it further disadvantaged those working-class residents whose houses were threatened by road building. The Regional Labour Party heeded the advice of their Working Party and called for an end to the safeguarding not just of the routes that the Green Paper proposed to discard, but of the Bridges Relief Road and the Central Area Distributor Loop also.[88]

Eventually the Regional Council voted to instruct their officials to prepare reports on the implications of abandoning the BRR and the CADL. They rejected by 31–16 a Conservative amendment that a decision should be delayed until after a major teach-in at which 'appropriate senior officials would be in attendance in order to acquaint the councillors with the recommendations contained in the Green Paper with regard to the removal of blight, and the consequences of any deviation therefrom'.[89] Councillor Catherine Filsell, Labour's Chairman of the Transport Committee, noted that the council's decision ran counter to the advice of their officials, but was in accordance with the wishes of the public.[90]

Previous chapters have shown that official advice on the transport issue had been rejected by elected members in the past. The change in the late 1970s was that a growing number of councillors began to see the transport issue as fundamentally a political, even a class, issue. In rejecting the advice of the officials they were not just seeing it as under-researched or insensitive to public opinion, but as a technical incursion into the arena of political choice. It was a trend viewed with dismay by some more traditionally-minded members of local government. Councillor John Gray, a Liberal on Edinburgh District, with a long interest in planning and environmental matters, became a vehement opponent of the way elected members substituted political decisions for technical advice. He noted, 'From henceforward it is no longer possible to accept any document on strategic planning, in either the District or the Region, as necessarily representing the views of the chief professional officers. Policy documents are now shaped partly by the policy decisions taken by elected members, and partly by public pressure.'[91]

The views of the chief officers nevertheless showed through in the next Green Paper, issued in May 1977.[92] Charged with drawing up a transport strategy based on maximum investment in public transport and minimum investment in new roads, the paper put forward a package of road proposals costed at £50.5 million, argued that a light rapid transit system was not a 'feasible financial proposition' and that public transport subsidies would be 'extremely expensive' and an ineffective means of trying to achieve positive discrimination in favour of deprived areas. Central government policies and statistics were frequently quoted to support the drift of the argument. Since the government's Document on Transport Policy published in 1976 recognized that personal mobility by car is the objective of a majority of the people, increasing car ownership and traffic volumes had to be the basis of the Region's policies. The fact that car ownership in Lothain (46 per cent of households) was 10 per cent below the UK average, meant it was 'not unreasonable to assume' that the rate of increase would be at least as great locally as nationally. Meanwhile, central government policy was that public transport cost increases should be met out of fares income and ideas for road pricing or supplementary licensing had been ruled out as means of restraining private transport.

After the public consultation, the Steering Group of Officers produced a further paper arguing a similar case.[93] The package of road proposals was advanced on environmental rather than traffic grounds, holding the possibility of pedestrianizing some central area streets, alleviating suburban problems, and developing 'attractive options for public transport'.[94] It conceded that some form of subsidy to public transport seemed almost unavoidable, given the limits to further productivity increases after the introduction of one-man buses and in view of EEC regulations of drivers' hours. However, 'any support should not be seen as a substitute for a fares increase, but as a supplement'.[95] Of various measures which might increase the attractiveness of public transport meantime, 'the most notable is the provision of bus shelters which can be done with comparatively modest capital investment'.[96] Throughout scant attention was given to the land use options associated with transport planning. The notion that the structure of land uses could be redesigned so as to influence the choice of transport strategy had disappeared somewhere in the economic recession and through the pecking order of regional departments.

The officials had asked to be instructed to 'advance the planning' of the West Approach Road, a Leith Docks Approach Road and the road through Craigmillar, now rechristened the Niddrie-Bingham Relief Road. Instead the Labour group successfully carried a motion that a feasibility study should be done on such roads, investigating their 'necessity and practicality or otherwise'. This change to the brief was resisted by the Conservatives, who urged early action on the Docks Approach Road in particular. The safeguarding of controversial remnants of earlier plans – the Morningside By-pass, the ICR and a relief road in Leith – was ended by a council decision on 20 December 1977.

In the circumstances the Structure Plan could not resolve the issue of Edinburgh's transport policy. It asserted the interdependence of land use and transport planning and noted that an element of road building remained an integral part of the strategy. However, the plan did not specifically propose a road network, but proposed to safeguard routes pending the more detailed investigation set in train by the decisions in December 1977.

The Examination in Public

Lothian's was the first Scottish Structure Plan to be subjected to an Examination in Public. This began on 9 October 1978. Five issues were selected by the Secretary of State for the Examination. These were:

1   The employment prospects for the Region, and in particular the consequences for the Plan of any possible employment growth as it would affect industrial and office building, migration into the Region, and overall demands on services, including the transport system.
2   (a)   The extent to which land for new office development is needed in the Region, taking existing commitments into account.
    (b)   The extent to which such development should be accommodated in Edinburgh City Centre, with particular reference to the implications of westward expansion.
    (c)   The choice of suburban and district centres for office development and the scale of such development for which local plans should provide.
3   (a)   The transport strategy for the Region: the policies for traffic management, public transport, cycling and pedestrian movement.
    (b)   The proposals to safeguard land for road construction in the City of Edinburgh District, and the relative priority of completing the outer city by-pass.
    (c)   The proposals to construct the regional section of the Musselburgh by-pass and an eastern approach to Leith.
4   The amount and distribution of land required for new house building during the Plan period, having regard to migration, household formation, demolition rates, density, market factors and other general planning objectives; the adequacy of the Plan's housing land policies for meeting the expected requirements.
5   Whether the Plan should indicate action areas with particular reference to Midlothian District.

At no stage, then was the strategy of the plan as a whole investigated as an integrated set of policies to achieve its four major aims. Nor did the Chairman, a Reporter from the Scottish Office, encourage participants to relate their contributions to such wider considerations. The focus was reductionist, isolating issues, then issues within issues. The 'informality' of the proceedings also influenced the way the plan was analysed. The venue (the august Solicitors' Library in Parliament Square, Edinburgh), the spotlights and the microphones were enough to make inexperienced public speakers feel apprehensive. The loose way that the discussion flowed, and the lack of cross-examination meant that the expected 'probing discussion'[97] scarcely materialized.

The various participants invited to the EIP by the Secretary of State are tabulated in Table 21. The pattern broadly fits that observed in early English EIPs.[98]

Professor Donald Mackay, a leading monetarist economist, had been invited to appear on the employment issue as an independent expert. Representatives of the trades union movement were not called to assist in the deliberations. On this issue, then, discussion was concentrated between the Regional Council and central government in the form of the SEPD, and Professor Mackay. Population and employment forecasts were debated, together with the provision of sites for industrial development and the availability of office accommodation. The issue was phrased to focus on the plan's ability to cater for employment growth: the relation of declining employment opportunities to the areas of social need to which the plan was supposedly directing resources was not a central concern of the participants.

The Reporter concluded that the Region had been over-pessimistic in their assessment of employment prospects up to 1983. He recommended that the population forecasts should be adjusted in line with the updating by the Registrar General and that 1983 employment estimates should vary within the range of 0 to 30,000 jobs above the 1975 level.[99] Thus unemployment was scarcely considered, despite the fact that even at the time of the EIP unemployment rates were well above those of the previous three decades. In so far as the matter was dealt with, the prescription was the provision of more serviced sites. Thus the Structure Plan was interpreted as a means of responding to market forces, which were seen as natural and apolitical. Even allowing for the limited powers of local government in the employment field, it is difficult to feel that the political priorities of Lothian's ruling Labour group had much influence on this part of the plan. It was also notable that neither the Scottish Development Agency nor the Manpower Services Commission were participants in the EIP, though their involvement is critical to attempts to generate employment in Scotland, especially in the areas of deprivation.

Representation on the office issue was more broadly based, as Table 21 indicates. The Chamber of Commerce and the firm of estate agents, Kenneth Ryden and Partners, could provide direct knowledge on market needs. The Cockburn Association and the three local action groups largely opposed the logic of meeting these needs. The other 'opposition' participant was the Labour Party's Planning

Table 21   *Participants at the Lothian Structure Plan EIP, 1978*

Participant	Issue				
	1	2	3	4	5
Lothian Regional Council	*	*	*	*	*
City of Edinburgh District Council	*	*	*	*	*
East Lothian District Council	*	*	*	*	*
Midlothian District Council	*	*	*	*	*
West Lothian District Council	*	*	*	*	*
Scottish Development Department	*	*	*	*	*
Livingston Development Corporation	*	*	*	*	
Scottish Economic Planning Department	*	*			
Professor MacKay ('Independent')	*				
Edinburgh Chamber of Commerce and Manufacturers	*	*			
Kenneth Ryden & Partners, Estate Agents		*			
Lothian Region Labour Party – Planning and Transport Working Party		*	*		
Cockburn Association		*	*		
Atholl–Torphichen Association		*			
Gorgie–Dalry Local Plan Association		*			
Portobello and District Community Association		*	*		
Spokes – Lothian Cycle Campaign			*		
British Rail			*		
Scottish Bus Group			*		
Edinburgh Outer By-pass Campaign			*		
Craigmillar Festival Society			*		
Scottish National Party, Trinity Branch			*		
Trinity Goldenacre Association			*		
Stenhouse/Whitson Action Group			*		
Leith Chamber of Commerce			*		
Forth Ports Authority			*		
Brighton Residents Association			*		
Associated Dairies Ltd			*		
National Farmers Union of Scotland			*		
Mr J. S. Wilson ('Independent')			*		
Mr J. G. Gray ('Independent')			*		
Lothian Region Housebuilders Committee				*	
London and Clydeside Estates Ltd.				*	
Bernard Thorp and Partners				*	
Law Society of Scotland				*	
Scottish Building Societies Association				*	
Dept. of Agriculture and Fisheries for Scotland				*	

and Transport Working Party, represented by John Russell, a lecturer at the Heriot-Watt Planning School. On this and all other issues the Region was represented by its Chief Officers, with no involvement of elected members. The presence of the Labour Working Party at the EIP was an indicator of the tensions between the political priorities of a substantial section of Labour activists and the policies to which elected Labour members had given their endorsement.

Again discussion focussed on land use, not social justice. The 'balance' that had to be struck was between the traffic generated by offices and the realization that, 'Potential developers and entrepreneurs in industry and commerce are free to go elsewhere if in Edinburgh or Lothian Region the shoe is made to fit so tightly as to pinch somewhere.'[100] Thus planning policies needed to be tailored to the reality of the unequal powers expressed through market forces; indeed, such policies were seen as an integral means of managing those forces in the name of neutrality. For example, the Chairman decided that, 'Some relaxation of office restriction policies must be accepted and that the consequential transportation problems must be solved, all in such a way that the integrity of Edinburgh is maintained'.[101] Modifications were recommended, endorsing office development in the Haymarket area, and easing controls in the central area.

There were more participants on the transport issue than on any others, as Table 21 indicates. This probably reflected the sensitivity of the topic, on which, more than any of the others, the Secretary of State needed to be seen to be giving objectors their say. The action groups generally opposed suggestions for new roads in the city, while supporting the early construction of the outer by-pass. The industrial and commercial groups invited maintained a low profile. However, in outlining their functional requirements in relation to transport they were broadly in the position of supporting new developments. Similarly, the Scottish Development Department, by indicating their intention to develop trunk roads adjoining the urban area, leant credibility to the argument that new roads would be needed to cope with the traffic disgorging from the upgraded trunk roads.

The most forceful critic of the transport proposals was Councillor Gray, who appeared with Mr McIndoe in support. He argued that the region should not abandon the safeguarding of the CADL and the Eastern Link Road or Bridges Relief Road. The decision to drop these routes ran counter to the advice and experience of chief officers and eminent consultants for over thirty years. Furthermore, Councillor Gray argued that it was wrong that the councillors who had forced these decisions were not present and could not be cross-examined so as to test the basis of the advice on which they had acted. Councillor Gray's position then was that transport planning problems could only be resolved by technical expertise and were not matters for lay dabbling.

Thus it was once more the transport question which highlighted the problems of managing urban change. Despite the acknowledged interdependence of land use and transport, the transport strategy of the Structure Plan was essentially on ice, awaiting the feasibility studies. The rationality of the plan was thus flawed. Safeguarding meant that blight would persist, not least in some of the areas of deprivation to which the plan was allegedly steering resources.

Councillor Gray's critique revealed some of the problems of legitimacy encountered by the scientization of practical concerns. If the issue was indeed purely technical, then the elected members would be mere ciphers, rubber-stamping decisions drafted by officials from their understanding of the space needs of functions that were integral to the well being of the settlement. Challenge could only legitimately come from other experts who could subject the assessment of functional requirements to further technical scrutiny. To question whether those functions benefited all equally, or to question whether those functional requirements should be met if it meant using resources on which there were other demands, was to act 'politically' and thus illegitimately. However, that ideology of scientism had been negated by the practice of the action groups and by the repoliticization of the Labour Party; in this process the ideology had been exposed as an unacknowledged form of political domination. The scientization had undermined the claim to democracy for a system based on accountable elected members; now the negation of scientism undermined the other side of that orthodox model, the notion of officials giving neutral technical advice. Thus, if advice could not be rejected, then democracy had been supplanted by technocracy; but if it could be overturned on political grounds then the advice itself was in part political, not an unbesmirched technical exercise.

Not surprisingly, with the real decisions still pending, the Chairman's Report largely endorsed the wait-and-see stance of the plan. He did however recommend that the questions should be resolved within a year.

The other major issue at the EIP was the amount of land needed for housebuilding. Like the roads question, though less dramatically, this question had rumbled throughout the history of twentieth-century planning in Edinburgh. As on the employment issue, representation of working-class and tenants' groups was notably lacking. In contrast, those bodies with a stake in the production and exchange of housing as a commodity were to the fore, with their professional consultants.

Predictably the Chairman's Report of the EIP catalogued and endorsed the priorities of the private housebuilding lobby. Owner occupation was depicted as the desirable norm, long upheld as an aim of government policy. The need for council houses was ascribed as a residue and left to the Housing Plans of the districts. The Report noted simply that, 'Local authority housebuilding programmes seem now to be curtailed, perhaps to be complementary to a rehabilitation programme.'[102] The building capacity 'no longer needed for building new council dwellings' might then be diverted to the construction of houses for other forms of tenure.[103] Apart from an implication that the promotion of the private sector at the expense of the public sector would help to correct 'social imbalance' that had resulted from past policies, the social consequences of the demise of council housing were not elaborated. The word 'homelessness' does not appear in the report.

The Chairman broadly sympathized with the housebuilders' criticisms of the region's estimates of housing requirements and land supply. The policy of directing development towards the inner city and away from greenfield sites was also undermined. The builders argued that inner city development, especially using designs and materials sympathetic to adjacent environments, was simply not a market proposition. The Chairman took the view that if it was not a market proposition, then it could not be relied upon as a key part of the plan. He argued that attempts to steer builders to difficult urban infill sites by restricting the availability of greenfield sites, would simply escalate land and house prices. As a consequence the region's ability to compete for new business or industry would be reduced. In essence, then, the redistributive aspects of the Structure Plan were rejected by the Chairman of the EIP on the grounds that they *were* redistributive rather than consistent with market forces, and thus could not be expected to succeed. The production of cities through the economic relations of capitalism was seen as a neutral, even benign process, not an exercise of political domination.

Central control

By the time the Report on the EIP had been processed through the Scottish Office there was a Conservative Secretary of State, Mr George Younger. Labour had taken overall control of Lothian Region in 1978, including in their ranks a number of younger and more radical councillors. A protracted struggle developed as central government cut back the region's allocation under Rate Support Grant in an attempt to force cuts in services and spending. Throughout, the fate of the Structure Plan was no more than on the periphery of the conflict. On the other hand, Lothian had held bus fares constant from 1976, as a part of Labour's pro-public transport stance, and the subsidy to the buses was clearly seen by central government as an area where cuts should be made. While struggles over the Structure Plan remained low key in comparison to the wider issues of finance, they were nevertheless clearly imprinted with the pattern of the developing political situation.

In 1979 Mr Younger issued a Direction requiring Lothian Region to review their assessment of housing requirements and land availability and to decide whether to construct or abandon the safeguarded radial roads in the Structure Plan. The region submitted a proposed alteration to the Plan in respect of these matters in April 1981, to which the Secretary of State responded in February 1982. The preparation and the response shows something of the way that land use planning was becoming more politicized.

The region's officials presented another Transport Green Paper in June 1979. It described the results of the feasibility studies on the safeguarded routes. The paper reasserted the position advanced by the officials in earlier papers, namely that some road building was necessary to bring the 'widest benefit' to 'the community'.[104] The surveys revealed that since central area parking controls became effective in 1974, there had been no increase in central area traffic levels. About 65 per cent of all peak period journeys by vehicle to central Edinburgh were by public transport, with a substantially higher proportion of work journeys being made by bus than in comparable cities.[105] Journeys by the elderly, blind and disabled (all of whom could get a pass entitling them to free bus travel) had increased threefold since 1970. Car ownership remained at 46 per cent of all households.

The officers' conclusion was that further car ownership and usage was therefore inevitable and that the benefits to be reaped from further subsidies to public transport or traffic management schemes were not commensurate with what could be had from investment in new roads. As the option of a central area road programme had been precluded by previous political decisions, the emphasis was put on suburban developments. The road proposals are listed in Table 22. In addition, the completion of the outer by-pass was endorsed. In all, the paper proposed investing £30.6 million in the by-pass and the Musselburgh by-pass. More controversially it proposed to build the urban roads through a capital expenditure programme phased over eight to ten years, costed at £33.9 million. In addition, £4.1 million was earmarked for provision of car parks. These figures were based on 1978 costs. In contrast, only £2 million was identified for capital programmes of traffic management and public transport improvements.[106] The report noted that the bus passes for the elderly, blind and disabled would cost £6.2 million of revenue expenditure for 1979, with a further £1 million being used to support bus operators providing services to the parts of the region not served by the Edinburgh buses. The subsidy to Lothian's bus fares was noted, but not quantified.

In effect the officials argued that new roads would be a bargain. They could largely be constructed along disused railway lines, thus affecting few properties while relieving congested suburban routes of traffic, noise, fumes and accidents.

Table 22   *Road proposals in 1979 discussion paper*

| | | Properties affected | | | |
| | Length | Requiring demolition | | | By noise |
	(km)	Dwellings	Industrial	Social	Dwellings
West Approach Road	6.0	1	1	1	80
Roseburn–Ferry Road Link	2.5	–	1	–	50
West Approach to Leith	4.4	–	4	–	110
Granton Spur	2.5	–	–	–	–
Northern Spur	1.3	–	1	–	–
Davidson's Mains By-pass	2.2	–	–	–	45
Niddrie–Bingham By-pass	2.9	–	–	–	–
St Leonard's Spur	2.3	2	–	–	–
East Approach to Leith	2.7	–	–	–	–
Totals	26.8	3	7	1	285

Source: Lothian Regional Council, 'Transportation in the Edinburgh Area' (1979), p. 10

The Lothian Region Labour Party submitted their own response to the Green Paper. They advocated that the proposals to build roads along the suburban railway lines should be withdrawn. Instead they pressed for a partnership between the council and British Rail to reopen some rail links and to build some new stations. They said that bus services should be extended and city centre parking controls tightened. Traffic management measures were also called for to force cross-city traffic out to the by-pass.

Opinion within the Labour group of councillors was divided, with a substantial number feeling that they were obliged to support their officials.[107] Support for the officials came also from the Chamber of Commerce, who called for the West Approach Road to be given priority and for more car parks to be provided.[108] Transport Action, Scotland, a body closely associated with the British Roads Federation, also called on the 'silent majority' to speak out in support of the officials.[109]

When the time for decision came, in December 1979, the council split along party lines over the transport issue. The Labour group, with the whips on, carried the day. The council voted to withdraw the safeguarding of all roads in the city, except for the East Approach to Leith and the regional section of the Musselburgh by-pass. They also decided to put into effect the other moves recommended by the Lothian Region Labour Party. The disused rail tracks were seen as having a potential for a light rapid transit system and meantime would be developed as walkways and cycleways.

Thus it appeared that the long running saga of Edinburgh's transport planning had finally been laid to rest. There was, however, a twist in the tail. The Secretary of State ruled that the entire roads plan should not be abandoned and that 'corridors' for at least three routes should continue to be safeguarded. These were the west approach through the Sighthill and Broomhouse areas; the Roseburn–Ferry Road Link, along disused railways; and the Niddrie–Bingham by-pass through Craigmillar. The modifications he proposed to the plan made no forecast of when, or even whether, the roads would actually be built.[110] The Secretary of State also made clear that his decision to end the safeguarding on the other routes did not imply support for the idea of a light rapid transit system. Thus the blighting caused by long-term aspirations to modernize the city was to be concentrated in council housing areas. In the light of the Secretary of State's decision, it is apposite to recall the observations of the Chairman of the EIP on the Niddrie–Bingham route, responding to evidence presented by Craigmillar Festival Society:

For some 20 years or more the future of certain houses, public open spaces, industrial sites and the site for travelling people has been looked as subject to the likelihood that a road will be built there. Young lives have been lived against this blighted background and some of these young people will now be approaching maturity. It is much too long a time for uncertainties of this kind to continue.[111]

On the housing land issue, the regional planners met with representatives of the private housebuilders. The result was an agreement that there was likely to be a need for an extra 40,000 new houses in the region during the 1980s. These were split equally between 1981–6 and 1986–91. Elected members had scant opportunity to influence the content of the Consultation Report containing these estimates.[112] As soon as the document was circulated it was strongly criticized by all four District Councils, and by Livingston Development Corporation. East Lothian's Director of Planning saw the report as constituting 'a radical reversal of approach on housing land', and as showing a 'flagrant disregard' for the green belt.[113]

Faced with the hostility of these authorities, elected members and amenity bodies, the planners escape hatch proved to be the subsequent availability of 1979-based population forecasts indicating a less dramatic rate of growth. Thus the alteration to the Structure Plan submitted by the Region in April 1981 put the growth in houses required by 1986 at 12,810.[114] In the months that elapsed while the Scottish Office deliberated the alteration, the major building companies put in applications for green belt housing developments, lodged appeals against refusals and inquiries were held in which the household forecasts were the central concern. Eventually in February 1982 the Secretary of State set down his proposed modifications. He called on the council to set aside land for a further 5000 houses by 1986 over and above the 12,810 figure of their alteration. His letter also spoke of the need to preserve the green belt as being a prime consideration, with encroachment being kept to an absolute minimum.[115] The housebuilders thus got substantially what they were asking for, with the pattern of allowing residential development within the green belt, while proclaiming the primacy of the belt. The pattern that characterized the planning of Edinburgh in the post-war period was reasserted.

The Royal Nurseries: a vignette for a decade of planning practice

This chapter has traced the shifting styles of planning practice in Edinburgh in the 1970s and into the 1980s. The underlying themes have been the search by planners for strategies which could defuse the conflicts over the development and use of land within the city, conflicts rooted in the inequalities of land ownership and market processes, though rarely being fought as class-based struggles. Economic recession, a mounting fiscal crisis and increasing centralization of power have compounded the difficulties which the local authorities faced in managing change in the city. In all this, the image of the city, that ambiguous summation of meaning associated with the historical environment and infused with the nuances of class relations within the Scottish capital, has been a recurrent focus. In an attempt to sum up the way these diverse yet structured factors have been worked through in day-to-day planning practice, we close this extended case study of planning practice in Edinburgh with one site and the practices associated with it.

The site is the Royal Nurseries, a heavily planted ridge some eighty-nine acres in extent, immediately west of the Craigmillar housing area. It provides a landscaped setting for the historic Craigmillar Castle, with important views from the Queens Drive in Holyrood Park. Abercrombie identified it as 'an essential feature of the composition of the landscape'. The land was classified as Grade A and A+ by the Department of Agriculture and Fisheries for Scotland, and was zoned 'agricultural land within the green belt' in the Development Plan approved in 1957. It forms part of a green wedge linking the open countryside to Holyrood Park.

The land had been used as a nursery, with the tree belts planted to provide shelter. It was purchased in 1961 by J. Miller, the owner of the group of building companies that had played such a prominent role in the development of the city from their founding in the inter-war period (see Chapter 5). He put the land in a trust for the benefit of his grandchildren. The transaction was registered in 1967 and the price paid was £250 per acre. Millers installed a tenant farmer who had the land rent free, but also, of course, had no security of tenure. James Miller and Partners lodged objection to the zoning of the site in the 1965 Development Plan Review, arguing that the land use should be residential.

At around this time the corporation were themselves contemplating using the site for council housing – the pressure for housing was intense and the land lay conveniently adjacent to existing council estates at Craigmillar and the Inch. Multi-storey blocks went up at the Craigmillar edge of the Nurseries site, encroaching on the green wedge and devaluing its visual integrity. Millers might well have won the day, had not the corporation's planning consultant, David Wishart, fought strongly against the development of the site and been able to produce a belated indication from Edinburgh University that they could use the land for playing fields. The site, in fact, adjoins their main playing fields at Peffermill. The Reporter indicated that he was first inclined to the view that the site should go predominantly for private housing, but that he eventually considered that university playing fields should have priority and that he could not make firm recommendations on the boundaries of any residential zoning. The Secretary of State agreed that priority should go to meeting the university's requirements, and invited Edinburgh Corporation to consider a Development Plan amendment which would allow zoning for a more definite purpose than just green belt.

On 27 May 1971, Edinburgh Corporation Planning Committee passed a resolution from Councillor George Foulkes (Labour) that the Town Planning Officer should consider what could be done to expedite corporation acquisition of land at Canal Field, in the south-west of the city, as a site for a new secondary school needed to relieve pressure on existing inner area schools. Canal Field, owned by Edinburgh University and used for playing fields, was zoned as private recreational open space. The university indicated that this land could be made available to the corporation, provided that Millers would let the university have a part of the land at the Royal Nurseries for playing fields. Thus the Royal Nurseries became, as the Town Planning Officer reported, 'the key to a series of negotiations involving a number of interested parties'.[116]

Not only would the transfer of land at the Royal Nurseries allow the Canal Field school to go ahead, it would also facilitate the exchange of another university playing field at Craiglockhart Terrace to the Merchants' Company to build a replacement for the George Watson's Ladies' College. The company owned the land at Craiglockhart and were keen to go ahead. Once this move was agreed the Merchants' Company could sell the Ladies' College site in George Square to the university, who had plans to expand there. Furthermore, the company also hoped to dispose of former school playing field land at Kirkbrae/Double Hedges Road, part of which was zoned for local authority housing in the 1965 Review, the rest being allocated to public open space. Millers were only prepared to release land at the Nurseries if the Merchants' Company would sell them a suitable piece of land at Kirkbrae/Double Hedges for private housing development. In effect Millers were holding the others to ransom.[117]

Thus while the fanfares were blaring for community participation and liaison government in Craigmillar, planning practice was proceeding as a means of resolving the conflicting development priorities within some of the institutions that made up the city's establishment. Nobody asked the people of Craigmillar what they wanted the land to be used for. The Planning Committee, meeting on 17 April 1975, therefore agreed to the Development Plan Amendment. As Millers were still holding out, the plan was to rezone 81.9 acres for Private Recreational Open Space (University Playing Fields). The remainder of the site, occupied by a quarry and a disused fireworks factory and owned by a Mrs Thomson, was to be rezoned to public amenity open space and acquired by the corporation in compensation for costs they had previously incurred.

Craigmillar Festival Society first heard of all this when a local councillor spotted the reference to the amendment in the Planning Committee minutes as they came to the full council. She wrote to the Director of Administration, requesting that a decision be deferred to allow local consultations. The amendment was submitted to the Secretary of State shortly afterwards. At this stage the author became involved as a member of CFS's Planning Workshop. CFS decided to lodge an objection to the amendment, on the grounds that the rezoning would pre-empt options for use of the land to the benefit of local residents. Millers also objected to the lack of provision for residential use.

The CFS began to lobby the new District Council. They argued that the eighty acres being zoned for playing fields at the Royal Nurseries far exceeded the land that the university would give up at Canal Field (8.7 acres) and at Craiglockhart (2.7 acres). The proposed use was seen as an under-utilization of land, which contrasted markedly with the unmet recreational needs of the disproportionately young local population, the vast majority of whom lived in flats. There was already an excess of private recreational open space around the area, to which locals had no legal access – the university's existing playing fields and those of Moray House College, as well as a golf club.

The District Planning Department did then carry out an assessment of open space provision within Craigmillar. This was done in response to the objection lodged by CFS and was therefore premised on the need to sustain a decision that had already been taken, rather than to assemble the evidence from which to plan to meet the open space needs in an area of social deprivation. The report divided Craigmillar into east and west sections. Its chief finding is shown in Table 23.

Table 23   *Open space in Craigmillar, 1976*

	Open Space (acres/1000 population)	
	West Craigmillar	East Craigmillar
Incidental open space	2.0	2.8
Neighbourhood parks	0.9	4.7
Total open space	2.9	7.5

Source: City of Edinburgh District Council, Planning Department, 'Open Space Provision: Craigmillar', Report to the Director of Administration, dated 16 March 1976.

The report noted that the Edinburgh Corporation had operated a standard of 2.5 acres per 1000 population in private housing areas, and that their Open Space Plan of 1969 had suggested adding 1.5 acres of neighbourhood park per 1000, bringing the figure up to four acres in all. Using these standards, East Craigmillar was seen as being more than adequately provided with open space, though there were slight deficiencies in the western area. A number of steps were suggested to address these deficiencies. The amendment itself proposed adding 7.3 acres in the old quarry site, which would put the neighbourhood park allocation up to 2.3 acres per 1000. Acquisition of part of the Nurseries for public open space was discounted on financial grounds and because it would prejudice the university's long-term needs. As an alternative it was suggested that part of a local primary school's playing fields could be converted to public open space and that the central courts of some of the housing blocks could be landscaped. The Planning Department thus were able to support their observations on the CFS objection.

The District Council therefore considered that 'there is no justifiable demand for additional large areas of open space in the Craigmillar area, and should any demand be proved it can be provided on alternative sites, whereas the University require the whole of the Royal Nurseries site'.[118]

Thus an 'objective' standard was established and shown to be met. As a contingency land could be transferred from local children as schoolchildren to local children as out-of-school users of open space. Measures like the rehabilitation of the back greens might be undertaken not because they were an eyesore and a frequent cause of complaint by the tenants, but as a fall-back position to meet the standard should the statistics alter. A park on the Royal Nurseries was out of the question, because the land would only be exchanged at a market price, and because the university wanted it anyway.

The assessment was questionable on a number of points.[119] No account was taken of whether the open space was actually 'effective', that is whether it was actually usable for either active or passive recreation, or made a *positive* contribution to visual amenity. Grass strips down a dual carriageway and on a traffic island, some (but not all) of the derelict back greens laced with electricity pylons, a paved footpath with grass verges and 'space left over after planning', were all included to make up the open space acreages. A park, mainly comprising thirteen football pitches booked out to teams from all over the city and to which local teams have no guaranteed access, counted as 54.5 acres of neighbourhood park.

The area of land was thus the prime consideration, rather than the use or access to it. No regard was given to social or economic needs of the people. The Open Space standards made no distinction between areas where houses had gardens and flatted areas. They had been refined in the 1960s, on the assumption that there would be increasing affluence and private mobility, assumptions which bore little relation to the reality of Craigmillar in the late 1970s. The political issue of how the benefit of the Royal Nurseries could be used had been reduced to the manipulation of technical indices. The powers associated with land ownership were taken for granted and seen as a neutral, 'practical' consideration. Furthermore the restriction of the indices themselves to crude areas of land and the adoption of city-wide standards strongly favoured those who could afford to purchase access to open space through markets. They could buy private open space with the house and the personal mobility to reach open space elsewhere, as well as getting their 'fair' share of local public open space as specified in the city-wide standards. Such planning therefore legitimates and compounds the existing inequalities within the city; it is not neutral, but rather a form of class practice.

The survey of open space in Craigmillar to rebut the claims of the CFS contrasted markedly with the ready acceptance of the university's estimates of *its* open space requirements. The convenience and desirability of the university's centralizing of its playing fields on one site and of its meeting UGC standards for provision seemed to be accepted without question. The planning therefore fitted the tradition of incremental and reactive response to the development priorities of institutions who owned or could purchase land.

'Community planning' and 'liaison government' began to give way to community action, as the CFS mounted delegations and demonstrations and began to mobilize local support. One effect was to reinject a political dimension to the issue. Paul Nolan, vice-chairman of the Society, accused the Planning Committee of 'acting as property agents for Edinburgh University'.[120] The District Council eventually divided 28–27 in favour of the amendment. The voting was on a party basis, with the Liberals and Conservatives supporting the amendment. The Planning and Development Committee of the Regional Council were persuaded to reject the advice of their Director of Physical Planning, and came out against the amendment. Labour councillors were quoted as saying: 'Our whole attitude should be changing so far as land use is concerned . . . the time has come when we should stop this nonsense in terms of planning in giving large acreages to minority groups', and that it was wrong for groups like golf clubs to have exclusive use of green belt land in densely populated areas of the city.[121]

The recession and the fiscal crisis intervened before the amendment reached a public inquiry. The Canal Field school was sidelined and the university deliberated on its playing field requirements. The Merchants' Company moved their Ladies' College and housing was developed at Craiglockhart. The university began to redevelop the freed George Square site. The old corporation had acquired the land at Kirkbrae/Double Hedges Road; now the district decided to sell 12.7 acres of it to private builders, retaining just two acres for sheltered housing. The cuts in local government spending threatened the financial support that Craigmillar Festival Society received and then the EEC grant ran out.

Negotiations continued unobtrusively between Millers and the university. By early 1980 the university were able to tell the owners of the land that 18.5 acres at the Nurseries would be sufficient to meet their long-term playing field requirements. James Miller and Partners put in a planning application seeking outline permission to develop 660 houses on 44.4 acres of the site. A further 17.7 acres were to be used for university playing fields, and 17.4 acres for public open space. Some of the housing, designated for 'alternative tenure', would be built adjacent to the high-rise blocks of Craigmillar at the east of the site. These would be divided by the open space from the housing for owner occupation in the west. Participation was extended to the CFS to the extent that they were informed of the application by the District Council and were invited to view the plans at the office of the consultant architects for the scheme.

CFS put in a formal objection and encouraged others to do likewise.[122] The Edinburgh Council of Social Service and the Inch/Gilmerton Labour Party did so. The Cockburn Association also objected. The application was refused by the District Council, who were supported by the region. The main grounds of refusal were the special landscape character of the site and the need to protect the green belt. Thus the recurrent confrontation in Edinburgh's planning was worked over again – that between the market forces urging the production of the city so that the environment can be sold and consumed as a commodity, and the preservationist opposition to the destruction of the special image of the city which that process entails. Millers, of course, appealed against the refusal of planning permission.

The Reporter at the ensuing inquiry was Mr Roberton, who had chaired the Lothian EIP. The main parties were the appellants and the local authorities. Thus the CFS did have the planning officials on their side this time, but objectively their position remained weak. Though discussions were held with the officials before the inquiry, neither the society nor the local elected members could influence the form and personnel through which the authorities chose to present their case. Nor could the district offer the society any support on any questioning of the adequacy of open space in Craigmillar. Indeed, CFS very nearly did not appear at the inquiry at all; some oversight within the district's administration meant that the third party objections were not notified to the Scottish Office and hence these objectors were not formally advised that the inquiry was imminent.[123] Furthermore there was no comparison in the resources which the Festival Society and the appellants could devote to preparing their cases.

The context of the inquiry, reflecting past planning practices, materially assisted the developers. The housing section of the Structure Plan was in limbo when the inquiry was held in October and December 1981. The Secretary of State had received the region's Alteration six months earlier, but not ruled on it. Similarly, there was no Local Plan for the area including the appeal site; survey work for a Local Plan had been initiated, but the exercise had been suspended pending the decision of the Secretary of State on the Structure Plan. There was the CFS's own Comprehensive Plan for Action prepared under the EEC programme, but it had no official status.

These omissions compounded the extent to which the inquiry procedures constituted a class barrier to those, like CFS, who were seeking to counter the logic of market forces. The discussion focussed on the physical characteristics of the site itself, the assessment of housing requirements in the city and the feasibility of meeting those requirements on other sites, notably in the inner city. Beyond an assertion that the development would 'help to create the right social mix in this type of area'[124] by the developers' planning consultant, scant attention was paid to the needs of the local people, or even to the context of the existing residential uses around the site. The Festival Society were allowed to present their case, but their ideas for the suitability of the site for a public park, or demonstration farm, combining education, work training and recreation, lacked credibility. The inquiry had been convened to decide whether housing and playing fields and associated public open space should be the use for the site, as the owners were suggesting, not to hear how a local community group might be able to use the land in the very improbable event of them being able to raise sufficient money to persuade the owners to release the land.

Similarly, notions like 'positive discrimination' fitted uneasily into the language of the inquiry, as did suggestions that the use of most public parks within Craigmillar for football pitches meant that there was underprovision of recreational opportunities for women and girls.

Sir James Miller had bought the land at Royal Nurseries for £250 per acre and put it into a charitable trust to benefit his grandchildren. Within Edinburgh in the early 1980s prices for land with planning permission for residential development were between £100,000 and £200,000 an acre. The city is renowned for canny financial management of the kind displayed by Sir James. However, the realization of the asset at Royal Nurseries will be delayed a while yet: the Secretary of State rejected the appeal against the refusal of planning permission early in 1983, primarily because of the landscape significance of the site. At the same time he upheld an appeal on two other green belt sites at Swanston, on the southern edge of the city, granting London and Clydesdale Estates permission for major residential development there, to the chagrin of local middle-class residents, their Conservative councillors and Conservative MP.[125] It also seems likely that the Canal Field site will now be sold by the university for housing development.

The Royal Nurseries saga illustrates several themes in this chapter. It shows the development of land as a commodity, and the class power of landowners. It reveals how development in Edinburgh perpetually threatens valued physical environments which are laden with identity and meaning for substantial sections of the city's largely middle-class population. The local state is fashioned by the economic structure of a city; here educational institutions such as the university, the Merchants' Company and property and building interests had close links with the local authority. Through town planning the local authority sought to mediate between its own development interest, the creation of development opportunities for other elements in the local state and conservation of the environment. The planning was carried out within the legislation established by the central state, legislation which was class-biased in the way it constrained the scope and powers of town planning. The Royal Nurseries also shows again the significance of central intervention through the Secretary of State's decisions. In so centralized a state as the UK it is difficult to see how power over urban development can ever be adequately comprehended purely at the local level.

The Royal Nurseries also shows how planners in the 1970s sought to build new relations with their public through encouraging 'community participation' and how the scope of that participation was circumscribed by the limited powers of the planners themselves *vis-à-vis* landowners and spending departments within central and local government. The consequent politicization of planning, as at the Royal Nurseries, further assailed the planners' credibility with elected members and fragmented the self-understanding of the professionals.

The Royal Nurseries also shows some of the complexities of the inter- and intra-class relations involved in town planning. Above all it shows that concepts like class, power and ideology are integral to an understanding of town planning practice. However, this study also warns against deterministic and reductionist approaches within a class analysis. Millers' appeal was turned down, and by a Conservative Secretary of State; the outcome was at least a partial victory for the Craigmillar Festival Society, a victory that would not have been possible without the support of the Regional and District Councils.

Town planning practice in Edinburgh has been one aspect of the day to day reproduction of class relations within Scotland's capital. It has been influenced by the overall balance of class forces both nationally and locally. The struggle for the city has made town planning a crisis-prone activity, reworking but not resolving contradictions between classes and fragmenting interests within classes. In the final analysis it is the class structure which is the source of the problems of rationality, legitimation and motivation which town planners have faced.

References and notes

1 Letter from John Byrom, Department of Architecture, Edinburgh University, published in *The Scotsman*, 13 Feb. 1970.
2 *The Scotsman*, 23 April 1970.
3 *The Scotsman*, 23 July 1970.
4 *The Scotsman*, 6 Aug. 1970.
5 *Edinburgh Evening News*, 1 July 1970.
6 *The Scotsman*, 23 April 1970.
7 *The Scotsman*, 11 Dec. 1970.
8 *The Scotsman*, 6 Jan. 1981.

9   C. Buchanan and Partners, and Freeman Fox, Wilbur Smith & Associates, *Analysis of the Problem*, City of Edinburgh Planning and Transportation Study (1971), p. 69.
10 *The Scotsman*, 22 May 1971.
11 C. Buchanan and Partners, and Freeman Fox, Wilbur Smith & Associates (1971), p. 2.
12 C. Buchanan and Partners, and Freeman Fox, Wilbur Smith & Associates, *Alternatives for Edinburgh*, Second Interim Report of the City of Edinburgh Planning and Transportation Study (1971).
13 *The Scotsman*, 2 Dec. 1971.
14 *The Scotsman*, 6 Dec. 1971.
15 *The Scotsman*, 24 Dec. 1971.
16 *The Scotsman*, 14 Dec. 1971.
17 C. Buchanan and Partners, and Freeman Fox, Wilbur Smith & Associates, *The Recommended Plan,* City of Edinburgh Planning and Transportation Study (1972).
18 *The Scotsman*, 4 Nov. 1972.
19 Ibid.
20 See the letter from Councillor Donald Gorrie (Liberal), published in the *Guardian*, 3 Feb. 1973.
21 *Edinburgh Evening News*, 25 April 1973.
22 *Edinburgh Evening News*, 27 April 1973.
23 Ibid.
24 City of Edinburgh, Joint Technical Working Party, *CEPATS An examination of the Recommended Plan,* Interim Report (1973). Also Joint Technical Working Party, 'The Recommended Plan' (1974).
25 City of Edinburgh Joint Technical Working Party (1974), para. 7.8, p. 11. One can only ponder whether the Working Party would have harboured such reservations about Buchanan's public participation programme if the expressions of public opinion had been equally vocal in favour of the scheme.
26 Edinburgh University, *Conservation and University Expansion,* Joint Report by the Factorial Secretary and the Planning Consultant (1969), pp. 1, 3, 4.
27 R. Jones, *Amenity-deficient houses in Edinburgh: 1967*, a Report presented to Edinburgh Corporation Housing Committee (1968).
28 I. W. Wintour, *Annual Report of the Sanitary Department, 1973* City of Edinburgh (1974), pp. 12–13.
29 *The Scotsman*, 6 April 1973.
30 *Edinburgh Evening News*, 1 June 1973.
31 C. Hague, 'Housing problems and policies in Edinburgh', *Open University Summer School Booklet for the Housing Module of D101* (1976), p. 7.
32 Edinburgh Corporation Housing Committee Minutes, 3 Dec. 1963.
33 Ibid.
34 Quoted in *The Scotsman*, 5 Aug. 1964.

35 *The Scotsman*, 31 July 1964.

36 *The Scotsman*, 24 July 1964.

37 *The Scotsman*, 4 Aug. 1964.

38 *The Scotsman*, 24 Feb. 1966.

39 *The Scotsman*, 21 Nov. 1969.

40 Letter to Edinburgh Corporation, date 13 July 1965.

41 *The Scotsman*, 15 Sept. 1965.

42 Edinburgh Corporation Housing Committee Minutes, 9 March 1965. Sir Frank Mears and Partners had also been consultants to the corporation on the earlier planning stage of the scheme. They appeared for the corporation at the Public Inquiry. Their brief for the plan included the requirement that it should achieve in 'twentieth century terms, some of the civic qualities of former times'.

43 Mr T. Jamieson of Sir Frank Mears & Partners in interview. Quoted in D. J. Laidlaw, 'Life at the Periphery: The Evolution of a Planned Housing Community', Unpublished BSc. Research Essay, Department of Town and Country Planning, Edinburgh College of Art/Heriot-Watt University (1976), p. 32.

44 Sir Frank Mears & Partners, *Wester Hailes: A Plan for a City Suburb*, City and Royal Burgh of Edinburgh (1968).

45 *Edinburgh Evening News*, 24 Nov. 1969. The Secretary of State asked for details of why the corporation had seen fit not to accept the 'best' offer, and there were calls for an inquiry. See *The Scotsman*, 31 July 1970.

46 'Wester Hailes speaks for itself', a report produced by representatives of tenants' associations, neighbourhood groups and the FISH Good Neighbours Scheme, 1977. See *Edinburgh Evening News*, 22 April 1977. Contracts for the eleven phases of development of the housing areas had been split between four contractors, Crudens, Wimpey, Hart and Smart.

47 *The Scotsman*, 17 Dec. 1969.

48 Edinburgh Corporation Housing Committee Minutes, 13 Oct. 1970.

49 Edinburgh Corporation Housing Committee, Vacation Sub-Committee Minutes, 22 Aug. 1972.

50 City Planning Officer, *Social and Community Development Programme for the City of Edinburgh* (1974).

51 *Edinburgh Evening News*, 6 June 1974.

52 The texts on the boards were often long and turgid descriptions. Some of the maps were almost incomprehensible to non-professionals, notably a traffic assignment map for the whole city.

53 The consultants argued that their proposals had elicited a considerable amount of public support. In reaching this conclusion though they tended to discount opposition to the plans voiced at many meetings as being emotive and prejudiced.

54 Councillor Smith in interview, quoted in A. Waterworth, 'Public participation in planning: an Edinburgh case study', unpublished MSc. Thesis,

Department of Town and Country Planning, Edinburgh College of Art/ Heriot-Watt University (1975), p. 64. Waterworth's was a participant-observer study: she was a member of the South Side Advisory Panel while doing the research. In considering Councillor Smith's comments, one should remember that local government reorganization was pending, which included a requirement for the establishment of Community Councils. The panel was probably a useful test-bed for this notion too. In a sense there had been an advisory panel before; the Princes Street Panel, a select grouping of distinguished architects.

55 Quoted in A. Waterworth, 1975, p. 55.
56 Ibid. p. 55. This statement was made to the second meeting of the panel in Feb. 1974.
57 A. Waterworth, 1975, pp. 80–1.
58 Quoted in A. Waterworth, 1975, p. 85.
59 Ibid., p. 113.
60 Details of the membership of the panel during this period are given in A. Waterworth, Fig. 3.4.
61 Quoted in A. Waterworth, 1975, pp. 57–8.
62 See A. Waterworth, 1975, p. 61.
63 This was Newcraighall, the village featured in Bill Douglas's auto-biographical film trilogy.
64 Quoted in H. Crummy (ed.), 'Festival of Change', Craigmillar Festival Society (1972), p. 40.
65 Lothian Regional Council, City of Edinburgh District Council, *Social and Community Development Programme: Progress Report* (1976), para. 3.3.
66 Lothian Regional Council, City of Edinburgh District Council, *Social and Community Development Programme: Progress Report* (1977), para. 4.2.
67 Ibid., para. 4.3.
68 *Edinburgh's Other News*, Sept. 1975.
69 See D. Laidlaw, 1976, p. 94.
70 Quoted in P. Wiberg, 'Public Participation, Community Development and the State', Unpublished BSc. Research Essay, Department of Town and Country Planning, Edinburgh College of Art/Heriot-Watt University (1980), pp. 66–7. The assessment was confirmed by Wiberg's own more extended analysis of the SCDP in Gorgie/Dalry. He showed that local groups were able to achieve some influence on back green improvement, setting up a city farm, and in their submission on the Structure Plan, but they could not exert influence to get low rent accommodation provided in the area.
71 P. Wiberg, 1980, p. 71.
72 Quoted in P. Wiberg, 1980, p. 66.
73 Ibid., pp. 71–2.
74 *Edinburgh Evening News*, 25 Nov. 1971.

75   Lothian Regional Council, *Structure Plan: Considerations Report* (1977), paras, 17 and 26.
76   Quoted in *Edinburgh Evening News*, 12 Oct. 1976.
77   City of Edinburgh District Council, *District Planning Report* (1977), para. 2.3, p. 18.
78   Ibid., para. 4.4, p. 31.
79   Ibid., para. 3.4, p. 26.
80   Ibid., para. 3.12, p. 28.
81   City and Royal Burgh of Edinburgh, *Report of the Technical Working Party into the Recommended Plan*, (1974) Section III, paras. 10.4 to 10.9.
82   City of Edinburgh District Council, 1977, para. 6.7, p. 47.
83   Ibid., para. 6.9, p. 48.
84   Ibid., para. 10.1, p. 63.
85   Lothian Regional Council, *Structure Plan* (1978), para. 27, p. 7.
86   Lothian Regional Council, Transport Committee, *A Paper for Discussion: Transport Policies and Programme, 1976*, para. 1. About 1000 copies were distributed, and 155 comments were received (Lothian Regional Council Minutes, 7 Sept. 1976).
87   *Edinburgh Evening News*, 16 July 1976.
88   *The Scotsman*, 14 June 1976.
89   Lothian Regional Council Minutes, 7 Sept. 1976.
90   *The Scotsman*, 8 Sept. 1976.
91   J. G. Gray, *Road End* (Edwina Press 1979), p. 29.
92   Lothian Regional Council, *The Development of Transportation Policy: Edinburgh Area* (1977).
93   Lothian Regional Council, *Transport Policy: Edinburgh Area* (1977).
94   Ibid., para. 3.10.
95   Ibid., para. 2.4.
96   Ibid., para. 2.7.
97   See Scottish Development Department, *Code of Practice for Examinations in Public* (1977), para. 40. The author's comments are flavoured by experience as a participant at the EIP, for the Craigmillar Festival Society. Councillor Gray, another participant, was especially critical of the EIP format, which he saw as a further triumph of 'public participation' over professionalism. See J. G. Gray, 1979.
98   See for example, C. A. Vielba, *A Study of Those Taking Part in Two Structure Plan Examinations in Public*, Institute of Juridical Administration (1976). Also S. A. Crane, 'The Examination in Public of Structure Plans: A Critique', Unpublished MSc. Thesis, Department of Town and Country Planning, Edinburgh College of Art/Heriot-Watt University (1977). For a comment on the pattern in Scottish EIPs see R. Boyle, 'Examinations in Public: Scottish practice reviewed', *The Planner, Journal of the Royal Town Planning Institute* (1980), vol. 66, no. 3, pp. 73–6.

99   Scottish Development Department, *Lothian Regional Council, Structure Plan, 1978, Report of Examination in Public* (1979), para. 2.15, p. 5.
100   Ibid., para. 3.15, p. 9.
101   Ibid., para. 4.9, p. 13.
102   Ibid., para. 9.18, p. 46.
103   Ibid., para. 9.18, p. 46.
104   Lothian Regional Council, *Transportation in the Edinburgh Area* (1979), para. 5, p. 1. This paper was prepared jointly by the Directors of Highways, Transport, Physical Planning, Policy Planning, and Finance and the Chief Constable.
105   Ibid., para. 9.
106   Ibid., para. 25, p. 8.
107   *The Scotsman*, 7 Sept. 1979.
108   *The Scotsman*, 19 Sept. 1979.
109   *Planning Newspaper*, 336, 21 Sept. 1979.
110   *Edinburgh Evening News*, 5 Feb. 1982. The Secretary of State had, in effect, forced an increase in bus fares in October 1982, through withholding rate support grant under the Local Government, Miscellaneous Provisions, Scotland, Act, 1981.
111   Scottish Development Department, 1979, para. 7.24, p. 34.
112   Lothian Regional Council, *Alteration to the Lothian Region Structure Plan: Review of Relevant Matters* (1980).
113   *The Scotsman*, 2 Dec. 1980.
114   Lothian Regional Council, *Lothian Region Structure Plan: Alteration, 1981*, p. 1.
115   *Edinburgh Evening News*, 5 Feb. 1982.
116   Para. 2 of a report entitled *Royal Nurseries*, attached to a Departmental Memorandum from the Town Planning Officer to the Town Clerk, dated 2 July 1971.
117   As the Town Planning Officer of Edinburgh Corporation observed: 'If the present owner refused to sell land to the University new and important development would be frustrated not only at Royal Nurseries, but also, Canal Field, Craiglockhart Terrace, and George Square. In these circumstances the onus would be on the Corporation to exercise its special powers of compulsory purchase in line with the Secretary of State's decision.' p. 3 of the report to the Town Clerk, dated 2 July 1971.
118   Scottish Development Department letter to Craigmillar Festival Society.
119   For a fuller discussion and critique of the open space assessment, see N. A. Lewis, 'Local Planning and Community Need: A case study in Craigmillar, Edinburgh', Unpublished BSc. Research Essay, Department of Town and Country Planning, Edinburgh College of Art/Heriot-Watt University (1976). See also D. Ward, 'Social Planning and Urban Differentiation: The Identification of Deprived Areas', Unpublished MSc. Thesis, Department of Town and Country Planning, Edinburgh College of

Art/Heriot-Watt University (1972). Ward derived an index to combine public open space and population under fourteen years of age for enumeration districts. His computer mapping revealed that Craigmillar EDs were in the most deprived category in Edinburgh.

120 *Edinburgh Evening News*, 15 Aug. 1975.
121 *Edinburgh Evening News,* 26 Sept. 1975.
122 For details of the objection and its drafting see D. West, 'Planning Aid: Theory and Practice', Unpublished BSc. Research Essay, Department of Town and Country Planning, Edinburgh College of Art/Heriot-Watt University (1980).
123 A telephone call to the Scottish Office, less than a week before the inquiry was due to start, revealed the oversight. CFS then informed the other third party objectors of the position. The Cockburn Association in particular protested vigorously at the mishandling of the whole affair. When the inquiry opened it was agreed that there would be an adjournment after a week to give the third parties time to prepare their evidence. The appellants initially raised objections to this arrangement.
124 Precognition of W. L. Love, Planning Consultant, p. 18.
125 *Edinburgh Evening News*, 3 March 1983.

9   Theory, practice and professionalism

This book has tried to explore and develop a critical approach to the theory and practice of town planning. The underlying thesis has been that the production, reproduction and planning of a city are dependent on the dominant economic and political interests within the society. Attempts to abstract the theory and practice of planning from that material base are seen as ideologies, which repress self-understanding, including that of their proponents. Since the book has focussed on places dominated by the capitalist mode of production, the critique of planning it contains has stemmed from theoretical critiques of capitalism and the capitalist state.

The extended case study attempted to study the planning of Edinburgh in terms of the concepts from the earlier chapters. A historical approach was adopted to draw out the links between the production of the city and developments in the mode of production. The broad pattern of planning and development in the city was seen to mirror that of the rest of Great Britain. However, the practice of planning was significantly shaped by the class structure and practices of a city with a disproportionately large middle class engaged in administration, legal services, education and finance. The city's unique physical environment was created, threatened and defended by this peculiar social structure, with planning the mediating mechanism, in rhetoric if not necessarily in practice. The particularities of planning in Edinburgh, even its parochialisms, are an antidote to over-generalization. They are consistent with and exemplify the notion that under capitalism development is uneven over time and space.

The methodology in the case study relied heavily on published reports, press cuttings and council minutes. This may have influenced the conclusions, leading to an overemphasis on locally-based political power structures and leaving the significance of economic change and of central state influence understated. The composition of the local power elite has not been established in detail or with consistency, though its broad and enduring base outside the working class seems undeniable. There is scope for further work on the financing of development within Edinburgh, the inter-relations between the local authorities and the Scottish Office and on the local power structure. Similarly this study has probed the workings of the development plans, but given less attention to development control. Doubtless readers can compile their own list of omissions and oversights; after all knowledge and understanding should develop through debate and critique.

What was town planning?

Planning in Edinburgh has been a limited and reactive means of managing the use and development of land. It has been a mediating factor in averting more fundamental conflicts rooted in private land ownership and developments in the mode of production itself. The practice of planning has not surprisingly varied over time. However, the study showed that when attempts were made to foster a more holistic and initiatory form of planning, they could never be sustained in practice and thus degenerated into mere ideology.

Whatever the face of planning at any particular time, the debates about its form and content have been dominated by Edinburgh's *bourgeoisie*. The Labour Party only achieved formal control of local government with the advent of the Lothian Regional Council. Even then their attempts to infuse their political priorities into the planning of the city were largely directed into the transport issue, on which there had been substantial middle-class opposition to previous council policies for several years. It is also interesting to note that industrialist interests seem to have exerted relatively little influence over planning in the city, except in the immediate aftermath of the two world wars. For the rest of the time the politics of the city were dominated by a small trader interest, often with ties into land and property, by professionals, and by the serried ranks of those seeing themselves first and foremost as 'ratepayers', with a self-proclaimed insensitivity to the class basis of their politics. Where planning was promoted in opposition to the definitions provided by these power groups, it was done so most successfully by professionals with backgrounds in architecture, planning and the visual arts, and by cultured members of the Scottish establishment within the city.

For all these peculiarities the imprint of national legislation and of fashions in planning remains very visible. This underlying unity derives from the transformation of the liberal capitalist state into the advanced capitalist state. Town planning is but one example of the extended involvement of the state in providing the means of production, reproducing a labour force and ensuring civil privatism. The change has been grossly disruptive of existing environments and social relations. In the centre of the city government departments and agencies (including universities) have been significant clients for the spaces created by the intensification of land uses through redevelopment. The planning system was both a facilitator of this process, with the private capital accumulation which it entailed and a less convincing public guarantor against the worst environmental excesses which the process also entailed. The form and structure of Edinburgh has changed substantially during the period of statutory planning, but less than it would have changed without such planning.

These same underlying economic changes have also impacted on the institutions and interests within the city, so indirectly influencing the planning. Concentration and centralization of capital over the study period eroded distinctively local patterns of ownership and control. Local stores gave way to branches of retailing chains and the decline of Princes Street as a shopping parade was a recurrent lament in popular and professional circles alike. National and even international building companies began to intrude into the industry which, initially characterized by a multitude of small competitive operators, had come to be the oligopoly of two locally-based companies strongly linked to local political structures. The local political scene itself was changed. The Progressives finally transmuted themselves into Conservatives, then came the detested jolt when the central administration decreed that in the interests of managerial efficiency there should be a Lothian Region, overlord to the historic continuity of the city, the vestiges of the capital being a mere District Council.

Yet these forces have not reached their logical conclusion within the city: Edinburgh has not been reduced to the bland 'Anywhereville' that safe returns and standardized production runs decree. The city centre has yet to be reduced to the appellation 'Shopping City' as at Runcorn New Town, repressing all aspects of civic life beyond passive consumption. This very difference is itself an important commodity, purchased by tourists from all over the world. Furthermore, the city's distinctive physical environment remains one of the few semi-coherent symbols of Scottish national identity, though suffused in tartanry and antiquarianism, an exultation of the classless embrace of the past.

The planning of Edinburgh from the eighteenth century onwards has been underpinned and riven by such contradictions, just as the central relationships of feudalism and nascent capitalism produced the city in earlier times. Because of the contradictions policies have oscillated, vacillated and been dissipated. The statutory framework of planning has been an ideal accompaniment. The limited powers and scope of British town planning, its conformity with the protection of property rights, its protracted procedures for reaching decisions and its administration by orthodox professionals and civil servants – all these definitive aspects ideally matched the planning priorities of those wielding formal and informal power in Edinburgh.

The totality of place

The case study provides one interpretation of planning. It stops short of explanation, lacking the full rigour of hard data on the various relationships, and indeed some of the central concepts are not quantifiable. The study's ambitions for generalization and prediction are sharply curtailed. Rather it tries to understand the past practice of planning in Edinburgh through critique, thereby providing a more aware basis for action. A critical and interpretive approach to place is intrinsic to the very idea of town planning, yet it is precisely such an approach which has been repressed by statutory definitions and by the profession's own distorted self-understanding. The state curtailed the preserve of town planning, severing the planning of settlement from the planning of production within the settlement. Planners opted for a simplistic Whig version of their own history, or shunned such habits entirely, favouring the garb of action men, getting things done by elevating a technocratic notion of practicality. The statutory limits to planning were a safe haven, the pale within which a distinct profession could be secured. Thus environments have been reduced to physical entities, bearing only a functional relationship to human activity, to people as consumers not creators.

The reaction from social sciences was predictable and has echoed through the literature of the last two decades. Physical planning was berated as arbitrary and irrelevant, a folklore not a science. A binding concern with place was declared obsolete by the positivist ideologues who came to dominate planning theory. The physical decay of the cities has been paralleled by the decomposition of the notion of settlement within planning theory.

The case study has tried to reassert a concern with place as central to planning theory and practice. At a theoretical level the uneven nature of capitalist development produces glaring disparities between places, despite the uniformity decreed by the multi-national control of production and exchange. At a tactical level the planners' traditional concerns with land use and amenity and more recent ecological concerns, constitute an inherent critical opposition to the domination of capital, carrying the possibility of counterposing a potential community use value against the reduction of the local life world of people to a commodity.

Divisions of class and sex are deeply rooted in the physical environment of our cities, yet are so familiar as to pass unnoticed. The neuroses writ large in the comforting fakes which adorn so many suburban houses go unremarked. Naive basic questions have therefore to be asked. Why is the city structured in the way it is? Whose interests created that structuring and how? Who owned the land and why? Which buildings dominate the townscape and what do they signify? What are the social relationships of the place and how are they expressed in the physical environment? How does the day-to-day experience of place differ between the sexes? What does the place look like to a child? Why do we live like we do, in places like we do? What alternatives do we have? What restricts our choices? How can we change the rules of the game?

Answers come from theoretical study of the dominant mode of production and its associated political forms, from empirical research, from direct action and first-hand experience, from understanding our own past and from a study of different places. They add up to a reimmersion of planning theory and practice in the study and design of settlements, but with settlement seen as a totality.

The current crisis

The traditional concerns of physical planning were not really confronted and defeated in their own terms by procedural planning theory, rather they were sidestepped by a shift in knowledge concerns. So in their turn procedural theories have not been defeated by epistomological subversion, but have been left behind by recession, economic crisis and the ascendancy of monetarism over social democratic politics. The crisis in planning has therefore become more evident as the obfuscatory theory and initiatives in practice which characterized the 1970s have withered away. The social investment aspects of planning, like those of the rest of the 'welfare state', have been cut back and planning has increasingly become an explicit tool of the market economy. Practice has become increasingly dominated by the ethos of increasing material wealth, with the planner more and more having to woo investors and less and less able to make them accountable. Practicality becomes synonymous with facilitating private capital accumulation.

Plans are losing their meaning. In areas where there is still development pressure strategic plans can attempt to ensure an adequate supply of serviced sites, though implementation is constrained by the problems local authorities face in planning capital expenditure programmes within central government's annual financial noose. Where there is little market pressure, strategic plans can try to steer the council's own investment, trying to make less go further and to discriminate 'fairly' among the deprived.

Local plans are similarly fraught. Even allowing for the range of practice that has developed, the abiding features have been the pull of 'practicality' towards an incrementalism where the plan becomes a snapshot of the present and a catalogue of changes which would occur even without the plan. Development control, so long the cinderella, is left to go to the ball, albeit with unkind comments and a trimmed outfit. Red tape may not be universally admired, but it does give some protection against scandalous exposures.

The fate of the British planning system is precisely and necessarily that of the post-war political consensus in which it was moulded. Planning was one of a number of indirect means of tackling what were seen as the residual problems of a transformed capitalism; planners could apply their expert skills in pursuit of technical change around which there was a consensus. The consensus and the associated form of planning has been sundered by the deep and continuing economic crisis and changing class structures and power. Labour surplus on a massive and international scale has greatly strengthened the hand of capital and has further divided labour against itself, not least on a spatial basis, between countries, regions and areas.

The professional establishment has responded by trying to revamp the orthodoxy, much in the way that Thomas Adams and his colleagues had attempted in their reports to Edinburgh Corporation after the 1931 crisis. 'Entrepreneurial' is the buzz word, an indiscriminate thirsting to 'get things done', the prevailing aspiration. Conversion of disused buildings into units for 'seedbed industries' is hailed as 'industrial regeneration'. The language games are played with a seeming oblivion for their politics. Within orthodox professionalism this is the language of a neutral expertise. The President of the Royal Town Planning Institute told planners at the 1980 Summer School, 'Our job is to work with Governments to see how effectively we can work with the market, a combination of help, guidance and control, whilst at the same time encouraging enterprise, not stifling it.'[1] Such sentiments are seen as apolitical, while opposition to them is 'politically motivated'.

What can town planning be?

Picturing an idealized city has been an important part of the pedigree of town planning. This frankly utopian tradition was part of the professional superstructure most fiercely criticized by the social scientists. The critiques were helpful in that they exposed the arbitrary and anti-democratic elements of such personal visions of public futures. More recently the economic crisis has drained any idealization of urban form of credibility. One serious consequence of all this is that planners lack a coherent image of the kind of city they are trying to create. Indeed, the most influential idealizations within the profession over the last twenty years have been concerned with the methods, not the substance of planning. A consequence is that public discourse on the possibilities for urban living are dominated by the images of the media and the developers.

Nor has the question of urban form received much consideration in the neo-Marxian literature on planning and urban development. Such authors have usually contented themselves with exposing the class basis of existing developments, rather than positing clear alternatives. Similarly the community action movement has been primarily engaged in defensive struggles, seeking to prevent change rather than creating new environments.

The abiding features of the capitalist city are the subordination of generalizable needs and interests to the imperatives of capital accumulation, with the associated fragmentation of the population which is reflected in the environment. The precise built form of the tendencies has changed through time, with each city remaining a unique historical and spatial entity, but the underlying rationale remains. A radical ideal must therefore negate and replace these criteria.

How would urban development proceed if structured around use values rather than exchange values? There would be greater equality between regions and between settlements within a region and a townscape freed from the domination of the symbols of corporate power, characterized instead by the collective activities of the people themselves. The planning of settlements to meet generalizable needs would require a harmonious relationship between man and the natural environment and between man and man. Conservation of energy, agricultural land and other natural resources and protection from pollution in all its forms would be central concerns at all scales of planning.

Cities as a form of settlement are rooted in the spatial structure of labour markets. The relationship between home and work is central to any urban structure. In contemporary Britain this means the growth of relatively small, free-standing settlements, in pleasant environments and mainly in the South of England, through the in-migration of white collar workers. It also means the de-industrialization of the metropolitan cores and the confinement of the old, the unskilled, the unemployed and ethnic minorities in the rotting inner cities and barren peripheral council estates. It means a spatial division between home and work, which accentuates the sexual division of labour.

There is no necessity for cities to be like this. Rather, the need is to plan production as part of planning the city. All people should have access to socially worthwhile employment opportunities. A closer association of home and work would hold possibilities for strengthening community solidarity and for sharing roles. Similarly, all the people should be decently housed in safe and attractive environments. Such sentiments may seem banal, but they stand in marked contrast to the reality of living conditions for very many working-class households in Britain today. There should be a basic equality of access to facilities through provision based on need, not through markets. This would require strong positive discrimination policies and a good public transport system planned in association with the location of facilities. Public transport is more socially equitable and environmentally sound than car usage and should be a central concern of settlement planning. Similarly the plans should give much more serious attention to the needs of pedestrians and cyclists than is the case at present.

The city centre should be a focus for civic life, not a monument to multinational finance houses and retailing chains. Public space is integral, space which can be used when people want, not when the security guards hired by private owners deem it permissible.

The question of the kind of city that is sought is inseparable from questions of how the city is to be planned and by whom. The planning of the city should be the way that people democratically control their own living conditions and create new experiences and opportunities. The kind of prescriptions sketched above are clearly not 'practical' in the present political climate – they are frankly oppositional to trends presently categorized as 'practical'. They require wideranging social change within which town planning is also changed. Against the limited and bureaucratic planning of the post-war consensus, now shredded by monetarism, we need to counterpose a full, but accountable method of urban development. A radical change in the planning system is needed, along with a radical professionalism among the planners themselves.

The persistence of social and economic problems under social democratic policies, together with their exacerbation under monetarism, has prompted the formulation of an alternative economic strategy (AES) within Britain.[2] The central concepts are a planned alternative to market-led growth, expanded public sector programmes and more democracy and accountability in decision-making. However, AES remains a framework of ideas rather than a single strategy, providing a pragmatic basis for debate and political mobilization that is widely supported within the British labour movement. It has a twofold significance to planners. It shows the possibilities for oppositional thinking, for creating and organizing an alternative to the dominant ideology. Furthermore, it is a planning strategy, albeit one in which spatial and environmental concerns have been weakly developed. The AES thus constitutes the most logical inspiration for developing ideas about an alternative planning system, as well as being in need of some elaboration itself in respect of the planning of cities and regions.

The starting point must be a national plan – indeed, the notion that urban and regional development can be planned in the absence of such a plan seems quite perverse. The national plan would indicate how economic activity and resources are to be developed and distributed around the country and through time. Such a plan would aim to create greater regional equality and a more rational use of resources than is possible under unfettered capitalist development. The national plan would have to co-ordinate the proposals for sectors of the economy and give them an inter-regional spatial dimension.

The national plan would be an important input into regional plans prepared by elected regional councils. These would co-ordinate the major expenditure programmes within the region and would be important vehicles for positive discrimination policies. The regional plans would also provide the framework for the negotiation of planning agreements with private firms and statutory undertakings. The agreements would be reached through a collective bargaining process, involving management, employees, the public sector and the local community. Planning agreements are an important element of the AES, though there is a tendency to depict them primarily in economic and employment terms. The social need for the products, and their environmental acceptability, should be central concerns of planning agreements, and the local community should be represented in the bargaining process.

The national and regional plans should cover five-year periods, with annual reviews and updating. Their spatial dimension would be further strengthened by public ownership of land. This would prevent landowners frustrating publicly desirable projects, or expropriating unearned increases in value. The land would be vested in local councils and leased to users. In this way development could be controlled in a manner that took into full account social considerations and not just narrow physical criteria. The ownership of the land would also strengthen the implementation role of local councils in economic development. This would not stop at site assembly and development, however, but would also entail a planned investment programme within the local economy, with stimulation and support for community-based economic initiatives. Again social need and environmental acceptability should be key considerations.

The actions of the local councils should also be demonstrated to be consistent with approved community plans. Such plans would be generated within the locality by residents and mediated and approved by the local council. Such plans need not be restricted to physical and land use matters, though they would certainly include them. The form and content could vary widely and the preparation of the plan would be an exercise in mutual learning between local residents, their own activists and the planners and elected members. Just as planners' practices and professionalism are currently tailored to fit the priorities of the capitalist state, so a radically changed planning system would require a radical professionalism.

Radical professionalism

Many radicals totally discount the notion of professionalism, pointing to the conservative ideology of professions and their social structures. Such blanket dismissals both obscure the strains imposed by current ideology, the incongruous gap between rhetoric and practice and also sidestep the question of the application of knowledge in any changed social formation. Two related issues deserve to be explored; the interest served by the professional and the interaction of expertise and political will.

Orthodox professionalism proclaims that a planner's actions are overridingly directed by the professional interest. Thus the Royal Town Planning Institute's Code of Professional Conduct specified that 'A member must not undertake any duties or carry out any instructions of an employer, client or supervisor which involve making statements purporting to be his own but which are contrary to his bona fide professional opinion.'[3]

This clause could be read as a liberating force, freeing planners' practice from the domination of resources, places and people for the benefit of capital. In reality, however, 'bona fide professional opinion' becomes an elastic notion, so that even the crudest manipulations of the environment for profit or power can find professional apologists. The idea thus exists without any binding definition. Nevertheless orthodox professionals scrupulously dissociate social considerations from their interpretation of bona fide professional opinion. Likewise, moral concerns about the use of town planning knowledge are deemed illegitimate. Opinions shaped on such criteria are labelled 'political', the orthodox converse of 'professional'. Thus orthodox professionalism is a classic positivist rendition, cleaving a reliable world of facts from an arbitrary morass of values, while legitimating the status quo as both realistic and honourable.

The use of town planning knowledge to further the iniquitous social policies of apartheid is one substantive example of how the systematic ambiguities of 'politics' and 'professionalism' are worked out. In the late 1970s the Radical Institute Group campaigned vigorously to persuade the Royal Town Planning Institute to sever their links with the South African Institute of Town and Regional Planners. RIG's actions were condemned by the professional establishment for 'introducing politics into the profession'. Yet the counter-proposition, that links should be retained, was deemed to be non-political! Eventually the links were broken, though the institute retains an ambiguous relationship with planners whose practice is directly and voluntarily subservient to the social priorities of racist states.

Another evident contradiction between professional rhetoric and practice concerns the production and use of weapons, especially nuclear, chemical and biological weapons. How can a profession with its *raison d'être* supposedly in the protection and enhancement of the physical environment fail to condemn production specifically for the destruction and pollution of that environment?

A town planner's professional code should make explicit a duty to protect the environment and to promote a truely rational and thus harmonious relationship between man and his environment. Professional planners should also be bound by a moral commitment to use their skills to further social equity. The lack of such a commitment in an unequal society is not a neutral stance, it is an endorsement and sustenance for inequality and repression. At the very least the professional code should require all planners to produce and make publicly available as full an assessment as possible of the likely social, economic, environmental and energy consequences of any plan or development. It would be interesting to see how the Privy Council and the Charity Commissioners would react if the planning profession began to dismember the bona fide labour of their members from the demands of the market and the state in this way.

A critical and mutually enlightening interaction between planners, politicians and the public must be a central concern of a radical professionalism. The planner would thus retain an expertise, but that expertise would be rooted in self-awareness, with a consciousness of the ways in which the city is pervaded by ideology and sectional interests. It would be allied to the imagination to design alternatives and the technical ability to specify them. Planners would thus seek to help politicians and the public to judge what they want their city to be. The planner is thus involved in a drama where the city is, *par excellence*, the stage where the two faces of technical capacity (liberation or domination) confront the two faces of a popular self-understanding grounded in tradition (a sense of meaning and history on the one side and an enthrallment by the limitations and manipulations of that tradition on the other).

Just as individual planners are party to this discourse, so too are planners as a collectivity. The pseudo-neutrality of orthodox professionalism produces social ignorance. A radical professional body should be a critical and independent institution, producing and disseminating knowledge freed from domination by the interests of capital and the state. It would be a counterveiling agency, breaking down the barriers of the inner professional world and the constraints woven by media images of the way we can live.

Translating a radical professionalism from an abstract possibility to a reality is no easy task, nor are there grounds for expecting it to be so. The starting point is the dissatisfaction and frustration experienced with orthodox professionalism, with the gulf between its rhetoric and its practice. The struggle to make professionalism a critical and liberating concept is itself a learning process. The aim is to structure new social relationships for ourselves as planners. This is an essential component of any political advance, not an optional extra, or something that automatically comes packaged with the millenia itself.

The words 'town and country planning' hold out the possibility of democratic control over the environment in which we live, a dissent from the state of places as they are. Practice has contradicted, though not wholly obliterated, that meaning. The radical planner must confront realities with possibilities, opposing from within and building dialogues outside, seeing his or her own frustrations as part of a much wider and more vicious repression. In the end we are morally responsible to ourselves for the social uses to which our knowledge of town and country is put.

References and notes

1   J. Collins, 'The planning system – how will it look in the eighties?', *Report of Proceedings of the Town and Country Planning Summer School* (1980), p. 18, The Royal Town Planning Institute, London.
2   For descriptions of the basis of the Alternative Economic Strategy see Conference of Socialist Economists London Working Group, *The Alternative Economic Strategy – A Labour Movement Response to the Economic Crisis* (CSE Books 1980). For discussions of its applicability to planning see D.

Howl, 'Alternatives for planning: planning and the alternative economic strategy', *Department of Civic Design Working Paper 21* (1982), Liverpool University. Also H. McLeish, 'The alternative strategy at national and local levels', *The Planner, Journal of the RTPI*, vol. 67 no. 6 (1981), pp. 160–1.

3   Code of Professional Conduct, Royal Town Planning Institute, London.

Bibliography

Abbott, E. R., 'President's Address', *Town Planning Institute,* vol. IV, no. 1 (1917), pp. 1–13.

Abercrombie, P. and Plumstead, D., *A Civic Survey and Plan for Edinburgh* (Oliver and Boyd 1949).

Adams, T., 'Some recent developments in town planning', *Town Planning Institute,* vol. I, no. 10 (1915), pp. 141–52.

Adams, T., Thompson, L., and Fry, M., *Report on the plan for the development of the Granton–Cramond area,* Report to City and Royal Burgh of Edinburgh (1930).

Adams, T., Thompson, L., and Fry, M., *Final report on town planning,* Report to City and Royal Burgh of Edinburgh (1931).

Altshuler, A., *The City Planning Process* (Cornell University Press 1965).

Amin, S., *Accumulation on a world scale* (Monthly Review Press 1974).

Amos, F. J. C., 'The development of the planning process', *Journal of the Royal Town Planning Institute,* vol. 57, no. 7 (1971), pp. 304–8.

Amos, F. J. C., 'Presidential Address', *Journal of the Royal Town Planning Institute,* vol. 57, no. 9 (1971), pp. 397–9.

Amos, F. J .C., 'Planning Aid', Paper to the President's Committee on the Urban Environment, Royal Town Planning Institute, PC 72 (16) (1972).

Armet, H., 'Notes on the rebuilding of Edinburgh in the last quarter of the seventeenth century', *Book of the Old Edinburgh Club,* vol. 29 (1956), pp. 111–42.

Ashworth, W., *The Genesis of Modern British Town Planning,* (Routledge and Kegan Paul 1954).

Backwell, J. and Dickens, P., 'Town planning, mass loyalty and the restructuring of capital: the origins of the 1947 planning legislation revisited', *Urban and Regional Studies Working Paper 11,* University of Sussex (no date).

Ball, M., 'British housing policy and the housebuilding industry' in *Proceedings of the Conference on Urban Change and Conflict,* Centre for Environmental Studies CP 19, London; CES (1977).

Batey, P. J. W. (ed.), *Theory and Method in Urban and Regional Analysis* (Pion 1977).

Begg, J., 'The causes and probable remedies of pauperism in Scotland',

Chalmers Association for Diffusing Information on Important Social Questions (1870).

Bennett, A., *The Grim Smile of the Five Towns* (Penguin 1975).

Benwell Community Project, *Adamsez — The story of a factory closure* (Benwell Community Project 1980).

Berry, B. J. L., *Growth Centres in the American Urban System*. Vol. 1 'Community development and regional growth in the sixties and seventies'; vol. 2 'Working materials on the US urban hierarchy and on growth centre characteristics, organized by economic region' (Ballinger 1973).

Bhagwati, J. (ed.), *Economic and World Order* (Macmillan 1978).

Biarez, S., 'Ideological planning and contingency programming: the case of the Lille–Roubaix–Tourcoing conurbation '*International Journal of Urban and Regional Research*, vol. 5, no. 4 (1981), pp. 475–91.

Bidwell, L. and Edgar, W., 'Planning Aid: Who gains?', *Planning*, no. 358 (1980), p. 7.

Bingham, H. M., 'Land Hoarding in Edinburgh', MSc. Thesis, Department of Town and Country Planning, Edinburgh College of Art/Heriot-Watt University (1974).

Boddy, M. and Fudge, C. (eds.), 'The local state: theory and practice', School for Advanced Urban Studies Working Paper 20, University of Bristol (1981).

Boyle, R., 'Examinations in Public: Scottish practice reviewed', *The Planner*, vol. 66, no. 3 (1980), pp. 73–6.

Breugel, I., 'The marxist theory of rent and the contemporary city: a critique of Harvey', in Conference of Socialist Economists Housing Workshop, *Political Economy and the Housing Question*, (Conference of Socialist Economists 1975), pp. 34–46.

Broady, M. and Mack, J., 'Administrative problems and social development', mimeo (no date).

Bruce, G., *Some Practical Good: The Cockburn Association – One hundred years participating in planning* (The Cockburn Association 1975).

Buchanan, C. and Partners, *South Hampshire Study: Report on the feasibility of major urban growth* (HMSO 1966).

Buchanan, C. and Partners, Freeman Fox, Wilbur Smith and Associates, *Analysis of the Problem*, City of Edinburgh Planning and Transportation Study (1971).

Buchanan, C. and Partners, Freeman Fox, Wilbur Smith and Associates, *Alternatives for Edinburgh*, Second Interim Report, City of Edinburgh Planning and Transportation Study (1971).

Buchanan, C. and Partners, Freeman Fox, Wilbur Smith and Associates, *The Recommended Plan*, City of Edinburgh Planning and Transportation Study (1972).

Carney, J., Hudson, R., Ive, G. and Lewis, J., 'Regional underdevelopment in late capitalism: A study of the North East of England', in *Proceedings*

of the Conference on Urban Change and Conflict, Centre for
Environmental Studies, CP 14, CES (1975).

Carney, J., Hudson, R., and Lewis, J. (eds.), *Regions in Crisis* (Croom
Helm 1980).

Castells, M., 'Remarques sur l'article de P. Birnbaum: controverse sur le
pouvoir local', *Revue Française de Sociologie*, vol. 15 (1974), pp. 247–
56.

Catford, E. F., *Edinburgh: The story of a city* (Hutchinson 1975).

Chadwick, G. F., *A Systems View of Planning* (Pergamon 1971).

Champion, A. G., 'Issues over land', in R. Davies and P. Hall (eds.), *Issues
in Urban Society*, (Penguin 1978), pp. 21–52.

Cherry, G. E., *The Evolution of British Town Planning* (Leonard Hill 1974).

Cherry, G. E., 'The Housing, Town Planning etc. Act, 1919', *The Planner*
vol. 60, no. 5, (1974), pp. 681–4.

Chree, G., 'Planning Aid', MSc. Thesis, Department of Town and Country
Planning, Edinburgh College of Art/Heriot-Watt University (1981).

City and Royal Burgh of Edinburgh, *Report of the Burgh Engineer's
Department* (Edinburgh Corporation 1894).

City and Royal Burgh of Edinburgh, *Reconstruction Problems,* Report by the
Town Clerk (Edinburgh Corporation 1919).

City and Royal Burgh of Edinburgh, *Annual Report of the Education
Committee* (Edinburgh Corporation 1933).

City and Royal Burgh of Edinburgh, *The Future of Edinburgh,* Report of the
Advisory Committee on City Development (Edinburgh Corporation
1943).

City and Royal Burgh of Edinburgh, *Development Plan* (Edinburgh
Corporation 1953).

City and Royal Burgh of Edinburgh, *Major Highway Planning*, Report by
the City Engineer (Edinburgh Corporation 1964).

City and Royal Burgh of Edinburgh, *Development Plan Review – Report of
Survey* (Edinburgh Corporation 1965).

City and Royal Burgh of Edinburgh, *Development Plan Review – Written
Statement* (Edinburgh Corporation 1965).

City and Royal Burgh of Edinburgh, *Town Planning Brochure –
Development Plan Review* (Edinburgh Corporation 1966).

City and Royal Burgh of Edinburgh, *Annual Report of the Sanitary
Department 1973* (Edinburgh Corporation 1974).

City and Royal Burgh of Edinburgh, *C.E.P.A.T.S.: An Examination of The
Recommended Plan*, Interim Report of the Joint Technical Working Party
(Edinburgh Corporation 1973).

City and Royal Burgh of Edinburgh, *The Recommended Plan*, Report of the
Joint Technical Working Party (Edinburgh Corporation 1974).

City and Royal Burgh of Edinburgh, *Social and Community Development
Programme for the City of Edinburgh,* Report by the City Planning
Officer (Edinburgh Corporation 1974).

City of Edinburgh District Council, *District Planning Report* (Edinburgh District Council 1977).

Clapham, J., *An Economic History of Modern Britain, Volume 1* (Cambridge University Press 1930).

Cockburn Association, *Annual Report, 1933* (Cockburn Association 1933).

Cockburn, C., *The Local State: Management of cities and people,* (Pluto 1977).

Coleman, A., 'Land use planning: success or failure?', *Architects' Journal,* 19 January 1977, pp. 94–134.

Colenutt, R., 'The political economy of the property market', *Antipode,* vol. 8, no. 2 (1976), pp. 24–30.

Colenutt, R. and Hamnett, C., 'Urban land use and the property development industry', Unit 9, *Urban Change and Conflict* (D202), (The Open University Press 1982).

Collins, J. F. N., 'The planning system – how will it look in the eighties?', *Report of the Proceedings of the Town & Country Planning Summer School 1980* pp. 16–20 (The Royal Town Planning Institute 1980).

Community Development Project Inter-Project Editorial Team, *The Costs of Industrial Change* (Home Office Urban Deprivation Unit 1977).

Community Development Project Inter-Project Editorial Team, *Gilding the Ghetto* (Home Office Urban Deprivation Unit 1977).

Community Development Project Political Economy Collective, *The State and the Local Economy* (CDP Political Economy Collective/Publications Distribution Co-operative, 1979).

Conference of Socialist Economists London Working Group, *The Alternative Economic Strategy – A Labour Movement Response to the Economic Crisis* (CSE Books 1980).

Connerton, P. (ed.), *Critical Sociology* (Penguin 1976).

Corrigan, P. and Ginsburg, N., 'Tenants' Struggle and Class Struggle', in Conference of Socialist Economists Housing Workshop, *Political Economy and the Housing Question,* (Conference of Socialist Economists 1975), pp. 134–46.

Crane, S. A., 'The Examination in Public of Structure Plans: A Critique', MSc. Thesis, Department of Town and Country Planning, Edinburgh College of Art/Heriot-Watt University (1977).

Crispin, G. and Hamnett S., 'Planning Theory: a collection of syllabuses', mimeo, paper given to the Conference on Planning Theory, Oxford Polytechnic, April 1981.

Crossman, R. H. S., *Diaries of a Cabinet Minister: Volume 1*(Hamish Hamilton and Jonathan Cape 1975).

Crummy, H. (ed.), *Festival of Change* (Craigmillar Festival Society 1972).

Cullingworth, J. B., *Town and Country Planning in Britain* 5th Edition (Allen and Unwin 1974).

Cullingworth, J. B., *Environmental Planning 1939–69, Volume 1,* Reconstruction and land use planning 1939–47 (HMSO 1975).

Cuthbert, M., 'The role of theory in town planning', mimeo, paper given to Education for Planning Association Planning Theory Working Group, Polytechnic of Central London (1975).

Daiches, D., *Edinburgh* (Hamish Hamilton 1978).
Damer, S. and Hague, C., 'Public participation in planning: a review', *Town Planning Review,* vol. 42, (1971) pp. 217–32.
Darby, H., *An Historical Geography of England before 1800* (Cambridge University Press 1961).
Davies, J. G., *The Evangelistic Bureaucrat* (Tavistock 1972).
Davies, R. and Hall, P., *Issues in Urban Society* (Penguin 1978).
Dennis, N., *People and Planning* (Faber and Faber 1970).
Dennis, N., *Public Participation and Planners' Blight* (Faber and Faber 1972).
Department of the Environment/Welsh Office, *Streamlining the Planning Machine,* Circular 142/73 (DoE): 227/73 (WO) (HMSO 1973).
Dickens, P., 'Social change, housing and the state: some aspects of class fragmentation and incorporation 1915–46', in *Proceedings of the Conference on Urban Change and Conflict* CP 19, CES (1977).
Dos Santos, T., 'The structure of dependence', *American Economic Review,* vol. 60 (1970), pp. 231–6.
Dunleavy, P., *Urban Political Analysis: the politics of collective consumption* (Macmillan 1980).

Edel, M., 'Marx's theory of rent: urban applications', in Conference of Socialist Economists Political Economy of Housing Workshop, *Housing and Class in Britain* (CSE 1976), pp. 7–23.
Edinburgh and District Trades and Labour Council, *Forty-seventh Annual Report,* (EDTLC 1914).
Edinburgh and District Trades and Labour Council, *Fifty-first Annual Report* (EDTLC 1918).
Edinburgh and District Trades and Labour Council, *Our Unseen City Revealed: A Tale of Housing Atrocities. Report on conditions revealed by the 1921 Report of the Medical Officer of Health* (EDTLC no date).
Edinburgh and District Trades and Labour Council, *Sixty-fifth Annual Report* (EDTLC 1932).
Edinburgh Chamber of Commerce, *Quinquennial Review Committee's Report* (ECC 1963).
Edinburgh Chamber of Commerce and Manufacturers. *Memorandum to the Advisory Committee on City Development* (ECCM 1943).
Edwards, D. and Curtis, B., 'Planning Aid: an analysis based on the Planning Aid Service of the Town and Country Planning Association' *School of Planning Studies Occasional Paper 1,* Reading University (1980).
Elkins, S. L., *Politics and Land Use Planning: The London Experience*

334   *The development of planning thought*

(Cambridge University Press).

Engels, F., *The Condition of the English Working Classes in 1844* (Panther 1969).

Faludi, A., *Planning Theory* (Pergamon 1973).

Foley, D. L., 'British Town Planning: One ideology or three?' *British Journal of Sociology,* vol. 11 (1960), pp. 211–31.

Foley, D. L., *Controlling London's Growth: Planning the Great Wen 1940–60* (California University Press 1963).

Foot, M., *Aneurin Bevan 1897–1945* (Paladin 1975).

Forrester, J. W. *Urban Dynamics* (MIT Press 1968).

Foster, J., *Class Struggle and the Industrial Revolution: Early industrial capitalism in three English towns* (Methuen 1977).

Fothergill, S. and Gudgin, G., *Unequal Growth: Urban and Regional Employment Change in the United Kingdom,* (Heinemann 1982).

Free Church of Scotland, *Report on the Committee on Houses for the Working Classes in connection with Social Morality, to the General Assembly of the Free Church of Scotland* (Free Church of Scotland 1862).

Friedman, M., *Capitalism and Freedom* (University of Chicago Press 1962).

Friedmann, J., 'Planning as a Vocation', *Plan Canada,* vol. 6 (1966), pp. 99–124, vol 7 (1967), pp. 8–26.

Galloway, R. F., 'The Edinburgh Improvement Act, 1867', 5th Year Thesis, Department of Architecture, Edinburgh College of Art/Heriot-Watt University (1975).

Gans, H. J., *The Urban Villagers* (The Free Press 1962).

Garin, R. A., 'A matrix formulation of the Lowry model for metropolitan activity location', *Journal of the American Institute of Planners,* vol. 32 (1966), pp. 361–4.

Garside, P. L., 'Evolution or genesis? The British Town Planning Movement 1900–1940' Paper to the Planning History Group, Sheffield, mimeo (1979).

Geddes, P., 'The Civic Survey of Edinburgh', in *Transactions of the Town Planning Conference,* pp. 537–74 (Royal Institute of British Architects 1910).

Glass, R., 'The evolution of planning: some sociological considerations', *International Social Science Journal,* vol. XI, no. 3, (1959), pp. 393–409.

Goldner, W., 'The Lowry model heritage', *Journal of the American Institute of Planners,* vol. 36 (1971), pp. 100–10.

Gordon, G., 'Status Areas in Edinburgh', PhD. Dissertation, University of Edinburgh (1971).

Gray, J. G., *Streets Ahead: A brief study of highway planning in Edinburgh since 1945* (The Edina Press 1975).

Gray, J. G., *Road End* (The Edina Press 1979).

Gray, J. G., *The Capital of Scotland: its precedence and status* (The Edina Press 1980).

Gray, R. Q., *The Labour Aristocracy in Victorian Edinburgh* (Clarendon Press 1976).

Grieve, R., 'In Retrospect: 40 years of development and achievement', *The Planner*, vol. 66, no. 3 (1980), pp. 62–3.

Habermas, J. 'On systematically distorted communication', *Inquiry* vol. 13, (1970), pp. 205–18.

Habermas, J., *Towards a Rational Society* (Heinemann 1971).

Habermas, J., *Knowledge and Human Interests* (Heinemann 1972).

Habermas, J., *Theory and Practice* (Heinemann 1974).

Habermas, J., *Legitimation Crisis* (Heinemann 1976).

Hague, C., *Housing Problems and Policies in Edinburgh,* Open University Summer School Booklet for the Housing Module of the Foundation Social Science Course, D101 (The Open University Press 1976).

Hague, C. and McCourt, A. D., 'Comprehensive Planning, Public participation and the Public Interest', *Urban Studies*, vol. 11 (1974), pp. 143–55.

Hall, P., Thomas, R., Gracey, H., and Drewett, R., *The Containment of Urban England* (Allen & Unwin 1973).

Harris, B., 'The uses of theory in the simulation of urban phenomena', *Journal of the American Institute of Planners,* vol. 32 (1966), pp. 258–73.

Harris, F., 'Address by Councillor Harris', *Journal of the Town Planning Institute,* vol. XV, no. 1 (1928), pp. 15–18.

Harvey, D., *Social Justice and the City* (Edward Arnold 1973).

Heller, R. and Willatt, N., 'The bungle that cost the banks £2,000,000,000', *Business Observer,* 29 May 1977.

Heseltine, M., 'Secretary of State's Address', in *Report of the Proceedings of the Town and Country Planning Summer School 1979,* pp. 25–30 (The Royal Town Planning Institute 1979).

Hill, D. M., 'A growth allocation model for the Boston region', *Journal of the American Institute of Planners,* vol. 31 (1965), pp. 111–20.

Horkheimer, M., 'Traditional and Critical Theory', in Connerton, P. (ed), *Critical Sociology* (Penguin 1976), pp. 206–24.

Horsfall, T. C., *The Improvement of the Dwellings and Surroundings of the People* (Manchester University Press 1904).

Howl, D., 'Alternatives for Planning: Planning and the Alternative Economic Strategy' Department of Civic Design Working Paper 21, University of Liverpool (1982).

Hume, G., 'St. James Centre: Finance and Development', in Peacock, H. (ed.), *The Unmaking of Edinburgh* (Edinburgh University Students Publications Board no date), pp. 31–2.

Hymer, S., 'The multi-national corporation and the law of uneven development', in Bhagwati, J. (ed.), *Economics and World Order,* (Macmillan 1971).

Isard, W., *General Theory* (MIT Press 1969).
Issacharoff, R., 'The building boom of the inter-war years: whose profits and at what cost?', in *Proceedings of the Conference on Urban Change and Conflict,* Centre for Environmental Studies CP 19 (CES 1977).

Jones, R., *Amenity-deficient houses in Edinburgh: 1967*, Report presented to Edinburgh Corporation Housing Committee (Edinburgh Corporation 1968).

Kantorowich, R. H., 'Education for Planning', *Journal of the Town Planning Institute,* vol. 53 (1967), pp. 175–84.
Kaucz, J. R., 'Residential Location: The application of the social physics model and the behavioural model to Edinburgh', MSc. Thesis, Department of Town and Country Planning, Edinburgh College of Art/Heriot-Watt University (1976).
Keeble, L., *Planning at the Crossroads* (Estates Gazette 1961).
Keeble, L., *Principles and Practice of Town and Country Planning,* 4th Edition (The Estates Gazette 1969).
Keir, D. (ed.), 'The City of Edinburgh', *The Third Statistical Account of Scotland,* vol. XV (Collins 1966).

Laidlaw, D. J., 'Life at the Periphery: the evolution of a planned housing community', BSc. Research Essay, Department of Town and Country Planning, Edinburgh College of Art/Heriot-Watt University (1976).
Land Campaign Working Party, *The Lie of the Land* (Shelter Community Action Team no date).
Law, S. *et al,* *Planning and the Future* (The Royal Town Planning Institute 1976).
Lebas, E., 'Movement of capital and locality: Issues raised by the study of local power structures' in *Proceedings of the Conference on Urban Change and Conflict,* Centre for Environmental Studies CP 19 (CES 1977).
Lenin, V. I., *Selected Works* (1969).
Leven, C. (ed.) *The Mature Metropolis* (D. C. Heath 1978).
Leven, C., 'The emergence of maturity in metropolis', in Leven, C. (ed.), *The Mature Metropolis* (D. C. Heath 1978).
Lewis, N., 'Local Planning and Community Need: A case study in Craigmillar, Edinburgh', BSc. Research Essay, Department of Town and Country Planning, Edinburgh College of Art/Heriot-Watt University (1976).
Lewis, J. and Melville, B. 'The politics of epistemology in regional science', paper presented to the 9th annual conference of the Regional Science

Association (British Section), September 1976, and published in Batey, P. J. W. (ed.), *Theory and Method in Urban and Regional Analysis* (Pion 1976).

Liverpool City Council, *Iterim Planning Policy Statement* (Liverpool Corporation 1965).

Llewellyn Davies and Partners, *Unequal City: the final report of the Birmingham Inner Area Study* (HMSO 1977).

Lomax, K. S., 'Production and productivity movements in the UK since 1900', *Journal of the Royal Statistical Society*, series A, vol. 122 (1959).

Lothian Regional Council, *A Paper for Discussion: Transport Policies and Programmes*, 1976 (Lothian RC 1976).

Lothian Regional Council, *The Development of Transportation Policy: Edinburgh Area* (Lothian RC 1977).

Lothian Regional Council, *Transportation Policy: Edinburgh Area* (Lothian RC 1977).

Lothian Regional Council, *Structure Plan: Considerations Report* (Lothian RC 1977).

Lothian Regional Council, *Structure Plan* (Lothian RC 1978).

Lothian Regional Council, *Transportation in the Edinburgh Area* (Lothian RC 1979).

Lothian Regional Council, *Alteration to the Lothian Regional Council Structure Plan: Review of Relevant Matters* (Lothian RC 1981).

Lothian Regional Council, *Lothian Region Structure Plan: Alteration 1981* (Lothian RC 1981).

Lothian Regional Council/City of Edinburgh District Council, *Social and Community Development Project: Progress Report* (1976).

Lothian Regional Council/City of Edinburgh District Council, *Social and Community Development Project: Progress Report* (1977).

Lowry, I. S., 'A Model of Metropolis', RAND Corporation, Memorandum RM–4035–RC (1964).

Lyddon, D., 'Scottish planning in practice: influences and comparisons', *The Planner*, vol. 66, no. 3 (1980), pp. 66–7.

Macartney, W. A., 'Town Planning in Edinburgh from the 18th to the 20th century – and its lessons', *Journal of the Town Planning Institute*, vol. XV, no. 1 (1928), pp. 29–37.

Mackintosh, J. P., 'The city's politics', in D. Keir (ed.) 'The City of Edinburgh', *The Third Statistical Account of Scotland,* vol. XV (Collins 1966) pp. 309–19.

Macrae, E. J., 'Historical Review', in Abercrombie, P. and Plumstead, D., *A Civic Survey and Plan for Edinburgh* (Oliver and Boyd 1949), pp. 5–16.

Manchester City Planning Department, 'Employment and Unemployment in Manchester: a context for local economic and employment initiatives', *Economic Information Paper 1/81* (Manchester City Council 1981).

Mandel, E., *Late Capitalism* (New Left Books 1975).

Marriott, O., *The Property Boom* (Pan Books 1969).

Marx, K., *A Contribution to the Critique of Political Economy* (International Publishers Edition 1970).

Marx, K., *Grundisse: Introduction to the Critique of Political Economy* (Penguin 1973).

Marx, K., *Capital: Volume I* (Penguin 1976).

Marx, K., *Capital: Volume II* (Penguin 1978).

Marx, K., *Capital: Volume III* (Lawrence and Wishart 1974).

Marx, K., and Engels, F., 'Manifesto of the Communist Party', in Feuer, L. S. (ed.), *Marx and Engels: Basic writings on politics and philosophy* (Anchor Books 1959).

Massey, D., 'Towards a critique of industrial location theory', *Antipode*, vol. 5, no. 3 (1973), pp. 33–9.

Massey, D., 'Capital and locational change: the UK electrical engineering and electronics industries', *Review of Radical Political Economies* (Fall 1978); reprinted in Blowers, A., Brook, C., Dunleavy, P., and McDowell, L., (eds.), *Urban Change and Conflict: An Interdisciplinary Reader* (Harper and Row/The Open University Press 1982), pp. 50–62.

Massey, D. and Catalano, A., *Capital and Land: Landownership by capital in Britain* (Edward Arnold 1978).

Massey, D. and Meegan, R. A., 'Industrial restructuring versus the cities', *Urban Studies*, vol. 15 (1978), pp. 273–88.

Masterman, G. F. C., 'The Heart of Empire', in *British Empire: Discussions of Problems of Modern City Life in England*, (T. Fisher Unwin 1901).

Mawson, T. H., 'Some of the larger problems of town planning', *Town Planning Institute*, vol. I, no. 8 (1914), pp. 113–30.

McDonald, S. T., 'The Regional Report in Scotland', *Town Planning Review*, vol. 48, no. 3 (1977), pp. 215–32.

McDougall, G., 'The state, capital and land: the history of town planning revisited', *International Journal of Urban and Regional Research*, vol. 3, no. 3 (1979), pp. 361–80.

McDowell, L., 'Class, status, location and life-style', Unit 13, *Urban Change and Conflict*, (D202) (The Open University Press 1982).

McLeish, H. B., 'The alternative strategy at national and local levels', *The Planner*, vol. 67, no. 6 (1981), pp. 160–1.

McLoughlin, J. B., *Urban and Regional Planning: A systems approach* (Faber and Faber 1969).

Mears, F. C., *The City of Edinburgh: Preliminary suggestions for consideration by the representative committee in regard to the development and replanning of the central area of the city in relation to public buildings* (1931).

Mears, F. C., *A regional survey and plan for Central and South-East Scotland* (Morrison & Gibb 1948).

Mears, F. C. and Russell, J., 'The New Town of Edinburgh – Part 1', *Book of the Old Edinburgh Club*, vol. 22 (1938), pp. 167–200.

Mears, Sir Frank and Partners, *Wester Hailes: a plan for a city suburb* (Edinburgh Corporation 1965).

Mellor, R., 'The British experience: combined and uneven development', in *Proceedings of the Conference on Urban Change and Conflict*, Centre for Environmental Studies CP 14 (CES 1975).

Mellor, R., 'The capitalist city: Britain 1780–1920', Unit 1, *Urban Change and Conflict* (D202) (The Open University Press 1982),

Melville, C. E. B., *Futures and Social Interests,* mimeo (1976).

Merchants' Company of the City of Edinburgh, *The Merchants' Company Institutions: Landed Estates – notes and plans for the use of the Governors* (1891).

Merchants' Company of the City of Edinburgh, *Report of a Special Committee on the Building Trade in Edinburgh* (1918).

Merchants' Company of the City of Ediinburgh, *Report of a Select Committee of the Company on the Development of Edinburgh* (1919).

Meyerson, M. and Banfield, E., *Politics, Planning and The Public Interest* (The Free Press 1955).

Miliband, R., *Parliamentary Socialism*, 2nd Edition (Merlin Press 1972).

Milne, R., 'Planning aid papers over the communication cracks', *The Surveyor*, vol. CXLII, no. 4231 (1973), pp. 30–1.

Ministry of Housing and Local Government and Ministry of Transport, 'Town Centres: Approach to Renewal', *Planning Bulletin 1*, (HMSO 1962).

Ministry of Housing and Local Government and Ministry of Transport, 'Town Centres: Cost and Control of Redevelopment', *Planning Bulletin 3* (HMSO 1963).

Ministry of Housing and Local Government and Ministry of Transport and Scottish Development Department, *The Future of Development Plans. Report of the Planning Advisory Group* (HMSO 1965).

Moor, N. and Waddington, P., *From Rags to Ruin: Batley, Woollen Textiles and Industrial Change* (Community Development Project Political Economy Collective 1980).

Muchnick, D., 'Urban Renewal in Liverpool', *Occasional Papers in Social Administration*, no. 33 (G. Bell 1970).

Murray, D. K., Sir (chairman) *Scottish Coalfields: Report of the Committee,* Cmd. 6575 (HMSO 1944).

Nairn, I., (ed.) 'Outrage', *Architectural Review*, vol. 117, no. 702 (1955).

Nairn, T., *The Break-up of Britain* (New Left Books 1977).

Needleman, L., *The Economics of Housing* (Staples 1965).

Nevitt, A. A., 'Issues in Housing', in Davies, R. and Hall, P., (eds.), *Issues in Urban Society* (Penguin 1978), pp. 183–215.

Office of Population Censuses and Surveys, *Towns Report* (HMSO 1982).

Pahl, R. E., 'Urban social theory and research', *Environment and Planning,* vol. 1 (1969), pp. 143–53.

Pahl, R. E., *Whose City?* (Longman 1970).

Pahl, R. E., *Whose City?,* 2nd Edition (Penguin 1975).

Parochial Board of St. Cuthbert's, Edinburgh, *Report of the Chairman's Committee* (privately printed 1866).

Peacock, H. (ed.) *The Unmaking of Edinburgh* (Edinburgh University Students Publication Board no date).

Pepler, G. L., 'Economics of town planning in relation to land development', *Town Planning Institute,* vol. I, no. 5 (1915), pp. 63–77.

Perrons, D. C., 'The role of Ireland in the new international division of labour: a proposed framework for regional analysis', *Regional Studies,* vol. 15, no. 2 (1981), pp. 81–100.

Regan, C. and Walsh, F., 'Dependency and underdevelopment: the case of mineral resources in the Irish Republic', *Antipode,* vol. 8, no. 3 (1976), pp. 46–59.

Richardson, H. W., *Regional Economics* (Weidenfield and Nicolson 1969).

Royal Commission on the Distribution of the Industrial Population, *Report,* Cmd. 6153 (HMSO 1940).

Royal Commission on the Housing of the Industrial Population of Scotland, *Report,* Cmd. 8731 (1917).

Royal Commission on the Housing of the Working Classes (Scotland), *Report* (1885).

Royal Scottish Society of Painters in Water Colours, *Town Planning Exhibition: Explanatory and historical notes and catalogue of exhibits* (RSSPWC 1937).

Royal Town Planning Institute, *Examinations Handbook,* (RTPI 1976).

Royal Town Planning Institute, *Memorandum of observations submitted to the Royal Commission on the Distribution of Income and Wealth* (RTPI 1976).

Royal Town Planning Institute (1981), *Code of Professional Conduct,* (RTPI 1981).

Sarjeant, G. and Milner, R., 'To the brink of ruin and back', *Sunday Times,* 22 January 1978.

Saunders, P. *Urban Politics: a sociological interpretation* (Hutchinson 1979).

Saunders, P. Notes on the specificity of the local state', in Boddy, M. and Fudge, C. (eds.), 'The Local State: Theory and Practice' *School for Advanced Urban Studies Working Paper 20,* University of Bristol (1981), pp. 24–37.

Saunders, P., *Social Theory and The Urban Question* (Hutchinson 1981).

Schuster, G., Sir, (chairman), *Report to the Minister of Town and Country*

Planning of the Committee on the Qualifications of Planners Cmd. 8059 (HMSO 1950).

Scottish Council for Development and Industry, *Inquiry into the Scottish Economy* (James Paton 1961).

Scottish Development Department, *Code of Practice for Examinations in Public* (SDD 1977).

Scottish Development Department, *Lothian Regional Council, Structure Plan, 1978, Report of the Examination in Public* (SDD 1979).

Scottish Land Enquiry Committee, *Scottish Land: Report of the Committee* (1914).

Scottish Office, *Central Scotland: A programme for development and growth*, Cmd. 2188 (HMSO 1963).

Scottish Office, *The Scottish Economy 1965–70: A plan for expansion*, Cmd. 2864 (HMSO 1966).

Scott–Moncrieff, G., 'Plan for Edinburgh', *The Scottish Field*, vol. IXL, no. 42 (1943).

Secretary of State for the Environment, Secretary of State for Scotland, Secretary of State for Wales, *Policy for the Inner Cities* White Paper, Cmd. 6845 (HMSO 1977).

Sharp, T. *Town Planning*, (Pelican 1940).

Sharp, T., 'Planning Now', *Journal of the Town Planning Institute*, vol. XLIII, no. 6 (1957), pp. 133–41.

Sharp, T., 'Planning Planning', *Journal of the Town Planning Institute*, vol. 52 (1966), pp. 209–15.

Simmie, J., *Power, Property and Corporatism* (Macmillan 1981).

Smith, C. J., *Historic South Edinburgh*, vol. 1 (Charles Skilton 1978).

Smith, J. L. (ed.) *Last Poetic Gems: selected from the works of William McGonagall* (David Winter & Son 1971).

Smith, P. J., Site selection in the Forth Basin, PhD. Dissertation (University of Edinburgh 1964).

Smith, P. J. 'Rural interests in the physical expansion of Edinburgh', in Minghi, J. V. (ed.), *The Geographer and the Public Environment* B.C. Geographical Series no. 7, Occasional Papers in Geography (Tantalus Research Ltd 1966) pp. 55–67.

Smith, P. J., 'Planning as environmental improvement: slum clearance in Victorian Edinburgh', in Sutcliffe, A. (ed.), *The Rise of Modern Urban Planning 1800–1914* (Mansell 1980), pp. 99–133.

Spence, N., 'The evolving metropolitan area', Unit 8, *Urban Change and Conflict* (D202) (The Open University Press 1982).

Steven, W., *History of George Heriot's Hospital*, 3rd Edition, (Bell & Bradfute 1872).

Stilgoe, H., *Proceedings of the Institute of Municipal and County Engineers*, vol. XXXVII, no. 44 (1910-11).

Sutcliffe, A. (ed.), *The Rise of Modern Urban Planning* (Mansell 1980).

Swann, P. B., 'Dock Revival?' *Planning*, no. 363, 11 April 1980.

Taylor, E. G., 'Leland's England', in Darby, H., *An Historical Geography of England before 1800* (Cambridge University Press 1961).

Thornley, A., 'Thatcherism and Town Planning', *Planning Studies* no. 12, School of the Environment Planning Unit (Polytechnic of Central London 1981).

University Grants Commission, *Review of University Development 1962–66* (HMSO 1966).

University of Edinburgh, *Conservation and University Expansion,* Joint Report by the Factorial Secretary and the Planning Consultant, (University of Edinburgh 1969).

Urry, J., 'Localities, regions and social class', *International Journal of Urban and Regional Research,* vol. 5, no. 4 (1981), pp. 455–74.

Vielba, C. A., 'A study of those taking part in two structure plan examinations in public', *Institute of Juridical Administration,* (University of Birmingham 1976).

Walkden, J. S., 'Notes on the work of the Department of Town Planning, Edinburgh School of Architecture, Edinburgh College of Art', *Journal of the Town Planning Institute*, vol. XXVI, no. 3 (1940), pp. 85–91.

Wannop, U., 'Scottish planning in practice: four distinctive characteristics', *The Planner*, vol. 66, no. 3 (1980), pp. 64–5.

Ward, D. 'Social Planning and Urban Differentiation: The identification of deprived areas', MSc. Thesis, Department of Town and Country Planning, Edinburgh College of Art/Heriot-Watt University (1972).

Ward, S., 'The Town and Country Planning Act, 1932', *The Planner*, vol. 60, no. 5 (1974), pp. 685–9.

Waterworth, A., 'Public Participation in Planning: An Edinburgh case study', MSc. Thesis, Department of Town and Country Planning, Edinburgh College of Art/Heriot-Watt University (1975).

West Central Scotland Plan Steering Committee, *West Central Scotland Plan* (1974).

West, D., 'Planning Aid: Theory and Practice', BSc. Research Essay, Department of Town and Country Planning, Edinburgh College of Art/Heriot-Watt University (1980).

Wiberg, P., 'Public Participation, Community Development and The State', BSc. Research Essay, Department of Town and Country Planning, Edinburgh College of Art/Heriot-Watt University (1980).

Williams, R., *The Country and The City* (Chatto and Windus 1973).

Youngson, A. J., *The Making of Classical Edinburgh* (Edinburgh University Press 1966).

Index